II0670094

DISCARDED
THE
UNIVERSITY OF WINNIPEG
PORTAGE & BALMORAL
WINNIPEG 2. MAN.   CANADA

The Story of Ernie Pyle

PN
4874
.P86m
53

THE STORY OF

Ernie Pyle

BY LEE G. MILLER

NEW YORK · 1950

The Viking Press

COPYRIGHT 1950 BY LEE G. MILLER

PUBLISHED BY THE VIKING PRESS IN AUGUST 1950

PUBLISHED ON THE SAME DAY IN THE DOMINION OF CANADA
BY THE MACMILLAN COMPANY OF CANADA LIMITED

SECOND PRINTING BEFORE PUBLICATION

A magazine version of this book appeared serially
in *McCall's Magazine*.

The quotations from Ernie Pyle's columns in this
book are reprinted by special permission of the
Scripps-Howard Newspapers.

PRINTED IN THE U.S.A. BY H. WOLFF BOOK MANUFACTURING CO.

Foreword

IT WAS an extraordinary thing, and it may seem an incredible one some day after all of Ernie Pyle's contemporaries have made their exits, but it is true that the life and work of this newspaperman had an enormous impact on millions of Americans. No other journalist ever evoked such mass affection as was accorded him during his meager tenure as a national figure.

There was, of course, a reason for this. He bridged a gap in our knowledge of the great war and of the men who were waging it—a gap of which we were not actively conscious until his reporting began to span it. Many others were as enterprising, as brave, as impeccably accurate in their war dispatches as he; *none* told the story of the soldier with such insight and such moving, though unmawkish, sympathy. And his personality so permeated his column, as it had done in peacetime with a smaller audience, that readers came to think of him not as a stranger, but as their friend, their friend Ernie.

In this book his professional writings are quoted only fragmentarily, since the best of them are available in five works of his own—*Ernie Pyle in England, Here Is Your War, Brave Men, Last Chapter,* and *Home Country,* all of which were assembled from his daily newspaper pieces. What follows draws more heavily on his private correspondence, in some of which may be discerned the processes of soul-searching that made him so intuitive a recorder of the nobilities and frailties of other men.

I come to the stand, in this chronicle of his life, as a biased witness, since he was my friend for more than twenty years, during the greater part of which he worked under me. It may be that

I have been over-scrupulous in trying, because of this acknowledged predilection, to keep out deductions of my own. But it has seemed preferable to let the story tell itself, as far as possible, through the letters and recollections that a number of his friends and kinsmen generously made available. This generosity was manifested most especially in the cooperation of his wife (who was my friend for nearly as many years as Ernie was) when she gallantly subordinated her privacy to her sense of history and handed to me the very personal correspondence which is so vital to this story.

LEE G. MILLER

Washington
January 1950

Contents

Contents

Ernie (*far left*) with co-workers around the newsroom copy desk at the *Washington News* in 1924 or 1925. The others (*left to right*) are Charles M. Egan, Lee G. Miller, Willis Thornton, Jr., Paul McCrea, and John M. Gleissner, then editor.

Ernie and his Ford, laden with gear, on a desert road in central Washington State. This was in 1926.

Fred Payne, *Memphis Press-Scimitar*

Jerry

Harold Davis, *Knoxville News-Sentinel*

Ernie

At work in a Nor-
mandy apple
orchard during
the post-D-Day
campaign in
1944.

Acme Photo
by Bert Brandt

With Bradley and
Eisenhower, at
Bradley's head-
quarters in
France in 1944.

Acme Photo

The Story of Ernie Pyle

CHAPTER I

Boyhood of a Hoosier

WILL PYLE was plowing up a blackberry patch on the Elders' west place, which he was tenanting with his bride, when Sam Elder walked over from the white frame house. With a few words Elder brought the plowman on the run. Dr. Otis Keyes and some neighbor women were summoned by telephone, and about five o'clock in the afternoon a boy of a little under seven pounds was born to Maria Pyle. It had been a hard time for her. She was thirty, and this was her first (and only) baby. She called him Ernest Taylor Pyle—Taylor after her maiden name, Ernest just because she liked the sound of it. And Ernest he always was to his mother and father; never Ernie, not even after Ernie Pyle had become a famous name.

That was August 3, 1900. The two-story Elder home where Ernie was born still stands, set back from the dust of a gravel road, a mile and a half south and a little west of the pleasant town of Dana, in Helt Township, Vermillion County, Indiana. A few miles to the west is Illinois, and a few miles eastward the Wabash River flows south to join the Ohio. The countryside is generally flat, occasionally rolling; fields of grain alternate with woods and pastures.

Ernie's forebears had lived in Helt Township for many years before the first building in Dana went up in 1869. Will Pyle, born in '67, seldom strayed far from home. But his father, Samuel Pyle, who had been brought to Helt Township as an infant from Chillicothe, Ohio, sailed around the Horn and worked for several years on a brother's California ranch before coming home and marrying a neighbor seventeen years his junior, Nancy Hammond.[1]

Ernie's mother, Maria Taylor, was born across the Illinois line in 1870. Her father, Lambert Taylor, was Hoosier-born, and in 1895 moved his family back to a one-story frame house a mile or so east of Ernie's birthplace. Lambert Taylor is supposed to have had a strain of German blood; other than this, Ernie's ancestors on both sides appear to have been of Scottish and English origin.

Ernie's parents did not get past the eighth grade. Will attended a one-room school along with thirty or forty other "scholars." One of his earliest memories was of his teacher lifting him up into the engine of a work train on a new railroad the Baltimore & Ohio was laying from Indianapolis to Decatur, Illinois, past the schoolhouse. Samuel Pyle sold wood to the railroad for crossties.

The Samuel Pyles had seven children, of whom five reached maturity. Will was twelve when his mother died, and a couple of years later his father married a widow with three daughters. Will and the rest were put to the chores and the plow as soon as they were of a size. Will was a well-behaved boy. He never took but one chew of tobacco in his life, from which he was sick in bed half a day. Later on he used to smoke a Sunday cigar or two, but quit before he married. He never was a drinker, although his father liked whisky and always had some in the house. There was much work, and no luxury, on the Samuel Pyle farm. When Will got a chance to make a little money he took it: he worked over in Illinois all one autumn cutting broom corn and husking field corn. Then he hired out to a farmer north of Dana. It was during this period that the widowed Lambert Taylor came back to Indiana with his son John and his daughters Mary and Maria.

On a Saturday night in the fall of '95 Will came down by buggy for a festival at the United Brethren church. There his sister

[1] Nancy was a granddaughter of Thomas Hood, a Virginia veteran of the War of 1812, who was said to have been the first settler in the Dana area. Members of the Hood clan have inherited a tradition that they stem from Robin Hood himself.

"Frankie" introduced him to the red-haired newcomer from Illinois, Maria Taylor. Will was slight and short—five feet seven and one-half, but taller than Maria. He was twenty-eight, she twenty-five. He didn't see her home that night. Maria played the violin and was in demand to play for square dances and schottisches at gatherings in the neighborhood, along with another violinist, a pianist, and a bass fiddler. It was the other violinist, a friend of Will's, who arranged the first date for them—a date to go to church. Soon Maria found herself in a dilemma. She liked this gentle farmer with the curly brown hair, but she had a "fellow" in Illinois. Eventually, as Will Pyle said half a century afterwards, "I cut him out. It made him mad, too."

Will went out to Hamburg, Iowa, to visit an uncle, and he and Maria wrote to each other. One icy day he slipped and broke a kneecap, and he came back to Dana on crutches. Perhaps his hobbling melted Maria's heart; at any rate, soon after that she agreed to marry him. On Saturday nights Will, who had been hired by a farmer across the Wabash to break his wheat ground, would row across to his brother Quince's, where he kept a bicycle, and pedal seven miles to the Taylors' to spark Maria. On November 1, 1899, they were married, and in the spring they moved to the Samuel Elder farm on a sharecropper basis. Ernie was born the following August. When he was eighteen months Maria's older sister Mary fell sick; there was no woman to take care of the Taylor household, so the Pyles moved in—to stay, as it turned out.

Ernie's boyhood was not unlike that of thousands of Indiana farm boys, except that he was an only child and was left to himself a good deal. Years later he told of a recurring dream that used to frighten him as a boy at nights—a dream that the world was on a pinpoint, "way out somewhere," spinning around, and it seemed to him that at any moment it might let go. He would awaken terrified.

There was no plumbing in the Taylor homestead. There was a

backhouse, and Ernie took his baths in a washtub near the wood-stove in the kitchen, in water fetched from a deep well. There was a party-line telephone but no electric lighting. Not until about 1919 were plumbing and electricity installed. When Ernie was a child the lack of such things was not considered a deprivation by respectable Indiana farmers.

Ernie liked "stories" and loved to have his mother or Aunt Mary read to him. And he enjoyed being taken to visit the neighbors, especially Lucy Campbell, a woman of some education. It was his mother who exercised the profoundest influence on him. Maria was more articulate than Will, and perhaps more sensitive to Ernest's moods, which then, as later, ranged from exuberance to moodiness. She had no intention of spoiling him just because he was her only child; she was tender to him, but there was little idle sentimentality about her; while she had a ready laugh, her tongue could be severe.

Ernie recalled in print, thirty years after, the time she whipped him when he was four or five years old: "My father was plowing at the far end of our farm, a half-mile from the house. I was walking along behind the plow, barefooted, in the fresh soft furrow. He had just started the field and was plowing near a weedy fence-row. Red wild roses were growing there. I asked my father for his pocketknife, so I could cut some of the roses to take back to the house. He gave it to me and went on plowing. I sat down in the grass and started cutting off the roses. Then it happened in a flash. A blue racer came looping through the grass at me. I already had my horror of snakes at that tender age. It must have been born in me. I screamed, threw the knife away, and ran as fast as I could. Then I remembered my father's knife. I crept back over the plowed ground till I found it. He had heard me scream and had stopped. I gave him the knife and started back to the house. I approached the house from the west side. There was an old garden there, and it was all grown up in high weeds. I stopped on the far side and shouted for my mother to come and get me. She said for me to come on through by myself. I couldn't have done that if it had killed me not to. She ordered me to come through, and I began to cry. She told me if I didn't stop crying, and didn't come through, she would whip me. I couldn't stop, and I couldn't come through. So she came and got me. And she whipped me. One of the two times, I believe, that she ever whipped me.

"That evening, when my father came in from the fields, she told him about the crazy boy who wouldn't walk through the weeds and had to be whipped. And then my father told her about the roses, and the knife, and the snake. It was the roses, I think, that hurt her so. My mother cried for a long time that night after she went to bed."

Ernie's second and last whipping came several years later. The family had a sorrel driving horse, Cricket, and his mother had warned him against riding Cricket too hard. He disobeyed—and got a tanning.

The child's golden-red hair was allowed to grow long until he was three or four, and Will Bales, down the road, whose widowed father presently married Aunt Mary Taylor, hung a nickname on him—"Shag"—which stuck for years. He went to Sunday school regularly, at the little Bono Methodist Church a couple of miles from home, and was baptized—sprinkled, not immersed—in the Methodist faith. Blessing was always asked at table in the Pyle home.

A tiny "crick" ran through a pasture half a mile or so from the Pyles', and Ernie used to walk there barefoot, to fish or to doff his overalls and go "mud-crawling"—the water was too shallow for swimming. The biggest fish he ever caught actually surrendered: it swam inside Ernie's loose underwear, and he ate it for dinner. Once he fell between the slats of a hay wagon and was hanging suspended by his head, barely able to touch ground, when they found him. If he had been an inch shorter he would have hanged himself, Aunt Mary said.

In 1906 he entered school at Dana. Will Pyle provided a horse, a neighbor supplied a buggy, and one of the teachers drove Ernie and two other children to the schoolhouse and back. Six-year-old

Ernie felt suffocatingly self-conscious among the town boys of tiny Dana, but by next year the new consolidated school at Bono was finished, and he was transferred.

His best friend was Thad Hooker, a year older. "We thought the world would end if we didn't see each other every day," Ernie wrote later. "We went through the giggly stage. It got so we couldn't sit down at the table, either at his house or mine, without choking from the giggles. Our mothers would want to know what we were giggling about, and of course we weren't giggling about anything, and our mothers would get provoked and make us leave the table." Other playmates were the six Saxton kids, his cousins, sons of Aunt Frankie and Uncle Oat, "the coon-hunter who had a laugh like a bell ringing." With assorted Saxtons he used to coast down a slope and through a creek on the running gears of an old buggy, pretending he was an automobile-race driver at Indianapolis. Sometimes he would stay all night in the Saxtons' log house, where there would be four or five in a bed.

A favorite game was Knights of the Round Table. Thad had a Shetland pony, Ernie would get one of his father's horses, and, equipped with daggers of lath, rug-pole spears, and wash-boiler lids for shields, they would engage in tournaments.

Ernie was of such slight physique that he shied away from baseball and basketball. But he was always ready for a prank, and if there were repercussions his air of frail innocence usually turned suspicion aside. His voice tended to be high-pitched and to break or squeak when he was excited. He developed a habit of clearing his throat—"no-squeak insurance," he called it—before making a remark.

The copybook in which Ernie learned penmanship paraded such maxims and bits of learning as "A noble deed is a step toward God"; "Bicycles were used as early as 1815"; and "Columbus sailed from Palos, Spain." His marks were good. His over-all average in the eighth grade was 90.9.

When he was nine his father put him to riding an Oliver sulky plow behind three horses. His mother was uneasy, he was so little, but Mr. Pyle had learned to plow at that age, and on stumpy ground. "I remember that first day perfectly," Ernie wrote later. "My mother had gone to a club meeting, but she came home in the middle of the afternoon and brought me a lunch of bread and butter and sugar out to the field. And also, I suppose, she wanted to make sure I hadn't been dragged to death under the harrow." He never was good at milking, so Mr. Pyle would milk while his son fed the hogs and horses. Ernie was handy with tools and helped his father build a corn crib. In summer he was up at four; during school months they let him sleep longer. As a young man he was to look back on his farm days as a period of unusual hardship; he actually talked, in his early newspaper days, of writing a book about his rugged boyhood, when a puny kid did a man's work; but it is unlikely that he was pushed even as hard as custom warranted. He just didn't like farming.

He had a dog that he never forgot. When he was managing editor of a newspaper he wrote a nostalgic tribute to "Shep": "The most human of all dogs seems not to be a dog at all. At least not according to the American Kennel Club. The animal in question is the plain unadulterated American Shepherd, found on farms throughout the country. Probably the greatest Shepherd dog that ever lived was part of the household of an Indiana farm. If there is a human being in this world who is kindlier, more understanding, more faithful, or more intelligent than that dog, then the little boy who was then his master has spent twenty-five years in vain looking for him. The little boy had no brothers or sisters to play with. His dog was his constant companion. And in all that vast prairie there was no one who understood the child's mind better than did the dog Shep. . . . When a little boy whose feelings were hurt would go out into the yard and lie down and cry, the dog would go and lie beside him, and lick his face and whine in the most complete and understanding sympathy."

Ernie hunted rabbits occasionally, with cousin Lincoln Saxton, and set steel traps for muskrats, though he trapped more rabbits than muskrats, and sometimes a skunk or a cat. His "travels" started early. When he was eight Aunt Mary and some others took him to Ringling Brothers' circus at Terre Haute, and he was greatly excited when elephants were brought up to budge circus trucks out of the mud. When he was about ten his father drove him in a "rig" to a circus at Clinton; a downpour shooed them to the shelter of a covered bridge, but they finally made it. And his mother and Aunt Mary took him to Chicago to visit his great-aunt Nancy Miller, a sister of Grandpa Lambert Taylor.

He was fourteen or so when he had his first date. He and Thad Hooker went together on a Sunday night to take June West-brook and Marie Igo to church. Thad had made the engagement. Ernie "worried about it all week, and would have backed out, but my mother made me go. It took me all Sunday afternoon to get dressed. I had on a Charlie Dawes hard collar and a new brown suit." They drove behind Thad's pony, in a surrey that towered above the tiny steed. The girls, Ernie related, "were as scared as we were. We took them rather formally to church . . . and got stuck in the mud, and had to get out and lift. When we got back to the girls' house we played 'Authors' for a while. After that the whole thing sort of bogged down. We couldn't think of anything to say, and we wanted to go home but didn't know how to get started." Finally Mrs. Westbrook summoned her daughter, who reappeared holding up an alarm clock. "She didn't say a word, just sort of giggled. We said something about not knowing it was so late, and rushed out."

In 1914 or '15 a great event occurred—Mr. Pyle bought a car. It was an Overland, and Ernie learned to drive. He was more adept than his father, who once oiled the brakes to cure a squeak, though he said Ernie's story that he consequently drove through a plate-glass window in Dana was exaggerated. Next year Mr. Pyle bought Ernie a car for himself—a new Model-T runabout (around four hundred dollars then). Ernie and Thad and two other boys, driving to a skating rink, collided with a buggy, over-turning it. They got out of the scrape, the car was fixed up, and Mr. Pyle didn't say a word.

Thad and Ernie learned to smoke together—cornstalk at first, out in the fields or in an attic; then tobacco in corncob pipes. They smoked on the way home from school and hid the pipes in a woodpecker hole or in a grass-covered rabbit hole. Then Ernie got careless and left his corncob on a windowsill. His mother handed it to him. "I see you're smoking now," she said. "Yes," he answered, and that was that.

Ernie took various summer jobs. One year he drove a team behind a slip-scraper, used in building a grade for a spur track to a coal mine. Will Pyle took on the scraper job himself for a day so that his son could go to Indianapolis and see Resta win the five-hundred-mile automobile race. Ernie never got over that race. He wanted to be a driver himself. The speed kings of the Indianapolis classic were the ultimate in heroes to him. He cut out and preserved their pictures. In later years he attended the annual race whenever he could, and listened to it by radio from as far away as Alaska. "I would rather win that race than anything in the world," he wrote. "I would rather be Ralph De Palma than President."

A year before Ernie's graduation from high school the United States declared war on Germany. He wanted badly to get in the war, particularly after Thad left for the Army. At the commencement exercises "there was an empty flag-draped chair on the stage for him. I could hardly bear to go to commencement, I was so ashamed that I wasn't in the Army too." His parents had insisted that he graduate. A few weeks after getting his diploma he took leave of a tearful mother and went over to Peoria, Illinois, where he enrolled in the Naval Reserve. He was sent to the University of Illinois at Champaign for preliminary training. Here the undeveloped letter-writer of the future wrote home on a Sunday night in October: "Another boy and I went up town this afternoon, and sat out in front of the depot, on a dray wagon, and watched the trains go by. He likes trains about as well as I do, and we set and talked about how we would like to be on one of the engines firing."

He was about ready to move on to the Great Lakes Naval Training Station when the Armistice was signed.

CHAPTER 2

From Rhinie to BMOC

IT WAS a green and diffident youth, unprepossessing in bearing and dress, who in 1919 said good-by to the farm and went over to Bloomington to enroll at Indiana University. Times and horizons had changed vastly since his father's boyhood, when an eighth-grade education was above average for a country boy. The University, while tracing its origin to 1820, had begun to build its permanent establishment only thirty-five years before Ernie's entrance. If he was immature, so was the University, although the fifteen buildings clustered on the campus were impressive to him. So were the coeds. So were the many automobiles in Bloomington. "There is a lot of big fine machines down here," he said in a letter home. "Well, I've wrote about all I can think of."

He and a Dana schoolmate found a room just off the campus. The fraternities, in whose handsome houses the elite among the students dwelt, in less luxury than the pretentious façades suggested, showed small interest in the unsponsored farmer boy. There is a story that during "rush week" the Kappa Sigs made overtures to Ernie but changed their minds without bothering to inform him, and that he sat disconsolately on his rooming-house porch, waiting in vain for one of the fraternity boys to pick him up, as arranged, for a party.

He had little idea what he should study. One thing he did know —he wanted to get away from farming. On the way to Kirkwood Hall to register he fell in with other freshmen, or "rhinies," as they were called on the campus. One of them was saying, "Well, why not sign up for journalism? At least you don't have to add and subtract. It sounds like a pipe." That was Paige Cavanaugh, a salty farm boy from Salem, Indiana. It turned out that journalism wasn't open to freshmen, and Ernie signed up to major in economics.

The first year was uneventful. His grades were neither good nor bad; he had a keen memory and took careful notes at lectures in a fine stylized script that he had worked out. In his English class he discovered such verbotens as the one concerning split infinitives, but he was slow to give up—actually he never did entirely abandon—the Dana flavor in his language. He wrote Aunt Mary: "Glad your hogs did so well. That will help a right smart with your machine." From college he wrote his folks once a week and went home for an occasional week-end.

At first he engaged in few extracurricular activities, aside from gradually getting acquainted with people and briefly attending a dancing school. He met the Dean of Men, Dr. Clarence E. ("Pat") Edmondson, a comfortable Hoosier scholar, who took a liking to him. Soon Ernie was dropping in often at the Edmondson home for long talks, and he picked up the Dean's practice of rolling his own cigarettes. According to Mrs. Edmondson, Ernie "always had a sincerity in his eyes—he had very fine eyes—that made you forget he was homely." Ernie was to write of the Edmondsons: "They were never deans to me. They were people. We were friends, and I believe they taught me more of what life is about than anybody else in my youth, except my parents."

He and Cavanaugh became intimates. Cavanaugh had served two years in the Army, much of it in France, and Ernie liked to hear him talk of soldier life. He was also a rapt listener to the reminiscences of an old Dana friend, Walter B. ("Shorty") Lang, who had interrupted his schooling in '17 to join the French ambulance service. "Ernie had a hero complex," Cavanaugh recalled later. "He and I both had a good eye for phonies around the campus, and we used to sit around and mimic them, but nobody who had been overseas could do wrong in Ernie's eyes, no matter how big a blowhard he was. And the race drivers! He tried to get me to go to Indianapolis just before the five-hundred-mile race. He said, 'We'll hang around where the drivers are for a few days and hobnob with them, and maybe one of us will get a chance to ride as mechanic.' "

In his first year Ernie didn't do much dating. "We were just farm boys and didn't know how to operate," Cavanaugh said. Like everybody else, he spent a share of his time sipping Cokes in the Book Nook, a soda fountain where a student named Hoagland Carmichael would sometimes sit down at the piano, turn a sheaf of music upside down, and play endlessly by ear.

As the school year ended, Ernie and a college friend heard of a chance to make big money as tool dressers in an oil field at Bowling Green, Kentucky. So off they went, but it appeared that tool dressing required experience, and they went hungry for a day or two before getting work unloading bricks. Finally they were signed on as members of a team erecting steel tanks. His friend went home after a few weeks, but Ernie stayed on, was put in charge of his tank-setting crew, and given a raise. "I had to fire a man last night," he wrote to Dana. "It's quite a sensation for a kid like me to be able to fire a fellow twice as old, but I'm mighty good to them if they are any account."

Back at Bloomington as a sophomore, he began to branch out. Shorty Lang got him a bid from Sigma Alpha Epsilon, and he moved into the fraternity house to live—and to suffer occasional whalings with a paddle, which as a novice he was required to buy and to produce on demand, until his formal initiation. He paid more attention to the coeds. He wrote Aunt Mary about a dance: "We had a wonderful time and everybody was carried away with the music." He enrolled for his first journalism class, and in the second semester became a member of the staff of the college paper, the *Indiana Daily Student*. A colleague on the *Student*— Jack Stempel, later head of the University's department of journalism—remembered him as sensitive and shy in those days, but "he covered it up with a hard-boiled manner." Journalism, at first, was just another course to Ernie. When he dreamed of the future he dreamed of travel—not as a reporter but as an adventurer, working his way on ships. He showed an aptitude for newspapering, however, even if some older hands on the *Student* considered his writing style too simple.

He was still in the Naval Reserve, and in the summer of '21 went to Chicago for a three-week cruise on the training ship *Wilmette*. Most of the cruise he spent in the galley, cooking. During a stop at Mackinac Island the Navy invited the public aboard to look around, and Ernie, shirtless and aproned, looked up in dismay from his hot stove to find a coed from the University laughing at him. The *Wilmette* went as far north as Duluth, his longest bit of travel so far.

At the beginning of his junior year he was made city editor of the *Student*—the only time in his life that he possessed this title. The *Student* was a member of the Associated Press, and in November 1921 carried the AP's famous series of dispatches by Kirke Simpson, describing in glittering prose the burial of the Unknown Soldier in Arlington National Cemetery. They brought tears to Ernie's eyes. It was probably Kirke Simpson, as much as anyone else, who influenced Ernie's decision to become a newspaperman.

He was admitted to the Sphinx Club, an interfraternity social group, and to the journalistic fraternity Sigma Delta Chi, and to the staff of the University yearbook, the *Arbutus*. The country boy was beginning to be a BMOC—a "big man on the campus." He was having fun too, although he was by no means altogether contented. "I remember him many times as a sad little guy," Cavanaugh was to recall. "I don't know what was the matter with him. He wasn't particularly interested in what he was doing in college, either socially or in class. And sometimes just the thought of the behavior of some smart aleck on the campus would give him the blues. Then again, with the right girl and the right music— soft and sad—he would be carried to the heights, only to fall flat on his face after the dance was over, in a kind of poetic sadness. What was life all about anyway?"

That year the I. U. football team was playing Harvard at Cambridge. Ernie wanted to go, so he switched jobs for a few days with the sports editor of the *Student*. He and several other boys chipped in and acquired a car, a veteran Lozier, and drove to Boston. The car caught fire and burned up. Some of the party made the trip back by rail; Ernie and a classmate hitchhiked. It took five days, and they rode in more than fifty machines.

Another big game that year was the one with Purdue. Ernie's father and some other Dana men, including "Doc" Sturm, drove to Bloomington for it. Doc's son Paul came down from Purdue. Later Ernie wrote his folks: "I got a letter from Paul Sturm and he is all worked up. He said Doc called him home and accused he and me and the rest of us of being drunk when they were down here for the Purdue game. It is an outrage and makes me so mad I can't see straight. It's just like someone said once, no matter how hard you may work to get to the top, there's always someone waiting there to kick you down. I can account for every minute the boys spent here. . . . I wonder how he thinks I could spend eight hours a day working on the *Student,* make the highest grades in the fraternity, and go with one of the most highly respected girls in school if I was a drunkard? There are three forms of dissipation that I absolutely do not participate in, and those are gambling, drinking, and running with wild women, and I defy anyone to say they ever saw me do any of them. I guess papa ought to know whether I acted like I was drunk or not."

It may be that Ernie was bending the truth a little for home consumption, for he was finding out about hard drink, though he was certainly no addict. Once he and Cavanaugh set some prunes and apricots to fermenting in Cavanaugh's room at the little Tourner Hotel, where Cavanaugh was a bellhop. The result was more a jelly than a drink, so they ate it with spoons. "We got higher than a kite," Cavanaugh said. Another time, a fraternity brother recalled, Ernie "took on a load and crawled up on a closet shelf and went to sleep." But this is the sort of thing a college boy does not advertise to his parents.

Ernie found occasion to state a conservative view about the

coeds. The following pontification was apparently designed for submission as an editorial in his journalism class:

THE IDEAL GIRL

Would you, a man, care to marry the present-day "popular" college girl, care to have her be the mother of your children, to have her become mistress of your household? Personally, I would not. I am not an idealist, far from it, but it has appeared to me that there is much needless frivolity and tittering about among the young ladies of the present day.

The girls who are most popular on the campus are those who can dance the most superbly; who can "spread the best line," so to speak; who can wear the most out-of-the-ordinary clothes and get by with it; and who titter aimlessly about, not knowing what they will do next nor how they will do it. . . . Personally, I like this type of girl—to frolic about with. What average young man doesn't? They show you a good time, take your mind from your troubles, (and your studies), and the money from your pocket, and still we like it. I think it is all right to use this type of girl as a play-thing during a college career, but when a man reaches the age, and the position in life when he begins to think seriously of a wife and home of his own, his mind turns to an entirely different type of girl. The type who is willing to share your troubles, sympathize with you in your periods of adverses, and makes your interests her interests.

He was sure that he had found the girl to fill his editorial prescription. He fell in love with a pretty red-haired coed, Harriett Davidson. He was mad about her.

Meantime Ernie was doing so well scholastically that he was excused from mid-year examinations, so that he could work full time on the *Student* during exam week. "Twelve of us have been picked to do the work of the regular staff of fifty," he wrote to Dana, "which means that we will have to work continuously from eleven in the morning until one o'clock at night." And he was learning one of the usufructs of the fourth estate—free admission.

"I went to a dance at the Student Building last night but couldn't get a pass for it. I think it is only the second dance I have had to pay for this year. I ran onto some girls coasting down Indiana Avenue yesterday afternoon, and coasted with them for about an hour. I sleep with one of the boys now, and he is just like a furnace, I never get the least bit cold. . . . *Tol'able David* [a movie] was here but I didn't get to see it as I always have to work."

He and Jack Stempel were promoted to news editors. They worked nights in alternate weeks, and on his off-duty weeks Ernie had plenty of time to circulate with Harriett. He wrote home: "Yes, it was pretty hard to lose the Purdue [basketball] game, but as usual I didn't let it worry me much. I guess there was a bunch got drunk after the game. I took my girl to the dance and there was such a big bunch of fellows there without dates that I sold two dances for a quarter apiece. It didn't cost me anything to get in in the first place, so I made money. I think everybody in school knows about it by this time, and they all think it was quite original. If I had been her I expect I would have gotten mad, but she didn't. . . ."

Harriett wanted him to go to Indianapolis for the state dance of her sorority, but he wrote home: "I told her I didn't have enough money. I expect I could make the trip on six or seven dollars but I didn't care much about going anyway. . . . That dance where they tried to dance by wireless music was last Saturday night at the Student Building. They had their wires all strung and were going to catch some music from Pittsburgh, but the air was so damp that they couldn't do it, so they wound up a phonograph over in Science Hall and played into the amplifier and no one ever knew the difference."

A few days later he wrote that his long hours were cutting his weight so that he could barely keep his pants on. And a postscript: "I didn't send my laundry this week." His custom was to mail his laundry home, in a canvas satchel, not only from Bloomington but later from Washington and New York, even after he married. To his mother it was always like getting another letter from Ernest.

One letter home indicated that he had definite ideas about a newspaper career: "Stuke Gorrell, my Kappa Sig buddy who worked on the *Student,* is coming back to visit this week-end. . . . I would like to go into the newspaper business with him sometime because he sure is good. . . . I hear from Doris about every week. I think she must be getting to the crazy stage, the way some of her letters sound. She talks a right smart about men and that makes me sick. I still like the women and like to play around, but I guess I have gotten old enough not to lose my head over everyone I see. How are your lambs and chickens getting along?"

CHAPTER 3

Adventure

IN MARCH 1922 Indiana University accepted an invitation
to send its baseball team to Japan. "I've just got to
go!" Ernie told Cavanaugh. Dean Edmondson, who with
Mrs. Edmondson was to accompany the team, gave his approval
on condition that Ernie make up his schoolwork during the summer session. Ernie's parents were upset, but there was no stopping him. He borrowed two hundred dollars, the note for which
was endorsed by Dean Edmondson.

Three of his fraternity brothers—Harold Kaiser, Joel Benham,
and Warren Cooper—got similar sanction, and the four boys
set out by day coach for Seattle. There, after sleeping four in a
bed at the YMCA, they talked themselves into menial jobs on
the liner *Keystone State*. Ernie wrote home: "I am in perfect
health, and I think I have a pretty level head, so there is not the
slightest cause to worry about me. I have trotted around this
old globe considerably, and I think I should be pretty well quali-
fied to handle myself wisely."

The twelve-man baseball squad arrived with the Edmondsons
and the two coaches, and on April 1 the *Keystone State* steamed
out into Puget Sound. An article mailed to the *Student*, signed
"Ernest T. Pyle, '23"—his first by-line—reported that most of
the party, including himself, were soon seasick. And "about
five days out a storm was encountered, many sailors saying it was
the worst they had ever seen on the Pacific with the exception
of a typhoon." The article continued: "A word about the

21

four adventurers. Kaiser and I are serving as bellboys. Since we
two are the only bellboys on the ship, we take turns about working, so that neither of us is overburdened with our labors. We
carry ice, water, shine shoes, deliver packages, fix bath tubs, and
tend to innumerable queer wants of the passengers. Benham is
assistant bartender. . . . Cooper is steward in the tea-room. . . .
We all have comparatively easy work, and are treated well by the
officers, passengers, and crew."

Ernie didn't mention a certain exception to the pleasant
treatment. One member of the baseball party insisted on regarding the boys as of a low caste and once gave Ernie a tongue-lashing
for spilling something. Ernie never forgot it. Joel Benham had
better luck. During the storm he upset a tray of drinks in the
lap of Efrem Zimbalist, the famous violinist. Zimbalist just
laughed.

The boys discovered to their dismay, after signing on, that
they had to stay with the ship after it touched Japan and thus
could not make the baseball tour. So in Japan they said good-by
to the team. They got a chance to tour Yokohama, Tokyo, and
Kobe during the ship's stopover and then went on to China and
the Philippines.

On an earlier voyage the crew of the *Keystone State* had struck
at Hong Kong for more pay, and a new crew had been signed on.
Now the strike had been settled, and at Hong Kong the old
hands were taken aboard. The temporary crew included a number
of Filipinos who were to be dropped at Manila, but several of them
wanted to go on to the States. Among these was a bright young
steward named Eugene Uebelhardt, son of a Swiss father and a
Spanish-mestiza mother. Ernie and the other collegians helped
him stow away. At least six stowaways were caught, but Ernie
and his comrades hid Gene in a clothes locker during the
daily inspections, carried food to him, and kept a constant watch.

At Yokohama the four rejoined the baseball party and with the
athletes were banqueted at the Imperial Hotel in Tokyo before
embarking for home. The adventurers, now idle, were quartered

in steerage. Joe Sloate, second baseman on the team, recalled later: "When we got on the ship at Yokohama and found they were supposed to stay in the filthy, stinking steerage compartments we decided to do something about it. It worked like this. Nobody paid much attention to Ernie and his pals in the daytime, so they came up to our cabins to sleep. During the night they would stay on deck, away from the sickening steerage. We brought our pockets full of food out of the dining room every meal, and fed them."

As the ship neared Seattle the boys got nervous about their stowaway. However, when the *Keystone State* docked, he walked off unchallenged. The four comrades chipped in to pay his fare to Indiana, and he went to Dana with Ernie, who was quite proud of "his boy." The home folks liked him too. Ernie would borrow the family Overland, drive it slowly until out of sight and sound of the house, and then say to Gene, "You think your Filipino drivers are pretty wild. See how you like this!" Whereupon he would open the throttle and scatter dust over half of Vermillion County.

In June, when Ernie entered summer school, he enrolled Gene in Bloomington High School. For a while that summer Ernie and a friend, "Nemo" Crowder, earned a little money by working at the Kappa Sigma house—Ernie washing dishes, Nemo waiting on table.

Ernie was made editor-in-chief of the *Student* for the summer session—during which the paper appeared twice a week rather than daily. He also was in charge of an innovation, the *State Fair Student*. Ernie and six or seven reporters set up shop at the fairgrounds at Indianapolis, and ten thousand copies were run off each day for distribution there.

When the fall term opened—his senior year—he found himself a big man on the campus for sure. Nearly everybody knew him and liked him. He had never been one to vie deliberately for place or popularity, but his quiet industriousness, his good humor, and his lack of "side" were esteemed. His sloppy clothes grew sloppier, if anything. He didn't move about with many of the campus big shots except in line of duty; his real friends were relatively obscure students. And there was, of course, Dean Edmondson. It was the Dean who recommended Ernie for the managership of the football team, which won him a varsity "I," and for membership in the premier campus organization, the Aeons.

The football managership led Ernie into one predicament: "They got me up by surprise in front of three thousand students at a football rally one night and made me make a speech. I had said about two sentences, and gone into my first extended-arm gesture, when out of the sea of faces I had to pick out Nemo Crowder, sitting way back there, laughing at me. That threw me off. I went completely blank. And there I was, stuck, in front of three thousand students, with my arm sticking out to one side, and not another word would come out. I finally walked off the stage, with my arm still sticking out. Everybody howled. I swore then it would be my last speech." And it was—almost.

SAE turned down a boy from Dana, proposed for membership by Ernie, who thereupon moved from the fraternity house to a rented room shared by Joel Benham and Gene Uebelhardt.

Ernie continued to be devoted to Harriett, and took her to Dana to meet the folks. And when Mr. and Mrs. Pyle and Aunt Mary came to Bloomington for the Michigan Aggies game, they were dined by Harriett and her mother. Aunt Mary remembered a quarter of a century later that Mrs. Pyle picked up a dollar bill in a Bloomington street.

When the University band needed money for a trip to Purdue, Ernie, the auto-race fan, and some friends conceived the idea of an auto-polo match, with admission fees, to raise the necessary funds. They attached steel hoops to two jalopies, so that the cars could roll over without hurting the poloists. Ernie and Bill Pierce, in a car called "Methuselah," were matched against Barrett Woodsmall and Joseph F. Breeze in "Apollo Jr." The score was one to one when the Pyle-Pierce car, which Ernie drove while

Pierce swung the mallet, got engine trouble and the contest was ended.

Just before the Purdue game at Lafayette, Ernie is said to have donned a scholar's robe and an old slouch hat and preached the traditional funeral sermon for "John Purdue." He helped found a monthly "razz sheet" called "The Smokeup," which poked fun at campus personages. In the 1923 *Arbutus*, among ten men singled out for caricatures and jingles Ernie was the first. The verse read:

This brilliant gem which blushed unseen in Dana,
Long since globe-trotter, Student Ed., Aeon and who-knows-what,
Still wears the same old hat, is still the same good fellow,
Lo, this man's name heads all the lot.

His successes turned to ashes for Ernie when his pretty red-head threw him over for another man. He was crushed. His heart and his vanity were badly hurt. It was the Edmondsons who, he wrote later, "sat in understanding and talked in their calm slow voices" that night he "thought the world had come to an end."

About this time the *La Porte* (Indiana) *Herald* asked Professor Joseph W. Piercy, head of the journalism department, to recommend a reporter for its staff. Ernie heard about it and went to see the Edmondsons. The understanding Dean broke a rule of his own against approving premature departures from college and gave his blessing to the project. Ernie took it up with his parents. They were firmly opposed, but in the end he simply notified them that he had taken the job. In late January of 1923 he went to La Porte to work, at twenty-five dollars a week. He was twenty-two, and he intended never to set foot on the Indiana University campus again.

CHAPTER 4

The Cub

THE first-blush estimate of the new reporter by the city editor of the *La Porte Herald*, Ray E. Smith, was not flattering: "Mr. Beal[1] and I thought we had picked a lemon. This young man, bashful and unimpressive, didn't look like a newspaperman to us. But we needed a man, so after finding him a room at the YMCA we put him to work covering the courthouse, fire and police stations, city hall, and a few other offices. People liked him immediately." Those months in La Porte were crowded with educational opportunities in basic newspapering, which a small-city newspaper often affords a cub in greater variety than does the metropolitan daily.

The Ku Klux Klan, soon to swell into enormity in Indiana, was in its organizing stage. Ray Smith was tipped off about a Klan recruitment meeting, and since Ernie had been in town only a few days and was known to few people, assigned him to attend. "Word got around that this stranger was there," according to Smith, "and he was followed to the YMCA by several men, who questioned him in his room. He was warned not to publish anything, but refused. His story was printed." There was no reprisal; the reborn KKK was at this time more puerile than sinister.

Among the friends Ernie made was Art Wegner, a blacksmith near the *Herald* building. Wegner, who occasionally contributed a letter in dialect to the paper, remembered years afterward: "I knowed one time when he ketched a feller doin' a trick he

[1] Charles A. Beal, the editor.

26

shouldn't a did, an' Ernie talked me into takin' him to South Bend that night for a kinda alley-by so's there wouldn't be no trouble. An' all tha time tha little redhead preached to tha other feller in the back seat. That feller is a deacon or su'thin' in tha church now."

Not long before Ernie left college, the Scripps-Howard newspaper chain installed Earle E. Martin as editor of both its newly founded *Washington Daily News* and its newly purchased *Indianapolis Times*. Martin was also head of the Scripps-Howard feature service, NEA (Newspaper Enterprise Association), at Cleveland. He was a man of energy and ideas, and he wanted "bright young men" for his papers. To this end he visited Indiana University and talked with, among others, Nelson Poynter, editor of the *Student*. Poynter suggested various possibilities, including Ernie. In May Ernie was invited by Martin to come to Cleveland and talk about a job. The *Herald* had raised him to twenty-seven fifty a week, but Martin's offer of thirty dollars as a reporter in Washington— the traditional mecca of American newspapermen—was quickly accepted. Poynter took a similar offer.

The city room, indeed the entire editorial working space, of the *Daily News* was a shabby, littered, ill-ventilated rectangle congested with secondhand desks and constricted between the clattering United Press bureau at the front and the even more clattering composing room and stereotype foundry to the rear, on the third floor of a narrow old five-story building at 1322 New York Avenue, Northwest, a few blocks from the White House. The paper had been launched eighteen months before, in a wave of expansion that followed Roy W. Howard's appointment in 1921 as chairman of the board of the newspaper chain, after an extraordinary success as president of the Scripps-owned United Press. It was a one-cent tabloid, an experiment inspired in part by the phenomenal growth of Captain Patterson's *New York Daily News*, and in part by remembrance of a Scripps fling with adless journalism, the *Chicago Day Book*, which had made a small start when World War I caused its abandonment. The *Washington Daily*

News, in fact, started as an adless paper, but after some months accepted such advertisements as could be cajoled out of skeptical merchants. The paper ran to only a dozen pages, dowdily illustrated with castings from NEA's syndicated matrices, since there was no engraving equipment. There were three or four typesetting machines, which along with the other composing-room equipment were presided over by foreman Jim O'Malley, a jovial citizen imported from the *Cleveland Press.*

The managing editor of the moment was a harried but good-humored product of the UP, Herbert W. Walker. The young staff was fluid, to say the least, as Earle Martin experimented with men and methods; shortly before Ernie's arrival there had been a succession of three city editors in a single day. Nevertheless, there was a real *esprit de corps* among the staff. The content of the paper was meager, but within the limits of its shoestring budget it was enterprising and sprightly. We[2] tended to look down our noses at the sedate *Evening Star,* Ned McLean's slipping *Post,* and of course the Hearst *Times* and *Herald.*

Among those present around the time of Ernie's arrival were Martha Strayer, who was to outstay all the rest (she was still a kingpin of the writing staff nearly three decades after she joined it); Milton MacKaye, a crack young reporter from Iowa, now a magazine man; Harold Keats, a lusty and resourceful fellow (he resolved the speculation pro and con the hotly rumored pregnancy of middle-aged Mrs. Nicholas Longworth by simply asking her and getting a yes, which was quite something in pre-Winchell days); Luther Reid, city editor for a time, and later a State Department executive; Willis ("June") Thornton, a future city editor, whose Monday-morning penance was a straight swig, without chaser, from a bottle of castor oil he kept in his desk; Bob Burkhardt, on makeup, who went on to movie-writing in California; Leonard Hall, whose sparkling drama-and-movie column was the paper's top attraction; Charles M. ("Chuck") Egan, a big fellow out of Notre Dame, later an executive of the *Washing-*

[2] I had joined the staff a month before Ernie.

ton Evening Star; Ralph D. ("Polly") Palmer, an ebullient kid from Akron, who stayed on to reign for years as city editor and managing editor; and many others, coming and going. There was a boy from the Missouri School of Journalism, who called a galley a "tray" and thought a stick of type was a single slug from a linotype. There was, for a few weeks, Steve Hannegan, an Indiana lad who left the *News* to strike it rich as a public-relations genius. Another Hoosier, Emerson ("Abe") Martin, from Elkhart, Indiana, was city editor for a while.

Ernie was a reporter at first. Soon, however, he was to be betrayed by a facility at headline-writing and copyreading into spending years on the desk. As a reporter, he had the advantage that a small staff offers—a wide range of assignments. A special attraction, until it palled, was the opportunity for free meals while covering luncheons or dinners.

Those were rather harum-scarum days. When the last edition had been put to bed, about five o'clock in the afternoon, it was common practice to push a couple of desks together and start a game of poker or blackjack. Ernie never tangled with poker, but he liked blackjack. And sometimes after work we would phone a bootlegger to fetch a half-gallon Mason jar of gin, on which reporters, printers, and stereotypers would collaborate. Ernie developed a formidable ability to hoist the jar and, instead of stopping at a single swig, keep it aloft while his Adam's apple registered two or three consecutive swallows. One time, at what turned out to be the final annual dinner of something called the Deadline Club— a very informal association of newspapermen whose sole function was this yearly binge—Ernie and everybody else got plastered. The dinner started at midnight, on a Saturday, so that both morning and evening staffs could attend. When I got to my YMCA room at dawn I found Ernie unaccountably asleep in my bed. How he got into the room I didn't know, and he wouldn't say. But it was nearer than his own place.

We were all young and could rebound easily from such dissipations. Ernie was always on the job at seven o'clock. And seven o'clock on the *News* was an institution. The others would insist that they couldn't start the day right without Ernie's morning gun—a resounding belch. He would demur on the ground that his gullet couldn't do him justice unless he ate an apple first, but even if this were not provided he would eventually oblige with a Gargantuan burst. Then, as often as not, Harold Keats, whose puckishness was belied by a ministerial front, would lead in singing "Rock of Ages," or some other hymn, to an unchurchly rhythm. After that we settled down to saw wood.

Earle Martin was succeeded as editor by John M. Gleissner, a fine and able man plagued by a hatful of complexes, and Herb Walker gave way to Merton Burke as managing editor. "Burkie" was a lovable and sometimes brilliant little guy who had his troubles and liked his dram.

There was no Newspaper Guild, and nobody computed his hours. We worked hard, but seldom minded this. We had a real affection for the paper—"the Interesting Little," as we used to call it, mimicking the writers of letters to the editor who referred to "your interesting little newspaper." Our off-work conversation was largely shop talk. Most of us knew few people in Washington except for our colleagues on the paper, and much of our off-duty time was spent in the office or in the UP bureau, where there was usually a poker or coon-can game or a bull session during the evening. The UP staff was small in those days, but it included Raymond Clapper, Tom Stokes, Frederick Kuh, Larry Martin, and Paul Mallon.

That first year was the year of President Harding's death, on August 2; Ernie and the rest of us worked all night and all the next day, and a few days later went down to the Treasury corner to gape at the cortege. It was the year the *American Mercury* first appeared, in December, under the co-editorship of H. L. Mencken and George Jean Nathan, and Ernie devoured it as presently he devoured *The New Yorker*. And it was the year that Ernie was invited to dinner, on Halloween, by a friend from Indi-

ana University, Anita Hanna, who was living with a pretty little
blonde of Ernie's age from Minnesota, Geraldine Siebolds. Ernie
had to leave soon after dinner to cover a community Halloween
party, and it was about a year before he saw Jerry again.

We used to eat at the Blossom Inn, a cafeteria across the street;
at Child's, a few doors from the *News*; at the Allies Inn; and on
festive occasions at Herzog's on the waterfront, or the Occidental,
or Harvey's. Few of us belonged to the National Press Club. I
think we were awed by the old-timers.

We did a little singing—perhaps at the Reynolds sisters' room-
ing house on Nineteenth Street, where June Thornton and Len
Hall lived, or perhaps in the composing room over a jar of gin.
Ernie had a sweet, high voice that was good on such favorites of
his as "Marquita" and "Back Home Again in Indiana" and "If I
Had My Way." Once in a great while the editorial side and some
printers would chip in for gin and sandwich stuff and give a cooperative party at the home, in suburban Hyattsville, Maryland, of
Jim O'Malley and his wife. These were called "Over the Hoop"
parties for some now obscure reason connected with a sort of pit-
fall in Jim's back yard. Sobriety did not prevail. But there were
sedater pastimes too. Washington had several legitimate theaters in
those days—Poli's, the Belasco, the National, and one or two
others. Ernie used to go as often as he could get passes or afford to
pay his way.

We had no qualms about the future, no feeling of insecurity,
although we seldom had more than a week's pay in our pockets.
We thought we were good, and our bosses sometimes humored our
vanity. Ernie took himself seriously enough in those days to talk
about writing the story of his life. Later he talked of writing a
seventy-five-thousand-word novel, each word to be the same
certain impolite monosyllable; he said he was stumped for a title.
He had all or most of his hair then, and June Thornton used to
delight in blowing a mouthful of cigarette smoke into his crisp
pink poll, from which the smoke would curl slowly for minutes.

Ernie was no Beau Brummel. He would come to work in winter wearing such items as a white woolen stocking cap and a loud plaid lumberjack shirt. Once Roy Howard, down from New York to give the struggling paper a squirt of energy, caught sight of Ernie thus attired at a desk, and demanded of John Gleissner, "What's *that*?"

CHAPTER 5

Jerry

IN THE autumn of 1924 Ernie met Jerry Siebolds for a second time, and this time something happened, emotionally, to both of them. It was the beginning of a love story.

Geraldine Elizabeth Siebolds was born August 23, 1900, at Langdon, Minnesota. Her father, a native of Germany, had been brought to America as a child by his mother, a schoolteacher. He married a sweet and gracious woman of complex ancestry—Dutch, French, and Scottish. During Jerry's childhood Mr. Siebolds had a mill at Langdon. Later he was foreman at the state hospital in Hastings, Minnesota. Jerry was a brilliant student at high school and was active in the Presbyterian Church and the Christian Endeavor Society. She played the piano and sang in the church choir and as soloist at "functions."

In March of wartime 1918, when the government was calling for more and more clerks in Washington, Jerry and a friend, Dorothy Myer, secretly took a Civil Service examination. One evening the Hastings telegraph agent got wires for them from Washington; jobs were waiting. The telegrapher guessed the girls would be at choir practice and delivered the messages to them in the middle of a hymn. Breaking the news to her parents was a hard thing for Jerry. Her mother "had a sort of fainting spell when I told her," Jerry remembered later. "Dad had to call the doctor. I couldn't bring myself to tell Dad that night. Next evening I went to him while he was reading his paper. 'I'm going to Washington,' I said. He was very kind about it. He said he had no sons he could send to the Army.[1] He had tried to get into the Army himself, but his health was poor. So he said it was all right for me to go."

The girls' jobs were as clerks in the Civil Service Commission. Dorothy left after a year, but Jerry stayed on. She had learned to value independence, and she had met people she liked. In fact she became engaged to one of them. She was engaged at the time she met Ernie again. Ernie, like his father before him, cut the other fellow out.

One night I was invited along with Ernie to have dinner at Jerry's. We found the apartment dimly lighted; she had neglected to pay her light bill, the electricity had been disconnected, and she had defiantly resorted to candles rather than make peace with the electric company. She liked candlelight anyway. Also, there was in her a stubborn, almost a morbid, nonconformism. Externally she was poised and calm, with a quick wit and a quick smile that was gracious or gay or mischievous as occasion suggested. She seemed unusually self-sufficient; she could spend long hours alone in apparent contentment, reading or writing verse or just dawdling to defer the domestic chores that she never learned to like. But there were depths in Jerry where dark waters struggled to engulf her.

Ernie and Jerry long remembered December 25 of that year as their "Cecil Alley Christmas." They had got the name and address of a poor Negro family in Cecil Court, a slum area near the Potomac in Georgetown, and had bought quantities of food and dolls and what not, planning to deliver them on Christmas Day. But they celebrated the Eve too well, and on Christmas felt so bad they finally arranged to send the stuff over to Cecil Court rather than play Samaritans in person. They felt so bad, in fact, that they arrived four hours late for a dinner party and feasted on nothing much but the skin of a no longer festive chicken, in an atmosphere of disapproval.

In the spring of 1925 Ernie was feeling run down. He asked for two months' leave and went to Dana to rest. He and Jerry wrote

[1] Jerry's two brothers were not old enough.

each other daily or oftener. He asked her to come out and visit. In May she took her vacation and stopped off for a few days in Indiana before going on to Minnesota. They continued to write constantly—letters repetitive with endearments. Then Ernie met Jerry in Chicago and they returned to Washington together.

They had decided to be married. Jerry was reluctant; in her anti-conventional eyes marriage was not for her. But Ernie shrank from offending his parents. So she agreed, while stipulating that the marriage be kept from their Washington friends. They took a day off and were married by a justice of the peace at Alexandria, across the Potomac in Virginia. Next day they were back at work. And for years they made a fetish of insisting they weren't really married.

They rented a dowdy first-floor-and-basement apartment in an old white brick house at 456 N Street, Southwest—"N the Little Letter," as Ernie's friends got to know it, since that was the way he always gave directions to visitors and taxi drivers. In January 1926 they moved to an apartment on downtown Connecticut Avenue—one big room and big bath, no kitchen, and no furniture except for two Army cots, a grill for making breakfast, and eventually a wicker chair or two. That was quite a place. Both Ernie and Jerry rolled their own cigarettes, and tobacco accumulated on the floor like sawdust in an old saloon. On Saturday nights they would clean up. Saturday nights also they would get a bottle of bogus Bacardi rum and mix sticky red cocktails of grenadine and rum that would leave rings on the window sills until the next clean-up a week later. Being eccentric became a ritual. They kept pretty much to themselves and probably were drinking more than was good for them. They would drop in of an evening on one friend or another, but after a few minutes would announce that they had been "insulted"—this was just a gag, of forgotten origin—and stalk out with the walking sticks they both affected.

Ernie was getting tired of his job—he was on the desk, pinned down by his skill as a copyreader. An urge to travel kept gnawing at him. Finally he put it up to Jerry—said they should quit their jobs and do something interesting for a while. She agreed. Her bosses at the Civil Service Commission let her go with regret, for she had been not only efficient but popular and had risen to be a supervisor. And everybody at the *News* was sorry too. The Pyles pooled their savings, about a thousand dollars, and Ernie bought a Ford roadster for six hundred and fifty dollars. He also bought a tent, white coveralls and helmets for himself and Jerry, and assorted camping equipment. In June 1926 they set out to drive "around the rim of the United States."

They headed southward, through Virginia, zestful for come what might. At night they camped by the roadside, inexpertly pumped up their little stove, and cooked. "We both cooked," Jerry said, "but Ernie was more experienced than I." They drove across the deep South, and through Texas to El Paso, and crossed the border to visit Juárez. Then across the Southwest, which they "loved at first sight." At Los Angeles, Paige Cavanaugh and some other young men hopeful of movie jobs had taken a house, and here the Pyles stayed a week. Then on to San Francisco, and up the coast to Portland, of which their first impression was unfavorable: when they stopped at a suburban roadside stand for a bite, an old man lectured them for "smoking cigarettes and eating watermelon on Sunday afternoon." At Seattle they turned eastward, and ran into a nightmare: somebody had strewn tacks in the road, and Ernie made thirteen tire changes in a single morning. At Jamestown, North Dakota, they bought four secondhand tires for a dollar apiece.

One night in August, ten weeks and nine thousand miles after leaving Washington, they camped at Elizabeth, New Jersey, and a storm blew their tent down on them. They were so tired they just lay there on their cots and let the rain soak them. Next day, bedraggled, they drove the Model T to New York and, in Ernie's words, "up Fifth Avenue, in a downpouring rain, on two cylinders, with knots as big as teakettles on all four tires, and had to sell the precious thing for a mere hundred and fifty dollars in order to get something to eat." They phoned Shorty Lang, of Dana and I.U., who was working in New York. He got them located tentatively in a theatrical hotel in the east Forties.

On his second day of job-hunting Ernie found work on the copy desk of the *New York Evening World*—the lobster trick, midnight to eight in the morning. He and Jerry moved into an apartment in a dingy brownstone house (since torn down) at 25 Abingdon Square, which is at Eighth Avenue and Twelfth Street on the edge of Greenwich Village.

No. 25 was presided over by Mrs. Daye Remington, a fancier of cats. She was a most respectable woman, but with her apartments usually occupied by young newspaper people she didn't always succeed in maintaining a perfect decorum. Nor did her cats serve the utilitarian purpose they might have, for Ernie and Jerry were occasionally awakened by rats. The Pyles had one big room, with nondescript furniture and torn window shades, and a bath. There was no kitchen. When Ernie came home from work Jerry would prepare his breakfast on an electric grill. They dined out, usually at the Shipshape, a block away, but by Thursday nights they were ordinarily so low in funds that they would go to Child's and eat "the vegetable dinner with Savita sauce"—those were the days when Child's was trying to reform carnivorous America. After dinner they would play double Canfield, night after night, unless they were out visiting or being visited. Sometimes "the newspaper gang would come after work and listen to the phonograph and talk gravely about things they weren't informed on." Sometimes they would climb through a trap door and sit on the roof with a bottle and talk, "and almost drive Mrs. Remington crazy because she was afraid we'd fall off."

Abingdon Square was bleak enough physically, but it could be gay—too gay once in a while. On Christmas Eve that year Ernie and Jerry and Milton MacKaye, then on the *New York Post*, celebrated with some bootleg drinks at a restaurant and were sick in bed all Christmas Day.

Ernie would get home from work about nine, eat his breakfast, and go to bed. Since he always had to have air, the windows would be open, which left Jerry, who was wide awake, shivering in a comforter. As winter closed in and her daytime discomfort grew, she decided this couldn't go on and got a job as receptionist at a business school in the *World* building, accepting in lieu of pay a course in shorthand and typing. Ernie, going off duty, and Jerry, on her way to work, would meet every morning across the street from the *World*.

Before this, MacKaye had persuaded Ernie to move over to the copy desk of the *Post*, then reputed to be New York's ablest desk. First he had to go through a tryout of some days, during which he played safe by working both jobs—the small hours on the *World*, then directly to the *Post* for the day shift.

The *Post* was then owned by the Curtis interests. Ralph E. Renaud was managing editor. The staff included such well-known journalistic names as Byron ("Barney") Darnton, Bruce Gould, Raymond Daniell, and Lindesay Parrott. James Thurber had left the *Post* not long before; the soon-to-be-famous humorist was, according to MacKaye, "always being sent over to Jersey to write features about cats that ate spaghetti."

The *Post* paid five dollars for each week's best headline, and Ernie often won it, averting a Thursday-night dinner at Child's. A headline remembered by *Post* old-timers was the one he wrote over a squib about a motorist who had been left abandoned after a struggle with robbers:

THIEVES ROB MAN,
THROW HIM AWAY

Ernie was uncertain what he wanted out of life. If he dreamed of being a columnist, there is no record of it, and in New York he must have perceived the difficulties of getting such an assignment. Colleagues regarded him as very sensitive. He seemed to have a chip on his shoulder. "He was quick to resent a slight, or an

THE UNIVERSITY OF WINNIPEG
DISCARDED
WINNIPEG 2. MAN. CANADA

imagined slight," MacKaye recalled. "He disliked many people. But he would take anything off a friend." It was during those days that *The New Yorker* made its debut, and Ernie became and remained one of its ardent readers. Some fragments of manuscript that he wrote later on might have been intended for submission to *The New Yorker*; they were found in a manila envelope with his notation, "Early Writings—No Good."

Ernie and Jerry used to visit an old-fashioned apothecary shop on Twelfth Street, run by Dr. Uhfelder, an elderly Viennese, who would rather be listened to than wait on customers. Ernie described him as a man "windy and wild with a gleam in his eye, who didn't know half the time what he was doing because he would get carried away in his own tall tales of how he had sat at Heine's feet, and studied under Hegel and Nietzsche, and been around the world in great ships. But he was grand if he liked you, and he did like us."

In late summer sad news came from Dana: Aunt Mary's husband, Uncle George Bales, died. Ernie wrote: "Dear Auntie—It is so easy to philosophize about the sweetness of death and all that, but when it comes home that is always a different matter. But death had to come sometime, and Uncle George had lived a long time, well and happily, and with little to regret. I think in his way Uncle George had had a good time, had enjoyed his life, and he had all the friends one could wish for. And that's about all there is to measure a life by—the happiness you've had and the happiness you've given."

While Ernie was in New York I succeeded Merton Burke as managing editor of the *Washington News,* and some time after that Lowell Mellett succeeded John Gleissner as editor. Mellett wangled a more liberal budget. We were shorthanded, as usual, and badly needed a good telegraph editor. I suggested Ernie. Lowell agreed, and I wrote him. Ernie wired that he would come only If I was going to be retained as managing editor. That was a rather embarrassing wire for me to hand to Lowell, but he grinned and said to tell Ernie okay. The *Post* offered Ernie a raise if he would stay, but by this time he was eager to change his scene again.

He and Jerry found that the second-floor apartment at their old address, 456 N Street, Southwest, was available. And on Saturday, Christmas Eve, 1927, they returned to Washington. The *News* office was deserted when they looked in, but they found most of us at a party, and there was a proper homecoming. At six a.m. Monday Ernie was back at work.

CHAPTER 6

Washington

ERNIE did a superior job as telegraph editor, for which he received sixty dollars a week. Some of this went to Dana, where the farm was not doing well, so there wasn't too much money. What there was, he and Jerry spent without thought of budget or future.

He was as fast and clean a copy-handler as I ever knew, and worked a hard, tense shift of eight hours. But he asked one day if he could try writing an aviation column on the side—he was developing a veneration for aviators that was reminiscent of his devotion to automobile racers. The project was approved, and on March 26, 1928, there was launched what may have been the first daily aviation column in the country.

Ernie would finish his office work at two or three in the afternoon, then prowl the old Washington-Hoover Airport, the Army's Bolling Field, the Anacostia Naval Air Station, and sometimes the smaller airports such as the one at College Park, Maryland. At home, in the evening, he turned out an aviation story, and from the office in the morning he would phone the airports for a list of arriving and departing planes. Such a roll call took only an inch or two of type in those days, when Eddie Rickenbacker is said to have remarked while watching a mail plane take off, "There goes another postcard."

Ernie's acquaintanceship among aviation people grew. The apartment at 456 came to be a haven and rallying place for pilots and their wives and girl friends, and for others connected with

41

aviation. Later on, when Lowell Mellett started to introduce Ernie to Amelia Earhart, Miss Earhart protested, "Not to know Ernie Pyle is to admit that you yourself are unknown in aviation." The column was marked by a preoccupation with people and with "little things." It made good reading, even for many with no intrinsic interest in aviation.

It was in May of 1928 that an air-mail line was inaugurated between New York and Atlanta, with Washington as one of the stops. The original pilots on the line, Amberse Banks, Verne Treat, Sid Molloy, Johnny Kytle, and Gene Brown, flew little open-cockpit ships that had few of the fancy devices later available, and they ran into plenty of trouble, of which Ernie was a zealous chronicler. One snowy night when Treat had to parachute, north of Washington, his first call upon reaching a telephone was to the postal service; his second was to Ernie.

In June one of Ernie's pilot friends, Herb Fahy—who was killed two years later—went West to ferry a Ryan monoplane from San Diego to Washington. Ernie arranged for him to bring Paige Cavanaugh to Washington for a visit. Cavanaugh was shocked on seeing his friend for the first time in two years: "He looked like an old man." Of course Ernie was working too hard, filling two jobs. "We were both feeling kind of sad," Cavanaugh said. "We didn't see much point to anything. Ernie had a crazy idea about him and Jerry and me going to Africa and driving across the Sahara and writing some pieces."

Presently Ernie was allowed to give up his copy-desk duties and devote his full time to aviation. After that he was less harried. The next few years may well have been the pleasantest of his life. His hours were his own, and the flying men whom he hero-worshiped were his friends. He was finding that people attached importance to him, which was gratifying even if he was not too interested in importance as such. Once a Washington hostess telephoned Jerry to invite her and Ernie to tea. Jerry begged off and said she was afraid Ernie's answer would be the same. "But you don't under-

stand," the lady is said to have protested. "I'm trying to help
Ernie Pyle get someplace." "But Ernie doesn't want to get someplace," was Jerry's reply. The Pyles were definitely uninterested
in society-page society. They had a social register of their own,
and 456 teemed with its members—aviation people, newspapermen, and a miscellany of other unpretentious people, including
cops.

One day a test pilot's plane disintegrated over Washington.
Ernie, at his desk, had two phone calls about it before the para-
chuting flier had reached the ground. A few days before Christmas in 1929 he scored a clean scoop on the crash of a Fokker in
which a congressman and several other people were killed. We had
a complete extra on the street before opposition papers could find
out what had happened. Here is a United Press item about it,
written by Raymond Clapper:

Washington, Dec. 20—(UP) Ernie Pyle, aviation editor of the
Washington Daily News, was talking by telephone with the Naval
Air Station today.

"Wait!" shouted the party at the other end of the line. "A plane is
crashing over at Bolling."

Bolling Field adjoins the Naval Air Station.

Pyle obtained first details of the crash, in which Rep. Kaynor, Mass.,
was killed. He was the first newspaper reporter to arrive at the scene.
Guards closed the field just after he arrived and no others were admitted.

That year Ernie got two five-dollar raises.

In 1929-30 a young naval lieutenant, Apollo Soucek (later an
admiral) was trying to set an altitude record. When he landed at
the Naval Air Station after his first high flight and asked for a
cigarette, Ernie was the first to hand him one. Another day, following a second flight, Ernie was there again with a cigarette.
Still later, "Soakum" stepped from his plane after another altitude flight—but Ernie wasn't there. Soucek refused to smoke until

Ernie was located, at Washington-Hoover Airport across the river, and rushed by taxi to do the honors. Soucek's highest flight was 43,166 feet, a world record then.

In June 1929 Transcontinental Air Transport started a coast-to-coast passenger service, utilizing planes by day and trains by night. Ernie made the first flight. In Los Angeles he saw Cavanaugh, who was leaving the next day for Germany to enroll in a glider-pilot course. Cavanaugh returned to the States in late December, having decided after a few crashes that gliding was not his dish, and he visited the Pyles for six weeks. As he remembered that period: "Ernie was still yearning to bust out and travel, even though he felt that he had the best job and the best bosses in the world. He wasn't particularly ambitious. He was just kind of melancholy. I think he was troubled because he had nothing to complain about. His apartment was a busy place. Aviators were always coming in or telephoning. I made the rounds of the airports with him sometimes. And we would go to places like the Bureau of Aeronautics. I was terrifically impressed with all these big people being so nice and friendly to Ernie. They didn't put up any false fronts with him."

The aviator visitors at 456 didn't drink much, although a drink of sorts was usually available. Of a Friday night Ernie would get a gallon of alcohol from a bootlegger, mix it with water and glycerin and a touch of juniper and other oils, and pour it into Gordon gin bottles. Once, though, when he had undergone a difficult tooth extraction and was in pain, there was nothing to drink but a few inaccessible ounces in a Maryland-rye keg. Some resourceful aviators pounded the keg apart to get at the final spoonful. Even after a night when there was a good deal of drinking Ernie was always at the office on time.

Jerry had no job, went to the movies seldom, if ever, spent little time on housework, and seemed to find everything she needed in her friends and her books. An observant friend who met the Pyles about this time, AnnieBelle DePriest Moreton, has contributed an interesting memoir: "I was a brand-new hostess for Eastern Air

Lines. Bunny Davis was ground hostess. She said to me as I stepped on the plane, 'There's an important reporter going to New York; name's Ernie Pyle. Be nice to him.' It was the first time I had ever thought about anybody being more important than anybody else. I didn't know what I was supposed to do outside my regular duties, which included the same interested, courteous treatment for all aboard. But as is so often the case, Nature took care of the situation. We went through quite a wind and some slashing rain. I must have looked uneasy, for as I walked down the aisle Ernie looked up questioningly. I sat down in the vacant chair beside him. He took my hand, smiled that sweet smile, and said, 'Is this your first storm, Miss DePriest?' It never seemed the least bit odd that *he* should be comforting *me*. And before I knew it we were out of the rain into the sunshine again.

"One night I was stricken with appendicitis. I don't know how he found it out, but anyway Jerry came to see me. Ernie had asked her to come. She brought some old-fashioned flowers, and after arranging them in a vase she sat at the foot of my bed, and all the while we were making conversation she had this sort of funny smile that made me unable to tell whether she was laughing at me or not. She asked me to come stay at their apartment when I left the hospital, since my base was in Newark and I was going to be away from work for a month. The day before I was to leave the hospital Ernie came and asked if I needed money to pay my bill. Fortunately I didn't. While living in their apartment for three or four weeks I learned that this was nothing unusual for them. They were always helping people out.

"When I would awake in the morning I would hear a piano [1] softly playing. There was a subdued quality about it that made me a little uneasy. There was something about it I couldn't understand. I lay in bed wondering about Ernie and Jerry.

"I would stay in bed until Ernie had gone to work. When I got up Jerry was always sitting in her chair looking up words in the

[1] This was a Christmas present to Jerry, bought by Ernie at ten dollars a month.

dictionary. Always reading something and marking things in books. Then she would bring my breakfast on a tray, and while I ate we talked. She drew me out: my ideas about things. At noon we had eggnog. Really a glass of milk, egg, and a tablespoon of whisky. It gave me a delightful sensation. We talked and talked and talked. Ernie would arrive quietly, always with the day's paper under his arm. Jerry served supper on trays, in the living room before the fire, and they discussed the day's activities. The fire became to me a symbol of their love and devotion to each other. It was never huge, extravagant, and roaring. It was a steady, dependable, trustworthy fire that burned continuously until we went to sleep.

"There was never any kind of emotion or upset about anything. No loss of tempers, ever. There was an unspoken but plainly visible love, admiration, and respect for each other. I gradually saw that it was the biggest thing about both of them. There was such a fusion of Jerry and Ernie in my mind that I was never able thereafter to think of one without instantly thinking of the other.

"Ernie bathed in the smallest bathtub I have ever seen. They always laughed about it. Jerry's habits were frugal almost. She and Ernie acquired the least in the way of material possessions of any persons I have ever known.

"People were always dropping in. Some telephoned to see if it was convenient, others just came. Sometimes Ernie was tired and really did not want anyone, but nobody was ever refused. Drinks would be served. Someone might ask Jerry to read some poetry. We would sit around, some on the floor, all at her feet the moment she began to read. It was an enthralling experience. We were suspended in space, living the beauty of her voice, the richness of words loved, caressingly spoken."

In 1930 I was transferred to other Scripps-Howard operations, and "Polly" Palmer became managing editor of the *News*. A letter from Ernie to me told the old story of wanderlust: "Jerry and I have the miseries from going around all huddled up. It isn't really so cold here, but us being as skinny as we are, it doesn't take much of the Arctic to do us. . . . Last Sunday afternoon we sat at home before the wood fire and got ourselves tighter than hell. . . . We have so far reformed that such a carousal as that is practically unique. . . . But I'm afraid the winter depressions are upon me. Oh for the South Seas. . . ."

When Polly Palmer got into some troubles as managing editor in 1932, Lowell Mellett decided Polly must go. He pondered three possible successors, eliminated two of them, and called in Ernie, who was aghast. He didn't want it. He liked what he was doing. He hated the routines and responsibilities of the office. At last he agreed, with two conditions: Polly must be kept on, and Jerry must be consulted first. He asked her to meet him for lunch. "He sounded queer," she told me later. "I found him at a corner table, looking pale. I said, 'You're sick! Why didn't you come home?' Ernie could hardly speak, but finally he said, 'Lowell told me this morning he wanted me to be managing editor.' We sat and discussed it. In the end Ernie said he guessed there was nothing to do but take it." The aviation colony was dismayed. Ernie and Jerry were invited over for a little ceremony at Washington-Hoover Airport, where Amelia Earhart made the presentations, a jewel case for Jerry, a fine watch for Ernie. He was wearing the watch thirteen years later when he was killed.

He wrote in his final aviation piece: "This column has tried to feel with those who fly. It has recorded the surprised elation of those who have risen rocketlike into renown, has felt despair with those who have been beaten down by the game, has shared the awful desolation of those who have seen their close ones fly away and come back only in the stark blackness of the newspaper headlines. This column has made enemies too. But they were enemies who wouldn't have been very good friends anyhow. The good friends—and they can be counted by the thousands—are what signify. . . . This is the end of what to me has been an epoch. . . ."

As managing editor Ernie inherited some assets and some liabilities. The staff was too small, and there was friction here and there. But there was a youthful bounce in the outfit, part of which could be attributed to a system of hiring as copy boys only young fellows just out of college or high school who wanted to become newspapermen and who looked as if they might. Such a lad would fill paste pots and fetch sandwiches until a vacancy as reporter occurred, after six months or a year, and then get a tryout. This procedure prospered, largely because of the extraordinary qualities of Polly Palmer, whom Ernie made city editor, as a mentor of green youngsters. Polly was a fine newspaperman, and he also had an enthusiasm with which he was able to infect his youngsters. The *News*, in effect, operated its own school of journalism, and Polly was dean.

Many of the old reliables were gone. Bob Horton, later a top government public relations man, was telegraph editor. Other hands were Walker Stone, later editor of the Scripps-Howard Newspaper Alliance, and John O'Rourke, who became editor of the *News*.

Ernie took over as managing editor just before the Roosevelt-Hoover campaign. Times were hard, and Scripps-Howard applied a blanket pay cut. Mellett had slyly anticipated this by giving raises to nearly everybody. And for the copy boys, cut from ten dollars a week to nine, Ernie fixed things by writing each of them a weekly expense voucher for a dollar. The Newspaper Guild was organized around this time. Ernie was "old-fashioned" about the Guild, but while he did not like it, he never tried to obstruct it, although once he did bawl out a reporter who attended a Guild meeting when he should have been covering a fire. Apparently the only person he ever fired was a miscast copy boy.

The comparative freedom of the aviation days was gone. He had to wrestle with personnel and budget problems; fuss over typography and edition times; pass judgment when city side and telegraph competed for space and display; sit in "the slot" or go to the composing room to make up the paper when someone was ill or on vacation; deal with cranks as well as sensible visitors;

handle the temperaments of Polly and some of the rest; and a thousand other things. He had no secretary, no private office; his desk was within whispering distance of the city editor, news editor, and telegraph editor. It was interesting, of course, but hard and confining, and while he met his responsibilities faithfully they weighed heavily on him.

Although Washington was the political center of the country, and from 1933 on the economic center as well, Ernie had more of a headline-hunter's than a thinker's interest in the stunning changes and bitter controversies of the Roosevelt Revolution. For one thing, editorial-page policy was out of his jurisdiction; the *News'* editorials, except those on purely local affairs, were handed down from the Scripps-Howard Newspaper Alliance. And the *News* did not undertake its own news coverage of national affairs; this was left to Scripps-Howard and the United Press. Ernie's concern with the great events of 1932-35 was basically that of a newspaper technician engaged in processing hand-me-down reportage and opinion. Perhaps if it had been otherwise he would have outgrown his distaste for politics. Perhaps, also, it is just as well that his own predilections as well as the circumstances of his job left his mind uncluttered with problems of state, free for his eventual task of exploring the simple humanities of peace and war. This is not to imply that he was uninterested in the Hoover-Roosevelt campaign of 1932, or the rise of Hitler to power in '33, or the sudden descent on Washington of the Brain Trust and the Alphabet; but his interest was scarcely more than that of the man in the street.

Ernie's aviation friends still came to 456, and later, after he and Jerry moved in 1933, to their apartment at 2007 Q Street, Northwest. He tried to keep in touch with aviation. When the government canceled the air-mail contracts and the Army lost a dozen pilots carrying the mail, Jerry sat through the Senate air-mail hearings in order to give him a report on them. Just before the bank holiday of March 1933 Ernie got worried and to play safe spent his savings on a Ford coupé. A few days after that he had an emergency appendectomy, performed by a Washington surgeon, Dr. Oliver C. Cox, nicknamed "Buttonhole" Cox because of the minute incisions that were his toolmark. Dr. Cox wrote Ernie ten years later: "When I really want to 'blow,' I stick out my chest and say, 'I took an appendix out of Ernie Pyle almost as big as he is!' "

There was little time to write, except for an occasional editorial, but he did undertake a personal survey of the relief problem in Washington and turned out a perceptive report which was spread, unsigned, across page one. By and large, his typewriter was idle in the three years of his managing editorship, and the daily indoors routine depressed him. "I too have failed to achieve my ambition," he wrote to his Filipino friend, Gene Uebelhardt. "In fact my life the past few years has gone in such a routine and deadening way that I am not sure any more just what my ambitions are. I think maybe I haven't any material ambitions—rather my ambition is to be free enough of material and financial worries that I can just sit and read and think. But to do that one has to get rich, and the prospects of me ever being rich are very slim indeed. I am still managing editor, but it is not a job that I like. It is hard and fatiguing work, and I get no chance to do any writing. I think that is where my greatest satisfaction lies—in writing—in expressing my feelings in print, and I don't get a chance to do it now. Maybe things will change later."

CHAPTER 7

Roving Reporter

IN DECEMBER 1934 Ernie had a severe case of flu, from which his convalescence was slow. The doctor told him to go "someplace warm, like Arizona." Apparently neither the doctor nor the patient was aware that Arizona in winter could be cold. At any rate, the Pyles set out in their Ford to seek a warm, dry place in which Ernie could recuperate. It was a wild-goose chase, though it had a happy ending.

Heading south, they found no heat. In Birmingham it was four above zero. In Mississippi they drove through a blizzard. At El Paso, traditionally hot and dry, it was raining. In New Mexico and Arizona, more rain. Even in the desert, at Indio, California, it was raining. At Los Angeles, the same. They made two hopeful sorties back into and around Arizona and New Mexico and never found decent weather. But they did find friends. From a hotel in Albuquerque Ernie phoned E. H. Shaffer, editor of the Scripps-Howard *Tribune*, and "Shafe" came dutifully to call. They asked him to stay on for dinner, but he declined and was on his way out when it occurred to them that there might be a Mrs. Shaffer. Ernie caught him in time to expand the invitation, and this time it was accepted, which inaugurated a long and warm relationship with Shafe and "Liz."

In Los Angeles once again, they abandoned the hunt for a vacation spot on land and signed up to sail to Philadelphia on a freighter, the nine-thousand-ton *Harpoon* of the Shepard Line. It was raining as they went aboard, but they were glad to settle

51

down for three straight weeks and six thousand miles on the
same premises, after living in some thirty-five hotels since leaving Washington. "I wish it had taken three years," Ernie wrote.
There were five other passengers, notably an elderly globe-
trotter named Walter A. Folger, of Medford, Oregon, who introduced himself to the Pyles at their first breakfast on board
by writing out a little verse and handing it to them. They
quickly made a friendship. Ernie said of "Mr. F": "He seems more
nearly what I would like to be someday than anyone I have ever
known. . . . He is one of the few old men . . . who, by mere
example, take the horror out of growing old. After knowing him
for a little while, I came very close to wishing sincerely that I
were already old. It all seemed too simple; all the trouble behind,
nothing important ahead, and the present quite good enough."
Nearly every morning Mr. Folger would produce another verse,
such as:

> If all the poems I have written
>   Were piled upon a pile
> And with a candle litten
>   You could see the blaze a mile.

> But the gold that I have gitten
>   For the poems I have wrote
> Wouldn't hurt the feeblest kitten
>   If poured molten down its throat.

As the *Harpoon* steamed steadily south it grew warm, and
Ernie was in paradise: "I wish I could put into words the in-
formality of life on a freighter, the timelessness it seems to gen-
erate, the beauty of a relaxed purposelessness. There was no
routine whatever, except eating. The days went by without pattern. You did what you pleased, which was usually nothing. . . .
It didn't make any difference. Nobody cared."

At Philadelphia there was some delay in unloading their car.
While they waited, a heretofore taciturn ship's officer returned
from a quick but unstinted visit to a waterfront bar and tipsily

offered to toss Jerry overboard. "I've spent this whole trip look-ing at you crinkle up your silly nose," he said, "and I'm sick of it!" Captain McKown of the *Harpoon* intervened.

About the time Ernie resumed work, Heywood Broun, whose syndicated column ordinarily was spread across the top of the *News'* opposite-editorial page, went on vacation. Ernie sug-gested to Lowell Mellett, or perhaps Lowell suggested to him, some articles about his trip to fill the Broun space. He turned out eleven pieces, and they were an instant hit. That was in April. Four months later Ernie had convinced Mellett that he could never be contented again as managing editor, and proposed a roving assignment. Lowell took it up with G. B. ("Deac") Parker, editor-in-chief of the Scripps-Howard newspapers. Deac had found in Ernie's vacation articles "a Mark Twain quality that knocked my eye out." He gave his blessing to a tryout trip. Ernie was relieved as managing editor and shifted to the Scripps-Howard Alliance staff, of which I was managing editor. His pay was raised from ninety-five a week to a hundred. With a high heart and no doubt some trepidation he prepared to launch a career as roving columnist. He wrote Gene Uebelhardt: "I've had a good stroke of luck. I've finally been transferred from this man-killing job I've been on for three years. . . . I will go where I please and write what I please. It's just the kind of job I've always wanted and I hope I can make a go of it."

On the day before Ernie turned thirty-five he and Jerry set forth from Washington. His instructions were to drive wherever he liked, write six columns a week about anything that inter-ested him, and mail them to Washington for distribution to the two dozen Scripps-Howard newspapers. It had been agreed that there would be no ballyhoo to the editors. The *Washington News* would print the stuff, for Ernie's by-line was already popu-lar in Washington. As for the other papers, the copy would arrive without fanfare on the editors' desks and take its chances in com-petition with everything else that was available from day to day. At Ernie's suggestion, he would pay forty dollars a week of his and Jerry's travel and living expenses and Scripps-Howard the remainder.

He was used to traveling cheaply. Here are the opening entries in his daybook:

Thursday, August 2

10 gals gas (Washington)	1.80
2 lunches (Conowingo, Md.)	1.00
10 gals gas (Devon, Pa.)	1.80
2 dinners (Farm near Doylestown)	1.20
	5.80

Friday, August 3

Room for night	2.00
2 Breakfasts	.75
Gas (Andover, N. J.)	1.06
Fruit	.94
2 Dinners (Perona Farms)	2.20
	6.95

The first column to be printed—on August 8, 1935—was datelined Flemington, New Jersey, where Hauptmann had been convicted of the Lindbergh kidnap murder. The people of Flemington, Ernie wrote, "feel very sorry for Mrs. Hauptmann," whose baby was "just starting to talk a little now, and one of his few words is 'Daddy,' and that makes Mrs. Hauptmann feel bad." This was nearly a year after Hauptmann passed the note that led to his arrest. At that time Ernie, bored with wolf-wolf alarms in the Lindbergh case, had buried the Hauptmann item on an inside page. But it is not true, as has been printed, that this had anything to do with his departure from the managing editor's chair.

From New Jersey on it was one dateline after another in a procession that was to continue for years; step by step through the New England states, across the Bay of Fundy to Nova Scotia to talk with the fabulous fishermen of Lunenburg and Mahone

Bay, to the Gaspé Peninsula, and on through Quebec and Montreal to Callender in Ontario, where they saw the Dionne quintuplets on display to tourists and sat up late with little Dr. Allan Dafoe. Then across the border and down by stages to Dana, where Ernie wrote the childhood story of the roses and the snake and his spanking.[1] Deac Parker pronounced it "one of the finest jobs of writing ever done in our concern." That particular column, along with several others about his family, dissipated any doubts in Washington about the usefulness of this roving assignment.

During the next five years, almost always with Jerry at his side, Ernie crisscrossed the United States and the rest of the Americas. As his confidence and skill grew, so did the number of his readers. Many Scripps-Howard papers at first used only an occasional piece but gradually found space for him as a daily fixture. The largest Scripps-Howard paper, the *New York World-Telegram*, was the slowest to give him such recognition; its management used only items that appeared to have "news value"—a policy that ruled out most of those marvelously human columns to which readers in other cities were warming.

Ernie gave himself his own assignments, with only infrequent suggestions from Deac and Lowell and me, even when he would touch home base in Washington for a week or two. Picking interesting assignments in Washington that will not be duplicated by some of the hundreds of other correspondents is not simple, but Ernie could take on such a thing as a hearing on potato production and make it come alive. He attended the first session of the Supreme Court in its blindingly new marble temple: "I defied both tradition and good taste and wore my white and brown checkered racetrack coat, with the green sweater and the gray pants." (He didn't equal the later *lèse-majesté* of Heywood Broun, who sipped gin from a hip flask during a session in the Supreme Court chamber.)

The column had a good change of pace. Sometimes it was fairly straight reporting, such as accounts of his visits to the

[1] Quoted on pp. 6–7.

Passamaquoddy tide-harnessing and Florida ship-canal projects and the Tennessee Valley Authority. Sometimes it was purely personal musing, sometimes farfetched whimsy, sometimes side-splitting comedy, and occasionally a piece of moving poignance. He went down to Lorton Penitentiary in Virginia, for example, to write sadly about his old friend Fred Hisey, a life-termer. Hisey, an elaborately tattooed Regular Army veteran, used to be a compositor on the *Washington News*. He was a quiet fellow and a steady worker, with a passion for his flower garden. But now and then he would take a day or two off and with sober deliberation get drunk; on the last of these sprees he shot and killed a girl.

Ernie described press conferences with such men as Cordell Hull, Henry Wallace, Harold Ickes, and Harry Hopkins; years later Robert E. Sherwood, in his book *Roosevelt and Hopkins*, was to say: "A description of [Hopkins] at a press conference was written by the immortal Ernie Pyle in the *Washington News*: 'And you, Mr. Hopkins, I liked you because you look like common people. I don't mean any slur by that either, because they don't come any commoner than I am, but you sit there so easy swinging back and forth in your swivel chair, in your blue suit and blue shirt, and your neck is sort of skinny, like poor people's necks, and you act honest too. And you answer the reporters' questions as though you were talking to them personally, instead of being a big official. . . .'"

One of the funniest columns Ernie ever wrote—requests for copies of it came in for years after its original publication—concerned his misadventure with a pair of pants.[2] The column was based on a very real incident involving a faulty zipper. Here is what happened, as set down by his friend Fritz Silber, who worked on the *News*. "One summer afternoon Ernie asked me to come over to his apartment on O Street for a drink. Jerry was away somewhere. Ernie mixed old-fashioneds, then he mixed some more, and so on for an hour. We were pretty happy and every-

[2] It appears in his book *Home Country*.

thing was coasting along fine. Then Ernie vanished toward the back of the apartment. About three minutes later he came out swearing. The zipper was stuck—at the top. He tugged and yanked, to no avail. After a few minutes of that he developed a truly mighty urge. We went to work on the problem. No pliers were to be found, but in the kitchen we located a big claw hammer. By getting the tab of the zipper into the claw we got good leverage. While Ernie pulled up on his pants, I pulled down on the hammer. The zipper moved slightly, and then the damn tab bent almost double and slipped out of the claw. To straighten it we had to get the tab on the edge of the kitchen table and flatten it with the hammer. By standing on his toes and h'isting his pants, Ernie managed to get the tab into position while I pounded it. Then we began all over again, levered the thing down another quarter of an inch, and it bent again. Tab on the table, pound, more levering, etc. Ernie was in quite a state, and neither of us was too steady of foot or eye. After repeating the whole chain of processes ten or twelve times the zipper was down far enough for him to work the pants off."

Ernie had found that in a strange city he could usually pick up ideas for columns by dropping in at a newspaper office. At the *Wilmington* (N.C.) *Star* he got a tip that led him into a shocking experience. He told about it in a letter to Dr. Wilburt C. Davison, dean of the Duke University School of Medicine:

". . . The newspaper boys in Wilmington told me I might find a feature story in a little boy there who had a very strange disease which the local doctors had not been able to diagnose. So I went out to see the child. The parents are extremely poor. They live in a disheveled suburb across the railroad tracks called 'Lingo City.' When I arrived the mother was out in the yard chopping wood and chewing tobacco. She is a young woman and seemingly quite intelligent. We talked a little while about the child, and she asked me if I wanted to see it. I told her yes, and we went in the house. She went over behind the stove, to a box about a foot high standing along the wall, and covered with blankets. She raised the blanket, and there was the most horrible sight I have ever witnessed, and as a newspaper reporter for many years I have seen some pretty bad things.

"The child is now twelve years old. He was normal (even above average in health and intelligence, his mother says) until he was four. Then something started on his foot that looked like a bad sunburn. Gradually it got worse and began to spread, and at the same time his weight began to dwindle away. This has been going on for eight years. Today it takes a long stretch of the imagination to consider the object lying there on the box a human being. The child has no flesh at all on its body. None whatever. Just skin, shrunk around the bones. Or rather, skin in some places. In others, the bone is showing through. . . . His legs and arms are no bigger around than my thumb, and they stick straight up in the air, wrapped around with gauze, like a mummy. The head is barely recognizable as a human being. There is no hair, and the scalp is an immense sore. The eyes have been destroyed by sores. The nose is gone. The mouth is just a little round hole, not resembling a mouth at all. The child can no longer talk, except for some slight jargon which the mother understands. It is able only to indicate to her whether it is hot or cold, and to tell her when it is hurting worse than usual. . . .

"Later I talked with the County Health Officer. . . . He said they had it in the Wilmington hospital for a long time, but couldn't do anything for it, and couldn't find out what was the matter with it, so they finally sent it home. . . . I have become extremely worked up over this case. It was too horrible to write for my newspapers, so nothing has been written about it, and nothing will be. . . . I am hoping that I have been able to arouse your interest sufficiently for you to make a trip to Wilmington to see the child; or send an assistant. I will gladly pay the traveling and living expenses for such a trip, up to say forty dollars, which should more than cover the trip. I feel that if you can once see the child, you could not let the case drop. . . . Please understand that I realize that the child itself cannot be saved, but maybe others could in the future if doctors knew what was the matter with this one. . . ."

Dr. Davison acted promptly. The child was taken to the Duke Hospital, studied, and treated, but nothing could be done for it. It died eighteen months later. Dr. Daniel J. Pachman, in an elaborate paper, said the case was "believed to be one of progressive generalized scleroderma with sclerodactylia and calcinosis." The Pachman paper was prefaced with an excerpt from Ernie's letter to Dr. Davison. "I doubt," Dr. Pachman wrote later, "whether any other scientific paper includes a layman's description of a disease; such was the excellence of his power of description."

By the time the Pyles arrived at New Orleans, Ernie was in one of his periodic moods of depression. "I'm in a slump for sure," he wrote me. And a few days later from Baton Rouge: "We came up here from New Orleans this morning, practically desperate. I had a lot of dope but hadn't been able to write a line. The old bean just wouldn't work. But I've been at it now since noon and have turned out five pieces. . . . I feel like I'm hitting a stride again and getting my confidence back. . . ."

They drove on to Laredo, Texas, the jumping-off point for a seven-hundred-and-sixty-mile drive over the new and not quite completed highway to Mexico City. The trip south of the border was easier than they had anticipated except for an unfinished stretch between Tamazunchale and Jacala, where the highway was a rocky and twisting ledge with sheer, unprotected drops of thousands of feet. "The most frightened I have ever been," Ernie wrote, "was driving over a fresh slide, during a rain, with just six slippery inches between my outside wheels and the bottom— two thousand feet below."

Bad news awaited them in Mexico City. Ernie's mother had had a stroke. He decided to fly to Indiana but, he wrote me, "I started coming down with aches and chills, had to have a doctor Saturday and Sunday, wasn't able to turn a wheel, sat up in bed last night and wrote two pieces with pencil, and am up this morning. My mother apparently is holding her own, so I am not planning to go." Of the columns he enclosed he said: "They're lousy. I'll start back as soon as we get ourselves squared away, then sell out and go back to the farm, which I never should have left in the first place." Deac and Lowell and I jointly telegraphed him that his stuff was excellent and urged that he take a rest in the lower altitude of nearby Cuernavaca. Ernie wrote back: "That was grand of you to send me that wire. I hate to think I have to be babied like the NEA cartoonists, but I suppose I do. I'm not worried about what anybody thinks of my stuff: I'm worried about the fact that when I sit down to write I haven't any emotion or enthusiasm. It's been that way on this whole trip. It is true that I haven't felt really good but a couple of times since I left Washington; but what I worry about is that maybe I'm just a flash in the pan, and that I'm written out. . . . I'm practically over my week-end sick spell, but continue to have these sickening, splitting headaches every afternoon. Maybe it's the altitude, I don't know. . . ." They did go down to Cuernavaca, and to primitive Taxco and Tepoztlán, and Ernie began to feel better and to fall in love with Mexico.

The next twelve months were a solid year of traveling within the United States, almost all by automobile. Jerry was an ideal traveling companion. Ernie didn't like much conversation while driving, and she didn't talk much. He did a lot of thinking at the wheel; he had long since given up his youthful zeal for speed and cruised at forty-five miles an hour or so. He seldom tired of driving, although occasionally he got so sleepy he would stop the car and walk up and down the road a few minutes to wake himself up, or even take a nap. They had become adept at living out of suitcases. While they carried half a dozen bags, these were packed with such efficiency that usually they would need to open only two. Ernie normally owned only one suit, a sport jacket, and an odd pair of trousers. He always wore white cotton socks, which cost a dime a pair, and no garters. He owned no more than three neckties at a time. He wore a years-old Borsalino hat, a lightweight felt with broad brim. Jerry, too, had a simplified wardrobe—two tailored suits and half a dozen blouses of varying degrees of dressiness.

One item of Ernie's equipment was a little wooden box in which he filed, by states, cards listing tips on possible stories. And he carried an old German camera. He sent back batches of photographs, with which the *Washington News* sometimes illustrated his columns; these were not distributed to the other papers—it was just a special service to his old sheet. He wrote on an Underwood portable, on which he had the normal and quite respectable two-finger speed of a newspaperman. His copy went to Washington by mail, and the postal service never lost a column. After the Mexico trip he and Jerry acquired a portable phonograph and a course of Spanish-language lessons on records, but they didn't get far with the Spanish. They carried a dictionary, but it was Jerry who used it—she was fond of crossword puzzles and double crostics. Sometimes the space back of the car seat looked like a lending library, for they bought a good many books. And they never missed an issue of *The New Yorker* when they could buy one.

Ernie never saw a paycheck. These and his expense-account checks were deposited in his Washington bank. Their wants were simple. Ernie was still rolling his own cigarettes, except while driving. Neither of them ate much; for Ernie a meal was more of a routine necessity than a pleasure to be anticipated and savored.

He leaned on Jerry a good deal—more, he realized later, than he knew at the time. She helped buoy him when he got into spells of depression and of dissatisfaction with the column. Sometimes, after he had worked over a batch of columns, rewriting and cutting and editing with a pencil, she would retype the finished product. She would praise what she liked, and where she thought he was substandard she would say so—unless he was in a low mood, when she withheld criticism. Her judgment was good, and he knew it. But then Ernie's copy was good, and Jerry knew that, better than he did; only rarely was she disappointed. He worked hard over his material. And if the result sometimes left him with a sense of inadequacy, at other times he felt a mastery of his craft. He wrote me in that year, 1936:

"Lee, I've been in a slump as you doubtless could see from my copy, and also terribly in the dumps. . . . I got that way partly because the last time I saw the *Daily News* I saw you were cutting so much of the 'little stuff' in my copy—the little personal phrases and opinions and asides, the stuff that I know was responsible for the success of the aviation column, and which I know readers like to see, maybe just a word here and there, but really the heart of the thing.

"I know that I have been very derelict about holding my stuff down. But I wonder if we could make a 'deal.' If I will absolutely promise never to send in anything over two pages long [about seven hundred words], could you be a little more lenient with the small phrases? I suggest that, because I feel sure you cut only for space, and not because there is anything especially wrong with these little things I put in. I'll never squawk, of course, over your cutting anything that you consider bad taste or bad writing.

"The reason I am so concerned is twofold: first, I think the whole success of the column depends greatly on that personal homey touch in the writing, and second, when I see my favorite phrases or lines cut out, it gives me an awful inferiority complex, and then I can't loosen up and write with any ease or freedom at all. And if I don't write my pieces with a swing and an ease for reading, they might as well not be written at all, for the subjects themselves of course are of no importance, and would be dull if not dressed up. And also (you'll probably think I've gone nuts from this) lots of times when I'm describing some scene or feeling, I try to make it sound almost like music, and I think sometimes it does, and I think it does to readers, even though they may not be specifically conscious of it. And often the dropping of a word or the cutting of one sentence into two shorter ones destroys the whole rhythm of it. I'm not trying to be any prima donna, as you must surely know, but I am so interested in the column, and I'm also cursed with such a touchiness and melancholia. I feel that my stuff at its very best is only just barely good enough—although I'll have to admit in private that I think it's better than some of our stars are turning out."

Ernie wrote to Dana at least once a week and kept up a correspondence with Cavanaugh and others. He often wrote letters as a sort of warming-up exercise before pitching in on his columns. These, by now, were giving to growing thousands of readers an escape from politics and punditry. He was transporting stay-at-homes, vicariously, to far places—places he peopled and illumined with interesting personalities and incidents and emotions. There were often a lot of "I's" in his copy (a critical editor counted them one day, and there were a score or more), but Ernie knew what he was about. People were reading the column as much to see what he was doing and thinking as to learn about what was going on in obscure corners of Colorado or Minnesota.

But he was hardly a celebrity yet. In most of the places he visited, people had never heard of him. He was often asked if he were "the bunion-derby man"—the promoter, C. C. Pyle. Often as not, new acquaintances thought his name was Pyles. When he got an invitation to address a University of Oklahoma dinner he was astonished. "Imagine that!" he wrote me. "I sent my regrets. Scared me even to think of it."

He was learning to his discomfiture that friends regarded his assignment as the world's cushiest job. He wrote me: "Takes me about half a day to write a column. Other half to dig it up. Other half seeing old friends in various cities. Other half traveling. Other half sleeping." His practice, actually, was to gather material for several days, then settle down in a hotel and write. Even though this might involve carrying a good many details in his head for a week or so, he rarely took a note except for a name, and his memory hardly ever failed him.

CHAPTER 8

Around and Around

IN THE summer of 1936 the Washington office, which had been faithful to the original idea that Ernie should follow his nose without assignments from us, suggested that he tour the drought-ravaged Dakotas. Reluctantly he dropped Jerry off in Minnesota at her mother's and spent ten lonesome days roaming that scorched and desolate area. He liked hot weather, but this time he got an overdose. From Kimball, South Dakota, he wrote Jerry: "I'm sure glad you didn't come—two days of terrific heat, then this afternoon a cloudburst, and tonight this dreary place. The road ahead is impassable with mud. . . . Today's rain was the first here in five and a half weeks, but it was only about thirty miles wide, and too late to do much good. . . . I really got lonesome today." From Rapid City, South Dakota: "It's now 104 or something, and was all day yesterday, with no rain in sight. . . . I think this is the last 'suggestion' for news behind the news I'll take, even if they don't like it. The roads have been gravel for the last two days, and the dust is terrific. I'm filled with it. . . . I'm sure glad I didn't stay on the farm."

In spite of the discomforts and the loneliness and the distaste for being "city edited" from Washington, he did a magnificent job. He started the series with a disavowal of the dramatic: "A drought is not a spectacular thing. . . . Crops are gone. Farmers are broke. The heat is terrific. The whole thing is awful. And yet I feel sure that a city-bred man, who had heard about the drought and who came out to see the devastation, would be disappointed.

People don't gasp for water. Houses don't catch fire. Cattle aren't dead on the road. Trucks aren't moving panicky-eyed families out before sunset. Farmers don't strike a pose and hang their heads in despair. . . . We think of farmers standing around in groups, making desperate decisions. A drought isn't like that. A drought never definitely passes a crisis. A farmer never knows just what day or even in what week he was ruined. . . ."

Since the drought was spot news, we had asked Ernie to telegraph his copy instead of mailing it. Western Union, for no apparent reason, ran his first two columns together, and they reached me in one piece. I concluded that he had been so moved by the disaster that he felt justified in writing at unusual length, and since the copy was impressive I sent the whole thing to the papers as a single dispatch and wired Ernie: "First piece a classic." When he learned of the doubling up he was pretty cross. He sent Western Union a sharp letter. To me he wrote: "I don't know why a mix-up like this should upset me so, but I'm so mad about it I can hardly see straight. You must have thought I had gone crazy sending in anything that length. . . . I've had a horrible afternoon. It is 110 in the shade here [Miles City, Montana] and I've been alternately collapsing on the bed, taking baths and trying to write a piece."

At the end of the trip he summed up: "Day upon day of driving through this ruined country gradually becomes a sameness which ceases to admit a perspective. . . . You arrive at a place where you no longer look and say, 'My God, this is awful!' You gradually become accustomed to dried field and burned pasture; it stretches into a dull, continuous fact. . . . You get to accept it as a vast land that was and is dry and bare, and was that way yesterday and will be tomorrow. . . . The story is the same everywhere, the farmers say the same thing, the fields look the same—it becomes like the drone of a bee, and after a while you hardly notice it at all.

"It is only at night, when you are alone in the enveloping heat and cannot sleep, and look into the darkness, and the thing comes back to you like a living dream, that you once more realize the stupendousness of it. . . . You can see then the whole backward evolution into oblivion of a great land, and the destruction of a people, and the calamity of long years on end without privilege for those of the soil, and the horror of a life started in emptiness, knowing only struggle, and ending in despair. . . . Sometimes at night when I am thinking too hard I feel that there is nothing but leanness everywhere, that nobody has the privilege of a full life, that all existences are things of drudgery that had better be done with. Of course, I am wrong about that. . . ."

Jerry rejoined him, and they drove to Canada and westward to Banff and Lake Louise, which Ernie pronounced "the most beautiful sight I have ever seen," and south to Glacier Park in Montana, where he hiked twenty-six miles across the Great Divide. They drifted around the West, to the Fort Peck dam in Montana, then being built; to Mount Rushmore, South Dakota, where Gutzon Borglum was at work on his mountainside carving of four Presidents; to Rapid City, South Dakota, where they happened onto President Roosevelt and his party, touring the drought area. Ernie wrote me: "I'll swear the reporters and photographers following the President actually make you sick. With the exception of a few decent ones like Tom Stokes and Ulric Bell and Arthur De Titta, the photographer, you'd almost be ashamed to be seen with one of them. And they're all so goddamned smart and know everything—just a bunch of super boys out looking down upon the country hicks. Christ, they haven't even got good manners."

Ernie and Jerry cut down through Nebraska and Wyoming— the forty-sixth and forty-seventh states Ernie had visited—and stopped at Denver with Jerry's sister Po (Mrs. Willard Jones) and her family. A few days later to Utah—state number forty-eight for Ernie, who "did considerable gloating over the girl who rides with me, because she is just a homebody and has only been in forty-five states." From Pocatello, Idaho, Jerry apprised the Shaffers that everybody in Salt Lake City "was very swell to us—and I believe friendliness and kindliness toward the stranger within the gate is the rule and practice of the entire cult." She said Ernie was "out at the moment, seeing an old chap who has a sign on his gatepost saying he will take on anyone in the world who cares to play poker with him—hope Ernest doesn't care to, for I doubt he's ever played a game in his life, and I need a new hat—the little gray model has a hole right in the front of the brim. I'm not proud, but it lets in the sun." Ernie had been reading *Tom Jones*, she said, and "the hearty chuckles I hear now and again from the other chair please me mightily." In Portland they had a reunion with old Mr. Folger, who was about to leave on another of his freighter trips around the world, and took him for an Indian-summer drive up the Columbia Gorge.

There were some months of drifting down the Coast, and a rather frustrating sojourn in Hollywood, though Ernie did manage interviews with Clark Gable, Ginger Rogers, Shirley Temple, Joan Crawford, Fredric March, and others. Then they turned eastward, bent on Christmas with the Shaffers in Albuquerque. Ernie wrote his parents and Aunt Mary: "Well, we have certainly been making hay since we arrived in Phoenix. I have turned out nine columns and got off some correspondence, and Jerry has done practically all of our Christmas shopping and got it wrapped. . . . I picked up a cold in San Diego (that wonderful air-conditioned climate is enough to drive a fellow to his grave—hot as summer for about three hours around noon, and like the North Pole at night). When we got to Phoenix I had to stay in bed a day. . . . Am sending you a snapshot of Gene [Uebelhardt] and his wife and little boy. Also sending you a little check. I figure it this way: I told papa I would send you $250 twice a year. I sent $100 in November, and my share of Aunt Mattie's estate, which was $105, makes $205. And this $50 makes up the $250."

The reunion with the Shaffers was fully as warm and gay as they had anticipated. Jerry wrote Liz and Shafe from Santa Fe: "Darlings—Never was such a Christmas—you were all so swell to us—I could weep to think of it. . . ." And Ernie wrote: "We never had such a good time anywhere."

They kept on across the continent to Washington and were planning a vacation in Florida when word came that Ernie's mother had had another stroke. He flew to Indiana and found that she was entirely helpless and could say only a few words—"wants to die and can't. It is heartbreaking. All we can do is make her as comfortable as possible, and that we are doing. I got in a full-time nurse, hospital bed, loads of supplies, and what not. The doctor says the next stroke might hit her next week, or it might be six months. It sounds cruel, but we all, including her, hope it is soon."

Ernie's boyhood friend Thad Hooker was in Dana and has described how he stood with Ernie at Mrs. Pyle's bedside: "She tried to talk but we couldn't understand all of it, though Ernie had enough composure to ask her questions, to which she would nod her head. She made us stand there and hold hands just like when we were kids and promise to be always the same kind of friends. It couldn't have been any harder on me if it had been my own mother lying there in such a pitiful state, so I broke down completely and blindly staggered out of the room." It was on this occasion that Mrs. Pyle gave Ernie a brooch which he had bought for her when he was a child; he was puzzled at first but finally divined that she wanted him to give it to Jerry. Jerry wrote her:

Dear Ernie's Mother:

Thank you for the beautiful little pin that you cherished for so long. I shall cherish it too.[1] How glad we were to be near enough so that Ernie could get home quickly. It was hard on him to be so far away from you last spring. You know how deeply I hope that you are comfortable and gaining strength.

I have told you before, and I want to tell you again, Ernie has never been other than dear and sweet and good. There's no one else quite as fine, and I realize how much it is due to you and to Mr. Pyle—to your wisdom in his early training. And because you didn't ever try to hold him back, but always encouraged him to go on, you have kept him closer to you than most parents keep grown-up children. And because you were always so understanding, he has never grown

[1] A few months before Jerry's death she showed it to me; it was one of her favorite possessions.

away from you in his thoughts. He has made me very happy. It has made me happy, too, to know that his affection for me has never changed his feeling toward you. He has always been your boy.

Love,
Jerry

After ten days, Mrs. Pyle's condition having improved, the interrupted holiday was undertaken—in Washington and New York instead of Florida. Jerry wrote the Shaffers from New York: "This week was vacation for Ernie, so he spent it in bed with a lousy cold. He's out and about today, however. And has gone to see *The Women*. From what I've read of the play, I think I'd better clear out before he gets back. I understand they tell all, and leave us without a leg to stand on. Saw *Tobacco Road* last night. I thought it was swell, though, timid soul that I am, I expected to blush redly through my rouge. I didn't even cringe or look away once. Some people who were DRESSED, and sat behind us, kept bemoaning the fact that 'There's simply NO ONE here, my dear! But what can you expect after a show's run this long?' It seemed to me that the place was packed, but people don't always see eye to eye on all things. . . ."

It had been agreed that Ernie should go to Alaska in the spring, leaving Jerry behind in view of the expected rigors of the trip. Meantime they drove together through Pennsylvania and Ohio. At Toledo they parted, Jerry returning to Washington. Ernie wrote Cavanaugh: "That there Miss Geraldine is all right, and it sure was tough to see her go."

What went amiss with Jerry is not likely ever to be known. Psychologists who sought later to explore her mind were unable to isolate a specific origin of her trouble. Perhaps there was a remote and forgotten incident or situation of earlier days that bedeviled her subconscious. Perhaps it was something in her relationship with Ernie; during some of their years together theirs was a non-physical union, due to a functional incapacity on Ernie's part which was eventually redressed. Conceivably Jerry

was affected by an unrealized jealousy of Ernie's growing importance; in a way, she had for years been the dominant member of
the household, on whom Ernie leaned for comfort and morale; but
now, in print at least, she was simply that anonymous "girl who
rides with me." Whatever the cause, something malevolent was
gnawing at her. And with Ernie gone, with their constant contact broken, she was alone with her thoughts and her imagination. She steeped herself in morbid verse. She slipped into protracted periods of brooding. On the surface, to her friends, she
usually seemed much the same old Jerry, bright and full of a fey
wit. But sinister moods drove her, for forgetfulness, to private
drinking, to the use of sedatives, and later to Benzedrine, on which
she came to depend for an illusory energy.

It was during the months-long separation that began with their
parting at Toledo in April of 1937 that her melancholia first
reached really serious proportions. But she had reserves of
strength that enabled her to regain a comparative calm after
these periodic sieges. She managed to accomplish the tedious business of storing the furniture and giving up the apartment, which
she and Ernie had decided was too seldom used to be maintained
any longer, and after a visit with Ernie's parents at Dana joined
her mother in Minnesota.

Meanwhile Ernie, after quitting Toledo, had spent a little time
in Indiana, both at Dana and traveling around. He had a dream one
night, a dream that may have derived from his diffidence about
meeting new people: "I dreamed I was at my boyhood home in
Indiana, and I went into my bedroom, and there was President
Roosevelt lying on the bed. He was dressed but had a bathrobe
over his clothes. He was lying with his back to me and was reading
his annual budget report, which was as big as the Chicago telephone directory. He turned and looked at me and said coldly,
'How did you get in here?' So I said, 'Why, your secretary said he
didn't think you were very busy, and it being just before lunch, he
said for me to come right on in without being announced.' The
President said that wasn't the proper procedure. . . ."

Ernie took his father with him to Evansville, for the ride, and picked up a couple of features. Driving back north, circumstances brought them to Bloomington. It was Ernie's first visit there since he left the University fourteen years earlier. He had intended never to return, but the road on which he planned to by-pass Bloomington was in bad condition. "The hills of southern Indiana roll and sweep and are beautiful beyond speech in the springtime," but "the hills were old ghosts of memories to me. Ghosts of people I'd known. And things I'd done. And girls I'd loved. Ghosts of another world that is now forever gone. Things piled up on my memory, and I drove in an excited misery of old thoughts. We stopped in the village of Lyons, and I asked a kid if he knew Joe Benham. The kid said he did, and I drove away fast, full of fear that I might see him. I didn't ask at all after another memory—a girl I knew—I wanted to ask, but somehow I couldn't." Nevertheless, they stopped in Bloomington and visited for an hour or so with Dean and Mrs. Edmondson. "It was wonderful to see them again. . . . We didn't talk about school. We talked about ourselves. And talked fast, for time was short. They gave me their pictures. And went to the car with us. And told my Dad I belonged partly to them. And said they didn't know when they'd been so glad to see anybody. It was dusk when we left. I hadn't looked at the campus or the new buildings as we came in. I didn't look at them as we drove out. I had come back, but I hadn't come back. And never could. . . ." That was one of his rare references in print to the University; he preferred not to poke the coals of those memories.

He stored the car in Dana and moved on to Seattle, where he wrote Jerry: ". . . went down to a waterfront sailor's store today and bought me a pair of high-topped shoes. They're about to kill me, up around my ankles. And a pair of dungarees like Cavanaugh wore (look pretty hot in them). . . . Got into Portland yesterday morning right on schedule. Rode the cab of the UP streamliner through Wyoming, had a nice night's sleep, then was up at six yesterday morning and rode the cab all the way into the Portland station. It was beautiful, sitting up front there, coming down the Columbia Gorge so early in the morning. Went right past the Bonneville dam, and could almost look in the window of the place where we had lunch with Mr. Folger that day. I wrote him this afternoon. . . . Lee says he put up my drought series for the Pulitzer Prize, but of course didn't get a nibble. . . . Today is the first chance I've had really to get lonesome, and I feel sort of lost and forlorn in Seattle by myself. Do wish you were here."

He wrote the Shaffers that Nelson Poynter was out as publisher of Scripps-Howard's *Columbus Citizen,* and commented: "These rapid-fire checkerboard changes seem to me insane, and how can the reading public feel any stability in the paper or home-town affection for it when New York sends in a new man twice a year? Nuts. Think I'll try to get and stay far away from Washington for at least a year, as they surely wouldn't fire me if I were in Hawaii or someplace and they'd have to pay my way back."

The Alaska trip was rather more protracted than it should have been, for sustained interest, although it produced many good columns. He saw Wrangell and Juneau, Skagway and White Horse, steamed ten days down the Yukon River to Dawson and Nenana, then went on by rail to Fairbanks, by truck three hundred and seventy miles to Valdez, and by air six hundred miles to Goodnews Bay, an arm of the Bering Sea in remote western Alaska. "At Goodnews," he wrote Cavanaugh, "the tide left our plane high on the beach and we couldn't get away when we planned, and the next day the fog was so thick we couldn't fly, but finally we got away, and flew the hell out of that old Bellanca clear back into Anchorage. Hit one bump coming over the pass through the Alaska Range that laid us right over on our side, and boy for about two seconds I wouldn't have given you three mills for the whole bunch of us. The pilot was a beginner and the old crate was patched up and I deserve to be killed for riding in the son-of-a-bitch. . . . Just realized I forgot to put any filthy words in this letter from Alaska. I know you'll want to put it in your scrapbook, coming from so far away—so here are just a few [he recited half a dozen]. Maybe I'll be in a better humor the next time I write, if ever."

Ernie and I had had some palaver about the possibility of another raise for him, and I had suggested he write a letter requesting one. "The truth is," he wrote me from Anchorage, "I've been so busy for the last three weeks I haven't even had time to compose a letter asking for that raise. Hope to do so soon, however, although I have a feeling the office is mad at me, and I'll get fired for even asking. . . . Sorry you haven't liked the Alaskan pieces, but I done the best I could." I had written him at an early stage of the trip that "your stuff has been right interesting but I wouldn't say sensational."

At Nome he boarded the Coast Guard cutter *Northland,* and from Dutch Harbor in the Aleutians he wrote: "Jerry dear —God but I'm a long way from home. Have just been looking at the map, and if you were to draw a line straight south from here, it would run about two hundred miles west of Hawaii. Which is where I've just written Lee asking for us to go next, but I have a feeling somehow that the answer will be no.

"Captain Zeusler has just been wonderful to me. I'm the only 'passenger' aboard, and I eat with him in state in the privacy of his own quarters. Have a cabin of my own, and nobody ever bothers me. We have a movie every night, and we have seen some dandies, even if they are three or four years old.

"A day and a half out of Nome we hit St. Lawrence Island, and landed at two villages there. No tourist has ever been there, and no white residents except the schoolteacher. We could look across the water and see Siberia very plainly, about twenty-five miles away. Another day and a half and we were at Nunivak Island (zig-zagging back and forth across the Bering). Nunivak is just the opposite from St. Lawrence, poor and primitive and filthy. The people are terribly poor looking, and it really turns your stomach to go inside one of their shacks. From Nunivak we went to the Pribilofs, to see the seals. But weather was against us. It started fogging and blowing just before we got there. So we just lay there and waited. For forty-eight hours—two whole days—just sitting there waiting. But around midnight the second night the boat started rolling at anchor, and the barometer kept going on down, so the captain said to hell with it, and we pulled up and started a run for Dutch Harbor at three o'clock in the morning.

"We were twenty-six hours on the way down here, and except for that storm we hit going to China fifteen years ago, the roughest twenty-six hours I've ever spent. Everything had to be lashed down. I had to get out my book straps and tie up both chairs and my traveling bag and secure every loose thing in the cabin, clear down to papers and toothbrush. I didn't get seasick, but it took so much will power to keep from it that I was exhausted when we got here. Went to the post office this morning and had one letter from home, but none from you. . . ."

That afternoon a letter from Jerry did arrive by packet boat. He was so pleased he wrote her again, reporting that he had just made arrangements to transfer to the new cutter *Ingham* for Juneau and Seattle. During this voyage he "stayed in bed most of the time to keep from getting seasick, and finally got around to reading *Tom Sawyer* and *Huckleberry Finn*, and thought they were mighty good."

The *Ingham* reached Seattle on August 5, and Ernie found both Jerry and a twenty-five-dollar raise—that made it a hundred and fifty[2] a week—waiting for him. "Some girl keeps wandering in and out of my room," he wrote in a column about his homecoming. "And the strange part is that I don't know her, although she acts as though she knew me. I notice she wears an ivory necklace I bought in Nome, so there must be some connection. She says she's the girl who used to ride with me all the time in the car, but I don't remember anything about it, although her face is sort of familiar at that. She says I went off and left her sitting in a rail-

[2] He had been raised in mid-1936 from a hundred a week to a hundred and twenty-five.

road station in Toledo last spring. . . . I'm not throwing her out just yet, anyhow."

He wrote Cavanaugh: "Miss Geraldine got here some twenty-four hours ahead of me, coming direct from Minnesota, and I tell you she's a mighty fine-looking woman. And a good woman too, in her way. She was somewhat delighted to see the wandering Jew again, in fact her spirits were so high she even admitted that Cavanaugh is a pretty good feller. . . . Maybe Seattle ain't the hottest town on earth, but it smells like attar of roses to me after my forty years in Alaska."

And he wrote me:

"I reckon you are a mighty fine boss, Mr. Miller. I get way off in the sticks and down in the mouth and mad and write you nasty letters, and you come back with a pleasant epistle as though I hadn't been shooting off the mouth at you. I say that's the kind of a boss to have. But you know me and these damn moods I get into, and I guess I have to have 'em to keep going, so just go on excusing them as long as you can.

"That was good news about the raise, and thanks a hell of a lot; you know I appreciate it. But how about you? Do you get yours? You didn't say anything about it, so I wonder. I'll feel plenty cheap if you got one for me and not for yourself. If you did I'll split with you; no foolin.

"Delighted to hear that Denver has put in the column. If somebody could just get the *World-Telegram* and the S.F. *News* to do it, the path would look brighter. I'm sincere in believing it would go good in New York if they'd just put it in for a few months. Had some mighty nice fan letters in the mail forwarded to me. . . ."

Then he threw his portable into full throttle and within two weeks or so had ground out his final Alaska copy—thirty-odd columns, enough to put him a month ahead. "Some of these pieces I think are pretty good," he wrote me, "and some pretty dull; but good or bad, Christ what a relief to finally get out from under. Never again will I let columns pile up on me like that."

It was decided in Washington that a trip to Hawaii would be all right later in the year. As for the present, Deac Parker suggested that Ernie seek out some small "typical" city and do a series on the relief problem—concerning which Ernie wrote Cavanaugh: "I don't like the idea, it sounds too important." And, dispirited by the long siege of writing, and possibly also by the contagion of Jerry's growing sense of futility, he added, "Life looks pretty glum to me and I see less sense to it than I ever did. . . . Miss Geraldine spends all her time working on a crossword-puzzle book, never goes out for a walk, and is even less interested in living than I am."

They took a train to Portland, for Ernie to get a clinical checkup, and to meet Mr. Pyle and cousin Lincoln Saxton, who had agreed to drive Ernie's car west from Indiana. "I told them to take about nine days," Ernie wrote the Shaffers, "and to go past Yellowstone Park and just take their time and see the world. But when we walked into the hotel the clerk said, 'Your Dad's already here.' They came through in five and a half days and didn't see a damn thing. So just for that I sent them right off again on a little thousand-mile round-trip jaunt down to California (to see Lincoln's brother Paul at Scotia). They're due back Sunday, by which time I hope to be able to venture as far as half a block from the bathroom, so we'll show them the town for a couple of days." He explained that he was being plied with Epsom salts and castor oil, "so I feel about as gay as a chicken with lice. Tomorrow they're going to run about thirty feet of electric-light wire, with a bulb on the end of it, down my throat and into my stomach to see what they can see inside there. The whole thing takes five days and costs seventy-five bucks and I know damn well they'll wind up by telling me I feel great, and will I be sore then!

"We are both anxious to get to gypsying in the car again, because that way we feel so free. . . . One night out on St. Lawrence Island I had a spending streak and bought three spotted-seal skins from some Eskimos (at $1.65 apiece) and they smelled so bad you couldn't keep them in the cabin all the way back, and in Seattle I had them tanned and they arrived today and look pretty good. In the above sentence I see you can't tell whether the Eskimos or the seal skins smelled so bad and now that I think it over I don't know that there's any way of telling which smells the worst so we'll just let it go. We're thinking of making Jerry a sort of short sports jacket and hat out of the things. What with Mexican necklaces and New Mexican Indian bracelets and Guatemalan dresses and Siberian ivory beads and Bering Sea seal coats and New York tailored suits, my little woman certainly is hot stuff. Maybe I could put her on exposition and not have to work any more. . . ."

CHAPTER 9

Leis and Lepers

"THE clinic," Ernie wrote his mother, "couldn't find anything fundamentally wrong with me—heart, lungs, stomach all o.k. except don't have the proper amount of acids in my stomach. They said the main thing seemed to be nervous tension and exhaustion, but I don't know any way to remedy that. They've given me some medicine, and instructions on eating, but it's exactly the same eating diet I have always followed."

He and Jerry drove to Idaho in search of some real loafing. And at the new St. Georg Hotel in the little town of Ketchum, near the Union Pacific's lush Sun Valley Lodge, they found it. Ernie climbed a few mild mountains, dropped an occasional dollar at roulette, made friends with the hotel staff, and had, altogether, a wonderful fortnight. He also picked up material for fifteen columns, so his big cushion left over from Alaska remained undepleted.

It was out of season for skiing, but he looked over Sun Valley Lodge and found it "the kind of place where I'd be miserable all day for fear one of the imported New York bellboys would catch me in a social error." But the shoe was on the other foot: the Pyles had dinner with one of the lodge executives, and a waiter spilled soup on Jerry's suit.

They drove nearly a thousand miles to North Platte, Nebraska, to grapple with the relief problem. After a day or two Ernie wrote me: "Did you know that a new depression has already started? I'm serious. I've been picking it up for nearly a month now. The snowball of public fear and tightening up has started to roll, and we're on our way down. Hang on." He was right. What he perceived was the start of the 1937 recession. A hard week's work in North Platte resulted in a detailed and thoughtful series in which his prime conclusion was that the relief problem was a long-term affair and should be dealt with accordingly. He summed up: "People on relief today are living in a world that has no place for them. The dumb guy has had his day in our country. We don't need him any longer. It's easy to look down upon the people on relief and give them hell and call them chiselers and deadbeats. We can criticize all we please, but the simple fact remains that jobs for these people do not exist. It goes around and around in a frightening circle. The most enlightened person I talked with in North Platte said: 'This thing has been centuries in the making. It won't be solved in two or three short years. And no one man is going to solve it.' " A Scripps-Howard editorial endorsed this report as "a more thorough study than has ever been made by any-one but professional social workers and relief officials." Ernie confessed to me that he "was sort of proud of it" himself.

Getting a definite go-ahead from Washington for the trip to Hawaii, they headed for the Coast. From Reno Ernie wrote: "Have almost had to quit drinking. Got so bad that even two drinks before dinner had me on the ropes all day. I've been seeking for a theory for my sudden drinking collapse, and I've decided this medicine they gave me in Portland just doesn't mix with liquor. Or maybe it's the altitude. I'll put that theory to a good test when I get down to sea level at S.F. . . . Is everybody in Washington awful serious, or does anybody have any fun? I've been away so long that I now picture everybody around the shop going around thinking heavily, and never smiling."

Jerry wrote Liz Shaffer: "RENO, my dear, RENO! A heady place. Gives one all sorts of ideas. What fun to get a divorce and start all over again. But since I can't imagine starting out with anyone but

Ernst,[1] it would be a waste of money, as well as time, and we haven't too much of either."

In San Francisco Ernie told of sending his friend Harold Talburt, the Scripps-Howard cartoonist, in Washington, a collect telegram "thanking him for inviting me to the Gridiron banquet, which would be while I was in Hawaii and he hadn't invited me anyway." In Los Angeles, Cavanaugh and his wife received the following:

Mr. and Mrs. Ernest T. Pyle
wish to announce an
"At Home"
for Mr. and Mrs. Thomas Paige Cavanaugh
aboard the "S.S. Lurline" of
the Matson Line
at
Pier 157-158 of the Harbor of Los
Angeles at Wilmington, Calif.,
or some such Goddam place—
from
10 a.m. until approximately 9 p.m.
of Saturday, Nov. 13.
Refreshments will be served, although Mr. Pyle
wishes it understood here and now that he
prefers not to get tight. However, he
cannot speak for Mrs. Pyle.

So, when the *Lurline* put in at Wilmington after the run from San Francisco, the Cavanaughs came to visit. Ernie was getting fed up with the job, he told them. He talked seriously of quitting— he had a notion about founding a costume-jewelry business, with Jerry as designer and himself as manager.

At Honolulu, the Roy Howards' daughter Jane, then a reporter on the *Honolulu Advertiser*, came out on the tug to drape them with leis. They liked Honolulu at once. "Now we're all torn between retiring in Taxco, Idaho, New Mexico, or Ha-

[1] This was one of Jerry's pet variations on her husband's name.

waii," Ernie wrote the Shaffers. "We have a little one-room apartment, but very nice, out on the beach at Waikiki; we've already decided to 'miss' the Jan. 1 boat and catch it Jan. 15—and Roy Howard will be here the 16th of this month [December] and I suppose I'll have stage fright so badly I'll go into a total eclipse and never be able to write another line. I've already been lying awake nights in a cold sweat merely because of the proximity of Jane. I believe she's a good kid, though, at that. . . . Jerry has been in the throes of Christmas shopping. I beat her every night for her un-American attitude—she's practically bought out all the Japanese stores in Honolulu. But it sure does save money!"

He rented a Ford in order to get around the island. Columns came hard at first, and his cushion grew thin. "Can't seem to find anything 'human' to write about," said a letter to me. "It's all either information or scenery." A break came when he read in the paper that Ernest Gruening, director of the Division of Territories and Island Possessions, had just arrived. Ernie had known Dr. Gruening slightly in Washington, so he telephoned him. "They came right down to the apartment," he wrote me, "and then had us up to the governor's mansion for dinner last night. Just like old home folks with the governor [Joseph B. Poindexter] and his very nice daughter. I like both Ernest and Mrs. Gruening, and they are damn smart folks. Think I was very lucky in crossing his path, for I was trying to get to the Molokai leper colony, and it seemed practically impossible. But Gruening spoke some magic word, and it's all fixed." Harry A. Kleugel, Superintendent of Hospitals, demurred, "but I just sat back and listened, because I knew and he knew he had to let me go. Later he became quite friendly and threw the doors absolutely wide open to me."

He left Jerry at Waikiki and flew with Kleugel to the Kalaupapa leper colony, situated on a spit that juts out from the base of a cliff on the island of Molokai.

"What an experience this has been," he wrote Jerry a few days later. "It's as weird as though you suddenly got to a monastery in

Tibet. Just this afternoon I talked for two hours with a Japanese leper, a graduate of the University of Hawaii, a highly intelligent man. He is horribly disfigured, it's almost impossible to look at his face, but we sat and talked like any two ordinary people. He was the kind I could ask the most intimate and personal questions of, and get an answer. When I left he said our conversation had given him the happiest day since he had been at Kalaupapa, because there's nobody of his education for him to talk to here. . . . Everybody has been grand to me; I'm practically a part of the community. I haven't felt any fear at all; and not much revulsion. You sort of get used to it. . . . When I go out tomorrow I'll have to ride up a continuous switchback trail that appears to go right straight up a perpendicular cliff two thousand feet high. It can't be quite perpendicular, but it looks like it. . . ."

It was at the Kalaupapa colony that the famous Father Damien, a Belgian priest, contracted leprosy and died of it (in 1889). Ernie met there a little old French priest, Father Peter, who also had caught the disease and had been cured by a prompt operation. But it was the Japanese patient, Shizuo Harada, who impressed him most. They later exchanged letters several times.

Ernie found that he could comprehend the self-sacrifice of Father Damien and Father Peter: "For I myself wandered into the foothills of martyrdom. Roaming Kalaupapa, I felt a kind of unrighteousness at being whole and 'clean'; I experienced an acute feeling of spiritual need to be no better off than the leper. My feeling will likely impress you as ridiculous fiction. But I did experience it. . . . The emotion itself was an adventure in desire, and I am glad that I have had it. But I am glad also that I must go on. For I know that in real life I am a 'sprint' martyr; the long, steady pull is not for me. I tire of too much goodness, and wish to dart off and chase a rabbit."

He wrote me about the Kalaupapa copy: "I'm proud of the series. First, because I think it is probably the first newspaper stuff ever written on the leper colony that hasn't been distorted, overdramatized, and fictionized. Second, the superintendent says that in his memory nobody, newspaperman or otherwise, has ever stayed in the colony as long as I did, or made such a complete study. I was there four days. Most get to stay only a few hours. The series is dramatized in spots, but there is not one word of manufactured drama in the whole bunch. Every word of feeling and emotion I've written about the place was my actual feeling. Of all the places I've ever been, Kalaupapa to me is the most powerful and dramatic experience."

He went on to other of the islands, Maui and Hawaii. He had hoped that Jerry might join him on "the big island," Hawaii, but she wrote that she had been drinking too much and did not feel like making the trip. He wrote her from Hilo: "I've started and thrown away two or three letters, because I've been in one of my dark helpless moods, and I knew my letters would sound as though I were catecizeing (can't spell it) you for your 'relapse,' which wasn't the case. But this evening I gave up and went to a movie, and now I feel better. For two days I haven't been able to write or even talk to anybody. I don't know what put me in it— it wasn't you; I guess it was the letters from Washington. They were certainly far from flattering. If they're so afraid I'll stay in Hawaii too long, I might as well hurry through, I reckon. I'm sorry you have been so miserable. I have so little understanding of anything . . . that I wouldn't have guessed it if you hadn't told me. Seems I'm too thick ever to learn. . . . (One day later) Your letter came today. I feel so terrible about the suffering you have gone through—please be happy and contented from now on till I get back. Going to Volcano House tomorrow. Hope it's warm so you can swim. All my love and don't worry."

He got back to Honolulu just before Christmas, after nearly a month on the outer islands. Jerry was better. "Miss Geraldine is still a mighty fine woman," he wrote Cavanaugh, "although she swum too much the other day and strained her heart, and now it stops two or three times every night and damn near stays stopped

and she thinks she's going to die. . . . Mellett got sore and quit
. . . . I don't know whether I've still got a job or not. I'm still
considering that jewelry business."

The Roy Howards had arrived, and Ernie's "stage fright"
soon disappeared. He wrote me: "The Howards, seriously,
were grand to us. I wish we hadn't even seen them, for I
figure the farther I can stay away from acquaintance with the
brass hats the better off I am. But—oh hell let's see, Mrs. Howard
had Jerry to lunch; I had two sessions with Roy lasting about
four hours each, listening to him talk about everything under
the sun (but not a word about me, for which I was glad); and
they had us to two cocktail parties, one a big important one, and
the other a little intimate family affair, with just them and Jane
and her feller and us, and then we all wandered out to dinner at a
corner hashhouse. Matter of fact, he is one of the pleasantest and
most fascinating talkers I've ever seen, and Mrs. Howard is just
grand. You can't help but enjoy being with them, even though
you know he's cold-blooded and would fire you tomorrow morning with a smile. I don't know whether he likes my stuff or not,
and don't care, for I don't want him taking any interest in me.
And I'm sure he won't, for this over here was purely social. . . .
The leper stuff seems to have had a good response. Roy Howard
read it in carbon, and all he said to me was that maybe it was too
long (which is doubtless correct); but word kept coming back
from other people in Honolulu that he'd told them he thought it
was great."

Ernie's worries about Jerry seemed to disappear after his return
to Honolulu. Certainly he was not so concerned about her drinking as to eschew the stuff himself by way of example. He must
have sensed, even then, that what disturbed her from time to
time was something deeper than any mere drink-craving, and he
was ever hopeful that, whatever it was, it would work itself out.
They did their share of holiday imbibing. "Last evening was New
Year's," he wrote me, "and despite the fact that I am a good
Christian missionary interested only in the eternal salvation of

the natives, a swarm of little *menehunes*[2] got into my bed last night, and poured some nasty liquid down my throat, and this morning I have awakened dazed and hazy. . . ."

There was a radiogram from cartoonist Talburt: "Be careful those lepers don't catch something from you."

He looked into the defense situation, insofar as the reticence of the military permitted, and wrote, among other things: "Long-range planes could spot an enemy fleet days before it reached Hawaii. It might even be possible for our planes to destroy a fleet before it got within a thousand miles. On the other hand, enemy planes might do the same thing in reverse." One night he dreamed that "the Army had my Dad in jail because of the columns I wrote about the Army and Navy in Hawaii." He wrote me: "Had a hell of a time with these Army and Navy columns, and they're not much good. They simply won't talk now, and despite my friend-of-a-friend introductions, they still wouldn't talk. And then, after not telling me anything, had the audacity to request that I submit my copy before sending it. I got my back up over that, so finally went to Roy Howard and asked him what to do." Howard told him that ordinarily he would refuse to submit the copy, "but that at present he felt matters in the Pacific were a lot deeper than we knew, and that a little twist here and there might do harm all around, so to go ahead and submit it and not make an issue out of it. So I did, and the funny thing was that they made practically no changes in fact, but were terribly, terribly hurt that I had mentioned their disinclination to talk. I could see it was merely a matter of some under-officers being scared to death they'd be called on the carpet, so I said oh well, I'll cut that stuff out. So after all the laboring of the mountains, here are the molehills."

Their sailing on the *Lurline* was festive—and sorrowful, for they hated to leave. Friends draped them with more than twenty leis apiece, and the traditional crying and kissing were wholesale. "Everybody has to come down to the boat and cry when you

[2] Hawaiian leprechauns.

leave Honolulu," he wrote me, "and our bunch cried more than anybody else's bunch, by God!"

On arriving in San Francisco Ernie found that the management favored another visit to Hollywood. "I'll see what I can do with [Walt] Disney right off," he wrote, "but somehow I never relish the hero of the moment, and he's been written up so damn much lately. . . . I don't think there's any danger of me finding even one new item about him, but maybe we can freshen it up by running it upside down or something."

He got a good batch of mail, containing "bouquets all over the place for the leper series.[3] Makes me feel very good. . . . I know I drive you nuts, and myself too, for being so long-winded. But, by God, when I have a good one and it goes out in full (thanks, Dr., you've been mighty lenient) they're the ones that bring in the letters. So maybe editors ain't so smart just because they're editors."

---

[3] I tried to plant that series with the *Reader's Digest* but had no luck; a decade later they were to use it as a condensation from *Home Country*. I also put Ernie up again for a Pulitzer Prize, with no result.

CHAPTER 10

Too Many Friends

THE column had been running now for nearly two and a half years, and with increasing success. Most of the Scripps-Howard papers were printing it regularly. There had been some informal talk about offering the feature to papers outside Scripps-Howard, which would mean more money for Ernie, but certain members of the management felt strongly that at least some of their popular writers should be kept as exclusively Scripps-Howard attractions. Robert P. Scripps himself was loath to see any more of the concern's product peddled on a come-one-come-all basis. Soon after Ernie's return from Honolulu, however, two things occurred which were to point the way to the release of his copy for general syndication. First, in February 1938 the enormously circulated columnist O. O. McIntyre died. I telegraphed Deac Parker, who with other of the chain's executives was conferring with Bob Scripps at Miramar, the Scripps ranch in southern California, and suggested that if serious thought was being given to general syndication of Pyle, the death of McIntyre might provide an exceptional opportunity for marketing Ernie's column—if the opportunity were seized without delay. Second, Ernie and Jerry had arrived in Hollywood for a few weeks' stand, and, either by coincidence or as a result of my wire, Deac telephoned, inviting them on Bob Scripps' behalf to lunch at Miramar.

Ernie wrote me: "Jerry says she never thought she'd come to driving two hundred and sixty miles just for lunch. We both had stage fright amidst all the big shots, but everybody was so pleasant we sort of got over it. And Jack Howard [1] was there, which made it a little better.

"Deac and I talked for some time after lunch. He said he had brought the subject up out there even before he called me, that they had discussed the wisdom of trying to syndicate the column, and that all he wanted me to know was that the traditional ban against syndicating anybody out of SHNA[2] has been lifted as far as I am concerned. Getting even that close to an actuality of syndicating the thing scared the hell out of me, and I went on telling Deac why it *shouldn't* be syndicated. I think it'll be a damned hard column to sell in the first place; and for best effect it can't be cut like other columns; it takes readers several months to realize it's a part of the family. Deac said that if they did syndicate it and it failed, not to worry that that would make him feel the column wasn't worth what SHNA is paying, and we would keep on using it. But he said nothing would be done till he got back from his trip. He said he'd never yet talked with Carlin[3] about it, and didn't even know whether United Feature would take it or not. I don't know what the hell to do. I told Deac I wasn't ambitious to be a great name or make a preposterous amount of money; that all I wanted was to make enough to build up some security for myself. The thing that frightens me worst is that if the thing should go over and get to running in a lot of papers, then a fellow would feel like he couldn't quit if he wanted to (or I'm afraid I couldn't), and that's always been part of my happiness on the job, that I felt the independence to quit a job any time I felt like it, even though I haven't exercised it but once or twice. And if the column was read by more people there would be more letters, and some arrangement would have to be made about that, for I can't physically handle any more than I do now. In fact it takes far too much of my time the way it is."

[1] Roy Howard's son, who had worked under Ernie in Washington.
[2] Scripps-Howard Newspaper Alliance.
[3] The late George Carlin, head of the United Feature Syndicate, a subsidiary of the United Press.

(Two weeks after the Pyles' visit, Bob Scripps, who had taken Deac on a fishing cruise, died aboard his yacht in the Gulf of California.)

Ernie wrote Shaffer: "I enjoyed seeing the ranch, and I am sure you're very jealous at us hobnobbing with such names. . . . But I am very sad about the whole business, for I have gone along for fifteen years now without knowing any of the bosses well enough to be recognized on the street, and now that they know me I suppose I'll be fired in six months, just like an editor." (The tenure of Scripps-Howard editors in recent years, especially during the depression, had been precarious.)

Hollywood presented its difficulties. Ernie did a long series on the Walt Disney studios, which was comparatively smooth going, since Disney and his staff were as cooperative as could be. After that it was rough. "We've been here a couple of weeks," he wrote the Shaffers, "and it's terrible. It's all I can do to face a movie star. They make me sick. And the worst part is that my private life interferes so seriously with my work! We have eight million friends and they keep coming to see us." And to me: "This Hollywood stay has been the worst problem I've ever faced, and one that frightens me because I don't know of any way to avoid it in the future—unless we hereafter confine ourselves exclusively to the back roads and avoid the big cities. The problem, of all things, is our friends. Here are some of the people that we have had to see many times during our stay here:—Aubrey and Mrs. Graves; Sally Campbell and a girl from Denver, who drove to California from Denver unexpectedly; Ben Hoy and his sister (the flier who lost his leg), who just showed up suddenly one day from New Jersey; Albert Moss and Johnny Palm from Alaska (couple of old sourdoughs); Duane Bush from San Francisco (met him in Alaska last summer); Tal and Marguerite; Ruth Simpson, a girl who used to work at the airport in Washington, and whom I simply bumped into on the street here one day; Nell Greenstreet, a friend from the old New York days, whom we crossed in Hawaii, and who is now back here; Chuck Egan is due here tomorrow for the Santa Anita

Handicap. In addition to those, there are all of our friends who live here:—Roy Chanslor (now out of a job); Paige Cavanaugh (ditto on job); my Filipino boy Gene (whom I haven't even yet seen, but must); and many people around the studios.

"The thing is so damned hard because people can't realize that I actually have to work; they feel that I'm practically on vacation; they don't realize that I work at reporting all day and must have the nights for writing. The only way I could have full time for myself would be simply to refuse to see or talk to any of my friends, and Christ I can't do that. For in the first place I like them and do want to see them, and in the second place I'd be put down, and correctly, as a horse's ass if I started that. . . ."

Next day he wrote again: "Lee, Jerry and I had a long talk last night about what to do in the future. We're both afraid of stepping into the big-time stuff, if that should come about. . . . So I wish you would ask Deac not to take any steps at all about syndication until I get back and we can talk it over. . . . I'm afraid of being built into a position where I can't quit. . . . As Jerry said, probably what I need most is a six-months mental vacation—but if a column is dropped for six months, it has sunk. So I don't know."

Another letter to me a few days later: "We'll be out of here in an hour. . . . Jesus I'm glad to get away again. Terribly shocked about Bob Scripps' death. Deac and Waltz[4] were to arrive at Long Beach at five this morning on the liner *Pennsylvania* with the body. I'd have gone down except it might be presumptuous and I guess there is nothing I can do for Deac anyway. I feel awfully sorry for him. Wonder what will happen in the concern now."

In Hollywood he had managed interviews with, among others, Norma Shearer ("She is the one I have always loved") and Olivia De Havilland ("So beautiful I couldn't do anything but stand and stare at her"). But he left Hollywood in an uncordial mood, as the last of his columns about the place attested: "A

[4] Edwin C. Waltz, Scripps' secretary.

friend of mine in Winnemucca, Nev., once said that the next time I came to Hollywood he wanted me to find out if Myrna Loy is really as sweet in person as she is on the screen. He said she was the only movie actress he cared about, and he just knew she had to be wonderful in real life or she couldn't be that way in pictures. Well, I certainly tried to find out. I think my Winnemucca friend is right, but I can't prove it. It's sort of hard to tell in sixty seconds whether a woman is sweet or not.

"Myrna Loy was working in a picture called *Test Pilot*, with Clark Gable and Spencer Tracy. After a week of negotiating it was finally arranged that I should spend half a day on the set, and sandwich in my 'interview' between scenes. Well, I'm no good at this kind of formal reporting. It's too stiff and hurried. And in this case there weren't any between-scenes for our interview anyway. Miss Loy was on the set nearly all the time, while I stood around on the edge trying to look as though I had kept my vanished dignity. But finally she did move out of the set and sit down in a nearby canvas chair. At that point her man, who had the jitters almost as bad as myself, hauled me over and introduced us. We said 'Howdy' or something, and then the director said 'Quiet,' because he was rehearsing somebody else. So we sat there about a minute, neither of us saying a word, and then she had to go back to work. At that point I said to the man, okay, let's kill it. . . .

"Around the studio they say Myrna Loy is very sweet, and very quiet. My Winnemucca friend will have to get along with that. As a matter of fact, I am sick unto death of trying to write about the great women stars of the movies. It is true that those I have finally been permitted to see have been very nice. But the rigmarole you have to go through, the stalling around and waiting, the few little precious minutes they finally give you, their apparent inability to break down and talk plain talk, all gives me a pain. . . . The stars are harassed to death, I know, and they do have to put up with all kinds of impositions from reporters, and they are justified in being suspicious and cagey about what they say, and you can't blame them for trying to preserve some privacy. What I'm sore about, you see, is that they don't distinguish between ordinary newspapermen and a fellow like me with polished manners, a learned mind, and a heart of gold! But they can't see it. So may the Lord forgive them; for they know not what they do.

"And on that sad and philosophical note let me leave Hollywood and trail off into the desert like a burro, alone and with head down, seeking peace and a new grip on life."

After a brief visit with the Cavanaughs they headed eastward in the face of severe flood conditions, and Ernie wrote me, from Barstow: "We're leaving here in the morning, but don't know where in hell we're going. We're starting up a dirt road into Death Valley, but don't know whether we'll get there or not. All other roads are closed (except one straight east to Needles), and this road of ours is so back that nobody's been over it for a year, I think, so we can't find out whether it's washed out or not. But I want to see Death Valley, and try to see Scotty, so we'll give it a try."

The day after that note was written Hitler marched into Austria. If Ernie felt any concern about this ominous step, none of his correspondence so indicated. He was having more immediate troubles of his own: "Lee: We're laid up at a place called Death Valley Junction, and I am about two-thirds down with the grippe. Roads all over this section are washed out, and we just sort of have to feel our way around. Yesterday we went to Scotty's castle and had one hell of a time. It took us an hour to go half a mile, and then we got stuck in a washout. We would have been there yet, I guess, except a car came along and helped us— the first car in three days! . . . Finally we got to Scotty's, and the sonovabitch was in Los Angeles! (Signed) Death Valley Ernie."

It was a week or so later when I heard from him again, this time from El Paso. He said the Gateway Hotel, where he had stopped various times before without commotion, "is practically tearing itself down because we're famous columnists. Two people came up today requesting autographs. In case you would like my autograph, I will sign my full name, just like I write it on checks and things. Ernest T. Pyle." One of the autograph seekers, he admitted in the column, was a small girl who, after being accommodated, asked him, "What do you do? Write, or what?"

They drove through a brisk sandstorm to visit and describe the spectacular Carlsbad Caverns in New Mexico, and on through some of the Billy the Kid country. At Roswell Ernie mailed Ed Shaffer a clipping from the local paper, which unaccountably identified Pyle as a former editor of the *Rocky Mountain News* of Denver. He wrote Shaffer: "What I told the reporter was that I had been appointed editor of the *Albuquerque Tribune* [Shaffer's job], but he got it mixed up, as reporters do."

And so on to Albuquerque and a joyous reunion with the Shaffers.

Shafe told Ernie that at a conference of Scripps-Howard editors the column had been given high praise by Ed Leech, editor of the *Pittsburgh Press*; Shafe himself considered it "the best column in America." Perhaps this gave Ernie heart to write me: "What would be your personal advice on the urgency of me getting back to discuss syndicatin'? As you know I am up one day and down the next, and although I am afraid of the consequences of syndication, I know also that I don't want to quit and go back on the rim [copy desk] somewhere, and a guy has to eat. So I suppose the thing to do is try to get syndication."

At Santa Fe, besides writing some columns about the artists, aborigines, and atmosphere, he complained in print of having searched the society pages "for a simple little item which should have read: 'Governor Clyde Tingley and Mrs. Tingley entertained at dinner at the Mansion on Saturday night for Mr. Ernest T. Pyle, the renowned roving reporter, and the girl who rides with him. Both dress and conversation were informal. A good time was had by all, observers close to the Governor reported.'" The picturesque "Ting" made Ernie a New Mexico colonel.

They drove and wrote their way eastward to Dana, where Ernie's mother was much improved from her second stroke. He wrote a piece about her: "Stories about my mother have appeared in this column before. And I'm afraid I've made a publicity hound out of her. For she said last night, and it sounded just like a Washington politician, 'I don't want you to write anything about me, but there are a lot of people who would like to know how I am.'

"Of course I'm merely joking about my mother being a publicity hound. She doesn't even know what the words mean. But I know what put the thought into her head. At Christmas and Easter she received 'Get Well Soon' cards from readers of this column in far-distant cities. And once last summer a young couple from the East, touring in this part of the country, dropped in to see her. Those things touched her, and so she feels that some people who don't even know her are interested in her. . . ."

After an absence of fifteen months, during which Ernie estimated he had traveled twenty-eight thousand miles, they drove into Washington and to my house, where sitting space was at a premium during the next ten days as old friends dropped in. The visit was described later in a letter from Ernie to Cavanaugh: "During that time I wound up the columns, did a few errands, and gradually got weaker and weaker from staying up all night and drinking too many iced teas. If we had stayed another twenty-four hours we would have been dead. Honest, we were in a hell of a shape. Jerry worse than I, and she hadn't done any sneak drinking either. In fact she was swell in Washington. But ten days of it straight will kill a guy, and I thought for two days her heart wasn't going to pull through."

He had written me again, shortly before arriving in Washington, about the syndication business: "I don't much give a damn one way or the other. It seems you have to be a demagogue and whale the air like Pegler and [General Hugh S.] Johnson to get anywhere, and I can't do that." He also told of a chat in Indianapolis with Ludwell Denny, editor of the *Times*: "You should have heard him raving about the following of the column in Indiana—although his paper gives it almost the worst butchering it gets in the whole outfit. I reckon the column's just so damn good that if he ran it in full it would set Indiana on fire and burn everything up. Yeah!"

Deac Parker, who was always to be found in Ernie's corner, had consulted with George Carlin of United Feature—indeed it is not unlikely that in his capacity as one of the three trustees who governed the Scripps empire he applied a little pressure. Accordingly, Ernie and I flew to New York and conversed with Carlin, who was civil enough but obviously unexcited at the prospective privilege of adding the relatively unknown Pyle feature to his stable of big names, which at the time included Pearson and Allen, Pegler, Raymond Clapper, and General Johnson, as well as innumerable comics and miscellaneous circulation-builders. Carlin said business conditions were so poor that he would prefer not to tackle the column until autumn and suggested that in the interim I could work up some promotion material. So it was left at that. The syndicate business is a unique one: the general practice, although there are exceptions, is to look down the nose at the unestablished but to welcome ardently an already accepted "big name" who is willing to divide the proceeds of certain success with the syndicate on a fifty-fifty basis.

Ernie was due for a vacation now—a joke, of course, to many friends who thought of his job as a perpetual holiday—and I decided to keep the column going for a few weeks by redistributing some of his old ones. Many of these were new to some cities, where the papers had been slow to give the column daily space. The vacation was as elusive as a will-o'-the-wisp, for its start coincided with the Memorial Day week-end, but after some unrestful prowling around Virginia in search of a pleasant place to relax—Warrenton to Charlottesville to Richmond to Williamsburg ("Every room in town was full"), to Yorktown ("We got a room in the oldest house in Yorktown and slept on a four-poster torture rack"), to Nags Head in North Carolina ("Cold and rainy and blowy"), to Norfolk—they returned to Williamsburg. The week-end crowds were gone, and they found a "lovely corner room" in the Annex of the Williamsburg Inn.

There Ernie wrote Shaffer: "Our vacation is over. I have been writing columns for two days, and we leave tomorrow for Washington. Lee phoned me yesterday. Deac got a long telegram signed by all five editors [of Scripps-Howard's Ohio papers], plus the Ohio group business manager, requesting that I come to Ohio immediately for an indefinite period and tour the state. So I said I'd go, but for Deac to let them know I wasn't going to write Chamber of Commerce stuff or recite their industrial figures, and I wouldn't stay in the state over two weeks and a half."

The Pyles drove back to my house for a week-end of too many friends and too many drinks. They planned to leave early Monday morning, but when the time came and the bags were all stowed in the car, Jerry decided she wasn't up to it. She had been having some painful trouble with abscessed wisdom teeth but was putting off the dentistry, and she really looked ill. Her bags were brought back to the house. In the meantime Ernie had been nursing his hangover with heroic doses of whisky. I had to go to work, so I said good-by to him. When I returned for dinner he was still there, still nursing, teetering a little, but insistent on making a start—which he did.

In two days he wrote Jerry from Parkersburg, West Virginia: "Darling: I wish I knew this morning just how you are. I'm not in any too good shape this morning myself. Not so sick, but in this terrible daze. It's all I can do to write a letter, and I couldn't possibly write a column or do anything else today. But I have definitely come to the end of this enforced spree, and it's going to be the last one for a long time. I'm going to walk the straight and narrow through Ohio, and I mean it. Everything since last Friday is such a haze to me and so confused that I can hardly remember the details of anything. . . .

"When I left Washington I stopped in Falls Church to see Bunny's[5] sister. I intended to stay only a few minutes, and then go on to Winchester for the night. Well, we talked a while and I needed a drink, so went and got my bottle out of the car. We drank and talked for nearly an hour, and finally, as I was getting ready to go, she said why not stay a little longer as her husband Ray would be home in a few minutes. Well, he came, and he is a very nice fellow, and we got to talking some more, and time just went on till the first thing it was daylight the next morning! It was certainly a crazy night. They had dinner ready to cook, but we never got around to eating it till the next morning just before going to bed! I piled in about five-thirty and at seven Ray awakened me, and I was on the way about seven-thirty. Didn't feel very bad either, as a matter of fact. We hadn't had a boisterous evening and only drank a pint between the three of us.

"Well, I never was out of the car from the time I left Falls Church till I pulled up here at Harriett's.[6] I completely forgot to eat a breakfast or lunch. . . . Harriett and LaRue are, of course, terribly disappointed that you couldn't come, but I promised them you would stop past on your way to join me later. . . . I've got a new love now, which is Claire.[7] She is absolutely the most beautiful thing I've ever laid my eyes on. We've got quite a crush on each other. Harriett says she never will have anything to do with anybody, but she'll hardly let me out of her sight. Very flattering. . . . We sat up and talked till after midnight last night, and although we drank very little I'm so weak and exhausted that last night's good sleep wasn't enough to pull me out. For, after all, I've seen the dawn come up three of the last four mornings. . . ."

Another letter came to Jerry, from Chillicothe, Ohio: "I've been so damned homesick and melancholy, clear down to the depths. . . . Maybe I'll feel different when you're with me again.

[5] Bunny Davis, a friend from aviation days.
[6] Mrs. LaRue Hendrixson, a girlhood friend of Jerry's.
[7] Small daughter of the Hendrixsons.

. . . I love you more than anything else in my life, as you must know even though sometimes I don't act like it, and I'm completely lost without you. When we're together again, let's try to work out something that will permit us to be ourselves and lead a life with some placidity, even if it does mean quitting my job. . . ."

Jerry, in the meantime, instead of going to the dentist, was keeping to her room. A tray would be brought to her, but she ate hardly anything. She was drinking. Her old friend Rosamond Goodman finally came over and persuaded her to go into a rest home, where she could be given proper care for a little while. Ernie wrote me from Cincinnati: ". . . got the word from Roz of Jerry's having to go to the sanitarium . . . and although I'm glad she went, I am sick about the horror she must have been through. I wish I could have stayed there with her to help her straighten out, but it was impossible. If I thought she was still bad off, I'd chuck everything and fly back, but Roz assures me that she is all right now but just needs solitude and rest and food. . . .

"This wild, spontaneous demand for Pyle in Ohio was so unanimous that Cincinnati, after a week of brain-racking, hasn't been able to think up a single tip for Pyle, and has decided there isn't anything in Cincinnati to write about. So I guess I'll have to go into the streets alone tomorrow and find something.[8] I was going to drop into one of the Chillicothe papers and ask for tips on some columns there, but lost my nerve for fear they'd think I was acting as advance agent for my syndicate self or something."

By the time he got to Columbus his spirits had risen, and he wrote Cavanaugh: "This is the first time in recent memory when I was completely written up on my columns, all clear on letters, have read everything in the room, and don't feel haunted by all that should be done. The reason for all this accomplishment is that . . . I've been leading an ascetic life, resisting all tempta-

[8] He visited the Procter and Gamble plant and wrote about the making of soap.

tion, and find myself able conscientiously to condemn all drunk-ards and evil-livers."

Jerry joined him in Akron. She "didn't have to have as many teeth out as she expected," he wrote his parents. "But she had a pretty tough time of it, and her jaw still hurts continually."

In Toledo a lot of mail caught up with him, including a letter from Harcourt, Brace and Company, suggesting the possibility of publishing a collection of the columns in book form. He asked me to have copies of all the material sent to Harcourt Brace, which was done, but nothing came of it. He wrote me: "When and if United Feature definitely goes on the market with the column, I think I can get a little write-up in the Press section of *Time*, which would do plenty good. I used to know the guy who writes it. . . ."

CHAPTER 11

South America

I T SEEMED time for another sortie outside the States, and a tour of South America was agreed on. The Pyles had a few days in Washington before setting out for Miami, their jumping-off point. The necessary nuisances involved in the trip, such as vaccinations, were sandwiched among hail-and-farewell parties. Finally—this was in September of 1938—they put their car aboard the overnight boat to Norfolk and were seen off by a handful of friends in a bedlam of last-minute drinks, bouquets, chatter, and, on Jerry's part, tears.

Ernie wrote in the column: "Once more we have come and gone from our home city—all in a flurry. Our visits to Washington seem almost like dreams. When people over the country ask us where we live, we say Washington, D. C. We carry District of Columbia tags on our car. We put down Washington on hotel registers. Yet we really have no home at all. We have friends all over the map. But it is in Washington that our friends are massed. And our visits to Washington are so infrequent and so brief that each one is like a daze we swim through, and we always leave with a feeling of frustration. For out of the hurry and tenseness and excitement, our visits can't be what we want them to be. We realize at the end that we have talked to lots of friends, yet individually we have talked to nobody. It isn't our fault, nor our friends' fault. We are prodigal sons, home for a brief moment, and if we are to see our friends at all, we have to see

100

them all at once. It isn't successful. There is no time just to sit down with one alone and say, 'All right, now let's talk about old times.'

"We feel the hurt in ourselves. But we also feel that our friends will gradually come to think we aren't worth bothering with— we are too hectic and ill composed; we do not conduct ourselves placidly, because of haste and many little duties; we are not ourselves. Always, after we leave Washington, we have a little talk to ourselves, and we visualize the day when disappointment in us will have wearied all of our old friends, and we see ourselves eventually returning to Washington with nobody at all to speak to us."

There were a few days of writing in Miami, and then began a three-month swing around South America by air. The trip was not notably successful; Ernie was half sick much of the time, and his unfamiliarity with Spanish tended to confine his copy to travelogue stuff and pieces about Americans living abroad. This was particularly unfortunate since United Feature had at last put the column on sale to all comers—who were slow in coming.

They flew first, via Cuba and Jamaica, to Barranquilla, Colombia, then to Cristobal in the Canal Zone, to Cali, Colombia, and across the Equator to Guayaquil, Ecuador—"which makes me a veteran of the Arctic Circle, the International Dateline, the Equator, and the Wabash River." The first night they were in Guayaquil, Ernie wrote in the column, "a local newspaperman came over to see me under the impression that I was a famous American engineer who had come to build a new railroad in Ecuador. I tried to straighten him out on that. But the next morning, according to the newspaper, I was a big American journalist, and editor of all the Scripps-Howard newspapers, including the *New York World-Telegram*. And two days later, in a Quito newspaper, I had been elevated to 'president of the great organization of North American Newspapers known as Screps-Howard.' As a result of these heady items I have just sent an air-mail letter (in Spanish) to Mr. Roy Howard, telling him to get the hell out of 230 Park Avenue by Christmas, or suffer the consequences."

From Lima, Peru, Jerry wrote me: "Ernie is trying to finish up the last of a bunch of columns—of which he's, as he says, so ashamed he could cry—and he almost has—I'm sorry to say I think he's somewhat justified in his feeling—though I haven't said so to him—The truth is that he somehow caught a heavy cold in Guayaquil—and if we'd been at home—and we hadn't been pressed for time—he'd have been in bed—If our arrangements hadn't all been made—we'd have stayed on in Guayaquil until he felt well—but he wouldn't ask Pan-Amer. to make a change for us—So we came on here, and it's very chilly—no heat at all—It's been so unpleasant that we've had to move the desk into the bathroom—run a tubful of hot water (which there is, thank God) and gather what warmth we can from that—I've tried to make him stay in bed at least until noon—but he wouldn't—he sits there and freezes and turns out what he feels is terrible."

Something interesting to write about—altogether too interesting, it must have seemed for a while—was provided on the next leg of the tour, from Lima to Santiago, Chile. Two hours out of Lima, at ten thousand feet and above the Andean badlands, Jerry touched Ernie's arm and said, "There's something wrong with this motor over here." As Ernie put it in the column: "In one tiny fraction of a second I went weak as a cat. I don't know whether I turned white or not, but I felt mighty white. For That Girl is not an alarmist, and I knew by her face that she wasn't fooling. I jumped up and looked. The motor nacelle was covered with black oil. By the way the sun caught the propeller, you could tell it was turning slowly. The passengers all looked, and the steward went forward into the pilots' compartment. But naturally they already knew all about it. Had known, even before we realized it. And in half a minute or so Co-Pilot William Baxter came back, looking as gay and happy as a June bug, and said to each passenger: 'We're making a safety landing at

Camana, down on the coast.' " Within half an hour or so the plane came to rest on a sea-level strip of desert.

As Jerry wrote to the Shaffers later: "The pilot[1] did a beautiful job of getting us down—We were scarcely on the ground before people came dashing from all directions—on foot, mule and horseback—old and young—mostly Indians—We were there for two and a half hours—sitting on the sand or walking about—constantly surrounded by chattering children—who stared at us and discussed us among themselves—pointed at our red fingernails—fingered our jewelry. . . ."

Another plane picked them up and flew them on to Arica, Chile, whence they proceeded to Santiago. A week later they made the big jump by air across the Andes to Buenos Aires, and presently took a leisurely boat trip up the Paraná to Asunción, Paraguay. Ernie wrote to "Dear Folks & Auntie" from Rio de Janeiro: "Our boat trip from Buenos Aires to Asunción was pleasant but not especially thrilling. The country was very flat and uninteresting all the way. We did have one very interesting morning, when we went through alligator territory. For miles and miles—nearly half a day—the banks of the river were just lined with them, out sunning themselves. One morning before breakfast I counted forty-five in about five minutes, and then all of a sudden there was a bunch that must have had a hundred in it, so I quit counting."

Ernie wanted, above all things on this trip, to visit Devil's Island, at the famous penal colony in French Guiana. It was decided that Jerry would do better to pass up this part of the trip and wait for him in Trinidad. So, after they had flown together from Rio to Pernambuco and Pará, Ernie dropped off at Cayenne in French Guiana and Jerry went on to Port of Spain, Trinidad.

He spent a week in Cayenne and never got to Devil's Island. Actually he discovered that of the eight or nine thousand convicts, only eighteen were on Devil's Island, and that, in fact, "it is a lovely tropical island, the kind we all dream about owning and

[1] Byron Rickards of Panagra.

settling down on. You have to be a big shot to be sent to Devil's Island." Having straightened that out, he proceeded to write a fine series about the penal colony and its almost forgotten men.

He wrote the Shaffers from Cayenne: "It was our plan that when I joined Jerry [in Port of Spain] tomorrow we would sort of vacation there for a week. But I had a radio from her saying on acc't of having come from south of the Equator, she had to report to medical authorities in Port of Spain every day, so she was going to Puerto Rico and wait. . . .

"You will read about this place when the columns come along. There are three toilets in this city of fourteen thousand. The hotel, unfortunately, does not own one of them. Thank God I haven't been caught with dysentery, with the only bathroom in the place being a bucket under the bed. Chickens stroll up and down the dining room as though they were waitresses. Vultures walk up and down the streets the same as people. During the big rain the other night I finally had to take refuge in the clothes closet and sit there from two a.m. until six because the rain all came right through the roof. I am so mauled by mosquitoes that my hands and ankles look as though I had elephantiasis."

He flew on, expecting to meet Jerry in Puerto Rico. At Port of Spain he mentioned this to a pilot he knew, who exclaimed, "Puerto Rico? She isn't in Puerto Rico. I took her to Miami last Monday."

A few days earlier a telegram had come to me, in Washington, from Jerry, in Miami, asking me to send some money. A letter followed: "I hated like the devil to have to wire you for money— but I didn't know what else to do—I had plenty to last if I'd stayed on in Trinidad—but I couldn't see staying on there and reporting to the Medical Inspector each morning at 8:30. . . . I cabled Ernie that I'd wait for him in San Juan [Puerto Rico] —I got there on Saturday—A nice enough hotel—but right on the ocean—It's the rainy season—a storm each morning—and the sea boomed and thundered so I couldn't sleep—Too close to home, no doubt—

"On Sunday my phone rang—at seven—They'd erred— Thought I was going on with the rest of the Pan Air passengers —Apologized when they realized their mistake—But I was awake —and had been, most of the night—Why should I stay—I called the airport and asked if I might go to Miami—The plane was full —but the airport manager who was a grand man said he'd arrange for me to go on Monday which he did—So here I am—

"I know it was crazy to pass up all the interesting islands on the way—but I feel, for myself, that I've reached the point of saturation—I may never see them again—but right now I don't care—I'm feeling well—but I'm tired— . . ."

From Miami, in a few days, Ernie wrote me: "I arrived from Haiti Sunday evening. I thought it was strange Jerry wasn't at the airport to meet me. When I got to the hotel she was in a pitiful state. She barely knew me and could only speak a little. She must have lost at least fifteen pounds. I don't know how long she had been drinking, or without food. But two days have passed now, and she hasn't been able to eat yet. It will take many days yet to get her back to normal.

"She had been so good all through the long trip; never a bobble. Today when she began to make sense again, she says she is ready, even eager, at last to go into a hospital or asylum or anywhere. An asylum of course is exaggerating it. But since she is at last willing, I think it imperative that she have something done with her. She feels that maybe there is something physically as well as psychologically wrong and is ready for a clinical going-over. She is so afraid and so melancholy that I wouldn't think of having her go anywhere by herself. So last night I wired her sister Po in Denver, who is a swell girl, a former nurse, and also knows about Jerry. She wired that she would either come, and go somewhere with Jerry, or see about the facilities of Denver hospitals for such things. I expect it would be better if she went to Denver although I hate for her to make the trip alone. We won't know for a few days, and I'll let you know.

"There's no reason I'm burdening you with all of this, except—

Christ! I have to tell somebody. . . . I've been nearly frantic with worry and despondency over Jerry's future, which of course is my future too. I've got an unbelievable amount of work to do—two or three score letters, Christmas presents, baggage sorting, little errands, and six columns to write; and can't do any of it until Jerry is back closer to normal again. So it is, all in all, a very charming homecoming. . . .

"If you should get a long sinister-looking package by air express one of these days, you are to open it, select one of the four instruments contained therein, place it upright on the floor, and then fall heavily forward upon it. And save the other three for me. [They were Indian arrows] . . ."

CHAPTER 12

The Open Road

THINGS turned brighter now—and it was high time. Jerry unexpectedly made such a rapid recovery that arrangements for her sister to come to Miami were abandoned. Ernie decided to drive to Key West, where friends from Washington, Burt and Betty Garnett, were vacationing, and write out the tag ends of his Latin American material. A note to me told of the changed situation, and he added: "I've decided this is the last complaining troublesome letter I'm ever going to write you. I just realized last night that I'm always griping, or moaning or weeping about something, trying to stir up sympathy for myself. My lot, of course, is a damn good one, and I'm going to try to appreciate it more than I have. And if I don't succeed, I'm going to try to quit weeping about it on your shoulder."

They got the car out of storage and, with the top down, under a hot December sun, took the Overseas Highway to Key West. "When I sit again at the wheel of our car after being away from it for months," Ernie wrote, "I feel like busting, it is so good." Key West was warm and restful, and he found, after catching up on his writing, that he was two weeks ahead. By doing a few pieces on Key West, he was able to prolong their stay to nearly a month. It was what they both needed badly. Ernie even went deep-sea fishing and played golf, and helped his backlog with such whimsies as his reply to a reader who asked if the columns had been put into book form:

"No, Mr. Brickel, they have not. And do you want to know

why? I'll tell you why. It's because there is a conspiracy against me. I am followed by dark men in derby hats with cold stumps of cigars in their mouths; at night I see shadows on the window curtains; I get strange indigestions after eating lobster salad. It is this conspiracy. . . . I understand that Simon & Schuster has one vice-president, drawing two hundred thousand dollars a year, whose sole duty is to keep anybody in the organization from mentioning the name Pyle, or anything that rhymes with it. Macmillan's have removed the letter 'O' from every typewriter in the building. They meant to eliminate the letter 'P,' but the typewriter man brought the wrong wrench. Stackpole Brothers have a man named Soskin hired to lean out the window and hiss all day long, just on the chance that I might be walking along Park Avenue. And I am informed that the firm of E. P. Dutton (my own initials are E. P., you know) has gone to court and had its name legally changed to 'Jack Dutton, Gen. Mdse.' Wherever I go, a cordon of silent, ugly men surrounds me, to keep the public away and to make it look as though crowds weren't trying to get my autograph. . . ."

The vacation over, they put themselves and the car on a boat to Tampa. From there they hit the road, bent on exploring the Old South. And now Ernie was in good stride again—in telling about, for instance, old Chase S. Osborn, the amazingly versatile former governor of Michigan, who was found at his remote Georgia hideaway, Possum Poke; about the Warm Springs Foundation; about Tuskegee Institute in Alabama, and its great Negro scientist, Dr. George W. Carver; and about all kinds of out-of-the-way odds and ends. They were escaping for the most part the big-city problem of "too many friends," and both the copy and their constitutions were the better for it.

In a letter to Dana from Mobile, Ernie described the country of southern Alabama: "It is the most backward section of America. About eighty per cent of the farmers are tenants. Most have no more than one mule; sixty-five per cent of the children have hookworm; there isn't one farmer in ten that has ever been out of debt in his life; they live almost like animals, both white and black; the majority are families of five to fifteen in a one-room cabin, eat nothing but side meat and corn grits, and are filthy dirty. And that's the case across three states as big as Ohio, Indiana, and Illinois. The government is trying to do something about it, but the people are so ignorant they don't want anything done."

In Louisiana Ernic was shocked to find his own kin living in circumstances comparable in part to those he described above. He wrote the Shaffers: "We dropped past to see my uncle (Dad's brother) in Louisiana. Hadn't seen him for twenty-five years, when I was a kid. I didn't expect to find him doing very well. He lived in Imperial Valley in California for many years and did pretty well with cotton, but had gradually been moving back east, to poorer farms. They had four girls, and all are married now, and gone. Dad hears from Uncle Clarence about every two years or so.

"We had a hell of a time finding the place. We'd pass some poor Louisiana farm shacks, and I remarked to Jerry that they probably lived in something like that. But I was badly mistaken. When we finally found them, they were in a one-room shack. Two old people, cooking, eating, sleeping, all in one room. They have one mule; twelve stumpy acres. They haven't a rocking chair. Uncle Clarence has no clothes but overalls. They came there from Arkansas, where his last farm was so poor he just walked off and left it. They are at the bottom. Out there all by themselves, in bleak country, lonesome. And Uncle Clarence is so good and kind and honest. It goddam near killed me.

"I had supposed that he would barely remember who I was. But he knew me before I got to the door; they were so tickled to see us; they dug out old family pictures and pictures of me when I was a kid; and most amazing of all, under the one bed they had a great stack of my columns out of the *Albuquerque Tribune*, sent by their teacher-daughters in eastern New Mexico. And when we left, Uncle Clarence stood on the old gate, smiling, and said what 'an honor it was to have a visit from Ernie Pyle.' My own uncle, and considering it an honor for me to stop and see them! I have never been so heartbroken in my life, and I just can't get over it. He says his one ambition in life now is to make a trip back to Indiana and see my folks. I'll see that he gets that; but we can't bail him out into a normal standard of living. Not that he asked anything of me—he was cheerful, and didn't complain, and he had the grace to not even apologize for the place. All of which means nothing to you, but it has saddened me so I can't think about anything else.

"My Filipino boy lost his wife and baby; our beloved little hotel in Ketchum, Idaho, burned down, leaving poor twenty-one-year-old Pete, the owner, straddled with a twenty-five-thousand-dollar loss; I have eczema and impetigo on my face and ringworm on my foot, haven't had a raise in two years, and don't even know who my boss is; United Feature isn't trying to sell the column and I am paying a secretary out of my own pocket to help answer letters; and if I can think of any more gloom I'll send you a telegram tomorrow."

Later, something happened in Oklahoma City to relieve his concern about Uncle Clarence and his wife, Aunt Axie. He wanted to do a few columns about Oklahoma's Boomer-and-Sooner days, and went to a library to look up the background. He wrote to Dana: "The young lady in charge was very helpful. When I went back this morning to continue my reading, the first thing she said was, 'Didn't you stop in Louisiana about a month ago to see your uncle?' And when I said yes, she said, 'Well, my mother is Aunt Axie's sister!' She said she knew that if I had seen them I would probably be upset and worried over the way they are living, and the main reason she spoke about it was to tell me not to be upset, for apparently they are living the way they want to live. Her mother was down to see them last summer and came back appalled at the way they lived; but they didn't mind or even seem aware that they weren't living as well as the rest of us. And she said also, that when they had money out in California they lived about the same way and didn't seem to know they had any money. She says that once in California they were worth between seventy-five and a hundred thousand dollars; that at that time Uncle Clarence was building better houses for his hired hands than he was living in, and letting them borrow from him as much as four thousand a year. She says they just frittered it away. . . . The girls all have good jobs and are willing to help them as much as they want to be helped. . . ."

Ernie sent his father money to finance Uncle Clarence's trip to Dana, and the old man was said to have been almost overcome at seeing the splendid stands of Indiana corn.

From Fort Worth I had a long letter from Ernie. (I was taking a sort of sabbatical year off the desk and was writing pieces of my own instead of handling others', so Ernie had less frequent occasion to communicate with me during this period.) He wrote: "We have reached a new low in discouragement and a feeling of frustration about the work. The column is No. 1, above all other columns, in a majority of our papers. That isn't my imagination— it's the record of one survey after another, and the written word of the editors. And yet nothing happens. We wonder what to do when you apparently have been successful, yet the people who sign your check decline to be interested."

In the same vein he wrote from Oklahoma City to the Shaffers: "We've been so low, as we heard somebody say in Texas the other day, we could sit on a cigarette paper and hang our legs over the side. United Feature can't (or doesn't) sell the column to anybody; despite the fact that a survey two months ago by the *Oklahoma News* showed my column topped by far everything else in the paper, yet the *Oklahoman* bought every column but mine when the *News* folded; I haven't had a raise in two years and understand I have reached my salary ceiling on SHNA, which is less than they are paying half a dozen of the seals around there. . . ."

A few weeks after these lugubrious letters he received the following from Deac Parker: "We are raising your salary twenty-five dollars a week. At the risk of your thinking I am trying to substitute words for cash, I want to say I wish it could be more. But times, as you may suspect, haven't been so good in newspapermaking, or anywhere else for that matter, and the 'service of supply' has been having its difficulties. If you will take this increase not only as twenty-five dollars per week more money but also as an expression of appreciation of the excellent job you have been doing, I shall be happy and so will everyone else concerned in the management."

That welcome letter from Deac was waiting at Denver when they drove in, and Ernie wrote me: "It came at a very funny time—almost telepathic. Jerry and I have been talking it over for several weeks and I had decided to write Deac (in fact had already started the letter) and ask for a little man-talk (as Cavanaugh would say) when I come East. . . . I seem to remember that Deac gave me to understand a year or more ago that I had reached my financial ceiling on SHNA. So what I had intended to have out with Deac was whether that financial ceiling could be rejiggered, or else put some real heat on United Feature. And that is the point which I still think should be thrashed out when I come East. The fact that they have sold only two or three papers in six months of course chagrined me, and I more or less took the blame for it upon myself. And then I began to hear a few things. For one, that there has been no promotion by them since the original blast. That editors who are United Feature clients were absolutely unaware that the column was for sale. And then came the following little item which made me goddam curious: When Peg [Westbrook Pegler] went on vacation, the *Tulsa Tribune* asked for my column. United Feature wired back and asked if they wouldn't take Clapper instead. They answered no, goddam it, that they asked for my column. So then they got it. Now what the hell does that mean? All put together, it looks to me as though somebody hasn't been wanting to sell the column. You and I both know that a sales organization like United Feature could sell mummified whales to more than two editors in six months if they were really pushing it, even in hard times. . . .

"I hear there've been a lot of dirty letters about the Southern pieces. I expected them. The pieces were absolutely authentic, and I take back none of them. . . . I expect there were dirty letters from whites about the Tuskegee pieces too. I was delighted to see the picture of Roosevelt shaking hands with Dr. Carver printed practically everywhere you looked."

For a long time Ernie had been nursing an idea for a transcontinental ride aboard a freighter truck, but he had decided to compromise and limit the stunt to a trip from Denver to Los Angeles. He also proposed to cover the San Francisco and New York World Fairs. Jerry was to stay with her sister until he got back from these enterprises.

The truck trip was rather rugged. He wrote Jerry from Los Angeles: "We got here at four o'clock this morning and after reading your letter I piled into bed, and then was so sleepy I couldn't go to sleep for half an hour or so. I kept thinking you were here, and the room was full of thousands of other people too, all making the most ridiculous statements.

"The last part of the trip was pretty much a nightmare. I had grown so sleepy and so weary that I hardly was able to sit up. The drivers weren't very generous with their sleeping quarters (though I can't kick, for after all they have to have their rest in order to work), but the result was that I had two short naps of an hour each in the 'sleeper'—two hours' sleep out of the last forty-eight, and you know I'm not very good at not having sleep. . . . Out of Banning it started raining, and we came on through one of those typical California rains, mists, fogs, and a general all-round hellish weather. Couldn't see ten feet ahead of you, yet the driver came plunging right through at about forty miles an hour. Any other time I would have been paralyzed, but I was in such a state of exhaustion I just said the hell with it, and catnapped in my seat and didn't even look at the road ahead."

United Feature had decided, possibly under pressure, to give the column a little more plugging, and unfortunately hit upon the idea of "sampling" editors all over the country with Ernie's reports on the two World Fairs—unfortunately because they turned out to be fairly routine rather than typical Pyle. In fact George Carlin showed me an indignant note from Stanley Walker, then editor of the *Philadelphia Evening Public Ledger*, berating him for having the nerve to submit such stuff. I didn't pass this on to Ernie, as he was already disappointed enough with the progress of the syndication.

He wrote Jerry from San Francisco: "They've taken so damned many pictures and been so slow about it that almost half of my time at the Fair has been wasted in picture taking. . . . Do wish you were going [to New York] with me. I suppose it would be foolish for such a short trip, but I can hardly bear to go East alone, without you to lean on and 'protect' me. I mean it. . . . I've managed to stay thoroughly sober and get plenty of sleep, yet feel lousy; my head swims and my eyes feel like they were balls of lead. . . . Truthfully, I'm disappointed in the Fair. But of course I mustn't say so in print. Not awfully disappointed, but it just isn't as fine as I had pictured it as being."

After covering the New York Fair he went West again and, rejoined by Jerry, took to the road. Albuquerque as usual drew them like a magnet. Ernie prevailed on Shaffer to go along with him, while Jerry stayed behind, on a two-week tour of the almost uninhabited desert country in the area surrounding the point where New Mexico, Arizona, Utah, and Colorado touch one another. The trip included a hair-raising passage in a small boat through the rapids of the San Juan River with the famous riverman Norman Nevills; a tour of the immensely spectacular Monument Valley, straddling the Utah-Arizona line, in the special big-tired automobile of desert-expert Harry Goulding, and a visit to the Grand Canyon.

Shaffer subsequently wrote two articles about their experiences, wherein he said in part: "People in out-of-the-way places are slow to warm up to strangers. Those out here have the reserve of their implacable open spaces and their impassive mountains. But not once did we leave a place where someone wasn't hanging on the car door, talking to Ernie and hating to see him go.

"While I was with him he talked to scores of people about almost as many different things. And he never took down a note. Each night he would jot down names and initials, but that was all. I think someone has said that Ernie absorbs scenes and situations through his pores and later lets them run down through his fingers onto paper. (Or maybe I thought that up myself.)

"He works methodically on those stories that read so easily and casually, sparing no effort to get what he's after. He keeps a tip book, in which he notes down names, addresses, and ideas as he hears about them. He clips newspapers and pastes items in the book. Perhaps a year or two later he'll be at the place where one of those items originated, and then he'll go and get a story about it.

"At Monticello, Utah, Ernie said suddenly, 'This is where a story is.' So he got out his little book, and, sure enough, there was a clipping about a hermit named Roy who had trapped some incredible number of mountain lions. We asked around, and someone said the hermit was in his cabin, high up on Blue Mountain. So we went up Blue Mountain, which is twelve thousand feet. There's a one-way road, twelve miles long, and you can't turn around on it until you get to the end. Well, we got to the end, and there was the cabin, but it was abandoned—apparently hadn't been occupied for months. I'd have squealed like a pig caught under a fence if it had been I that had driven up that mountain after a story and found no story. But Ernie just rolled a cigarette and said, 'Shucks, it probably got too crowded up here for Roy.'"

Shaffer returned to Albuquerque, and Ernie holed up at a tourist camp in Flagstaff, Arizona, to wait for Jerry. She brought a letter from me listing the total result of the syndication effort—eight newspapers: *Akron Beacon-Journal, Juneau Press, Los*

Angeles News, Miami Herald, Ogdensburg Advance News, Pontiac News, St. Petersburg Times, Toledo Blade.

There followed a considerable survey of some of the national parks, Zion and Bryce Canyon in Utah, and Glacier in Montana. Equipped with a knapsack fashioned by Jerry, Ernie hiked all by himself the fifty miles from Sun Chalet in Glacier Park to Waterton Lakes in Alberta, Canada. Then it was Helena, Montana, and the copper mines at Butte, and so to Boise, Idaho, where Ernie took time to write to the Shaffers: "Boise is only twenty-six hundred feet high, which is the lowest we've been in a couple of months, and it's really got us. I was going to do great gobs of work today, but have actually lain here on the bed most of the day, in one of those deadly stupors. It's hot and muggy, and we feel like we're suffocating. . . . Something terrible has happened to me. Haven't had anything to drink but beer for three weeks or so, and the last couple of evenings haven't even had beer. And I'm on no wagon, I'll have you know. It's just that I don't hanker for a drink. It's got me worried sick. Yesterday was my birthday. And I'm thirty-nine years old and don't give a good goddam who knows it, and within another year there won't be a hair on my head. In addition to having achieved sort of a lack of personal vanity, I have also reached a pleasant state where I don't care whether they sell the column, give me a raise, or anything. I never knew advancing age had such compensations. . . . I have a whole sack full of rock for the rock-mad Shaffer children. It is seventy-five per cent copper, and I mined it myself out of a mine twenty-eight hundred feet under the city of Butte. Someday I'll have to go back and start mining for that two dollars I lost at roulette in one of their gambling joints the other night."

He also mentioned his birthday in a letter to me: "One more year and I'll be middle-aged. I'm looking forward to it." As the years progressed, however, and birthdays rolled around, he would keep deferring that mythical borderline beyond which yawned middle age.

It was not long after this, on August 21, 1939, that the announcement was made of an agreement by Germany and Russia to sign a non-aggression treaty. I was at sea at the time, on the way to France for a vacation. Ernie wrote me from Seattle: "We haven't been able to do anything all week, except just sit and wait for the next edition to come out. Bet I've bought eight dollars' worth of papers this week. All the crises over the couple of past years we've never paid much attention to; but something got in us about this one, and we've felt right from the first day that this one was going to be war—not a war to end war, but a war to end everything. I've even been dreaming about it and couldn't half sleep at night. . . . If war breaks out you better stay over there, and Jerry and I will come over and join you, and we'll become famous war correspondents. Dr. Miller can go to the front and be a hero and I will write 'homey stuff' from Wales or Denmark."

CHAPTER 13

A Taste of Fame

THE Pyles were in Portland, Oregon, when the declarations of war were issued. Ernie wrote next day to "Dear Folks & Auntie": "I can't see anything but a longer and more terrible war than the World War, and although we can undoubtedly keep out of it a long time I feel we will have to go in if it lasts longer than two years."

From San Francisco he wrote Cavanaugh: "I guess we're in the same state of mind over the war. Geraldine now says she will jump out of a high window if I go. She is terribly upset about the war, and now the heat has got her, and she's a little cross this evening. As for me, I eat the heat up, and if the damn war lasts long enough, I'll bet I get some kind of a look at it."

Again to Cavanaugh: "This is just between you and me and not to be mentioned to her, but the other night Miss Geraldine broke that 'unspoken stalemate' I wrote you about by announcing out of a clear sky that she was ready and willing for me to go cover the war if I wanted to. I know it was a terrible decision for her and she had rassled with it a long time, and I thought it was pretty fine of her to do it. But the war has begun to bore me, at least from this distance, and it seems like an awful lot of trouble to get over there, and apparently the censorship this time is so drastic you couldn't write anything readable anyhow, so I will put it up to the bosses, and if they say all right then I'll go, and if they say no I won't put up much of a fuss. . . . (Signed) Gen. Ernest Gamelin."

118

As they moved down the coast, they began to learn with a vengeance some of the inconveniences of being "celebrities." Ernie wrote the Shaffers: "I wouldn't tell it to anybody except you folks because the other people would think I was getting stuck up, which of course I am, but the point is that in San Diego the residents have somehow got it into their heads that there is only one true and living God on Earth, and that his initials are not J. C. but E. P. And I tell you it's the goddamnedest thing you ever heard of. They had a piece in the paper, and although the *Sun* didn't give out where we were staying, still enough got through so that it was like being a fugitive in a nightmare with fingers pointing at you and people 'just waiting to shake hands' and people wanting 'just two minutes' and 'just two hours.' It was wonderful of course but at the same time it was awful, and it really scared the living daylights out of me. I am now more resolved than ever to hurry right along and get retired as quickly and as firmly as the law of gravity will allow.

"Well, at any rate it was buoyant to a point but . . . it finally got us to the breaking point and we were a couple of hazy babies when we at last got out of San Diego and wobbled over the mountain. When we came out of the pass and down into the sand and wide-open spaces, that goddam old empty desert looked so good we could have got out and kissed it. . . . This is honestly the first day in two weeks that I haven't felt like a Memorial Day cartoon of ten thousand graves when I woke up in the morning. . . . People all say that Jerry looks younger and prettier and more animated every day, and I believe it is true. . . ."

Ernie got a letter from Wesley W. Stout, editor of the *Saturday Evening Post*, urging him to do some articles. The compliment delighted him, but he had to reply that the columns took all his time. Stout wrote again: ". . . We shall go on admiring the job you are doing and hope that we may chip a piece off of it some time. . . ."

They scratched leisurely around the deserts of Arizona and New Mexico, and then Ernie wrote me, suggesting a Central

American trip. He continued: "This past week in Lordsburg, Deming, and Silver City, N. M., all in the *El Paso Herald-Post's* circulation territory—I think every inhabitant of those three cities, and every rancher around, reads that column like a Bible. In none of those places did I ever come down from the room, or come in from the outside, but that there were people waiting to see us—just to say how much they enjoy the column. The first night in Silver City we tried to eat in the coffee shop, and never did get to finish our dinner. After gathering my columns I had planned to stay in Silver a couple of days and write them out, but it was impossible—we simply had to leave.

"I know it must sound awful to you for a guy like me to say this, but we actually know what it is to have to eat in our rooms and sneak out the back way. I'm not trying to overtoot my own horn and I certainly couldn't have the courage to be so immodest to anyone else, but I am just trying to show you that the powers-that-be have no idea what a hold the column really has—and what a basis for selling it if they were interested. The silly part of this whole letter is that I'm not suggesting that we do anything about it. I just hadn't mentioned it at all to anybody for so long I thought I'd just up and say it. I haven't any burning desire to be spread in every paper in the country. I'd gaily take a little more money if I could get it, but even that isn't on my mind, for we're able to save some as it is. I guess I'm just like an old screwball I wrote about up at Silver City—all I really want is to be appreciated."

The Central American trip had been approved, so they drifted to New Orleans and booked for Panama on the United Fruit liner *Sixaola*. He wrote me: "I hope the office won't even suggest that I do any military columns down there [in Panama]. . . . If there is one thing in this world I hate and detest, it is writing about the Army."

Besides being harassed by visas and vaccinations, Christmas shopping and unwritten columns, Ernie had some long-distance conversations concerning a sudden proposition by Fred Ferguson, head of the Scripps-owned NEA Service, who wanted to take over the column from SHNA and United Feature. Ferguson offered him a little more money than he was getting (which was now a hundred and seventy-five a week from SHNA and about twenty-five a week from United Feature), but, as Ernie said in a letter to me, "What concerns me more is the nebulous question of freedom, actually and in spirit. Ferguson said naturally they would leave the column alone—that you don't tinker with a locomotive that's running good. And I'm not afraid of their good faith, but I am afraid of their life-long trend and instincts on handling feature stuff. . . . It would be hard for Ferguson not to ask me to shoot somewhere and do something when he had one of his hunches. In fact, I fear it would be almost impossible. On the phone, he said why no, they wouldn't order me to do things. He said, as an example, that if there was a national political convention, they'd want me to go write about it as *I* wanted to write about it, not as all the other reporters wrote about it. And I told him he had just spoken the very thing I feared—he'd want me to go to political conventions, and that's the very thing I don't do, and the thing steady followers of the column don't want me to do.

"I suppose it would be possible to actually include in a contract that I was to be sole picker of my subject matter. But hell you can't put in a contract that the office isn't allowed to change your copy—that isn't sensible. And yet if they ever started monkeying with it, me and the column would be dead. I just don't know how to insure myself with them the same understanding and intimate feeling for the column and the feelings of the readers toward it that I have had under you and SHNA. [Ferguson eventually admitted he was licked, and the deal was dropped.]

"P.S. I've reopened this letter at Jerry's suggestion to tell you that she is feeling fine. She has always been a little concerned about her state of a year ago this time [at Miami] . . . but Jerry has had her battle out and she's won it. She has never drunk secretly since then; in fact, I don't believe she has really been tight since then (though I have, fortunately). She drinks as often and as much as we both always did, and enjoys it, but the psychosis or whatever you call it is gone. I'm no longer worried about it; her general nature and outlook on life is a thousand per cent better than it has ever been since I've known her; and I admire her tremendously for what she has done with herself. She kinda wanted you to know it."

The car was shipped to Miami, and two days before Christmas they sailed for Panama. The six-day voyage to Cristobal, via Havana, was uneventful to an extreme, "probably the most characterless ocean trip we've ever taken." But the Canal Zone was fascinating if exhausting. The Americans in the Zone, Ernie wrote to the Shaffers, "are so lonely for companionship (plenty of Americans there for company, but they're all the same kind of sheep) that they are almost pathetically eager to talk to you, and ashamed of themselves for staying there so long, and the result is that it's the drinkingest damn place under the American flag outside of Alaska, and I'm not sure *it* should be excepted. Also we hit it at New Year's time, and everybody was celebrating, and they damn near put us away from much roistering and no sleep. Jerry has got so extreme heat hits her just as hard as extreme cold. Don't know what we'll do with her, unless I can get her air-conditioned. Personally I think we're both sick of traveling, though neither of us would admit it. No, I guess that isn't true—what we need is to sit down and settle a bit and not write columns for six months, but hell you can't stop writing for six months and then start again. . . .

"I am tickled to death I didn't go and get myself involved [in the NEA offer]. . . . We'll stay where we are and be ready and free to quit at the raise of an eyebrow. As Jerry says, by watching our pennies we right now could live for more than five years on what we've got."

He wrote some columns about the unusual status of the several thousand Americans employed by the government to operate the Canal and the Panama Railroad, and in a note to me said that these pieces "will doubtless bring a flood of letters from Panama patriots and government officials accusing me of everything from shoddy reporting to rape." This was in reference to such observations as: "Next to doing his job well, the Canal worker's main idea is not to disturb the status quo. . . . One of their own, who sees them clearly, has called them 'stall-fed.' They have surrendered the important quality of egotism—the eternal conviction that you could do it better than the other guy. They have given up personal ambition, natural instincts of competition, all the lovely mystery of life, for a security that gives them a life of calm and a vague discontent."

His concern about the local reaction to this sort of comment was groundless, for the often pugnacious newspaperman Ted Scott wrote in the *Panama American:* "Ernie . . . is one of the few highly touted U.S. syndicated writers who have ever been through these countries on tour and have not made us look like a tribe of monkeys swinging from our tails in the tropical jungles."

In Nicaragua they underwent a slight earthquake, found out all about growing coffee, and had dinner with the American Minister, the famous Indiana novelist Meredith Nicholson. In Honduras they visited the quiet, cobblestoned capital, Tegucigalpa, and the Mayan ruins at Copán. In El Salvador, smallest of the Central American republics, Ernie wrote the astonishing story of a young boy, nicknamed Tarzancito, who had been lost in the jungle when scarcely more than a baby, and when captured at a presumed age of about five years had many of the characteristics of a wild beast; when Ernie saw him, six years after that enforced return to civilization, he was a well-mannered and gentle-voiced lad, prospering in his studies and fond of Tarzan movies. From Guatemala City Ernie made expeditions to ancient Antigua, once the rich and handsome capital of Guatemala, which in 1773 was shaken to the ground within a few minutes by an earthquake, and to Carmelita, in the heart of the great Petén jungle of northern Guatemala, source of most of the chicle of which chewing gum is made, and a habitat of the deadly fer-de-lance.

Here he had an experience which took some delicacy to describe: "This is a little odd to be putting in print, but I believe you won't mind my telling it. The one and only 'Chic Sale' in the settlement of Carmelita is merely a stockade of poles, forming an enclosure about six feet square. There is no roof. An old gunny sack hangs across the 'door.' The seat is made of sticks, tied together with vines. The back wall literally stands in the jungle. Weeds grow on the floor.

"Well, one day, things being what they are, Your Correspondent found himself in there. The sun beat down soothingly upon him, and there was no noonday sound in the jungle. And then suddenly—I hardly know how to tell it—there was a rustic scratching and scampering on Your Correspondent's leg. I don't mean that part of the leg down by the foot. I mean that part of the leg way up where it joins the body, around toward the back —a part which happened to be divested of covering at this moment.

"Well, Your Jungle Hero almost jumped over the stockade wall. Cringing and terrified, he looked back to see what had attacked him. And ladies and gentlemen, it is the truth, what had run so madly up the side of your bare, innocent correspondent was a lizard more than a foot long! A newspaper man does, indeed, meet so many interesting people, animals, and reptiles."

The Pyles had engaged passage by ship to Miami, but the sailing was canceled, and they had to fly. Jerry joined her mother, who was wintering at Lake Worth, Florida, while Ernie went on to West Palm Beach to write out in solitude the remnants of his Central American material. In nine days he turned out a record twenty-four columns and made a start on an article about his wanderings which a friend on *Collier's* had requested—and which the magazine subsequently rejected.

CHAPTER 14

A Home to Come Back to

THEY hit the road again, through Florida and Alabama to Memphis, where Ernie came down with assorted aches that finally forced him into a clinic. The tests showed low blood pressure and some anemia, stomach spasms caused by nerves, and "exhaustion." The doctors prescribed a month's rest. So they drove to Biloxi, Mississippi, where they had friends, and rented a house. Ernie told the Shaffers: "The doc gave me some vitamin B-1 or something which he said would make a rocking chair eat within a week, but I still have to force my food down. Haven't had a drink for a month. . . . Just don't seem to want any; the doc said I obviously didn't drink enough to hurt me. . . . I think, if I must be a self-analyst, that the war has considerable to do with my slow picking up.[1] I've been so saturated with horror and despondency over it that I couldn't see much point in living. The slaughter has been so terrible and the Allied efforts so discouraging. . . . Jerry is worried too about the war and the aftermath and feels more than ever that we ought to get some property, because we'll likely lose everything else, so you better resume your looking around for us. The way I feel now, I'm only good for about another year of column-writing anyhow. We thrive on the traveling, but the pressure of a thousand words a day is becoming increasingly a specter."

The Washington office had suggested a European trip. Ernie was lukewarm about it. He wrote Cavanaugh: "They say not

[1] This was written nine days after Hitler's invasion of the Low Countries.

125

to go if I don't want to—the hell of it is, I personally want to, yet I don't see how I could do anything but make a failure out of it. Can't talk the languages, censorship and mail communication terrible, everybody too damn busy fighting the war to monkey around with a nosey feature writer and I couldn't blame them." Then he got a letter from me: "Europe is OUT. Good God, there won't be any Europe in a week or two. In a few days the French government will be scramming for Bordeaux."

Refreshed by their sojourn in the sun, the Pyles drove to Dana, where home was anything but restful: "I don't know whether I can remember all the details, as it's pretty much of a blur. Or rather a nightmare. The crowd got bigger and bigger and worse and worse. I can't begin to detail the people who came. People I never saw before or heard of. Friday night we were ready to sit down to supper at five p.m., and finally got there at a quarter till nine." From Dana Jerry went on to Minnesota, and Ernie flew to New York to undertake a transcontinental trip by bus.

While in New York he took time to do some columns about the American Volunteer Ambulance Corps and the American Field Service, each of which had sent scores of ambulances and drivers overseas to work with the French Army. He got so interested that he telephoned me in Washington to say he was giving serious thought to signing up. I pointed out that the situation in France was fast disintegrating—in fact the Germans were in Paris a few days later—and counseled him to wait a while and see what happened. He wrote me: "Hope I didn't shock you too much with my phone call. As I meant to say, it isn't any sudden madness, but something I have been eating and sleeping with for a week or two before this guy suddenly took it right out of my mouth this afternoon. But we'll let it jell while I am on this trip. . . ."

Ernie fudged somewhat on the coast-to-coast bus ride, breaking it in the middle by taking a train from Chicago to Denver, which was just as well since the various buses he rode on provided nothing particularly interesting to write about. Cavanaugh, who was out of a job, drove to San Francisco to pick him up at the end of the bus trip, and they rode to Los Angeles together. Then Ernie flew on to Albuquerque, where Jerry was waiting at the Shaffers', and they went up to Santa Fe to look into the possibilities of acquiring a little house—a pied-à-terre for vacations, for housing their accumulations of books and travel souvenirs, and perhaps for their retirement. But the prices of available houses seemed high, and instead they bought two or three acres of ground with the idea of eventually building a cottage.

Jerry's mother fell and broke an arm, and it was decided that sister Po, a trained nurse, should go to Minnesota, while Jerry kept house for Po's family in Denver. Ernie flew on alone to Indianapolis. This was during the Republican National Convention, and he wrote Jerry: "Well, Willkie got it. Over Kansas last night we listened to the convention through our earphones." He also told her that before leaving Albuquerque he had been shown a plot of ground in the outskirts of the city, not far from the Shaffers'. "The statistics were that the two lots would be $760, and the house around $3000, but having heard so much about extras, I thought up every possibility of expense I could think of. . . . And the result was that our $3000 house, plus lots, extras on house, various assessments, grading, shrubbery, paving, furnishing, etc., would cost us close to $6000 and would probably run us $300—$400 a year to keep up! So I guess we have exhausted New Mexico for home possibilities. However, I did get kind of house-building crazy during my studies, so to give us a chance to talk it over, I deposited $25 to hold the two lots for forty-five days. . . . Somehow, I'm more set than ever on the necessity of us getting some place—and the fun of it too. But apparently any city is out, due to high cost. The only thing I see left is to buy a house in some small place where we could pick up a good one for $1000, spend another $1000 remodeling it, and have then a total investment of only $2000 or $2500. I really believe anything beyond that for us would be very foolish. . . ."

On a request from Washington, Ernie made a tour of Wendell Willkie's farms near Rushville, Indiana, before taking the first of several pleasant breathers in rustic Brown County, celebrated (at least among us Hoosiers) for its scenic hills and its colony of artists. He wrote Jerry: "When I was doing the Willkie farms, one of the businessmen of Rushville trailed around and took pictures of me all afternoon, and this morning he sent them to me. And they are really excellent. I look less like a fool than usual. . . .

"Louis Seltzer[2] called the other morning. Had just had a bright idea that I do the Mesabe range in Minnesota. Told him I'd only done about ten columns on it before he started using the column. He said his face was red for not appreciating the column at first, but they were making up for it now. And I guess they are at that. He said it was the most-read thing in the *Press.*"

Again to Jerry, a few days later: "The Democratic convention seems to me disgraceful[3] and everything Roosevelt does lately seems to me cheap and shameful. I've been for him, but he has run his course, and I am a Willkie man now. . . . Roosevelt's flabby statement last night that he has never had any desire or purpose to continue in office is such a downright lie it makes me blush that he could say it with a straight face."

On my way back to Washington from the convention I stopped at Indianapolis, breakfasted with Ernie, and drove with him down to my home town, Seymour. Next day he wrote Jerry: "Bob Elliott[4] wrote that the Panama-Pacific line was thinking of inviting you and me to go on the opening trip of their new coast-to-coast service with ships taken off the European run. Knowing Lee was coming, I waited till he got here and asked him if we could go. He said hell yes. . . . I had a nice day in Lafayette, stayed all

[2] Editor of the *Cleveland Press.*
[3] That was the one so clumsily stage-managed by Harry Hopkins, assisted by the famous "voice from the sewers."
[4] Of the *San Francisco News.*

night there, and then next day went on fifty miles north and spent the day with George Ade! He is a marvelous person—you'd love him. He's seventy-four and not well, but his wit and understanding and kind personality are just as sharp as ever, and it turned out he reads the column every day in Miami, where he spends his winters.

"Lee has a million stories from the convention, but the best one is a true one about Roy Howard. One evening after convention (they never could get taxis) Roy and Deac and Roy's secretary got on a streetcar. There was a delegate on the car from Wyoming, pretty far gone in his cups. He was gazing around, and suddenly he lit on Roy. He brightened up like a flower, staggered over, tapped Roy on the chest and said, 'You know, if you just had a walking stick, you'd be a dead ringer for that little sonovabitch Roy Howard.' Lee says Roy took it in good order. And later Deac said to him, 'Roy, you better start telling this as soon as you get to the hotel, because I'm going to get on the telephone and tell it to everybody I ever knew.'"

He wrote Jerry from Brown County: "This is really a fascinating place. It isn't like the Midwest at all. They're a peculiar, proud, somewhat backward hill people who have descended straight from English immigrants without any mixing; the country is as lovely as anything between the Rockies and the Appalachians; the town and countryside are full of characters and of artists in pretty log cabins stuck around under the trees. . . . I think I know a third of the inhabitants by their first names already. . . .

"You paid me a most beautiful compliment, darling, and I know that you meant it, but it is not true. I have not achieved anything within myself. You mistake a calm stupidity for a calm resignation. The only thing I have achieved is in learning a little bit about sincerity and about dignity from you. I mean that. . . . It will be wonderful to see you—I feel such a lack of somebody stronger to lean on when we are apart this long. My life, when I am living it just for myself, seems to get chaotic and all full of irrelevant things and I just thrash around. Maybe I should disguise myself as a French orphan and get somebody to adopt me. . . . I can't help but be pleased that you miss me. But it works both ways. I wish I were as great as you feel I am. You shouldn't have such ideas after fifteen years."

There were so many distractions that Ernie had to run over to French Lick Springs in order to grind out a dozen Brown County columns. Then he flew to Denver, picked up Jerry, and they flew on to San Francisco, where my wife and I joined them for a gay two-week cruise via the Panama Canal to New York on the liner *Washington.*

The four of us were invited to sit at the captain's table, the captain being the famous Harry Manning, who, as Ernie reported to Cavanaugh, "turned out to be a tough baby," but Jerry "sat next to him at table and she got him hammerlocked and all tied up in a knot until he was practically following her around like a baby." He was indulging in a little hyperbole here, but certainly Jerry did seem to have a softening effect on that rugged and not too social mariner.

At Balboa the *Washington*'s berth was near that of the British liner *Rangitiki,* on her way to Australia with hundreds of English children. "How close to pathos we were," Ernie wrote in the column, "as we so gaily slid past the grim and serious *Rangitiki.*" He was to be aboard her, in uniform, on a perilous voyage from England to North Africa.

The cruise over, Ernie and Jerry picked up the car in Indiana and took to the road once more, down through southern Indiana, and from Evansville Ernie wrote Cavanaugh: "Well, by God we finally did get to Salem, Ind., the home of the illustrious Paige Cavanaugh, of World War, Indiana University, and Mattingly & Moore [a whisky] fame. Yessir, we stayed all night Saturday night with Lee Miller's folks in Seymour, and then arrived in Salem at three Sunday afternoon, and I'll be goddamned if it wasn't six-thirty before we ever found your folks. Nobody knew where they were. So I figured they'd have to be home by four-thirty to feed the chickens, so we waited, and the fat bulldog took such a

shine to me she had to sit in my lap and lick my face all afternoon.
. . . It was getting on toward dark, so we drove downtown and
et (worst meal in five years of traveling too), and when we got
back to the house they were home.

"They seemed mighty glad to see us, and your Dad said, 'I'd a
knowed that mug anywhere,' and those were the last words he
got in for a while. He is so much like my Dad that it practically
haunts me. He looks a little like him, talks exactly like him, his
voice sounds like his, he's just about as deaf, and they have the
same sort of timid kindness. They both even say 'are-ow' for
'arrow.' And your house too has got a thousand and one little
things in it that are exact duplicates of ours. Your kitchen 'safe'
and the stove and the bathroom and the linoleum—although I
must say we haven't got any pictures to equal those dimpled,
reclining cupids in your folks' bedroom. Well, we sat around a
while, and Ida was on the verge of calling up half the county
and having them right over till I put a stop to that.

"Monday morning . . . your Dad and I got in the car . . .
and I'm sure I met half the people in Salem. It was a regular pilgrimage, from one store to the next. It was all very exhilarating
until we met one guy—the optometrist—who had never heard of
me or the *Indianapolis Times* either, and on top of all that he'd
never heard of you. So I says to your Dad '—— him,' and we went
on to the grocery store. . . . We left at ten-thirty for Evansville, and your Dad was really so disappointed that he almost
cried, and I felt like a low-down sonovabitch at going so soon. But
we actually had to, on account of me being desperate with the
columns. And also—this is exceedingly private—Jerry had had a
hard week and was about to the end of her resources.

"Despite fifteen years of living with one, poor Jerry has never
had any understanding of country people and simply can't adapt
herself to them. She had been three days with my folks at Dana,
which was an ordeal, and a day and night with Lee Miller's folks,
which further weakened her, so by the time we got to your
house she really had the screamies inside herself, and even wanted

to back out and not go at all. Your folks of course couldn't tell the difference, but I was scared to death she was going to blow.

"Well sir, we're agonna do it. Build a house, I mean. And apparently right away. In Santa Fe. We just decided all of a sudden, and sort of simultaneously. I really think it's the thing to do. It's foolish and an utter luxury, and yet I have a feeling it is gravely important for us. Somehow this past cut-up summer has sort of curdled our companionship, and Jerry, desperate within herself since the day she was born, has seemed to become more so. I have a feeling that the only possible peace for her, even though it may be only temporary, is a new interest and then an opportunity for solitude out there. When we started the boat trip, she said that when she went out to see that spot in Santa Fe the last time, she felt that if she could just be there with her books and piano and cigarettes and cold coffee, she would never want to leave it again. I am terribly afraid of our future as we're going now; if the business in New Mexico can offer her a minute of contentment, I'll jump at it.

"It isn't this job as such that's doing it, it's people and harassment and no time to think. We've thrashed it over a good many times, and I've been ready to quit, but we both realize that we're in a trap and I can't quit—actual responsibilities for other people's welfare upwards of two thousand dollars a year, responsibilities to ourselves, and worst of all the knowledge that a stepback into financial worry would throw us into a more helpless despond than we're now in. In other words it seems hopeless both ways. . . .

"I know I'm completely out of character in writing to you so intimately and so gravely as this, so please forgive me and skip it. For one thing, seeing my own folks—so old, so disappointed, so eager and helpless—and seeing your folks so exactly like my own —it kind of throws me. There is no sense to the struggle, and there is no choice but to struggle. . . .

"I hope the government takes your house away from you and that your wife runs away with a Japanese schoolboy. You're too old for the draft and too young for the pension and if you've got anything to look forward to I don't know what it is. . . . (Signed) Farmer Boy."

They drove to Cincinnati, where Jerry waited at a hotel while Ernie flew to New Mexico to arrange about building a house —but in Albuquerque, it developed, not Santa Fe. He wired her: "Have just ordered built magnificent baronial castle of three infinitesimal rooms on Crackerbox Row to be ready December first. Shaffers are dancing jigs and I am leaving at three o'clock before changing my mind again. Love and see you in the morning."

The World Series was about to start in Cincinnati, and to avoid the crowds they went on to Lexington, Kentucky, where Ernie took to his bed with a bad cold, "dragging up occasionally to try to write a piece." Then to Knoxville, Tennessee, an unpleasant journey, since Jerry was suffering from "nerves" and, as Ernie wrote the Shaffers, "It was a slow and twisty road, and me with the aches, and we were about done up when we got here . . . and then we couldn't get rooms, on account of eight million drunks being here for the Duke-Tennessee football game. At any rate George Carmack,[5] through some superhuman influence, did get us in here; but we couldn't get twin beds, so neither of us could sleep last night. . . .

"Have they started on the house yet? I suppose there'll be six complications per day, and queer things like amortizations and debentures, and I'll bet sure as hell I wind up in jail and lose every cent we put into it. . . . You might also make sure that they put floors in the rooms and a roof on the house, but since they are experienced builders they will probably think of that themselves."

A week later Ernie wrote from Gatlinburg, Tennessee, in the Great Smoky Mountains: "I am lying in bed—just an old middle-aged bastard about two-thirds exhausted from walking up and down a mountain. Yesterday I walked alone to the top of Mt. Le

[5] Editor of the *Knoxville News-Sentinel*.

Conte. Stayed all night and almost froze to death. Today I walked down by another trail. Fifteen miles altogether, and tough going. My life these past days has been full of turmoil. . . . Some of these days I am going to feel lighthearted again, and when I do I'll probably come back and jump clear over Mt. Le Conte."

He picked up a lot of interesting material in the Smokies, talking with picturesque mountain characters, including moon-shiners, and then they moved on to Washington. Their friend Richard Hollander of the *Washington News* concocted the following by way of greeting:

Welcome Jerry and Ernie
Home from your long journey.

But—
Where is home?
Nome?

Not when you eat Thanksgiving turkey
In Albuquerque.
And Christmas dinner with a Zulu
Or in Honolulu.

O.K. then, where *do* you squat?
Anyplace on the map that's a dot?
Like—

San Francisco
Or Mt. Kisco?
Kobe
Or Nairobi?

Can you, for instance, get crisp bacon
In Interlaken?

And if you have a pain

In Maine
Can you get a doctor there as good as the one in Cheyenne?
Or will he be about like the one in Cayenne?
And then—

Is butter better in Alaska
Or Nebraska?

And—
How is the toast
On the Coast?

And—
Where do you find that likker
Makes you tight quicker?

Or does it come down to this:
It's all hit or miss
In Pottsville and Pottstown
Plattsburgh and Johnstown
And all the other towns and villes
Where bad hotels charge heavy bills?

A week later Ernie wrote the Shaffers from Winchester, Virginia: "I'm going to London. Just tossed it off as a mild proposal to Deac the other night, and damn near fell out of my chair when he said sure, go ahead. Expected a lot of red tape and opposition, but both the State Department and British Embassy seem delighted and are doing everything for me. . . . Well, now that it's definite, I am scared half to death and Jerry is badly upset and really grieving (but don't ever say anything to her about it, for she's trying so hard, as she would, to be brave and indifferent about it).

"People were swell in Washington. Of course they're always swell—but this time it seemed like they were their old selves that we used to know; nothing changed, no swell heads, everybody just right. One of the nicest times we had was a long, chatty, intimate visit with Deac and Adelaide and Mary.[6] There is no question about it—they are wonderful people. . . . Phil Simms[7] sat one afternoon and told me the whole story, in most intimate detail, of his experiences at the fall of France. They say he had not told it fully to anybody before, and I was immensely flattered, and greatly moved, because the story of his actual and emotional experiences is an epic. . . .

"I imagine they are getting along pretty fast now [with the house]. I just itch to be out there and putter around with it, and wish Jerry was as eager. Please tell the contractors I would appreciate it very much if they would put hinges on the doors, so we could open them in case we wanted to go through. . . . I don't give much of a damn who wins the election. . . ."

He wrote Cavanaugh about the London trip and said he was "already so goddamned scared I wish I'd never thought of it in the first place. . . . Jerry has lost all interest in the house; is merely going out because somebody has to; but I think maybe she will get interested when she gets there and has to start fixing it up. . . . Better put your name on the envelope when you write again, for I've got a new secretary and she might get a shock. Jean [Mrs. Richard Hollander, who had been handling Ernie's fan mail] felt she couldn't do it any longer . . . so Roz [Mrs. Joseph L. Goodman] has taken it on. You remember her? Jerry's best friend. . . . Is my white stocking cap in that bag I left with you? If it is, I wish you'd send it to me. . . ."

Ernie had booked passage on a Pan-American Clipper, New York to Lisbon, for November 14. One of his letters in the interim was less than blithe: "I'm not going off on this trip as light-heartedly as on all the rest, for there are multitudinous dangers, and anyone would be a fool to deny it, but somehow I feel I have to go; Jerry is taking it pretty hard, but is stoic just the same, and of course willing for me to do whatever I want."

[6] Deac's wife and daughter.
[7] William Philip Simms, foreign editor of the Scripps-Howard newspapers.

Jerry wrote the Shaffers of her inner anguish about Ernie's trip: "I'm not going into any litany about my thoughts, feelings, and reactions, beyond this: I've almost recovered from the internal fainting spells I've had for the past few weeks; and I've overcome the constant jabbing from something in my brain that cut me off from even the small comfort of sleep. In truth, I have managed to creep up, and without reservations, to the place where I think I couldn't bear it if something were to happen now to what seems reasonably certain to eventuate. I've also been able to handle the maniac-urge I've been victim of, to kick people who think, 'isn't it WONDERFUL!' and who shout loudly of 'oh how I envy you,' right straight in their faces. In short, I think I'm wonderful.

"But to pretend that I give one single solitary good goddamn about a shack or a palace or any other material consideration in this world would be to foist upon everybody at all interested the greatest gold-brick insult a low mind could conceive. I've no doubt I'll go through all the motions of doing what must be done. I'll probably even double-hem and french-seam the window curtains. . . . And if I live through that, I'll know I'm good. For the truth is that the situation seems to me as diabolically ironical as any ever devised.

"And that I guess is the way I don't talk about matters I announce I'm not going to talk about. And here it is the first Tuesday after the first Monday in November, and the lives and futures of two great men are tottering on the scales. . . . Ah, well a day, I was ever one to say nothing is more important than the individual is to himself. . . ."

Back in Washington, they arranged to have their furniture taken from storage and shipped to Albuquerque, and Ernie wrote the Shaffers: "If they're waiting on the interior paint decision, tell them to go ahead with what Jerry calls an 'off-white'—I suppose Liz knows—not brown, or coffee or whatever—just something that looks almost white until you put real white up against it and then it looks kinda like cream, only not so much so. Oh for Christ sake, paint it yellow."

A troubled and fearful Jerry accompanied her husband to New York for the leave-taking. This, however, ran into delay, and the Clipper schedules appeared so fouled up that Ernie changed plans and arranged to go to Lisbon by sea, aboard the American Export liner *Exeter*, sailing November 16, 1940.

CHAPTER 15

The Blitz

THE *Exeter* sailed from Jersey City on a dark, raw afternoon. The Pyles had run into an old friend—Jim Moran, the professional screwball who capitalized such nonsense as selling an icebox to an Eskimo and publicly hunting a needle in a haystack in downtown Washington—and Moran went with them to the pier, but even his persiflage did little to relieve the pains of parting.

Good-by notes were exchanged:

Ernie to Jerry: "Darling—I hate the idea of being without you for a while much worse than you think. Fortunately for me I have had too much to do to think about it too much.

"I know you'll be all right—I know it will be hard for you, but still I know you will be all right. I've got plenty of confidence in your strength—when I get back we'll take a lesson from our experience and be happier than we have ever been. We love each other too much to throw it away. And I do love you, my darling, I do."

Jerry to Ernie: "Ernie darling—I more than love you—I adore you—You're so necessary to me that even thinking about you far away and me not with you makes me panic-stricken—but just because you are what you are—and because you are the only thing in this world that means anything to me—I'll be all right—and so will you."

The *Exeter* was only a few hours under way when Ernie opened his portable and wrote to Jerry: "I could see you off all right, but now reaction has set in, and I feel lonely and desolate. Not that I didn't hate to see you go—I could hardly bear it—but somehow the full significance of things never walks in on me until I am alone. . . . We sailed at exactly two. . . . At four we had boat drill, and they actually swung the boats out. No play business this time."

Jerry went to Albuquerque, and stayed with the Shaffers—where she was soon joined by her mother—until the bungalow was finished. Her mother remained for several months to help her get settled, and Jerry seemed to develop a real interest in the house, of which the Albuquerque paper wrote: "It's a trim little house, white with green roof and clean lines. The living room has a fireplace that looks west over the mesa to the Rio Grande. In an alcove is a baby grand piano. . . . One of the nicest rooms is Ernie's studio—paneled in knotty pine. Tall built-in bookcases reaching to the ceiling. Lots of fascinating things waiting for Jerry to decide the right place for them—Guatemala fabrics, a head carved in ironwood from French Guiana, a Conquistador silver cup from Peru, carved figures from Ecuador on the mantel, copper mugs used by Admiral Farragut to measure powder, which serve as ashtrays, a beautiful piece of Bagdad embroidery used to cover a big comfortable chair . . ."

Aboard the *Exeter* Ernie found there was another correspondent among the passengers—George Lait, a companionable Hearst man, on his way to the London bureau of the International News Service.

Seven days out Ernie wrote Jerry: "I have had a couple of bad nights of homesickness for you, once when I thought I just couldn't stand it, and as a result I haven't been sleeping very well. . . . Lait and I got very drunk the night we left Bermuda and I was good and sick all the next day. But have tread the righteous path since then. . . . I've played a lot of solitaire. In fact have now played a hundred and fifty-two games, and won only twice. . . . My columns aren't good; I never could seem to get in the writing mood. I keep wishing I were in New Mexico with nothing to do instead of on a boat with something to do. You know I have decided after all these years of thinking I liked the sea that I really don't enjoy being on a boat very much. . . . I know you won't have any trouble getting the house fixed up, and darling don't pinch your pennies on it. Get anything and everything you want. . . ."

And he wrote Ed Shaffer: "Don't show this to Jerry, for it would make her feel bad. But think you ought to know just what my affairs are, in case anything should happen.

"All stocks, policies, deeds, and everything are in my safety deposit box in Union Trust Co., in Washington. Lee Miller has the keys in SH office. Copy of will is also in box—made out by George Elliott, lawyer friend of ours, couple of years ago. . . . We don't owe a cent to anybody in the world." He enclosed a summary of his finances:

(We have $3,000 in stock losses, bad loans to friends, etc., which we can kiss good-by. But everything below should be convertible into cash.)

	Present Value
Scripps-Howard Stock—(Fifth & Sixth)	$ 2,500
Straight Gov't. Bonds	500
—(Interest coupons on above bonds)—	100
Baby bonds	3,000
Std. Oil Calif.—200 shares	4,000
Newsp. Savings Soc. (Cincinn.)	2,000
Santa Fe lots	2,100
	14,200
—Plus Albuq. house, all paid	4,000
	18,200
—Plus 3 life ins. policies of total	12,000
	$30,200

He had been instructed to air-mail his columns except for urgent copy, but in case of delays in the mails he was to use wireless or cable. Not being accustomed to these more expensive means of communication, he practiced on shipboard by "cableizing" the first of his columns about the trip and mailing this sample to me along with the orthodox version:

Unipress Newyork Pyle Proscripshow
Exeter Sailing of ship world over gay holidayish event ship carries people out reality into illusion people who go away ships going away for little while to better things but that not true as sailed today europe was no gayety on exeter never any ocean any climate have seen ship sail so drearily doubt single person aboard goes joyously anxiety on all faces certainly none going just fun of it this ship takes human cargo into land heavy reality rather from it. . . .

He said he hoped I could handle such copy myself, for it would take "a close familiarity with my crazy style to make it come out right. . . . Wish I knew if Jerry got to New Mexico all right. She took this whole thing awfully hard. I'm really worried about her."

In Lisbon no hotel rooms were to be found, nor were any seats immediately available on the British Overseas Airlines to London. Ernie and Lait found quarters in a *pension*, and began a wait which lasted twelve days. The *pension* being uncomfortably chilly, they moved after a few days into the Hotel Europa, but even here, Ernie wrote his parents, "it has been so cold I have had to run hot water on my hands every once in a while to limber them up so I can write." To Jerry he wrote: "We both took two baths each last evening, just trying to get warmed up. . . . Before leaving the boat, I had a bellboy wash me out a 100-pound sugar sack. So I am now going to put everything I can spare in my black bag and leave it at the UP office. And put the overflow in the sugar sack and take it. So the great journalist will arrive in England carrying a yellow bag, a typewriter, and a sugar sack over his shoulder. . . . George is a hell of a nice guy. It would be hard to pick up anybody as pleasant to live with as he has been. He's been everywhere and done everything, and has a million funny stories, and is good humored and never gets out of sorts. . . . Lots and lots of love, darling, and do try to be happy. . . ."

On December 9, 1940, Ernie and Lait, in a four-motored flying boat, were whisked by a tailwind to the English coast, and that night stepped from a blacked-out train into beleaguered London. The first words Ernie heard were from an aged station porter: "Well, he hasn't come yet, sir, he's more than a bit late tonight."

"He" was Hitler, or, more specifically, the Luftwaffe. Ernie wrote Jerry: "There wasn't a single plane over England the night we came in. I went to the UP, and then came on to the Savoy Hotel, found Ben Robertson here at the hotel less than an hour after I got off the train, and was I glad to see him! [1] He has been grand to me and has helped me more than I could ever say. . . .

"This hotel, although it has been hit three times, is running just as usual, and it is certainly a lovely place. I have a wonderful room—I wish you could see it. We've never had much nicer. And best of all, it is hot. . . . I am paying 23 shillings a day for the room ($4.60). But it's expensive living. This is a flossy hotel, and as Quent Reynolds says, 'They shilling you to death here.' But this is the center of things, and about twenty American newspapermen are here.

"Everybody has been wonderful over here so far—the Americans have been nice, and so have the British. Courteous and friendly treatment everywhere. And I fell in love with England the minute I set foot ashore. As soon as the war is over we must carry out our original plan to come over and get a car and drive all over the place. . . . The first night I was here I ate dinner with Ben and two young members of Parliament. One night we went to the Ritz for dinner with Frank Gowen, of the American Embassy, the one Mrs. Shipley[2] wrote me a note to. He was certainly wonderful. He left for the States yesterday, and he spent

[1] Ernie had known Ben Robertson when the latter was with the Associated Press in Washington; he was now with the newspaper *PM;* later he was killed in the crash of a Clipper at Lisbon.
[2] Mrs. Ruth B. Shipley, head of the Passport Division of the State Department.

his very last day here . . . writing letters to friends that would help me, and taking me to Scotland Yard and introducing me all around. One of the Scotland Yard inspectors is going to take me to the East End this week, where the heaviest damage has been done.

"It has been very quiet since I came. There wasn't a plane over the first two nights. Then for two nights a few were over, and the sirens blew and there was considerable shooting, but no bombs came in this part of town. Tonight the warning sounded about half an hour ago, and the first guns have just now gone off. They sound like thunder close up. I haven't been at all nervous, but undoubtedly will be plenty when and if they start coming close. Of course I haven't seen much of London yet, but they've cleaned everything up so beautifully that it seems much better than I thought. In fact London doesn't feel it has been hurt much at all, and all the stuff we've read at home about the people being wonderful doesn't half tell it. I suppose I'll be accused of being taken in by the British, but by God their spirit is just almost unbelievable. They have tough years ahead, but I don't believe they will ever crack. Except for one horrible night the very night before I got here (they say almost the worst of the war) the bombing has been very light the last two or three weeks, and has given the city a chance to catch up with its repairs. . . ."

He wrote me in the same vein, but added: "The other night, when it was fairly quiet, what apparently was a piece of shrapnel whizzed past my window with an awful swish, and damn near scared me to death. My heart stopped a few seconds waiting for the explosion, but it never came."

The columns from England were well received from the start. Mrs. Roosevelt wrote in "My Day": "I don't know whether any of you are reading about Ernie Pyle's trip to England with as much interest as I am, but I have read everything since he left. . . ."

The slow pace of the German air attack did not continue.

Twenty nights after Ernie's arrival there occurred the furious fire-bombing of Sunday, December 29. He had written me only the day before: "My only worry is that I haven't been able to get emotional about anything I've seen—for that reason I fear the columns are dull. So far I haven't been in any danger at all." Suddenly it was different. Ernie wirelessed:

"Some day when peace has returned to this odd world I want to come to London again and stand on a certain balcony on a moonlit night and look down upon the peaceful silver curve of the Thames with its dark bridges. And standing there, I want to tell somebody who has never seen it how London looked on a certain night in the holiday season of the year 1940.

"For on that night this old, old city—even though I must bite my tongue in shame for saying it—was the most beautiful sight I have ever seen. It was a night when London was ringed and stabbed with fire.

"They came just after dark, and somehow I could sense from the quick, bitter firing of the guns that there was to be no monkey business this night. Shortly after the sirens wailed I could hear the Germans grinding overhead. In my room, with its black curtains drawn across the windows, you could feel the shake from the guns. You could hear the boom, crump, crump, crump of heavy bombs at their work of tearing buildings apart. They were not too far away.

"Half an hour after the firing started I gathered a couple of friends and went to a high, darkened balcony that gave us a view of one-third of the entire circle of London. As we stepped out onto the balcony a vast inner excitement came over all of us—an excitement that had neither fear nor horror in it because it was too full of awe. You have all seen big fires, but I doubt if you have ever seen the whole horizon of a city lined with great fires—scores of them, perhaps hundreds. There was something inspiring in the savagery of it.

"The closest fires were near enough for us to hear the crackling flames and the yells of firemen. Little fires grew into big ones even as we watched. Big ones died down under the firemen's valor, only to break out again later. About every two minutes a new wave of planes would be over. The motors seemed to grind rather than roar, and to have an angry pulsation like a bee buzzing in blind fury. The bombs did not make a constant overwhelming din as in those terrible days of last September. They were intermittent—sometimes a few seconds apart, sometimes a minute or more. Their sound was sharp, nearby, and soft and muffled, far away. They were everywhere over London.

"Into the dark, shadowed spaces below us, as we watched, whole batches of incendiary bombs fell. We saw two dozen go off in two seconds. They flashed terrifically, then quickly simmered down to pinpoints of dazzling white, burning ferociously. These white pinpoints would go out one by one as the unseen heroes of the moment smothered them with sand. But also, as we watched, other pinpoints would burn on, and pretty soon a yellow flame would leap up from the white center. They had done their work —another building was on fire.

"The greatest of all the fires was directly in front of us. Flames seemed to whip hundreds of feet into the air. Pinkish-white smoke ballooned upward in a great cloud, and out of this cloud there gradually took shape—so faintly at first that we weren't sure we saw correctly—the gigantic dome and spires of St. Paul's Cathedral. St. Paul's was surrounded by fire, but it came through. It stood there in its enormous proportions—growing slowly clearer and clearer, the way objects take shape at dawn. It was like a picture of some miraculous figure that appears before peace-hungry soldiers on a battlefield. The streets below us were semi-illuminated from the glow.

"Immediately above the fires the sky was red and angry, and overhead, making a ceiling in the vast heavens, there was a cloud of smoke all in pink. Up in that pink shrouding there were tiny, brilliant specks of flashing light—anti-aircraft shells bursting. After the flash you could hear the sound. Up there, too, the barrage balloons were standing out as clearly as if it were daytime, but now they were pink instead of silver. And now and then through a hole in that pink shroud there twinkled incongruously a permanent, genuine star—the old-fashioned kind that has always been there.

"Below us the Thames grew lighter, and all around below were the shadows—the dark shadows of buildings and bridges that formed the base of this dreadful masterpiece.

"Later on I borrowed a tin hat and went out among the fires. That was exciting too, but the thing I shall always remember above all the other things in my life is the monstrous loveliness of that one single view of London on a holiday night—London stabbed with great fires, shaken by explosions, its dark regions along the Thames sparkling with the pinpoints of white-hot bombs, all of it roofed over with a ceiling of pink that held bursting shells, balloons, flares, and the grind of vicious engines. And in yourself the excitement and anticipation and wonder in your soul that this could be happening at all.

"These things all went together to make the most hateful, most beautiful single scene I have ever known."

Jerry, five thousand miles away, wrote a friend: "I think Ernie's column about the burning of London is the most terrible and beautiful I have ever read—I had a very curious experience the night it happened—I'd had a quiet day—just doing little odds and ends of things—and feeling reasonably content—Suddenly, and for no reason, I got really panic-stricken—Real terror—simply stark terror—Everything was quiet—not a sound anywhere—I couldn't think—I wanted to scream out—I didn't—I finally picked a scrap of my brain out of thin air—and went to bed—and after a while, I slept—I awakened calm—I guess that was the end of the panic my mind has been trying to deny."

Ernie wrote me about that night of fire: "I was never in any danger—although if chance had shifted us six blocks in either direction, I would have been. It was all more like just being a spectator at some huge show. You could hardly believe it was real." He added a bit of raillery for Talburt, the cartoonist, who was a great admirer of the London cartoonist David Low: "Tell Tal that Low comes up and has dinner with me almost every evening, and that I asked him for an original for Tal, and he said he never heard of the sonovabitch." As a matter of fact, Ernie did have a visit with Low, a little later, and did bring back an autographed original for Tal. Better still, somebody at the *London Evening Standard* had given Ernie a copy of a Low cartoon which had been on exhibition in a window of the newspaper office when a bomb fell in the street and blew a hole in the picture. As Ernie related it: "I took the cartoon with me out to Low's house. He had not known about the bomb incident. When he saw the hole, it was as though I had handed him the Pulitzer Prize, you never saw anybody so delighted. He thumbtacked the cartoon onto his drawing board and inscribed it to me. . . . And this is what he wrote, in the white space right next to the jagged hole: 'Dear Hitler— Thanks for the criticism. Yours, Low.' And he beamed like a child as he rolled it up and handed it to me."

Meanwhile Ernie was proceeding with a program he had outlined not long after reaching England, when he wrote me: "I feel a very keen desire to put the whole picture in columns—not at all for propaganda or because I think a 'message' needs to be got over, but because of the same old basis the column has always been written on, of making people at home see what I see. Everything has already been written by the other boys, but nobody has ever paused at this or any other moment to sit down and put the whole picture into words."

It was not always easy. One of his heavy colds put him out of commission for a while. And, as he wrote Jerry, "I seem to be suffering more than ever from timidity and an inferiority complex. It's just a horror for me to go out and talk to people. I feel like I'm conspicuous and ignorant and have reached forty years old with so little knowledge I can't even hold a conversation with twenty-year-olds. I am trying to take especially good care of myself. I do go out at night to visit the shelters and the ARP wardens' control posts, but don't sleep in the shelters, not even in the very flossy one we have here at the hotel. . . . I'd give half a year's pay to see you now. When I get back I think I'll retire from the writing business, which I never should have entered in the first place, and take up a career of living on a suburban corner in Albuquerque and reading books all day long—provided you keep me warm and well fed. . . ."

Roy Howard sent him a message: "Your stuff not only greatest your career but most illuminating human and appealing descriptive matter printed America since outbreak battle Britain. World Telly firstpaging and your stuff talk of New York these days. Scripps-Howard is and Britain should be proud job you doing. Your daily picturizations British character courage thrilling America. Congratulations thanks regards."

Howard also wirelessed his friend Lord Beaverbrook: "Ernie Pyle special Scripps-Howard writer reachable through United Press is daily cabling greatest most appealing descriptive stuff reaching America since outbreak war. Want you send for talk to him. Is shy modest unimpressive to look at but is one of greatest reporters and writers in American journalism as well as most meticulously honest and colorful. He is worth any assistance you can extend but don't bark at him because he don't know barking peers don't bite. Affectionate regards."

Ernie was far more interested in people than in personages, but he dutifully called on "the Beaver," who was Minister of Aircraft Production, and had a stimulating interview with him—although he insisted in the column that he had "always thought a member of the peerage gave off a constant white light like an incendiary bomb, and if you got caught in this light you became weak all over, your tongue froze, and you were sort of hypnotized."

Ernie devoted himself now to making perfectly clear to his readers in America just how the English were managing in this troubled and perilous time—how life went on in the blackout, in the shelters, in the anti-aircraft gun pits. He wrote Jerry: "I've been going like a steam engine all this past week. Have just finished eight columns on the shelters—I've spent night after night in them, been in about fifty I guess. They're not so hot. . . . The closest bombs we've had around here were last night, while I was miles away with the guns that were shooting at them! . . . I've honestly got like all the other people here—don't think anything about bombs really; just let em fall and if they're gonna hit you they're gonna hit you, although the chances are very great that they won't. . . . The last couple of weeks I've just been crazy for Bull Durham, but there isn't any in London. . . . It will be strange and wonderful to see you again. I can hardly wait. Love and love."

He moved out of London now, to an RAF bomber base and to York and Edinburgh and Glasgow, and soon wrote Jerry: "My trip north was good, except I ran into a terrible blizzard last week-end and the trains were running late, and I almost froze in the hotels with no heat. . . . Visited farms, fishermen, shipyard workers, and what not. I like the Scottish people. They seem almost like Americans. Everybody was grand to me everywhere. . . .

"Guess I've really worked harder this winter than for many a moon. In fact I've done nothing else. But I don't mind, for there's so much I want to do in such a short time, and also I haven't made any friends that I feel close to at all. Frequently I have dinner here in my room, in order to keep on writing and not waste time. . . . Haven't heard anything from the office since Roy's flamboyant cable. Wasn't that the damnedest thing? Mr. Willkie is due here in a day or two. Don't know whether I'll see him or not, but wish I could get him alone and take him on a tour of the East End some night, just the two of us. I'd show him what he's looking for. Haven't made any attempts to see Hopkins.[3]

"I've washed handkerchiefs and socks this winter till I hate the sight of them. . . . An American is such an oddity in Scotland

___

[3] Harry Hopkins had arrived a few weeks earlier as President Roosevelt's personal representative to establish a close liaison between FDR and Winston Churchill.

these days that they had a piece about me in the Edinburgh paper! . . . I've got to get started on this frightful bunch of columns in my head. Have about ten to do, I am afraid. And no notes. . . . Do hope you're well, darling, and as happy as is possible for you to be. I am both. But gee it'll be wonderful to get back again. The day I land in New York, and then in Albuquerque, will be two great days for me."

It was about this time that Ambassador Joseph C. Grew was reporting to the State Department in Washington that one of his diplomatic colleagues in Tokyo had "told a member of the Embassy staff that there were reports from many sources, including a Japanese source, that Japanese military forces planned a surprise mass attack at Pearl Harbor in case of 'trouble' with the United States."

Ernie made another trip which took in some of the industrial centers such as Birmingham and blitzed Coventry: "I was horrified. We walked and drove around Coventry for three hours. And late in the afternoon I realized that I had been saying to myself half out loud, saying it over and over again like a chant: 'My God, this is awful!' "

He wrote Jerry: "I got back to London yesterday afternoon, and was I glad to get back. I've never been colder in my life. And my schedule was so tight I've traveled for ten days without writing a line, and worked day and night. Was tireder last night than I had been in months. But fortunately I didn't take any more cold, and a hot shower, shave and clean clothes, and a long sleep last night resurrected me so I feel fit again this morning. I'll have at least fifteen columns to write out of my head. . . . Lee cabled 'Shelter series great. How you doing?' I do hope the columns are going over as big as reports from America seem to indicate. Lee said fifteen papers had taken the column on just for the duration of my stay over here, so I suppose they'll all drop when I get back. I don't give a damn. All I want to do is sit in Albuquerque about two weeks and not write anything.

"I saw Willkie once here, and ran onto their party again in Coventry and Birmingham. . . . England is all ready for invasion at any moment, but I am a lone wolf who thinks he isn't going to try to invade this spring. . . ."

He wrote to his parents and Aunt Mary: "I got a letter today from some fool reader in Los Angeles who said he knew I wasn't in London at all, but was writing the column from somewhere in the States. When you make the long trip over here and work hard and then realize you're writing for half-wits like that, it almost makes you want to give up." And to Cavanaugh: "Dear Mr. Spirit-of-America: Since writing the above salutation some eighteen hours have passed, during which I was engaged in 'pushing open a few doors,' as we say in Britain. The result is that I don't feel so good this morning, and trust you are feeling the same. . . . Things have been so quiet here the last few days I've actually got in the dumps, and have been lonesome, homesick, bored, fed up, and generally crotchety. For that reason I decided to do the door-pushing last night. It is yet too early to tell whether it helped or not.

"No, Mr. Cavanaugh, I haven't had the obscenity scared out of me yet, and consequently I'm not a broadened or completed man. But I'll bet I've been closer to bombs than you ever were in 1918, and you've been lording that over me for twenty years, so from now on you can cease and desist."

On March 3, after another period of hard reporting and writing, personal tragedy struck. As Ernie told it later, in the column:

"One drear evening in London a friend and I started out to dinner. We had gone about two blocks when we heard hurrying footsteps behind us. We turned and saw that it was a little bell-boy from my hotel. The lad's name was Tom Donovan, and he was the one who had showed me my room on that first strange night months before when I arrived in London.

" 'This telegram just came for you, sir,' he said. 'I thought maybe I could catch you.' I thanked him and he started on back.

"I stepped over to the curb, out of people's way, while I tore open the telegram and read it.

" 'What is it?' my friend asked. 'More good news from home?'

" 'Read it,' I said, and went on ahead. When he caught up he said, 'I'm sorry,' and we walked on toward Leicester Square as though nothing had happened.

"It was the cablegram that told me that my mother, far away in Indiana, had come to the end of her life.

"That night in London, back in my room alone, it seemed to me that living is futile, and death the final indignity. I turned off the lights and pulled the blackout curtains and went to bed. Little pictures of my mother raced across the darkness before my eyes. Pictures of nearly a lifetime. Pictures of her at neighborhood square dances long, long ago, when she was young and I was a child. Pictures of her playing the violin. Pictures of her doctoring sick horses; of her carrying newborn lambs into the house on raw spring days. I could see her that far day in the past when she drove our first auto—all decorated and bespangled—in the Fourth of July parade. She was dressed up in frills and she won first prize in the parade and was awfully proud. . . .

"I could see her as she stood on the front porch, crying bravely, on that morning in 1918 when I, being youthful, said a tearless good-by and climbed into the neighbor's waiting buggy that was to take me out of her life.

"The pictures grew older. Gradually she became stooped, and toil-worn, and finally white and wracked with age . . . but always spirited, always sharp.

"On the afternoon that I was leaving London I called little Tom Donovan, the bellboy, to my room. One by one the floor servants had come in, and I had given them farewell tips. But because I liked him, and more than anything else, I suppose, because he had shared with me the message of finality, I wanted to do something more for Tom than for the others. And so, in the gentlest way I could, I started to give him a pound note.

"But a look of distress came into his face, and he blurted out, 'Oh, no, Mr. Pyle, I couldn't.' And then he stood there so straight in his little English uniform and suddenly tears came in his eyes, and they rolled down his cheeks, and then he turned and ran through the door. I never saw him again.

"On that first night I had felt in a sort of detached bitterness that, because my mother's life was hard, it was also empty. But how wrong I was. For you need only have seen little Tom Donovan in faraway London, wretched at her passing, or the loneliness of Snooks [her little dog] after she had gone, or the great truckloads of flowers they say came from all over the continent, or the scores of Indiana youngsters who journeyed to her both in life and in death because they loved her, to know that she had given a full life. And received one, in return."

CHAPTER 16

"The Little House Is Wonderful"

ERNIE stayed on a few weeks longer and then flew home over the new four-continent Clipper route, by way of Lisbon, Portuguese Guinea, Brazil, Trinidad, and Puerto Rico.

I went to New York, and was at La Guardia Field before dawn when the Dixie Clipper put down in the Marine Basin. The flight had taken four days, and Ernie was tired. He was carrying an incendiary bomb (a dud which landed on the Air Ministry and from which someone had removed the thermite contents) and a bagful of bomb fragments. We caught a very little sleep in New York, called on a few people, flew to Washington for a crowded week-end, then Ernie went on to Dana. And once more he wrote a column about his mother:

"One winter night a few years ago I was sitting in the dark cabin of a westbound airplane high over the rolling hills of southern Ohio. . . . My mother had had a second stroke, and they said over the phone she might not live. I had taken the first plane from Washington that went toward Indiana.

"I had flown many thousands of miles before, but never had I flown in emergency. And for the first time I felt the full significance of what aviation science had given me and others like me suddenly faced with the need for desperate hurry.

"Perhaps I felt it too much, for my flight through the night

155

to my mother's bedside took on a touch of drama to me, and I built up the scene of my homecoming in my own mind somewhat as though I were seeing it on a screen. I was proud of myself in those days. I don't mean that I was big-headed, or thought I was better than anyone else. I was looking at myself more by the standards of those who stay at home in the neighborhood than by any specific accomplishments.

"Only you who have come from the intimate confines of a Midwestern farm community can know in what fear parents live of their children bringing shame and disgrace upon them. I was an only child. All my parents had was centered in me. I was young when I went away. They sacrificed to send me to school. I had gone from there on into the world, and my visits home, though regular, were brief and far apart. In twenty years my mother had not seen me a total of two months. But I had been good about writing, in later years I had been able to send a little money, but best of all I had never brought disgrace upon my parents. They had never seen me jobless or loafing, they had never had to swallow the bitter pill of gossip that their son was worthless, I had never been in jail or mixed up in scandal. And so, thinking of these things, I pictured in my mind my return to my mother's bedside. I saw her lying there, I saw myself rush in and take her hand. I could hear her whisper, just in her last moments, 'I am proud of you.'

"A car met me at Indianapolis that dramatic night and rushed the seventy-five miles through the night to the maple-hidden farmhouse where I spent my youth. My mother was conscious, but the stroke had wounded her tongue and she could not speak. I did not know until later that she didn't realize who I was. I stayed on and nursed her for many days. My father and Aunt Mary were usually up at five in the morning, and then I would turn in. I had been there almost a week, and one cold morning had been in bed barely an hour when Aunt Mary came in and awakened me. She was excited. 'Your mother has just realized you are home,' she said. 'She wants to see you. Get up and come in quick. She can say a few words.' So I jumped out, threw on my bathrobe, and went to her room. Her worn face went into a small smile as I came in, and her eyes shone. She reached out her hand for mine, and I sat on the side of her bed, and she squeezed my hand almost until it hurt.

"It was a long time before she could say anything. Her words came with great effort, and I had to lean over and listen closely to make them out. And what my mother said, there so white in her bed, laboring to produce each whispered word, was this: 'Are . . . you . . . proud . . . of . . . me?' . . .

"A great choking hatred of myself swept over me, and I could only squeeze her hand, give her a slap on the knee, and say, 'You bet I'm proud of you.'

"And then I ran to my own room and, I think for the first time in more than twenty years, lay on my bed and wept. . . ."

From Dana he flew to Albuquerque and Jerry and the new cottage. "The little house is wonderful," he wrote me. "It's no bigger than your thumb, but Jerry has certainly made a little gem out of it. She says she's never going to leave it, and I think she's a little more than half serious. . . ."

Just why they had chosen Albuquerque was explained some time later in an article he wrote for the magazine *New Mexico* at the request of its editor, George Fitzpatrick, and for which he refused any payment.[1]

"Why Albuquerque?" Ernie wrote. "Well, that's a hard question to answer. There are many little reasons of course, but probably the main thing is simply a deep, unreasoning affection for the Southwest. I guess it's like being in love with a woman. You don't love a woman because she wears No. 3 shoes or eats left-handed or has a diamond set in her front tooth. You just love her because you love her and you can't help yourself. That's the way we are about the Southwest. . . .

"And here are the things we like about living in Albuquerque:

"We like it because we have a country mailbox instead of a slot

[1] The article is copyrighted and is quoted here with permission.

in the door. We like it because our front yard stretches as far as you can see, and because old Mount Taylor, sixty-five miles away, is like a framed picture in our front window. . . . We like it because you can cash a check almost anywhere in Albuquerque without being grilled as though you were a criminal. And because after your second trip to a filling station the gas-pumper calls you by name. We like it because people are friendly and interested in you, and yet they leave you alone. To a vain fellow like me, it is pleasant to be stopped on the streets downtown by perfect strangers and told they enjoy your columns; and yet these thoughtful strangers do not ask anything of you and do not keep you standing in fretfulness. . . . And we like it here because you can do almost anything you want to within reason. . . . I go to the Alvarado Hotel's swell *Cocina Cantina* always in my overalls, and nobody raises an eyebrow. We like it because we can have Navajo rugs in our house, and piñon and juniper bushes in our yard, and Western pictures on our knotty-pine walls. We like it because you can take a Sunday afternoon spin into the mountains and see deer and wild turkey; and because I have a work bench where I make crude little end tables and such stuff for our house. . . .

"We like it because the meadow larks hidden in the sage across the road from our house sing us awake in the summer dawn. These meadow larks sing the oddest things. One of them says over and over 'Your face is awfully pretty!' And another one says 'Here comes the preacher.' [2] Every night around nine two rabbits come to nibble on our lawn. And about once a week when we rise early, there are quail in our front yard. We have actually counted as many as fifty. And when we go out onto the porch they don't fly away with a frightened whirring of wings, they just walk slowly across the road and inside the concealing sage as though to say, 'Don't get it into your head we'd leave if we didn't want to. We were through anyway.' . . . We have seen sunrises so violently beautiful they were almost frightening, and I'm only sorry I can't

[2] It was Jerry who translated those birdcalls into English.

capture the sunsets and the thunderstorms and the first snows on the Sandias, and take them East and flaunt them in people's faces.

"We like it here because no more than half our friends who write us know how to spell Albuquerque. We like it here because there aren't any streetcars, and because you see lots of men on Central Avenue in cowboy boots. We like it because you can see Indians making silver jewelry, and you can see sheepskins lying over a vacant downtown lot, drying in the sun. And we like it because the dirt street in front of our house washes into such deep gullies that not many people care to drive over it. . . . And we like it because you can drive half an hour from home and buy a burro for five dollars—in case you want a burro.

"We like it here because we're on top of the world, in a way; and because we are not stifled and smothered and hemmed in by buildings and trees and traffic and people. We like it because the sky is so bright and you can see so much of it. And because out here you actually see the clouds and the stars and the storms, instead of just reading about them in the newspapers. They become a genuine part of your daily life, and half the entire horizon is yours in one glance just for the looking, and the distance sort of gets into your soul and makes you feel that you too are big inside."

However, Ernie's very first visit to the little house fell far short of relaxation. Whenever he sat down to admire a sunset, his job was looking over his shoulder. Before he left Washington he and I had had a telephone conversation with Roy Howard. Howard thought Ernie was exhausted and should have a rest. But at the same time he thought certain of the tag-end columns about England were anticlimactic, and suggested that they be thinned out. It was these pieces, some already written and others in his head, which Ernie was counting on to afford him a cushion while he took a recess in the New Mexico sun. And George Carlin of United Feature was distressed lest a gap in the daily production play hob with his hopes of retaining on a regular basis those newspapers which had signed up for the Pyle columns about England. Carlin wrote me that Howard "pounced on me with a notion that Ernie was jittery and on the verge of a nervous breakdown and to ask him to do any further work was cruel and inhuman. He acted as if I were a Simon Legree trying to whip the tired slave beyond the last ounce of his endurance."

I wrote Roy, agreeing to drop a few of the columns Ernie had written, and to abandon some others still unwritten, and said further: "There is one point which I didn't make over the phone the other day: it is perfectly true that Ernie's copy lost considerable altitude, compared to his early weeks in London. But I think it should be borne in mind that most of his papers, unlike the *World-Telegram,* have been running his column day in and day out, hot, cold or indifferent, for years. His average reader is not conditioned to expecting something sensational every day. He looks on Ernie's column as a sort of cross between a travelogue, a highly personalized and humanized diary, and a reporting job. This typical reader will be interested in Ernie's reunion with his father. (Did you know, for instance, that when Ernie's mother died, the *Cleveland Press* had me telephoto a picture, and the *Indianapolis Times* asked me to write an editorial about her, and the *Boston Globe,* one of the new and 'temporary' clients, wired for details about Mrs. Pyle and where Ernie was when he learned of her death, etc.?)

"What I'm driving at is that, while I think you are right about sawing off the London stuff quicker than Ernie had planned, I think you are wrong if you regard a leisurely, 'trivial,' 'unimportant' piece by Ernie as a mistake or failure. Some of his most unpretentious pieces have evoked more interest and reaction than columns that have been really newsworthy. The fact is, in my judgment, that the great mass of Ernie's readers are a sight more interested in Ernie Pyle himself, and his reaction to things and people both large and small, than in the strictly objective reporting that Ernie does. . . ."

Ernie wrote me: "Your letter to Roy was a masterpiece. . . . Since I'll have to start out of here with at least a week's cushion of columns, it means I'll have to leave the very day I get through writing my two weeks' supply. . . . That still leaves unfinished several days of necessary personal secretarial work . . . and it still leaves unaccomplished any renewal of acquaintanceship at all with Jerry. What with the chaos of homecoming, and now my strictly imposed solitude for writing, I honestly haven't got to sit down and talk with her yet. If Roy just hadn't killed those extra columns I'd have had at least a week of rest. I hate like hell to skip, not that I am so hot about keeping new clients, but that it does put George [Carlin] in a hell of a position. We had to laugh over his letter about getting denounced by Roy as a slave driver. It sounded as though he were about to cry. I know that if I leave with all my personal stuff unfinished and no relaxation at all, I'll be frowny and tense all summer. . . . Goddamit, I don't know what to do. I wish you'd put on your boss-whiskers and make a decision and just write and order me to do one thing or the other. . . ."

He did manage to keep the column rolling without interruption, but only by resorting to stern measures. In one letter he said: "If this isn't irony—here we spend a lot of money building a refuge and then damned if I don't finally have to come down to a hotel and hide in order to get my work finished. That's a hell of a price to have to pay for a decent wage. I've practically become a goldfish. If I weren't afraid of the future, I'd quit this job and raise cactus for a living."

The evenings at home were usually jolly. The Shaffers would drop in, or the contractors who had built the house (Earl Mount and Arthur McCollum, who became fast friends of the Pyles), or "Barney" Livingstone of the Associated Press and his wife Moran. But there was the ever-impinging knowledge that this was only an interlude and that he must get on the move again.

About this time it was decided that Scripps-Howard should issue in book form a collection of Ernie's dispatches from England, for sale through the newspapers as a "promotion" enterprise. In those days the costs of manufacturing a book were low, and a deal was made with Robert M. McBride & Company in New York to produce *Ernie Pyle in England* in an edition of some twenty thousand copies at a cost to Scripps-Howard of thirty-odd cents each. These were readily sold, at fifty cents, of which ten cents a copy was allotted to Ernie. Of the approximate twenty-one hundred dollars he received he kept one-third, gave one-third to British War Relief, and gave me one-third, since I had put the book together. "This isn't solely because you handled the book," he wrote me, "but because for years you have been more or less my mentor, taken an interest in me, helped me get the things I want. . . . I've never been in any position to repay you in any way, and I know money is a poor and hard way to do it, but it's better than nothing, at least from my standpoint. So cash this check, you sonovabitch, and let's hear no more about it."

The book was dedicated to "That Girl Who Waited." McBride later issued it through regular trade channels at a higher price.

Ernie turned his old Dodge in for a Pontiac convertible and, leaving Jerry behind for a few days, drove to El Paso. There, at Fort Bliss, he found out how things were going with the men being drafted under Selective Service—by arranging to be put through the routine himself. They weighed him in at a hundred and thirteen pounds. He wrote Jerry: "Went out at noon today to try to buy a briefcase and wound up by holding a ducky little reception in the luggage store, giving out autographs like Rudy Vallee, and smiling and saying nice things all around. . . ."

She joined him, and then Ernie couldn't resist driving the two hundred and seventy-five miles back to Albuquerque to write in his own home the material he had picked up at Fort Bliss from the draftees and from the commanding general, Major General Innis P. Swift. Strangers had begun to seek out their new house, for he wrote his father and Aunt Mary: "If anybody should ask for our Albuquerque address, I wish you wouldn't give it to anybody except personal friends. We get little enough privacy as it is. Some tourists were here at six-thirty this morning!"

They drove to Los Angeles and visited the Cavanaughs, and between jollifications Ernie went through a number of factories, such as the Lockheed aircraft plant. But the friendly atmosphere of the Cavanaugh ménage was not conducive to work, and he had to move to a hotel to get the columns written. Then, his work caught up, he wired Cavanaugh: "Prepare for Armageddon about one p.m."

Jerry was rather distraught, and the reunion convivialities may have accentuated her nervousness. In any event, when Ernie returned to the Cavanaughs' one afternoon, following another session of writing in a rented room, he found a note on his pillow —Jerry had flown back to Albuquerque. The note gave no reason.

Ernie had felt close to a breakdown himself, what with his columns and the extra chore of reading the proofs of the new book. But in a few days he wired Jerry: "Just now getting head above water. Finished and mailed book proofs this afternoon. Do hope you're feeling normal by now. Things here as well as could be expected without you." He wrote her the same day: "Darling: I haven't written you before because I just couldn't. I've been in kind of a fret and am just now out of it. Have been working almost desperately. . . . I'll try to relate what has happened since you left. I didn't do any good at the motel that day. Got more and more frazzled as the day went on, and finally checked out and came home [to the Cavanaughs'] for the night about five-thirty. And found you gone. Tried to phone you at the airport at least to say good-by, and couldn't make the damn phone work. Seemed like everything went wrong. Also a bunch of complaints from editors and readers in the mail about swearing in the column and mentioning the name of the new car. I felt like flailing about as they say and kicking a few things. . . . I'm really quite disappointed in the book but shan't say anything. The latter part reads all right, but the early part lost so much in translation [from his wireless condensations] that it isn't my writing at all. And Lee has cut out so much of the 'little stuff' and the cracks and so on in his editing of it for the book. I don't know why he did. . . . I guess Lee just had too much to do at the last minute. But I can tell he put a lot of work on it, and the things wrong with it aren't his fault. . . . Wish you would buy yourself some new books, and anything that you want to get for the house. . . ."

He went on alone to booming San Diego, where he wired Jerry plaintively: "Am at Hotel San Diego case anybody cares to write." She did write, and he replied: "Darling: I was so relieved and grateful to get your letter. . . . I've decided to start [a vacation] just as soon as I wind up San Diego. . . . Boy it'll be good to get there and just collapse. I'm so damn tense and harassed by the deadline, I feel like I couldn't stand it much longer. . . . I'm sorry you don't feel the same about the house. I do want you to love it. Having me around for a month with nothing to do but bother you will probably end it all for you!"

The vacation turned out to be no unmixed blessing. Ernie had a fine time building a white picket fence around part of his yard. He got a nice puff in Mrs. Roosevelt's column; she had read that he was taking a month off, and she wrote: "I want to tell him that while I do not begrudge him a well-earned vacation, I shall miss him very much. . . . I have come to feel I know him and to wish that some day, on his vacation perhaps, he might drop in and sit before my fire." Best of all, his book on England was a complete sell-out in Albuquerque stores the day it went on sale.

But Jerry became increasingly morose and eccentric. As Ernie put it in a letter to Roz Goodman, "We have had certain illnesses in the family which have made my vacation a farce." He was more explicit to Cavanaugh: "Geraldine was drunk the afternoon I got home. From there she went on down. Went completely screwball. . . . One night she tried the gas. Had to have a doctor. Had to phone Po. She came on the next plane. . . . Feel just great starting another solid year of work. If a mouse squeaks I'll jump clear out of my skin and right out the window."

He finally drove Jerry to Denver and put her in the Presbyterian Hospital for an elaborate examination. "She's hating it ferociously," he wrote the Shaffers, "and is in quite a pretty state." And in a few days he wrote me: "They're almost through with the clinical tests—and they all show that there's nothing the matter with her physically. In fact it's amazing that she could be in such good physical shape after the way she has punished herself. . . . The doctor, who is good and a bit of a psychologist, says (and I agree) that it would be futile and possibly dangerous to put her in the hands of a psychoanalyst. He says one wouldn't get ten feet with her. It's got to come out of her own desires and will, and I don't know whether it's too late or not."

Jerry left the hospital after ten days, her health and spirits apparently recovered, and insisted on flying home to Albuquerque while Ernie, alone and dismal, resumed his travels. "Trying to get the columns started again is about to drive me insane," he wrote Roz. "If you run onto anybody in the market for a slightly used secondhand man, who weighs a hundred pounds, has gray hair and a tired look, let me know. The price is two bits."

He wrote "Dear Papa & Auntie" from Des Moines: "Day after tomorrow is my birthday. . . . Forty-one years old—I'll soon be middle-aged."

In Washington, as a result of a casual conversation I had had with a Canadian official, it was learned that Ernie would be welcome to make a tour of the new string of military airports then being installed in western Canada, as steppingstones from the States to Alaska, and Ernie somewhat unenthusiastically (because of his dislike of cold climates) agreed to go. In a letter from Toledo, Ohio, he said: "I'm not really keen on the trip—and yet I'd welcome a sudden trip to the North Pole to break up the present monotony of trivialities. I'm afraid being in England has spoiled me for the duration. I've got to be doing something a little exciting or I go nuts. And being selfish, I sit around and gloom about my own sad plight.

"My old life, I feel sure, is gone. But it is a hard thing to abandon forever a companionship that was as close as ours was for fifteen years. I don't know what the future will bring; I suspect nothing. And that life will go on pointlessly like this for years. . . . I don't truthfully know what Jerry's real feelings are. But she seems content now to idle and float and contribute nothing to a time of living which is pretty tough for everybody. She has always been noble inside; but in this new personality or character that developed while I was away, she seems less noble. I don't know whether she has actually got hold of herself again or not; or if she has, possibly she has had to so remake herself that she is no longer the person I used to know. . . . I have a horror that in these last few years of mental turmoil and fleeing within myself for escape, I have gradually developed into a state of permanent confusion and melancholy. . . . I suspect that possibly—if I could isolate it or put my finger on it—the constant background of the war has something to do with my wholly hopeless feeling about everything. . . ." (Within the past two months Germany had invaded Russia, and the Atlantic Charter had been proclaimed by Roosevelt and Churchill.)

In Cleveland he cleaned up his accumulated writing in preparation for the Canadian trip and stored the car. He wired Jerry to airmail his passport, but she sent it by train mail. "So I had to cancel my reservations [to Ottawa] and wait over another day. I don't know why the hell it is people are so goddamned indifferent about doing things for me. God knows I ask little enough."

He wrote Liz Shaffer from Ottawa: "Don't tell Jerry you've heard from me, but I can get so little out of her that I've just got to have some word of how she is before I set out on this trip to Alaska. So I wish you'd write me, airmail, at the MacDonald Hotel, Edmondton, Alberta, Canada, just as soon as you get this. . . . I've only heard from Jerry about three times since I left there [five weeks earlier]. When I do hear, her letters seem all right, except that they don't say anything. . . . I talked to her last Saturday night by phone. She sounded perfectly all right, except very sentimental and started to cry a couple of times, and said she had planned to come East to rejoin me. . . . She vowed faithfully that she would write me early Sunday morning and send it here. Still nothing had come by last night, and I got way down in the dumps again. Then at one o'clock this morning I was awakened out of a dreamy sleep, and it was Jerry calling from Albuquerque to say that she hadn't written at all, because 'she got involved with children,' whatever that means. One certainly isn't involved with children twenty-four hours a day for four days straight. . . . So I don't know what to think—whether she's getting on three-and four-day benders where she can't write; or whether such a change has come over her personality that she can't force herself to do anything. . . ."

That letter, written on a Thursday, saved Jerry's life. On the following Sunday night, having received the letter, the Shaffers went to call on her. At first she wouldn't let them in the door, but in the end she relented. Liz, seeing that Jerry was not herself, insisted on staying all night. About three-thirty in the morning she awakened, went to Jerry's room, and found her hemorrhaging severely from the mouth.

Ed Shaffer managed to reach Ernie by telephone in Edmonton, where he had arrived by air Saturday midnight, and told him that the doctor thought he had better come as quickly as he could. "I don't know how I did it," Ernie wrote to Dana later, "but I caught the seven o'clock plane—was in the air half an hour after Shafe called." Because of Labor Day traffic and bad connections, he did not reach Albuquerque until Wednesday noon.

"Jerry is out of danger now," he wrote his father presently, "but will have to be in the hospital quite a while. What happened is that an ulcer had developed without giving any indication of itself, and it ate into a blood vessel and she lost a good deal of blood. . . . I don't want to leave until she has completely recovered, so I have dropped the columns indefinitely. . . . I badly need a rest from the column too, so it works out all right. Jerry has a strong constitution and snaps back very quickly from illness. I saw her this morning, and she looks and acts as though she had never been sick."

The stress was almost too much for Ernie, and after Jerry was completely out of danger "I kinda gave way to the strain and got a little drunk (along with Earl; I think we were both downtown and making asses of ourselves all day). Anyhow, some time during the day, Earl said let's go some place. I said all right, let's go to El Paso. Earl said anywhere's all right with me. Then I said no, let's go to Los Angeles. Earl said okay. So by God we called up and were lucky enough to get seats on that night's plane. I wired Cavanaugh to meet us at one o'clock in the morning. On the way home to pack a few things, we staggered into Earl's for a drink, and suddenly I said let's take Shirley with us. Earl said to hell with her. I said by God we'll take her if we can get a seat, and we did get a seat. . . . We were there four days, drunk most of the time,[3] had a marvelous time, did a million things, and were still so tight when we started home that they damn near didn't let us on the plane. The Cavanaughs will probably never speak to us again." Ernie was tastefully attired during the whole trip in Levis, plaid shirt, and ten-gallon hat.

He had been given leave with pay by Scripps-Howard. But now he wrote to Deac Parker, Walker Stone and me in Washington: "Jerry is doing fine; will probably be home from the hospital the last of the week; but her escape was so narrow and her illness so serious that she will have to be under strict personal care and hospital surveillance for a year or more. I just found that out yesterday and she hasn't been told yet.

"And now to launch into the heartbreaking part:—I've either got to take a three-month leave of absence or quit my job. Whichever I do is up to you. I almost feel that it isn't fair to ask for that much leave on a continuing thing such as a column, so I will write this letter on the basis of a resignation. This decision is no flash judgment nor dramatic gesture—I've thought it around the circle of my bewildered brain a million times in the past month, and there is simply no alternative.

"If I am to leave Scripps-Howard after seventeen years of mighty fine association, I think it is only fair to give you the whole story, as much as I hate to. It is for your ears only.

[3] This, for the record, did not include young Shirley, Earl Mount's daughter, who didn't drink.

"For more than ten years Jerry has been a psychopathic case. In the past few months it has reached a stage in which you would have to turn your back to call it anything less than a form of insanity. She is a dual personality, you might say a triple personality—one side of utter charm and captivation for people she cares nothing about; one side of cruelty and dishonesty toward the few people she does care about; and another side of almost insane melancholy and futility and cynicism when she is alone, which is her true personality. She is a Jekyll and Hyde; even when not drinking she changes from one mood or personality to another, as the occasion demands; she is so adept at deceptiveness that only a few people (fortunately for me, her brother and sister are among them) know, or would even believe when told, her state. Because of her futility complex (I suppose) she is not permanently interested in anything. And without any interest, she frequently gets to wallowing in boredom and melancholy and hopelessness, and that leads her to progress from normal drinking to colossal drinking. . . . Lee knows a few of the troubles I've had with her secret drinking and her 'other-worldly' moods over the past few years, but even he doesn't know a hundredth of it. She has been much worse since I returned from England. . . . When she snaps out of one of her moods, and she can almost at will, she is so thoroughly normal and fine that even I, after hundreds of such experiences, think to myself my God I must have been wrong, and it *will* never happen again, just as she vows. She came out of the Denver hospital that way, thoroughly confident of herself, and assuring us that she was on a great highroad to recovery. Yet we found out later that she started secretly drinking within an hour after she left the hospital.

"From there on you know the story—she wanted to come back here until I got across the Midwest; she apparently did fairly well for about a month, and then she hit it up again in a big way, and here she is. Her sister Po flew down from Denver again last weekend at my request, to help me thresh out a course of some kind. The doctor assured us she was well enough to talk seriously about what we were going to do with her, and I felt a decision had to be made now for I had already gone three weeks on the payroll without doing anything. So Po came down, and Dr. Lovelace—one of the finest doctors and finest men in the Southwest—sat on our front porch for an hour and a half while we threshed the whole thing out. And we arrived at the decision that the only step left to try was to put her in a high-class private sanitarium for six months.

"This decision was concurred in by Dr. Richards of Denver, Dr. Lovelace of Albuquerque, Jerry's brother [Fred Siebolds], her sister, and myself. So we put it up to her, and in that dogmatic, autocratic way with which she has ruled ever since I've known her, she simply refused to go. It was as though she had said 'I will not go, you are now all dismissed.' And that was practically true, because we had thought we had the legal power to commit her to a private institution for treatment, but we found later those laws exist in Colorado, but not in New Mexico. And she is too foxy to let us coax her into Colorado now. She simply said that when she got out of the hospital she was coming home to her own house (she has developed a passionate love for our house out here) and that after a few weeks she would start traveling with me again. But of course she won't. For one thing, I think that deep down she never wants to travel again, or at least not until in her shifting interests she gets bored with this place. For another, a good part of my traveling until the war is over will have to be in places where she is not allowed to go. And last, the doctors will not let her make a move for at least a year.

"So we mulled over the realm of possibilities. One was to leave her here under strict care, and me start out again. But that is out, first because I would be a sonovabitch to leave her now in the state she is in, second because I have been so shattered by the awful strain of carrying on all summer with this nightmare weighing me down, and finally by the climax and this frantic searching for a solution when there apparently is no solution, that I honestly believe I could not write a coherent column within two months.

So the only thing left is for me to stay. Jerry says this is her renaissance; that because of the fact that she has been scared for the first time in her life, she will be all right from now on. I know she means it, but I also know she meant it all the other hundreds of times she said it. She has the most dominant will power of anyone I've ever known over everybody but herself. And even if she is kept from drinking, that isn't the fundamental; the fundamental is her mind and spirit and approach to life.

"Jerry's sister feels that she is hopeless; I'm afraid that deep down I feel the same way, yet I can't do anything but hope, and believe that through some miracle it will all turn out all right. I either have to stick here now or else abandon her, and obviously I couldn't and wouldn't do that. So I've got to stay here two or three months, both for her and because I myself am in no mental condition to resume work now.

"If I take a long leave of absence or if I resign, I want it to be made retroactive for three weeks, so that I can refund the salary you have been paying me while doing nothing. Also, I would like to buy the car and my typewriter from the office. Also, I have considerable office expense money. All in all, I would owe the office close to two thousand dollars. If I should stay out here permanently, I intend to do nothing for a couple of months, and then I suppose I can start picking up a few free-lancing jobs. There are even now some available, I believe, which I've turned down as 'on the side' work in the past few months. We would get along somehow, I'm not too deeply worried about that. But I am both too young and too financially 'unheeled' to think of retiring now to a life of whittling; and if I did while the war was still on, I'm afraid I might work into a complex of doing-nothing-while-Rome-burned that would be as evil for us as Jerry's is. Although I am completely sincere and determined in my decision to quit if it comes to that, I still hope that through your generosity something can be worked out to allow me to continue with Scripps-Howard some day when the storm is over. If my private life could be on a normal basis, I love what I've been doing, and believe I've done it well, and can't really picture myself doing anything else. Surely I can tell in a couple of months what direction things are going to take.

"I wish you would let me know just as quickly as you can. I realize that in the end the decision has to be mine, but because you are my employers, and because we are all close friends as well, I wish you would shine any of your light in my direction. Christ knows I've run out of light."

Deac Parker replied, directing Ernie to take a three-month leave: "During that time I do not want you even to think of the newspaper job. . . . My interest in this is great for purely professional reasons. I want you refreshed and able to swing with absolute freedom when you start out again. You won't be able to do that if, in the meanwhile, you have constantly in your mind —even subconsciously—the job and the future. I know that isn't an easy assignment for one of your conscientiousness. It will require resolve and considerable self-discipline. But I stress it from the concern's point of view, as an investment in you, carefully and coldly considered.

"Your leave of absence will be on full pay. . . . I know that this order is right and just and plain good business. Hence, consider it a ukase. . . ."

Ernie replied to Deac at once: "I'm a fine one to quibble when all you're doing is to be the finest employer a human ever had. But I do have to quibble over my salary during this three-month leave. . . . This leave of absence is to try to rejuvenate Jerry, one of the most important things in the world to me. It is also to build myself back up again, as you say, so I can swing hard when I start again. And to do either one, I've got to be absolutely free while doing it. I've got to know the time is *my* time—that I *own* the time because I've paid for it in absence of salary. If my salary goes on, I can't but consider it *your* time, and every loafed minute will be under strain, and I will be fretting and restless about getting back to work. . . .

"This is (I hope) the toughest battle I'll ever have to face in life, and I've got to feel that I'm fighting it with my own hands and my own money. . . . Your giving me the time to do it, and the knowledge of your friendship and intentions, is enough for you to contribute. . . . I'll be cooking and washing dishes and hammering and sitting and reading and loafing—that's the point in doing it—and I couldn't do it if my pay went on. Even the fact that I would undoubtedly be the highest-paid housemaid in the world probably wouldn't seem funny to me under the circumstances.

"So I ask you, Deac, to take me off the payroll. . . . I know that my chances of success will be far greater if you will let me do it my way. . . ."

Deac replied: "I understand—and you win. . . ."

CHAPTER 17

Crisis

JERRY convalesced steadily under the devoted care of the Catholic sisters at St. Joseph's Hospital, with whom she had quickly become great friends. She responded so well to a special diet that she soon outweighed Ernie. Letters came to her from all over the country, from friends and from Ernie's readers. Flowers poured in voluminously. And after almost six weeks, she was brought home.

She preferred to do without a nurse or maid, so Ernie did the cooking and other housework. He was kept so busy that the weeks flew. Among other things, he decided a guest room was more useful than his attached garage, and had the latter converted into an attractive bedroom and bath. He was beginning to look forward to traveling again and was giving much thought to the possibility of a swing around the Orient. He wrote to us in Washington suggesting a three-month tour beginning about December 1 and covering the Philippines, Hong Kong, Chungking, the Burma Road, Rangoon, Singapore, and the East Indies, plus possibly Australia and New Zealand. Concerning Jerry he said: "She looks fine and is fine most of the time. It is too early to tell whether she can solve her own terrific problem or not—we probably won't know that for many months. But she is trying and she is progressing, I can say that. She is up all day and does enough to keep active. She doesn't go out, and won't see many people, but she is trying gradually to regain a genuine interest in things.

"The reason for my leave of absence—to try to help Jerry over the hump—has either been done or hasn't been done, I don't know yet. But, regardless, I feel there is no necessity or possibility of gain by me staying on more than another month. Hence this beginning of talks about what I shall do when I resume."

As to the proposed journey: "Deac, I believe your one fear about such a trip is that we might get into war with Japan and I might get hurt. But actually I see little grounds for worry even if I were caught over there by war with Japan. . . . As far as personal danger is concerned, I feel it much less hazardous than last winter's trip. Jerry wants me to make the trip, so there are no complications there. And . . . I feel it important that we should kick the column off again with something big. . . . From the syndication standpoint George Carlin writes that practically all the old clients will renew (I've personally had letters from many of them), and I believe that if we resumed syndication with a trip like this, they should run the list up close to a hundred papers before I get back. Which of course would put a little more hay in my mow.[1]

"I'm rested, but my time here has not been a picnic or vacation, as many people seem to think. It has been a time of constant worry and bewilderment, and still is somewhat. It has been a change rather than a rest. But the mere change of type of responsibility has done me good I am sure, and I have a feeling that maybe I can grind exceeding fine again when I start out. . . ."

Deac approved the trip, and Ernie came to Washington to make his arrangements. It was the next day that Sumner Welles, Undersecretary of State, warned in an Armistice Day speech that "at any moment war may be forced upon us."

Ernie's week in Washington was overcrowded with both work and play. There were numerous visits with officials who could smooth his path around the Orient, and numerous parties given by friends.

---

[1] Some weeks before the column was suspended, Carlin had informed Ernie that his clients, including the twenty-odd Scripps-Howard papers, numbered forty-seven, with a total circulation of just under three million.

On a sudden whim he bought Jerry a little dog, a Shetland shepherd, and it went with him on the plane to Indianapolis and thence, after some difficulties, to Albuquerque. Ernie wrote Roz: "Our flight to Indianapolis was pleasant, although I had a sinking spell on the way (having eaten nothing since the previous noon) and had to call for hot chocolate and cookies. Then, before we landed, I felt something like the flu coming on. And I wasn't mistaken. By the time I got to the hotel I had to go right to bed. . . . Took the dog to the room with me, and she slept all night on the bed with her head on my stomach. I was too sick even to think to have a bellboy take her out—the result was that apparently she held everything from Sunday noon till nine a.m. Monday, and then she didn't hold nothing no longer. I spent my sick day leaping out of bed periodically and cleaning the room. To think that I lived through it and still loved the dog must prove that I am a man of the ages, or something. Late Monday I got myself up and got the train to Dana. Spent three days there. The dog was pretty bewildered and frightened by all the changes. . . . Everybody admired her and said she looked and acted exactly like a fox, which she does, and the farmers all said not to let her get out, or she would be shot for a fox. . . . I left [Indianapolis] by plane Friday night. . . . This country, so wide and empty and peaceful, almost made me cry as we flew over it. I am sure I could never again tolerate the East except on visits.

"Things weren't well when I got here. Jerry had cracked up again . . . but was again on the mend. I was pretty discouraged. But since then we have had talks and made some definite plans, and I feel honestly the most encouraged I have for months. She still is willing to fight her fight. And—she loves the dog! I haven't been so pleased in years. She's almost childish about it. And as for the dog, I could kick her from here to Los Angeles, for she won't have anything to do with Jerry. . . . Apparently through that horrible week of traveling and jumping from one strange and horrifying place to another I was her only protector. And she literally worships at my feet. She is two inches behind my heels day and night, even if I only get up to get a cigarette. . . . The dog is now known as Cheetah, since Jerry always wanted a real cheetah anyhow."

When Cheetah continued to be obdurate about transferring her affections to Jerry, Ernie bought another dog, a huge and affectionate Dane which they called Piper. He wrote to his father: "The arrival of the Dane has done wonders for the little dog. They immediately became friends, and since then she has blossomed out like a flower. She hasn't been afraid or trembly since he came, and the way she struts around and shows him things is very funny. She . . . can walk right under him and still have six inches to spare."

It was Ernie's belief that Jerry's latest collapse had resulted from her being suddenly deprived of Benzedrine pills. He arranged to have these restored in small doses and engaged a nurse for the winter. He told Cavanaugh: "Jerry hit the bottle for the first time while I was away, but I think not excessively. She told me that she drank just enough to scare the wits out of her."

Ernie was scheduled to board a Clipper at San Francisco for Honolulu on December 2, but now his booking and several others were canceled to make room for airplane propellers urgently needed by the Chinese. After much telephoning and telegraphing and pulling of wires, he arranged passage by steamer for December 9, and then the Army commandeered all passenger accommodations. He began negotiating for space on one of the bombers that were being ferried to the Pacific.

On November 26 at Washington, Secretary of State Hull had handed the Japanese envoys, Nomura and Kurusu, a proposed basis for a peaceful agreement between the two countries. Kurusu, upon reading it, said that the Japanese government would likely "throw up its hands." One day before this the Jap task force had left Hitokappu Bay for the waters north of Oahu. Three days later Hull told the British Ambassador that Japan "may move suddenly and with every element of surprise." On December 6 President Roosevelt, in a direct appeal to the Emperor of Japan, spoke of "tragic possibilities."

The next day the Japs struck Pearl Harbor.

The Pacific trip was now out of the question, and Ernie decided the best place to resume the column would be California, where invasion rumors were rife. He wrote Cavanaugh from San Francisco: "Are you scared? . . . I sat around Albuquerque at loose ends Sunday and Monday, getting jitterier and gloomier by the moment. Then Monday night when the rumor came there were two Japanese carriers off San Francisco, I just . . . went to the phone and got a seat on the first plane out. And got here yesterday afternoon. . . . I slept right through the raid alarm and blackout last night—just the same as I did in London the first night. Fine citizen I am. . . . Albuquerque is jitterier than hell. Everybody's chin is a yard long. Up here they're just badly confused. Some are scared to death, and others won't take it seriously. They will after the first bombs fall in. Today's Pacific news makes me feel like curling up."

He was dining with friends when another air-raid alarm sounded. They doused the lights, poured water into a flaming fireplace, and took a walk through the shrouded city. Ernie wrote a long piece about it for next day's *San Francisco News:* "I felt a certain sort of great pride. It was partly a shameful sense of egotism that I, one of the very few among these millions in this vast black space, was an old hand and had been through all this a hundred times before. And it was partly, and even more so, a pride that now we too, we here in America, were sharing in the knowledge of a universal catastrophe. Now we have ceased playing. . . ."

Immediately after Christmas, Ernie left San Francisco and drove northward in search of column material. In Oregon a letter from Jerry reached him; she had been feeling bad and had gone to the hospital for a few days. He wired suggesting that she stay a whole week. And he wrote her: "I'm awfully glad you went. Your letter was so frank and nice that I'm not worried about you. . . . I have felt that you were making progress (psychologically, I mean), for your letters seemed to show it. . . . Me, I'm so shriveled up even mentally from the dismal weather . . . that I can just hardly get my work done. I really don't know whether I can keep on going or not—writing has never been such a torture for me. The worst trouble is that I'm not interested in anything; I'll go a mile out of my way to avoid getting a column. Maybe it would be better for me to drop it and do some kind of defense work. I'm ashamed to write such a blue letter. But you know me— I have to wear my melancholy on my sleeve. . . . Last night I dreamed I was driving along up here in the Northwest, and I saw a toy Shepherd running alongside the road, and after awhile I realized it was Cheetah. So I stopped and got out, and she recognized me. Wonder what that means?"

From Seattle he wrote me: "Had a nice letter from Deac, telling me to follow my nose. But if I do, I'll probably just follow it to the bottom of a lake somewhere. I simply can't hit my stride. I'm almost desperate. Have been thinking seriously of quitting. I did have a little cushion ahead but have now lost it. Can't make myself get interested in anything. Jerry is in the hospital again. Has been for a week. They've given her a blood transfusion. Her blood count was down to fifty per cent of normal. In addition, she now has pellagra—from not eating properly. She wrote me about it and made it sound so matter-of-fact that I wasn't worried about it very much. But early this morning I had a call from Albuquerque—and the reason for this setback is that she's been doping and drinking to excess again. I don't know how much longer I can take it."

But next day he wrote Jerry: "Your good letter came this morning, and I was so pleased to know that you were getting along well. . . . I gathered a couple of quick columns this morning, and too the weather is warmer, so I'm picking up. . . . A reporter on the Butte (Mont.) paper wrote me the snottiest letter you ever read. I sat down and wrote him back a good hot one. It will undoubtedly cost me the column in Butte, but it was worth it to tell that guy off."

An item in Ernie's expense account: "Wartime stimulant, $5.00."

He drove two hundred miles to Portland and prepared to go up to Timberline Lodge, which he had visited in 1939 with Jerry, and for column-writing purposes learn to ski. "Now that the time is nigh," he wrote Jerry, "I'm terrified of going up there and making an ass of myself, but I guess I can't back out now, and anyhow non-military subjects to write about are scarce."

After his first day on skis at Timberline he wrote her: "My verdict is to hell with skiing. It's the hardest work I ever did. And so far it really isn't any fun. God, but skis are awkward things to be encumbered with. I've been down at least fifteen times today, but the instructor said I did far better than most beginners. The liar, I'm just too damn stiff ever to ski, and always was too stiff. But one thing, it sure makes you eat. . . . I hurt my ankle today in one of my falls, but it isn't serious. All the rest were nice soft, graceful falls! . . .

"Wonder if we couldn't make a living after the war by going into a very snozzy home-decorating business along Western lines, and at very snooty prices—and hire a few craftsmen to make stuff like is in this lodge. Charge rich bastards a thousand dollars a home and do about six a year. You could furnish the taste and imagination, and I'd furnish the—right off I can't think of anything I could furnish. I'll give it some thought."

From Portland two days later he wrote her again: "My skiing career . . . wound up in a blaze of glory (I like to think) in the midst of a raging snowstorm this afternoon. . . . When I got up this morning I was so sore from head to foot (not from falls, just from sore muscles) that I actually couldn't lean over to tie my shoe. Also it was blizzarding outside. So I just lazed around the hotel all morning." Friends, however, "insisted that I ride up the ski lift with them and ski back down. I said that was ridiculous, that I couldn't even make a simple turn, and it would be suicide to try to ski that long mountainside. But they said I could and had to, so I finally went and asked the instructor if it would be safe, and he said he thought so. So I gave in. . . . Well, we rode up, and started down. And the first thing I knew I was doing fine. We took our time . . . and out on those long slopes I soon found I was doing naturally what the instructor had been pounding into us."

Back in San Francisco, he got word from Jerry that Piper, the great Dane, was dead. He wired her at once, phoned her that night, and wrote: "Darling, your letter about Piper was beautiful, and I could hardly keep back the tears as I read it. I am broken-hearted about it because of course I did love him, but more especially for you. I know how much he was to you. . . ."

Another letter to Jerry: "I had the grandest letter from Lowell [Mellett, who was now one of President Roosevelt's administrative assistants], in which he sent his special love to you. The letter was the result of a semi-tight one I wrote him from Portland. I'm mentioning it especially because in it he said that if I wasn't happy at what I was doing (which I had intimated) they would dig up something for me to do in Washington. . . . Of course I have no wish to do so, but I thought it was grand of him. . . .

"Roz says she's getting overwhelmed with mail (she actually sounds scared for the first time) and also she's been overwhelming me with mail. . . .

"I've been having the oddest thing—apparently rheumatism in my ankles and wrists. . . . I suppose it's induced by the damp climate and the humidity of the booze I've been drinking. Otherwise I've been feeling great, and told you, I think, that I'd gained a lot of weight. I think it makes me look repulsive. Some flatterers say it makes me look younger. Even so, why look younger when you've reached the rheumatic age?

"It seems there is nothing but confusion in my mind about everything, and I'm afraid my letters must be depressing to you. I wish I could go and DO something. Either fight or retire from everything or something. If Lowell's offer were somewhere in the West, I think I might consider it. And yet—we've got to have money. . . ."

Jerry replied: ". . . (a) I've a notion to pick up and come out to California. (b) I feel that the great bulk of mail (plus the comments I get) proves that you should stay on doing what you're doing until you HAVE to do something else. I understand how it is that you feel you aren't doing anything much, what with things the way they are; but for once, I know I'm right. Everybody needs relief from thinking about one thing. And finally this business boils down to the point where everyone is thinking about himself. Your column gets them away from that. (c) And furthermore, what with an invalid woman on your hands, and God knows how many dogs, well, you just have to go on supporting us in the style to which you've accustomed us. (d, e and f) The wind is blowing a gale, and it's certainly March, and not February, as the calendars say.

"Seriously about money, dear. You've mentioned several times that we need it. You left me well provided for. I'm sorry as the devil that I've had to make such inroads into the amount. . . . I think by the fifteenth I'll be able to let the nurse go. I definitely decided today that I won't get another dog. Maybe later on I'll be able to relieve the budget. I've tried, not as hard as I might, to keep it down. . . . As far as I know we're still solvent, and better off than we would have been had we stayed on in Washington, and tried to keep up with the various Jones families. . . . I guess I'm just trying to defend myself where I know there's no defense. I should have done better, and I know it."

Ernie wrote Cavanaugh: "Well, my friend, if you expect to be seeing me week after next, I think it's about time you were writing and inviting me. . . . I've gained ten pounds and am approaching the status of a he-man. Let's you and me join the Navy. I will by God if you will, if they'll take us. . . ."

Expense account item: "Riotous living, $4.50."

Ernie was about ready to head south when he caught a touch of grippe which kept him in bed two days. Then he got grapevine word that some of the people at the *San Francisco News* thought he'd not been around there enough, and also thought he should be writing about more serious things. He told Jerry he was "so damn mad I could spit. . . . But at any rate I suppose now I've got to stay over tomorrow. . . . Such business nauseates me.

I was already pretty desperate on the columns, and now this grippe has thrown me two days further behind, which is just all I can be thrown behind without going for a loss. . . . The war news couldn't be worse, could it? [Singapore surrendered three days later.] It looks hopeless for me to get across anywhere now. . . ."

Soon he wrote me from San Diego: "I really don't see a damn thing to do but work my way slowly across the country toward the East Coast. . . . I'll stop in Albuquerque two or three days . . . and try to thresh out something specific with Jerry. I can't go on forever traveling alone and keeping a nurse with her just for company. But I suppose I will. . . . I'm glad you liked the recent stuff. I need encouragement. . . . Jerry called last night; was very lonely and sentimental. Made me feel bad. I'm not going to ask for any draft deferment at all. We've got enough to keep Jerry for several years but wouldn't have a penny after the war was over. But what the hell. . . ."

His struggle to build up his cushion of columns wasn't helped by a revenue man who volunteered to fix up his income tax "in ten minutes" and then gossiped and puttered for half a day, nor by some friends who dropped in for "half an hour" but upon arriving at the hotel dispatched their children to a double feature and stayed with him for three hours. "I really believe I'm going to turn hard," he wrote Jerry, "and not put myself out for a soul any more, and not ever call up anybody I don't want to. I'm leaving early in the morning to get away from it all. I've just talked to Margaret Miller [Mrs. Max Miller] and told them I'd stop for a few minutes in the morning on the way out. The people I want to see I give only a few minutes to. I guess it's just my own bad judgment. . . . If a person stayed around here long, he would have little hopes of us ever winning the war. Right here, in the supposed danger area, people don't seem to care whether we win the war or not. I'm not enthused about us being in the war, but by God if we don't win it life will be unlivable. . . ."

His mood was getting lower and lower, although a reading of the columns would hardly betray it, for he kept them on a light note. At Deac Parker's request he drove over to Palm Springs, the California desert resort pioneered by grandmotherly Mrs. Nellie Coffman, where he wrote the Shaffers in some awe that the tax on his 1941 income was nearly fifteen hundred dollars—"sort of frightened me to realize I had got that important." The letter continued: "I've been in a constant almost desperate depression ever since leaving Albuquerque, but for once I'm not going to dwell on that, other than to ask you to be thinking a little for me— it is humanly impossible for me to carry on much longer under the present setup; it's all too pointless, either from Jerry's stand-point or mine; I'm too desperately lonesome to continue; I feel sure that Jerry's recovery plans (and I'm sure she has tried and maybe still is) do not include ever traveling with me again; I believe what-ever affection there is left between us is only one that comes in bursts of sentimentalism about old times and long years of wearing the same shoe; I hear she's drinking again and she has not written me in three weeks; my presence there doesn't help even if I were to settle there. What would you do?

"There seems to be no long foreign trip I can take, for I can't get the columns back from anywhere. I might quit the column and go somewhere as a regular correspondent for S-H, radioing back pieces when and if I could. . . . Maybe the draft board will settle the whole thing for me. I hope so. . . . Clapper is taking a trip I should have taken [to Cairo, India, and China], yet I don't know how I could have gotten my column back. Mine ain't worth radioing all that distance."

With unaccustomed bluntness he wrote Jerry, omitting the usual salutation "Darling": "Jerry: I have waited and waited, but the letters you said were on the way never came. It has now been more than three weeks since I've had a letter from you. I know you have been able to write if you wanted to. I can't attempt any longer to know what motivates you in any certain direction, or what you really want from life. We've done everything as you wished it done, and apparently all in vain. You've always said you needed to have me in your background, but now obviously you no longer do. So I'm ready to call the whole thing off if you are. Maybe a drastic change or a fresh start would give you strength and interest. It might send me either up or down, I don't know which, but I can't carry on much longer under the present state of turmoil. I'm leaving here early in the week. I'll work into Arizona, but I don't know where I'll be. My traveling plans are indefinite. The columns are a daily torture. I know you are lonely, but so am I, often desperately so.

"I had got that far when your telegram came. I am relieved to hear from you. But it doesn't alter what I've been trying to say. I suppose neither of us could likely form a new companionship. For physical reasons alone a new one is forever denied me. But our old companionship is gone—revived only in our thoughts and in waves of sentimentalism—and possibly we might both be less burdened if we ceased to carry the empty carcass. We've discussed this before, and both have let the memory of old and better times overwhelm us. Actually we have contributed nothing to each other in two years. All I can suggest is that you think this possibility over, as I have tried to do. There must be some solution soon for both of us, or we'll both collapse completely. This is written with a heartbreak."

This letter crossed one from Jerry, in answer to which he wrote: "Darling—Well, that's irony. At the same time I was writing you a letter calling it all off, you were writing me one calling it all on. I don't know what to say, darling, I really don't. Naturally I'm moved deeply by your letter, as I've always been moved by every real effort you've made toward molding yourself into a normalcy which is unnatural for you. And yet, if you've pulled yourself out of the quagmire through your want for a child of *ours*, I am fearful over the grounds you've built your recovery on. For in the first place it seems to me unfair to a child to be born of parents our age; further, we're both a little neurotic by now; and lastly, and even making unnecessary the other two considerations, I *can't* give you a child, as you know. I haven't been lying when I've told you that the power of sex had gone from me.

"Frankly, I had come to the bottom of the well when I wrote you. I've been in a mental desperation these last few months that can't continue without me cracking up. And it seemed to be enhanced by a knowledge that, even should you recover, it was too late, for our old companionship was dead. In other words, I've looked and searched in a million directions, and I can see nothing but that we're trapped. I can't see any way out for us. I've no doubt that—without being actually conscious of it—I too have changed in these last couple of years, enough so that if you became ready to pick up again where we left off, I couldn't. I believe that in your heart you never want to travel again (and I can't blame you), and that if you did force yourself to, it would be such an empty and meaningless life that you would finally have to leave and flee back home, or else revert to the mental agony you're just now escaping from.

"As for me, I must continue to travel if I am to make a living that will support us. I would drop that in a minute, as I almost did; yet I know my own psychology, and I almost know that if I were to return to a settled life of office hours and drudgery and so much less of everything than we can now have, I would be wild within six months, which would destroy us both. . . .

"During our long years together when you were what to me was 'normal,' but which periods you have always said were actually 'unnormal' and you were just acting, it seemed to me that our companionship was the most ideal thing that ever happened; I know it was all I ever wanted if it could have been continuous instead of spasmodic; and I can hardly think back upon it now without crying. Nobody could ever have had such a perfect and comforting understanding of me as you have had; you carried me along and I leaned on you, although actually I didn't know it. And in my thoughtless way, I think I gave something to you too.

"But that is gone. It has been gone for two years. That's a thing also that makes me hopeless and desperate. Frankly I have considered, in my mind, the possibility of other companionships, and there again I run into hopelessness. I would almost be afraid to take another companionship because of a fear that I would always be comparing the new one's inadequacies to your companionship when it was full and best; that I would be obsessed for life with ghosts of regret and misery over not having myself done differently in some way to prevent, or maybe even not to have been the cause of, your wrecking yourself. . . .

"As for the way you feel now, darling, about a child and everything—I know you went through a soul-searing while I was in England, and I think you felt exactly this way when I came back, and I think the fact that I didn't feel that way and couldn't respond is what sent you down the last toboggan. I believe you had gone to the depths of yourself and had come out on top during the time you felt that you might never see me again. The tragedy of our lives is that I *did* come back alive from England, the same person, while you had remade yourself.

"Oh I've torn myself apart too, darling, thinking, thinking, thinking—but I've never come to anything. And I don't mean just thinking of us on a basis of what *you* do—I mean searching and weighing myself in it equally too, with the faults and psychoses that have by now become a part of my character. But I don't get anywhere. And I can't carry on much longer with my work or probably my sanity the way things are set up now. I'm not working *for* anybody; nobody dear to me is interested in me; my life is purposeless and tortured, and soon my ability to carry on and make a living will be impaired, and that will be the beginning of the end. There must be something definite soon; a drastic change; a recapturing of lightheartedness; a contentment through companionship, something. I don't know the answer. I hope to God you do.

"I do hope (if I were a prayin' man I would pray) that this seriousness and frankness does not throw you back into a relapse into futility; do try not to let it, darling; try to stay steady-minded and help think this thing through with me. And then write me whatever comes to you. . . .

"I'm running back to San Diego for a certain purpose. I hadn't told you. For some six weeks I've been going to the doctors in the faint hope of repairing myself. The treatments have been agonizing and cruel. I doubt that I have the courage to continue them much longer. And there seems little hope that they'll be successful anyway. . . ."

It turned out that Jerry was in no condition to face problems. From San Diego a few days later Ernie wrote Cavanaugh: "Speaking of Albuquerque, our fears were justified. I've talked with Albuquerque every night for the last four nights—one night twice. Jerry has been put under opiates for three days. Nurses around the clock again. Just went clear to pot again in the last couple of weeks. Fooling everybody in the daytime and drinking all night apparently." Again to Cavanaugh, from Phoenix: "Yes, I've got sense enough to know I'm headed for trouble, but Jesus Christ, what have I got *now*? . . ."

When he reached Albuquerque he and Jerry could come to no decisions, and in a few days he had to move along. A letter from *Reader's Digest*, inviting him to do some magazine pieces, failed to give him a lift; he declined. From Clovis he wrote to Jerry: "I suppose our trouble is that we still love each other despite everything; yet it isn't enough to sustain either of us. I try to look at it realistically, and accept the fact that we can't regain something that is gone, and yet I just can't bear to. . . . So as I see it, there is only one thing left for each of us (we used to think of it as just you, but now it's me too)—and that's for each of us to buck himself up and do his job and stand on his own feet until we gain a new sense of vitality through each one's own pride of victory over himself, or else just completely go to hell in a hand-basket. . . .

"I was ready to give up. But a person just can't *do* that. I've got to get back to the columns with a vim, and restore an interest in life in myself. I've got to work hard again, and brood less, and enjoy things more, and drink less. To be candid, I don't know whether my character is strong enough to do it or not. I've got to do it, and you've got to do it. The only question left is whether we can do it together or not. I'm terribly afraid we can't. But maybe I'm wrong, and I'm ready to try it together again if you feel it might work.

"I want you to join me again as soon as you are able, if you really feel that you want to. My fear of your doing so is that the monotony and senselessness of traveling the hick circuit, the deprival of the freedom and pleasures and help that you have there at home, and possibly my own inability to help you enough as we go along, will drive you off the deep end again. But if you want to try it on the understanding that you'll shoot back home to what is a kind of refuge if you feel yourself despairing, then I will too. Our lives have become tragic, there's no denying that. I really don't know why they should have become so. And despite the fact that your tragedy is so far more apparent, I have never in my soul given you all the blame. I have failed too. I suppose that's really the reason I can't quit. That, and a fear of facing the facts of life. . . . I feel so sorry for us both—if we only had each other to lean upon once more, but we haven't. Love to you, darling, try to cheer up, and whatever decision you make I'll go along with you on. . . ."

His problems still roiled his brain as he drove, through a hailstorm, to Amarillo, Texas. There, finally, he decided he could not go on. He made up his mind at breakfast and at once telephoned Washington that he had reached the end of his rope and must drop the column. He was urged to go on back to Albuquerque and try to relax for a while before doing anything decisive. The next day he drove three hundred miles back home. Three days later he wrote to "Dear Papa and Auntie" that the bosses "were very kind and sweet about it, as they always have been with me. . . . My plans still aren't definite, but I feel positive I will not resume the columns until after the war, and that may be several years. In the meantime I think I'll just stay here for a couple of months and try to get myself calmed down. . . . Some other type of work I could have carried on, but to write a column you have to put other things out of your mind and really think and create, and I just had too much on my mind to carry on any longer. . . ."

The next day Ernie and Jerry were divorced.

CHAPTER 18

The Unmarried

THE divorce was a step that Ernie and Jerry passionately regretted once it had been taken. Both of them had been distraught to the breaking point the night before, when they made the decision. It was Jerry who, out of the depths of self-criticism, precipitated the issue that night; it was she who suggested the divorce, after he had abandoned the idea "for lack of courage." But it had been much in his mind for weeks. At first, it may be, he saw it only as a means of escape from the torment of a love and comradeship now so deeply mired. But then he conceived the thought that such a drastic move might jolt her out of the irresponsibility in which she was floundering, and later make possible at least a partial restoration of their old life. "We finally decided on the divorce as an experiment," he wrote, "on the gamble that it might shock her into a realization that she had to face life like other people. It was concurred in by the doctors, the nurse, Earl, Po, and Jerry's mother. It wasn't a divorce of hate and was based on the premise that if Jerry would now get to work and cure herself, we could some day be remarried. It is the first time she has ever been put in a position where she'll have to work, and work like hell, to get what she wants—which is me. I don't know whether she can make the grade or not. If she can regain herself within a year or so, we'll likely be remarried. If she can't, then plans are made to take her to a sanitarium."

Ernie had gone alone to Joseph L. Dailey's law office to have the divorce papers prepared. Since they were residents, no waiting was required. "I've handled many divorce cases," Dailey said, "but I never saw anybody so distressed as Ernie." There was a brief hearing in court—Jerry remaining at home—and the decree was granted. On leaving court Ernie said to Dailey, "I'm never going to write any more—at least not a column." Then he went home. Jerry had packed to go away, perhaps to Po's at Denver, but was not up to it. So the two of them, no longer man and wife, stayed in the little house for two weeks, to the puzzlement of the neighbors. That first night some friends came over for dinner, and on the surface it was almost as if nothing had occurred. Once Ernie said, "Is there a draft on you, dear? Hey, what am I saying 'dear' for now!"

In the afternoon he had written me: "Jerry and I were divorced this morning. It seemed to be a necessary and last-hope form of psychological surgery. That's all I can say about it now, or probably ever. We are both terribly broken over it. I can't tell you yet when I can resume the columns, if ever. I don't know yet what I am going to do, or can do. You have all been very wonderful and patient with me, and if your patience can last a little longer, I will make a decision soon." This was on April 14, 1942.

He wrote his father and Aunt Mary, simply stating the fact of the divorce and offering no explanation. The press wires had carried the news, but Mr. Pyle and Aunt Mary knew nothing until the letter arrived. Aunt Mary, who was entertaining one of her clubs, handed it to Mr. Pyle. As he started reading it, she asked, "What does Ernest say?" Mr. Pyle said nothing, just read on, then handed it to her. "But what does Ernest say?" she asked. "Is Jerry worse?" Mr. Pyle was silent. Thad Hooker's mother put her arm around Aunt Mary; the ladies had all read the news in the paper but had said nothing. Aunt Mary wrote Ernie: "We are so broken up. An end like this to what we thought an ideal couple. Your father won't say anything about it. When he read the letter he just sat and stared. . . . We hope it is for the best. Am thankful this did not happen in your mother's time. Ernest, you know how deeply we feel about this. And how we love you. Please come home and make us a long visit. Please don't be too hasty about joining the Army." For he had written that he might volunteer.

A letter to Cavanaugh: "Dear Happy Man: I suppose you have seen the news, so I will spare you all the details. . . . I don't think I'll ever resume the columns, although of course I may. My moods and decisions change every hour on the hour. I tried to join the Navy Monday but was too old unless I knew a trade. I may come to Southern California for a couple of months, build up my weight, and join the Army. Actually, I don't know for sure what I'll do.

"Jerry . . . now plans to dismiss her nurse, get a maid, get a job, and buckle down to living. If she does, that's just what we wanted. But she probably won't. . . . If you can think of anything to live for, please let me know. You think you're cute as hell, don't you, eating your lunch in your patio like a millionaire, and laughing to beat hell, I suppose. . . . (Signed) Tommy Manville."

He executed an agreement giving the house to Jerry, keeping the Santa Fe lots for himself, and dividing fifty-fifty their savings, represented by securities valued at $22,625. Also, he deposited $2600 with a bank, to be paid out to Jerry at $35 a week.

The Washington office persuaded him to come East, and he wrote Cavanaugh before leaving: "Dear Dream Man: The office insists that I come to Washington and get arrangements started for another foreign trip. . . . I've expressed through my bag of nice wood and carving tools, and may whittle a little there. Also my heavy clothes and everything, for God knows where I'll go. I'm not taking any of my other personal things from the house, as I still feel there is some hope (though dim) of Jerry eventually recovering and we could start over again. She has been in a Christawful shape this week. Nurse and doctor here almost constantly. . . . She just can't accept the fact that we are divorced and that I'm going away again.

"We've looked up the Civil Service, and they'll give her a job here as soon as she is officially reinstated to the rolls. She has lifetime rating. I'll arrange it when I get to Washington. . . . Her only two courses left are to take a job and pull back to a normal human being through hard work and regimentation of her life; or to go to a psychiatric sanitarium for six months or a year, which Po is going to force the next time she blows up. But it's mighty hard to leave her in her present state of utter hopelessness and tragedy. . . .

"Mr. Mount has a new story he wants to tell you. It actually happened. A guy came into Dr. Connor's office the other day, and they were talking about a mutual acquaintance. The visitor said, 'Doc, So-and-so is a plain out-and-out no-good sonovabitch. And besides that, he has other faults.' (Signed) Magellan."

He left that night, first penning a note for Jerry: "My Darling—My heart is breaking too, but I know how much harder it is for you—for you feel we are going out of each other's lives forever, whereas I feel it is only a matter of time until we are together again—and that time, really happy. . . . As long as there is the slightest hope, there is no other woman in the world for me. . . . We are too intimately woven together to separate ourselves, really. And you *can* do what you *have* to do, I know you can. You still have the necessary will and character to do it. If your love for me is the dominant thing in your life, then you must never hesitate for an instant in your mission to cure and restore yourself. Instead of this being a hopeless day for you, let's let it be our first hopeful day in years. For now, for the first time, you really have a goal to fight and work for. It had to be done this way—cruel as it is upon both of us—for there was no other way left. But now I genuinely feel hopeful for us; more than that, almost sanguine about the outcome for us—you and me together as we should be, and happy. . . ."

He wired her on reaching Washington and presently wrote: "God, how I long for the open spaces. I've really been so sad and depressed about everything, I've felt that I simply couldn't endure it. And the mere fact of being in Washington is enough to drive anybody insane. . . .

"That first afternoon I went to see General Surles, head of Army information, and he confirmed the hunch that I should go to England instead of Australia. He said they were glad for me to go and that they would put me on the first convoy going out. It all sounded too easy to be true. Then yesterday I went to Deac's house and we talked the whole thing over, and he okayed the England trip, regardless of whether Walker found it would be too expensive or not. So everything was all cleared, and then this morning I dropped past the draft board to turn in my questionnaire and get permission to leave the country for six months. And goddamned if I didn't find that I'm in Class 1-A, and they're expecting to call me up in either July or August!

"Thus everything was instantly confused. I think it likely they would give me a six-months leave from now, but would then pick me up and induct me the minute I returned, around December. And Walker doesn't want me to start the column again at all, even with a trip to England, if it has to be dropped once more. He says it's been started and stopped already so much that the editors are getting fed up. So—the whole thing now revolves on finding out whether I would pass the physical examination if and when I was called up. . . . If I fail to pass, then I can go ahead with the column. If I pass, then I know I'm destined for the Army by late summer, and can either start work at some straight and non-by-line reporting until then, or loaf around a little while and then enlist. . . .

"I have your civil service letters (and are they wonderful, made me awfully proud of you, and nostalgic). . . .

"Actually I feel that my capacity ever to produce the column again has died; I don't truly want either to go to England, resume the column, or go into the Army. . . . I feel that if I could just run back to Albuquerque and start a life of utter simplicity I would be happy. But I guess I can't, and I have determined not to come back until you have won your great fight. . . .

"People have been very tactful about the divorce, almost nobody mentioning it at all. I anticipated there would be some sonovabitch opinions of me expressed around the circuit of editors, and Deac says there has been. They too can go to hell. . . . I miss you more than I've ever missed you in my life. . . .

"P.S.—Thanks so much for your thoughtful departure gift. Believe it or not, I haven't opened either one of them yet. Hope I'm not getting temperate."

A letter came from Jerry, and he replied: "It sounded more like you and I was cheered, but I could sense that you don't feel on top of the world yet. But I believe you will if you are firm and determined with yourself, darling. We've got everything to win, and not much more to lose, so you must try with a desperate tenaciousness.

"I don't want you to worry about me. But since coming here I realize that I have gone much farther down than I had known. In the way of loss of spirit, I mean, and flabbiness of decision or desire. It seems to me that my character and my will and my ability to go along a straight line have all deteriorated. . . . I believe I'm pretty far along in the very path of floundering that you were in. I seem to have messed up so much in my own life and others' that now I too don't wish to face anything, and just want to avoid the realities of everything. The reason I'm saying all this is that I'm scared, and *I've* got to take *myself* in hand, and I'm going to. I realize that one reason for my indecision about what I shall do is that I've got lazy and simply don't want to work at anything except watering our lawn and looking at the horizon, and shutting my eyes to all the grave and hard things of life. I'd got it into my head that I wasn't going to do anything in the line of work I didn't want to, and that by God I'd just quit if things didn't go my way. But now I'm scared, and I'm going to do whatever they tell me to. And it looks as if it might be something I don't like at all. . . .

"Walker wants me to work in the office until final word [about the draft] comes through. In fact, he wants me to start on the desk tomorrow, and work till Lee gets back. I sure don't relish the idea, but there it is. I know that at this stage of the game work is my only salvation (just as I had always felt it was yours), and since I can't write a column with my mind and soul consumed with despair, I'll simply do something that I can do, to keep from thinking constantly about myself and us. . . .

"I'm sure Dr. ——'s indifference is due to something else than that you are no longer living on the top wave of my popularity. That was never true in the first place; you lived on your own deserved popularity. And now my popularity is gone. There have been a good many hints dropped in my presence that show me I'm washed up with a good many people. It has just been insidiously creeping in. People can't keep their noses out, of course. I find some blaming you, some blaming me—none of whom, of course, know anything about us really. Somehow the result has been to make me feel closer to you than ever—as though the world had turned against both of us, so we'd have to work together and pull ourselves out and then stick up our noses at them. Of course there are people like the MacKayes and Roz and many others who accept what has happened as our business and still feel the same about both of us. . . .

"Darling, write me whenever you can, know that I appreciate, and also feel the necessity for knowing, that you are trying like hell all the time; and I'll try like hell too, and by God we will pull out of this thing. . . ."

He was so discouraged and sensitive that he began to think even his father and Aunt Mary were cool to him. He wrote them: "I haven't heard from you now for more than two weeks. I hope you haven't decided not to write me, for I've got worries enough without you turning against me. I've done nothing wrong. I know our trouble—especially without an explanation to you—was hard on you both, but you must accept my assurances that everything will be all right eventually, and not let yourselves get broken up over it. . . . Had a nice letter from Jerry yesterday. . . . I'm hoping she will be able to go to work in a week or two. She said Cheetah missed me so much that she had got sick, and they had to have the veterinary." He got a warm letter back from Dana.

Walker Stone persuaded his friend William E. Leahy, who

headed the Washington draft board, to arrange a special physical examination for Ernie in advance of his being called up for induction—in order to determine whether he would be accepted when his draft number did come up, or whether he would be free to resume the column. Pending this, he put in his time at copyediting.

The desk work did help for a few days, but a letter from Jerry's nurse plunged Ernie into despair again. The nurse said Jerry had seemed to be doing fine but in recent days had been "slipping rapidly." In a day or two Jerry phoned him that she had dismissed the nurse; at the end she broke down and couldn't speak, and he finally had to hang up. He sent five hundred dollars to Earl Mount in Albuquerque and asked him to get the nurse back on the job and to pay her from this fund. He wrote Jerry: "I took my Army physical at Fort Myer yesterday—the final one that puts you right in the Army if you're drafted or enlisting—and goddamned if I didn't pass![1] Everybody was amazed, and it complicated the situation. Now I don't know whether to go to England and join the Army immediately upon my return in the fall, or to join the Army right away. . . . I can't see anything clearly at all and feel absolutely incapable of making a decision. I think mainly I want to go into the Army because I simply can't bear the thought of writing daily columns again, even on a trip to England. . . .

"I'm sorry that you felt so badly Sunday when we talked, and that we had to stop talking. . . . Love to you darling—I hope and hope constantly that you are all right, and getting on top of everything, for yourself and for me. . . ."

Ed Shaffer had been very ill for weeks, and the management thought somebody should go out and get a firsthand report on how both Shafe and the *Albuquerque Tribune* were getting along. Ernie suggested to Deac that I go, since I was a friend of Shafe's, and this was arranged. Before I left Washington Ernie wrote me from Dana, where he had flown for a quick visit: "I'd give my

[1] He was one pound under the minimum weight, but the examiners waived this.

right arm to be going to Albuquerque with you tonight, but I guess all fun is over for the duration. . . . I still am no nearer a decision on myself. But looking at it from a slightly detached viewpoint out here, I'm getting a little chary of going into the Army right away. Deac is leaning toward that now, rather than going to England. What I'd actually like to do, of course, is come out to Albuquerque and loaf (or work at a piddling job) until the draft actually picked me off. But that doubtless would do Jerry more harm than good, by restoring the circumstances whereby she could lean on me instead of herself, so I guess that's out."

I had not seen Jerry in two years, and when I got to Albuquerque it seemed to me that she had aged a decade since 1940. She was haggard, terribly tense, and given to tears—though she tried to put up a front. Ernie had hoped that my visit would do her good, but she was unduly excited when I arrived and seemed to grow more so.

Ernie talked with Earl Mount and me by telephone and decided that at last he must act. He got Po to come to Albuquerque, and with the help of sedatives she and Dr. Connor took Jerry by train to the Woodcroft Sanitarium at Pueblo, Colorado. Ernie wrote Cavanaugh from Washington: "It should have been done long ago, but I never had the heart or the will power over Jerry. The first commitment is for six months. She should stay there a year. Po will return to Albuquerque in a couple of weeks, box up all our 'little things,' then rent the house. . . . As for me, I'm lower than all your gloom periods put together. I abhor the thought of starting to work again, of going to England, of doing anything."

But he made his decision now. He would go to England. The draft board gave him permission to leave for six months, and friends in the Air Forces told him that when he returned in the fall they would get him a commission in Air Intelligence.

A forlorn letter from Jerry pleaded that she be freed from the sanitarium and that they be remarried. Ernie wrote her: "As for our remarriage, darling, that too will have to wait. (This all sounds so cold when I write it). I, like you, would like to do it right now, but I won't. I can sense that what you want above all else is a complete return to status quo. But that failed too many times. The way I feel about it, our marriage is a goal, and not a thing to revert to automatically just because we both want it. . . . When we remarry we have to know that you are your old self again. . . . Whether you believe it or not, you are the only thing in the world that I care for. I've always known that, but I've rediscovered it in this horrible time since I left Albuquerque. . . . I've wanted to die. . . . A dozen times I was on the verge of throwing up everything and fleeing back to Albuquerque. . . . But I'm coming back (permanently I mean) when you are so far along the road of cheerfulness and normal outlook and usefulness to yourself and other people, that there can be no doubt about our future, and not until then. . . ."

The Army telephoned the surprising and welcome word that he was to go by Clipper, from New York to Eire, instead of by ship. He wrote Jerry: "I've been working hard at my 'woodcarving.' . . . Yesterday I mailed you my latest effort—it's a little one of Cheetah, and damned if it doesn't look something like her from certain angles, especially from just a tiny angle off direct front. It's made from that piece of mahogany I got in the Petén jungles. . . . My greatest desire is to be with you, but that can't be, so my love stays here with you. . . ."

From the Algonquin Hotel in New York he wrote her: "Darling—I am taking off within the hour. I came here because I couldn't stand to go to the Piccadilly[2] without you. I am not excited about going, but do feel a last-minute sense of fatalism or something. I am all alone. Be my old Jerry when I come back. I love you."

---

[2] The hotel where they had usually stopped.

CHAPTER 19

The Fringe of the War

IT WAS on June 19, 1942, that Ernie landed at Shannon Airport. There lay ahead half a year of recurrent homesickness and depression and illness before he was to find, in Africa, a tonic that would lift him, for a while, out of his unhappy preoccupation with his personal hell.

From Dublin he wrote Jerry about the trip: "We stayed overnight in Canada in a little town. The liquor stores had closed . . . so a fellow from California and a colonel and myself were walking around town hunting a drink. In a drugstore the other fellow went up to a Canadian lieutenant and asked him where we could get a drink, and he said, 'Down at my house.' So we three went down and spent the evening and had a grand time. We started early next morning and flew all that day and all that night. The actual ocean crossing was wonderful. We had only about four hours of darkness. There was a solid floor of clouds beneath us for eighteen hundred miles—the longest the captain said he had ever seen. They've abandoned their berths, so we slept in our chairs on the floor or on life preservers or wherever we could. A lot of the passengers knew the column, and the Army colonel told our Canadian friends I was the only 'celebrity' on board. I told him the rest must be a sad lot then. . . .

"I went to a little Irish town [Adare] and stayed the first day and night, to get rested up and get my bearings. . . . I was sitting in front of the Inn, and along came a woman with two little Shetland sheepdogs. I couldn't resist introducing myself, and she turned out to be Lady Adare, whose husband owns the whole countryside. But she was nice, and we talked dog awhile. They looked just like Cheetah, only were smaller. Yesterday I hired a car and drove to Limerick, only a short distance, and there took a bus for Dublin. It was a long, tiresome, packed ride—took us seven hours—but we went clear across Ireland, so I got a fine sight of the country. Ireland is beautiful. . . . I think about you so much. I think this is my last trip—unless I take one under Army auspices over which I have no control. I really feel that I can never be successful with the columns again, for my interest is gone. . . ."

In Dublin he bought a book on Irish history, eighteen shillings ninepence worth of lipsticks for presents in England, and, according to his expense account, a "whottle of Irish bisky, seventeen shillings." He explained that "lipsticks are practically extinct in England. It is even quite the thing nowadays for an American to give lipsticks to a man in England as a gift, for he in turn can give them to his girl friends."

To his surprise, the Dubliners were rather solemn. In fact, when he spent half an hour with Eamon De Valera, "I told him I'd seen so few Irishmen laugh that if he didn't tell me a joke or two I was going to feel very sad. He smiled and said he couldn't think of any jokes."

Moving on to Belfast, he wrote me: "The correspondents are all in uniform. I hope I don't have to get one, for it costs a lot, and I'd feel silly in one. . . . I haven't felt really well since leaving home. Takes me about two hours every morning to get the spark of life burning again. Was very depressed in Dublin, but now am starting to throw off a little of my depression." He had planned to pitch in at once with the American Army troops training in Northern Ireland, but they were in the midst of strenuous eight-day maneuvers, "and everybody was too busy to get my kind of copy from them," so, as he wrote Jerry, "I suddenly changed my plans and took the train to Londonderry to write about the new naval base. . . . Had a stroke of luck up there. I was invited to stay at an old house where several Navy and Marine officers stay and have their own mess right there. And it turned out that the Navy doctor staying there was in school when I was.[1] I didn't remember him but he did me, and he couldn't do enough for me. Made me take his own room, which was nicer than the spare room, took me everywhere in his car, and finally loaded me up when I left with two cartons of cigarettes and a bottle of American whisky, a whole carton of Hershey bars, and such assorted stuff as catsup, peanut butter, sandwich spread, cans of nuts, etc. . . . All the other officers were swell too, and made me feel very much at home. There was considerable partying over the Fourth of July weekend, and how I ever got around to doing any work at all I don't know. . . . Last Sunday I went along on a picnic with two busloads of sailors and Marines. We went along the north coast of Ireland, which is very beautiful, up to the famous Giant's Causeway. . . . They had two cases of beer which we drank on the way home, and they sang throughout the whole two-hour drive. I really had a good time. . . . I'll surely hear from some of you in a week or so. . . ."

The sailors, he found at "Derry," were taking drastic measures to keep the colleens from aspiring to dates with officers: "They told the girls that any man wearing gold braid had a contagious disease and should be avoided. And that red stripes on a man's sleeve (a petty officer) meant he was a criminal out on parole."

Expense-account entry: "Celebrating Independence Day, one pound."

He cabled from Belfast that his first copy was on the way to London to be censored and wirelessed home. The column was duly launched in the papers on July 16—just three months after it had been dropped. He wrote me: "You know, Dr. Miller, I've come to a worrisome conclusion about what I'm going to do—I've decided I don't want to be an officer, I don't want to be a private, and I don't want to be a civilian. What do you suggest?"

The next three weeks he devoted to the Army, which was dis-

[1] This was Lieutenant Commander John R. Phillips of Michigan City, Indiana.

persed in driblets throughout Northern Ireland. A jeep (it was being called "peep" in Ireland then) and an Army driver were always at his disposal, and he covered some five hundred miles in his rounds, usually spending his nights in the enlisted men's quarters. He would be in the field four or five days, then return to the Grand Central Hotel in Belfast to write. Many of the soldiers he encountered had known the column back home, which did his morale good. And here and there he would find an old friend. Officers and troops everywhere were hospitable, including Major General Russell P. Hartle, the Army's head man in Northern Ireland.

Ernie wrote the Shaffers: ". . . things are just beginning to open up for me here now. It takes so long to get acquainted and onto the ropes, and then about the time you should be leaving everything seems to unfold like a flower for you. . . . I'm getting interested in things again. . . . I haven't been warm once for a month and have seen the sun only a couple of times. I go around in three sweaters and a trench coat. . . ." He had heard nothing from Jerry—the overseas mail was erratic—except once when I telegraphed her offering to forward a message by cable. She wired me: "Feeling fine. Miss Ernie. Love." And she wrote me: "Distance and time have assumed such unpleasant lengths, I'll be delighted when the columns start. . . ." The regular habits imposed by sanitarium life were restoring her to an even keel, superficially, although the psychiatrists made little progress in penetrating the stubbornness with which she shielded her processes of thought. She was using all her resources of charm and wile to persuade Po, who came occasionally for a visit, to obtain her release.

Ernie was discovering that he and the American soldier were simpático: "I believe I get along better not being in uniform, bunking around with enlisted men as I do. An officer's uniform would scare them and put them on guard, and I couldn't lie around half the night shooting the bull with them. As it is, they seem to feel that I'm just another old broken-down guy from home and sort of a sight for sore eyes."

He told in detail how these troops lived and trained and played —the sort of thing their folks back home wanted to know. He saw St. Patrick's supposed grave at Downpatrick. He drove to Derry to revisit his Navy friends, and "it was almost like getting back home." He talked with a Baptist chaplain, Kenneth Ames of Minnesota, and pulled a boner in the column by writing: "If a wounded Catholic soldier is dying and there is no priest about, Baptist Ames will go ahead and give him the last rites of the Catholic Church." A church paper in Toledo, Ohio, admonished him for such "silly reporting," and used the opportunity to belabor him for his divorce and for what it chose to call his "endless puerilities" and "meager vocabulary." When I forwarded the pertinent part of the complaint to Ernie, he straightened it out in the column with the help of a friendly priest, but the incident made him chary of writing about chaplains.

Ernie at this time had no real expectation that he would become a front-line correspondent. He found the troops eager for action, but of course neither they nor he had any idea when it would come; it was only in this month—July 1942—that the Allies made their decision to invade North Africa, rejecting the American proposal to assault Europe first. He was still supposed to go home after six months.

From Belfast he wrote Jerry in high spirits: "When I went down to lunch here was your letter forwarded from London; my first from you and I'm almost beside myself with delight, for I had given up hope that you were going to write at all. You didn't say a word about yourself so I know you are not happy. But it's been so long since I've seen anybody who is that I guess all normal happiness is out for the duration. . . .

"Right now I'm in the miseries with a good old-fashioned American cold. Started taking it at Derry on Saturday; Dr. Phillips doctored me up with stuff and I came back to Belfast (clear across Northern Ireland) yesterday morning in my Army peep, with no side-curtains or anything. Have stayed in bed since then, except to go down to meals. . . . Was away six days on this last trip. Drove day after day in this open peep in unbelievable downpours, with wind and cold mixed in. . . .

"I am so glad you liked the books, and especially my carving of Cheetah, of which I was immodestly proud. . . . I do hope you can find it within yourself to write me at least once every ten days or so. The world is tough for all of us these days, so do your best to keep going. All my love."

CHAPTER 20

"Pyle Frontwarded"

ERNIE took the overnight boat to England. "I was excited at arriving here," he wrote me from London, "and riding through town from the station was an exhilarating thing, passing old familiar scenes and places, some of them gone now. But for some damn reason I let down afterwards, and today have been in a complete funk. London is cleaned up now, and the streets are jammed, and the place is full of Americans enjoying the war, and the London I knew when it was a close little tense group is gone." He complained of his cold. "The Army wanted to take me to the hospital in Belfast, but I was afraid they would keep me, so I resisted from day to day, and finally got up and about. But I'm still consumed with the damn thing, and my stomach is haywire. . . . Today is my birthday. Just an old broken-down, washed up forty-two-year-old sonovabitch. Wonder if I'll ever be forty-three, and if so why?"

He had gradually come to the conclusion that his cue was to continue indefinitely writing about the troops rather than to return home and enter the Army. "Nobody knows what is going to happen over here, but you can feel something in the air, and I believe it would be unwise to come home in October. The opening of a second front, of course, is anybody's guess. I am making my preparations, just in case, and if any such thing happens, I will go along. Not with the first batch, probably, but follow along after the first few days. . . . At first, of course, there will be facilities and wire space only for the press-association men." If no second front developed, he thought that by autumn the American Air Forces would "surely be in action, and by actually living with them and devoting almost all my time to them, I could become sort of an adopted unofficial biographer for them. They certainly will provide the best reading until a second land front comes. Probably no other person will actually take them on exclusively. In a way I could revive the old aviation column. . . . As for returning and going in the Army—I will of course if the office asks me to because of expense, or because the columns are failing. . . . I believe my field is right here, if I can keep the columns swinging to your satisfaction. I had one little spell of writing where I thought I was getting back into the old channel."

For a week he stayed close to his hotel, the Savoy, nursing the cold and concentrating on his writing. He wrote Cavanaugh: "There was an alert the first night I was here but no shooting. . . . I'm paying eight dollars a day for bed and breakfast, which I consider too much for a farmer. . . . I was among the guests at a big dinner party given the other night by Mr. Quentin Reynolds, at which one of the other guests was Mr. Randolph Churchill, but I don't think he ever knew I was there. . . . I'm getting fixed up so that if they go to France I go along. Ain't you jealous? Probably not. I wish I was settin' in your back yard in the sun. . . . I dropped from $22,000 savings down to $5000 in the past twelve months. . . . As soon as this mess is over, if it ever is, I'll betcha I'm gonna quit this goddam column and settle down to whittling. . . . We here in London know that you in America are giving your all. . . . (Signed) Hyde Park Percy."

He wrote his father and Aunt Mary: "I walked past the other day to look at an old, old restaurant where a friend and I used to eat a couple of times every week when I was here before. I was there the night I got the cable that Mama had passed on. The place is all gone now—it got a direct hit, and there is now nothing but a big hole in the ground. I understand there were no survivors."

And he wrote me: "I'm getting letters from soldiers whose

folks have written them from home, wanting me to come and see them. . . . The Army people are really very fine, I'm having no trouble at all, the censors are reasonable, and so far I haven't the slightest kick against anything." A few days later: "It seems expedient to get my War Department accrediting changed from 'recognized' to 'accredited,' in order that I can go along when there's some action. That means I'll have to get a uniform. . . . Whether it's Africa or here, it looks to me now that I definitely should stay on this side through the winter. Material of my kind is almost limitless, and awfully good reports are coming back (via letters of families to Army and Navy friends) on the column from your side. . . . The big Commando raid [1] has set us all up. . . . I'm quite comfortable, well-fed, and getting interested again."

He wrote Jerry that the figure of Peter Pan, in Kensington Gardens, seemed to him "the loveliest statue in the world." In another letter he told her: "I'm under no illusions that my writing does the country any good, and yet it surely does more good than my running a typewriter in a private's uniform in some camp in Louisiana. . . . I know how tough it is for you [in the sanitarium] but I can only hope and hope that you won't leave too soon. The whole future for both of us depends on how you come out of the hospital, and it's just like getting up too soon after an operation."

He had been in London more than a month, aside from a visit to Glasgow, before he began making excursions into the country. Getting his bearings and various credentials had taken a good many days. He wrote about the changes he had found in London, about the dullness of the food, and a series on the Red Cross hotels, which the Red Cross made into a pamphlet back home. He asked me to apply to his draft board in Washington for a six-month extension of his overseas leave. Since Scripps-Howard had taken the position publicly that none of its employees was indispensable and that exemptions would not be requested, we simply put it up to the draft board to decide whether Ernie would do the country more good as a soldier or as a correspondent. The board promptly

[1] The attack on Dieppe, August 19, 1942.

issued a new six-month leave. It was not long after this that the Army decided to stop drafting men past thirty-eight, which put him in the clear, and me too. My number had been about to come up, and I had put my house in order preparatory to being drafted, which led Ernie to write me: "Far be it from me to tell you how to run your business, but I've seen enough to know it would be foolish for you to go in the Army as a private. . . . I've seen a lot of privates of your and my stripe, and they're going nuts."

He spent a few days at Salisbury with an artillery outfit. Most of the men were from the Tennessee and Carolina hills. "There is a simple genuineness about them that shows in every word they speak," Ernie wrote. "They are courteous, friendly, and trusting— all by instinct. They don't have the city man's smart-aleck ways and suspicious outlook. [They] made me aware once more that a companionship with the earth and the woods breeds something fine in a character; and that sophistication is one of life's lesser virtues."

A disturbing letter came from Sister Margaret Jane, of the hospital in Albuquerque. Jerry had written her "giving way to her pent-up feelings" about being in the sanitarium, and Sister thought now that perhaps Jerry should stay in a full year. This no doubt helped put Ernie in the mood to dispose of a bottle of rye some Derry friends had brought him. He wrote Cavanaugh: "I've had hardly anything at all to drink the last three weeks, and yesterday I felt miserable and blue and couldn't write and a friend and I went out and sat in Hyde Park about half the afternoon. Kept feeling lousier and decided maybe the trouble was a lack of alcohol in my system, so came back to the room, opened the rye, and sat there and killed the whole damn bottle, the two of us, and never even got down to dinner. Sure thought I was gonna die this morning, but boy it felt good. . . . I do practically nothing over here except work. Go to a movie about once a week. Live with the enlisted men when I'm out at the camps. Do most of my eatin' and drinkin' right here at the hotel when I'm in town. Have got very economical with the office's money and ride the buses and undergrounds all the time instead of taking taxis. Am getting most of my stuff back by air-mail now instead of by radio. Know all the Army censors and don't have any trouble along that line. Got to get me a uniform. . . . Already have the caps, and look like a horse's ass in them. . . . (Signed) Richard the Lion-Hearted."

He spent a few days at a camp where enlisted men were being trained for commissions, and tried running their tough obstacle course with them, "but there was something queer about the high wall. For instead of scaling it, I found myself just leaning against it rolling a cigarette." That's the way he wrote it, but men who were there said he put in full days alongside them to get the feel of their strenuous schooling. From a big supply depot he reported: "It is a strange night, here in this American camp. . . . We are in a far country from home. Work is urgent and grave in this camp. The air is chill and damp, and ghostlike sentries walk their posts in the blackout. If there were only bon-fires about we might be a picture from Civil War days. I wander among the tents, picking up new friends here and there. Even in the dark the presence of a stranger draws soldiers as molasses draws flies, for an outsider in camp is a curiosity and anything that breaks the monotony is welcome. . . ."

Back in London, he was astonished to get a cable from Jerry say-ing that she was in Albuquerque, and well and happy. No men-tion of when she had left the sanitarium. She had prevailed on Po to authorize her release, and as the house had been rented was living in a cottage on the grounds of St. Joseph's Hospital.

A laudatory note from Deac Parker arrived at "an opportune time," Ernie wrote me, "for I've been badly in the dumps for about a week. . . . A trickle of mail is coming in from readers; all of it very encouraging."

In spite of his aversion to speechmaking or anything like it, he agreed to an interview with the cartoonist Bruce Bairnsfather, for transcription and subsequent broadcasting to America on the "Stars and Stripes in Britain" program. Bairnsfather was "such a nice guy I couldn't say no." Edward R. Murrow tried to get him to do a weekly program for CBS, but after mulling it over for several days he turned it down. He met General Dwight D. Eisenhower for the first time. The General "seems very nice. Asked me to take a trip with them one of these days."

A letter from Jerry arrived, but also a cable from her asking that he return the letter unopened. "It's a terrible temptation to open your letter," he wrote her, "since news from you and of you is so scant, but you asked me not to so I am returning it unopened. It's been over a month since your last letter." He told her that Gene Warner of the Red Cross, who "is my closest friend here, says they are having great difficulties in Washington finding the right kind of people for these camp and club-hostess jobs. What they want is somebody mature, intelligent, and with good personalities. It had struck me that you would be ideal for such a thing; and more, it would be a kind of job that would consume your time and thoughts, it couldn't get boring, and it is something you could feel was worth while doing. . . .

"Had a nice long letter from Julie Pegler. She said somebody gave him [Westbrook Pegler] two pointer pups for his birthday, and he named them 'Roy W. Howard' and 'Deacon Parker,' and when the one pup makes a noise he yells, 'Shut up, Roy W. Howard.'

"I seem to get along fine with the troops. I almost never hit a new group without finding somebody who read the column back home, so that gives me a good entree. . . . The way it looks now, I don't see how I can return to the States until just about a year from now. If I'm going on with the job I mustn't let the columns lapse again, even for vacation, for a year or more yet. . . . I know you'll have plenty tough going, but I know you can stick through it, and surely something good and fine for us must be there in the future."

Helen Richey, the aviator, took him to Claridge's to see General Jimmy Doolittle, with whom she was to have dinner. Ernie hadn't seen Jimmy in years; also, Jimmy had a bottle of rye. The upshot was a long reminiscing session in his rooms, and they missed dinner entirely. Most of the rye was consumed by Ernie. . . . On a later occasion Ernie visited General Doolittle at a headquarters outside London, and when Ernie got into his jeep to depart, according to his version of it: "Jimmy said, 'I really ought to kiss you good-by, you little So-and-so.' And I'll be damned if the So-and-so didn't."

Ernie was in heavy underwear by this time, but his chilly hotel room was uncomfortable for writing. He was thinking of going to Africa as winter approached, and possibly on to India and China; he had no inkling that Eisenhower was soon to invade Africa. I wrote him to use his own judgment.

In October he went out to see his old friend Ira Eaker, now a major general and head of our Bomber Command, and an Albuquerque friend, Colonel Ed Tracy, chief flight surgeon of Bomber Command. He was a guest at "Bomber Night," a gay monthly dinner with skits and speeches. General Eaker introduced him to the assemblage and beckoned to him. Ernie whispered, "For God's sake, don't ask me to make a speech. I can't talk." So the General announced, "Ernie says he can't talk. I've known him for twenty years, and I fully agree with him." Ernie wrote Jerry about the General: "He looks a little older and very tired around the eyes, but he is carrying an awful burden and working himself to death. I had to laugh at one thing—his aides were informed before I came out that I knew him, but as usual were skeptical I think. Then after we met he was so nice (he hasn't changed a bit in personality) that apparently the aides decided we were old bosom pals. Ira has a terrible cold and they've been trying to get him to take a couple of days' vacation, but he won't do it. So they asked me if I wouldn't tell him he looked tired and ought to rest a couple of days. I said I would but my suggestion would certainly have no weight. Anyway, I did. And a few minutes later he told one of his aides he was going to take two days off and stay in bed. . . . Ira said he and Ruth had talked about us a lot and were shocked at the news they saw about us. I told him that our feelings had not changed."

A letter from George Carlin reported that only about forty-five papers were running the column, and Ernie wrote Jerry: "Every new arrival over here reports that the column is just what the people want to know and nobody else is doing it, but it's the old story of not being able to get it past the editors. So to hell with it. I'll write as long as there seems to be any point in it, and after that I can go in the Army. . . ."

Ernie spent much of October visiting Army Air Force installations; getting acquainted, for instance, with his "favorite bomber crew"—the "House of Jackson." And now the word was passed to him that a military operation was impending; he agreed to go along. The direction and dimensions of the operation were secret, but I believe he was given some hint of the African project. "I'm thinking of moving from here," he wrote Jerry on October 23, "so you better wire Lee and ask him where to write me, as I'll let him know by cable. . . ." Three days earlier General Mark Clark had landed in North Africa from a submarine for parleys with pro-invasion French leaders.

Overseas mail was getting short shrift now, for the convoys to Africa were absorbing the ships. "I've still had no letters from you," Ernie wrote Jerry. "In fact nobody has had any from anybody lately. . . . I'm sort of marking time, doing some rather dull columns on rationing and fuel control and utility clothes. . . . Tonight Paul Manning of NEA Service and I are giving a 'combined operation' in the form of a little dinner for the American Division of the Ministry of Information, with a couple of Army officers thrown in. Paul has a nice apartment, we've used both our ration books to get enough food, and we and the guests will have to do the cooking. . . . It may be that you won't hear from me for quite a while, but don't be worried if you don't. Actually I don't know myself at the moment just what my plans are. . . . I suppose that you and our house and the big country out there occupy my mind fifty per cent of the time, and yet it all seems to be growing far far away, almost out of my grasp. I wonder if I will ever be a part of it again. Yearning for it has become almost a phobia with me. Nothing else is able to interest me. How I wish I could hear from you just once before I leave London. . . ."

A letter did come, the next day. "I am so elated," he replied. "Your letter was so good. It sounded alive and like you used to be. . . ." There were two more letters, and he wrote: "I've had three letters from you within a week and am practically beside myself with delight. I supposed all the time you were getting my letters but just weren't writing yourself. . . . Your remarks about the column were the first kind words I've heard about it in months, with the exception of a few strangers who arrive over here from the States and say everybody is reading it. . . . Your feeling that it's as good as you say, I think, must be due to the fact that you love me and are blind! Of course I'm pleased at your saying it, for I still want you to think everything I do is wonderful. But, truthfully, my one desire in life—next to being with you —is to put that column behind me forever. All this terrible business of the past year has been hard on me too, darling. . . . One thing I never took into account at the time was what it might do to me. I don't know why I never thought of that; too busy thinking about other things, I guess. But it has made my life a mental and spiritual bottomless pit. . . . We sort of seem to have traded positions. I'm sorry to have lost my regard for what other people think, for I think it is in a way a good balance, but I have. Now you care for their opinions, and I don't. I guess it's a defense mechanism probably, for I know that in our little thing most people think badly of me, and in order not to be hurt by it, I've just had to stop caring. . . . I only hope I won't disappoint you. As Sister says, I know I can be proud of you, but I'm not sure it will work both ways. . . ."

The first of a long procession of Ernie's friends to lose their lives in the war, Byron Darnton of the *New York Times,* was killed off New Guinea when an American plane attacked an American boat, through a liaison error.

He sent me a suggested editorial expressing concern over the "blabber-mouthing going on at home against England": "Such things as poking our noses into the India pie before we've won any battles. Such stuff as shouting that England is fighting only to retain her big-business empire. Such ignorant accusations as that she's sitting back and letting us pull her chestnuts out of the fire. When we raise issues like that, we are acting like madmen, for by that method we can create suspicion, distrust, and dislike for us in the minds of the best friends we've got. . . ."

The censor's stamp on that piece bore the date November 7. The next morning the invasion of Africa began.

On November 9 Ernie wrote to Jerry: " . . . Goodness knows when your next letters will get to me. But Lee will let you know where to write, and please, darling, keep on sending them, because they mean everything to me. . . ." That night he left London. Gwyn Barker, his best friend in the American section of the British Ministry of Information, reported to me: "I did have the fun of seeing Ernie off. Went round to dinner at his apartment, where were also Dick Hollander, Gene Warner, and Paul Manning. After dinner, with the door wide open, Ernie leapt into what he feared might be his last bath in months, carrying on a long conversation with us the while. He emerged, pink and shining and dressed in his military uniform, looking terribly attractive but very shy. There followed a fearful business of packing his stuff into the few bags allowed, distributing amongst ourselves the leftovers. Then we set off, a little sadly by this time, in a cab to the U. S. Army Headquarters, and at the door, in the black of London blackout, we left your little Ernie to set out on his big adventure."

The United Press advised me laconically from London: "Pyle frontwarded."

CHAPTER 21

Bad Dream in Africa

A N ARMY car took Ernie and other correspondents to a
suburban station, and an all-night train delivered them
to the big British transport *Rangitiki* at Newport Haven,
Wales. He "felt a little kinship" for the vessel, since he had
crossed her path at Panama in 1940. His cabinmates were Will
Lang, of *Time* and *Life*, and two censors, Lieutenants Henry
Meyer and Cortland I. Gillett. The others of the press were A. J.
Liebling, of *The New Yorker*; Gault MacGowan, of the *New
York Sun*; Merrill Mueller, better known as "Red," then of *Newsweek*; Ollie Stewart, of the *Baltimore Afro-American*, and Ser-
geant Bob Neville, of *Yank* and *Stars and Stripes*.

This is as good a place as any to confess that I deleted from a
Pyle column a handsome reference to Liebling wherein Ernie
wistfully avowed an inability to write as well as the magazine
man. It happened that Liebling had written for *The New Yorker*,
not long before, a caustic and one-sided series of articles about
Roy Howard. For Ernie to single him out for a puff might have
struck Howard as a gratuitous needling, and this I was sure Ernie
did not intend. As for Ernie's modest judgment of his own pen in
comparison with Liebling's, one book reviewer presently mentioned Liebling as "*The New Yorker*'s own Ernie Pyle."

Ernie was on his way to war, but almost as a tourist, a dilet-
tante. He still meant to take a look at Africa and then fly on to
the Far East. Certainly he had no thought of becoming a Boswell to the infantry.

217

The *Rangitiki*, after two days of loading troops, put to sea, tested her guns, then moved with seeming aimlessness for a day or two until she was fitted into her station in a convoy heavily escorted by British warships. By this time Ernie had come down with "one of the Ten Best Colds of 1942," which kept him abed for several days. Aside from that, and a false torpedo alarm, and a warning that fifty U-boats lay athwart the approaches to Gibraltar—"we all felt it was actually miraculous that we got through the way we did"—it was an agreeable voyage, especially after the convoy zigzagged out of British rains into calm sunshine. Sometimes he ate with the troops, crowded uncomfortably below. But "those of us in the cabins were awakened at seven every morning by the cabin steward, bearing cups of hot tea," and in the officers' mess "the headwaiter wore a tuxedo at dinner-time." There was even mixed company, for Army nurses were aboard, most of them with the Roosevelt Hospital unit from New York City.

Just two weeks after the invasion of Africa—the fighting by now had moved far to the east—the *Rangitiki* arrived at Mers-el-Kebir in Algeria. Down the gangplank to a long concrete quay went Ernie, lugging a barracks bag, bedroll, musette bag, gas mask, helmet, canteen, and typewriter. Gault MacGowan remembered him as looking "wan and miserable," and he was still self-conscious in his uniform with its "C"—for correspondent— armband. It was several miles to Oran, and no transportation was provided. While others shouldered their impedimenta and trudged toward the city, Ernie, waiting irresolutely among his gear, was offered a lift in a captured French car by a soldier—Sergeant Chuck Conick of Pittsburgh—who deposited him at II Corps headquarters in the Grand Hotel.

Ernie settled down at the Grand, wrote a series about the sea trip, and then devoted himself to talking with, and writing about, the troops who had made the original landings and the hospital outfits that had taken care of the wounded. "These first cable columns are confused and inadequate," he wrote me, but to us at home they were exciting.

Ernie's room was shared for a while with Joe Liebling, who has written in *Esquire:* "We had a double bed and an Army cot in the room. Most of the officers and correspondents slept two in a bed, reserving the cot for an overnight visitor from the field. Ernie, although he was ill, insisted on sleeping on the cot and leaving the whole bed to me because I was big and fat. One time Lowell Bennett, a youngster working for INS, came back from the young front in Tunisia and stopped over at Oran on his way out. . . . Bennett was gloomy about what he had seen at the front. Ernie, after listening to Bennett, thought maybe the whole expedition was a mistake. He said to me: 'Fellows like Bill Lang and you, who have roots in Europe, can work up a real hate about this thing, but I can't. When you figure how many boys are going to get killed, what's the use of it anyway?' War for him meant not adventure, as for Bob Casey, a crusade, as for Bill Stoneman, an enthrallment, as it did for Hemingway, or a chance to be a prima donna or get away from the sports department, as for a number of other fellows. He treated it as unalleviated misfortune."

Ernie wrote Jerry that the past year was one "I wish I could have omitted from my life. . . . You'd laugh if you could see my room. . . . When I'm out around the camps, I tell the people I know best to come and use my room and get themselves a bath at the public bath on this floor whenever they're in town. And today, all within a period of ten minutes, people from four different camps arrived to take baths—a colonel and a captain from one field hospital, a colonel and a captain from another one miles in the opposite direction, a private from Syracuse, N.Y., and two fighter pilots. My room began to look like Saratoga Springs. . . ."

His state of mind and heart continued bleak. On Thanksgiving Day he wrote Jerry: "I wish we could do by proxy what we've both thought about. If I only knew how you felt and what your wishes were I'd try to see if it could not be done. It wouldn't bring me home any quicker, but somehow I know I'd feel happier about things." This idea of a remarriage in absentia became increasingly engrossing, and he sought out Colonel Damon M. Gunn, Judge Advocate General of II Corps, who drew up a legal instrument appointing Ed Shaffer to serve as Ernie's proxy in a wedding ceremony. The document stipulated: "This power of attorney shall become effective . . . upon its delivery to [Shaffer] by Sister Margaret Jane, Mother Superior of St. Joseph's Hospital, Albuquerque, N. M., with whom the same shall be placed in escrow and whom I expressly authorize to determine in her discretion when this power shall be exercised." Ernie sent it off to Sister Margaret Jane, asking her to present his "proposal" as soon as Jerry's condition and attitude seemed to warrant the step.

Most of the correspondents in Africa at this time were basing at Algiers, where Eisenhower had his headquarters. Some of them had tried to send dispatches revealing the extent to which pro-Nazi Frenchmen in Africa were being permitted to retain responsible offices. The censors refused to pass such copy. One night when Ernie was dining at Oran with some friends in the Counter-Intelligence Corps they told him at length of the frustrating position in which they found themselves. It was their function to combat collaborationism, but their instructions limited them to action against Germans and Italians; a Frenchman could be arrested only by the French police, who were less than aggressive in these matters. Perhaps if Ernie were to expose the situation, it was suggested, things might improve. Ernie did, in a couple of political columns that created a sensation in America.

Possibly because the censors were used to regarding the Pyle copy as non-political, these were cleared without challenge. Washington was so startled that the War Department telephoned Scripps-Howard suspiciously to ask if the copy had passed censorship. "We have left in office," Ernie wrote, "most of the small-fry officials put there by the Germans before we came. We are permitting fascist societies to continue to exist. Actual sniping has been stopped, but there is still sabotage. The loyal French see this and wonder what manner of people we are. . . . Our enemies see it, laugh, and call us soft. . . . Our fundamental policy still is one of soft-gloving snakes in our midst." This was widely quoted. Raymond Clapper commented: "We have had practically nothing worth reading out of there on this funny business except Ernie Pyle's two highly informative and eye-opening dispatches. How they got through is a mystery. Somebody must have been napping, because nobody else has got it out."

With two lieutenants, Leonard Bessman and Max Kuehnert, Ernie visited the French Foreign Legion headquarters at Sidi-bel-Abbès, which yielded colorful copy. He was rebuilding his back-log, turning out thirty columns in two weeks, for he wanted some leeway when he headed east to Algiers and the front.

An attack of influenza put him in bed, where trays were brought him from an Army mess. Hal Boyle of the Associated Press recalled: "The first time I saw him he was lying in a big double bed in the cold and drafty Grand Hotel in Oran, mopping his nose and gently cursing all the people who had reported that Africa was a warm country. He wasn't famous then. He wanted a handkerchief more than he did anything east or west of the Suez Canal, and when I gave him two he was as grateful as if I had handed him the mortgage on a gold mine."

Once Ernie dreamed that Jerry had married someone else. The dream was so vivid, he wrote her, "that for days I couldn't believe you hadn't. It was horrible."

On Christmas Eve he sat up in bed, with his portable in his lap, and wrote Jerry: "This is our third straight Christmas apart. And I hate it. . . . I'm desperate to learn how you are. . . . I've had only one drink of whisky in seven weeks; a nurse gave me a swig out of her flask at one of the tent hospitals. . . . I actually don't miss it at all. Now if I were just to quit smoking, cussing, and thinking critical thoughts about my fellowmen, I'd be so god-damned pure I'd hurt. . . . If it's true that people's ears burn when somebody is thinking about them, then you and Cheetah must be burned to a crisp."

He said nothing to her about the proxy. By cable he asked me to send her his love and request a message from her. She wired me that she was "going to work soon" and that "I think of him constantly and send him all my love." That was his first word from her in two months.

Mastering the flu, he cleaned up odds and ends of columns and wrote me that he thought he would go to the front shortly and stay there "long enough to produce maybe a month's copy. Then I'm wondering if it might not be wise for me to start a two-or three-months trip on out to India and China. I sense a long lull and period of preparation coming up here, with not a great deal new to write about. I might get such a trip under my belt and be back for the works here, if any."

The initial successes of the invasion of Africa had petered into stalemate when the Germans, reacting with efficient speed, threw enough force into Tunisia to prevent Eisenhower's vanguard from racing on to Tunis and Bizerte. It was now a matter of waiting until the Allies could bring in men and weapons for a big push. Meantime the air forces of both sides were active, day and night.

From Oran, Ernie flew to Algiers, and then, in a C-47 with Spitfire escort, he went on two hundred miles to the southeast, to a desert airdrome called "the Garden of Allah," at Biskra, an oasis in the Algerian desert from which our heavy bombers were plastering Tunisia.

CHAPTER 22

The Infantry

W HEN Ernie stepped from the airplane at Biskra, in early
January of 1943, he was putting his foot on the thresh-
old of the great fame which was to envelop him. He
already had a considerable following. Some sixty newspapers were
printing the column, and thousands of soldiers were receiving
clippings of it from back home. His gift of friendliness made him
welcome anywhere. But he was not happy. His mind dwelt on
home. He was forty-two, a frail-looking ghost of a man, haggard
from recurrent illness and the tragedy of Jerry.

The soldier life he had seen heretofore had been that of the
garrisons and training areas. The perils he had experienced in London had had an impersonal quality quite unlike the intimacy of
German aircraft roaring down upon an open field or road. Now he
was to see, and live, war in the raw.

He had been at the Garden of Allah scarcely three hours when
German planes bombed the airdrome and he learned how hospitable a slit trench could be. And it was not long before he saw
the dead pilot of a returning Fortress handed by his comrades,
head downward, from his plane. He found that officers did not
have to nag their men into digging trenches deep enough or pre-
serving a perfect blackout.

Still, Biskra was not really rugged, for a reporter. While the airmen lived in tents, Ernie wrote Jerry that "I have a nice room in
a desert hotel with a little balcony where I sit in the sun." The
nights were cold, and there was no hot water, but the days were

bright and the remnants of his flu dissolved. The purple mountains of the Saharan Atlas range recalled the Sandias outside Albuquerque. "I dreamed about you last night, as I often do," the letter to Jerry said. "I dreamed that Piper had come to life. Isn't that a silly one. . . ."

The change to sunny weather, and the stimulating contact with bomber crews living at close grips with sudden death, began to lift him out of himself. The column came more easily. There was a particularly notable piece of writing about a bomber, the *Thunderbird,* that was overdue from a raid on Tripoli and was about to be written off as missing: "And then an electric thing happened. Far off in the dusk a red flare shot into the sky. It made an arc against the dark background of the mountains and fell to the earth. . . . Then we saw the plane—just a tiny black speck. It seemed almost on the ground, it was so low, and in the first glance we could sense that it was barely moving, barely staying in the air. Crippled and alone, two hours behind all the rest, it was dragging itself home. I am a layman, and no longer of the fraternity that flies, but I can feel. And at that moment I felt something close to human love for that faithful, battered machine, that far dark speck struggling toward us with such pathetic slowness. All of us stood tense, hardly remembering anyone else was there. With our nervous systems we seemed to pull the plane toward us. I suspect a photograph would have shown us all leaning slightly to the left. Not one of us thought the plane would ever make the field, but on it came—so slowly that it was cruel to watch. It reached the far end of the airdrome, still holding its pathetic little altitude. It skimmed over the tops of parked planes, and kept on, actually reaching out—it seemed to us—for the runway. . . . The wheels touched softly. And as the plane rolled down the runway the thousands of men around that vast field suddenly realized that they were weak and that they could hear their hearts pounding. . . ." The *Thunderbird,* its two port engines put out of action by flak, had shot down six Nazi fighters, fought off others, and staggered home across the mountains with a picayune twenty gallons of gasoline to spare.

Ernie accompanied a salvage party on a dusty drive of two hundred miles in open trucks across the desert, within twenty miles of German outposts, to recover parts from crash-landed airplanes. They saw mirages, and fraternized with lonely French garrisons, and Ernie helped dig slit trenches while the salvaging proceeded. A soldier said to him, "Five years ago you couldn't a got me to dig a ditch for five dollars an hour. Now look at me. You can't stop me digging ditches. I don't even want pay for it. I just dig for love. Any time I get fifty feet from my home ditch you'll find me digging a new ditch, and brother, I ain't joking. I love to dig ditches."

Copy about the adventures of the Fortress crews was abundant at Biskra. And he visited a fighter base to write about the P-38 pilots who were escorting the heavies: "It's interesting to sit in with a bunch of pilots in the evening after they've returned from their first mission. They're so excited they are practically unintelligible. Their eyes are bloodshot. They are red-faced with excitement. They are so terrifically stimulated they can't quiet down. Life has never been more wonderful."

In a few weeks it was time for a change of pace, from air to infantry. Tanned and in unaccustomed good health, Ernie left the Garden of Allah and made his way, for the first time, to mountainous Tunisia, to the town of Gafsa. He wrote Jerry: "I'm back where the goddam weather is no better than England's—dark, wet, cold, and disgusting. I have had my first bath in five weeks!" At Biskra, he explained, he had had "every comfort—good beds, good food—everything except hot water. And I simply can't take a cold bath."

It was plain that the excitements of life so near the front had worked a change in his outlook. Only recently he had written me that he still thought "it might be smart to go to India." Now he said: "I've temporarily abandoned the idea of starting to India in favor of staying on here until whatever happens is over." Africa was agreeing with him: "Outside of my horror of cold, I was never better physically in my life, I guess. I eat like an animal and have gained a little weight. I don't often have those tight feelings in the back of my head any more: I still get spells of being nervous, but not too bad. Actually I think the fresh air and the lack of drinking have been very good for me. I must admit that my new Christian purity isn't due to any spurt of will power on my part; it's due solely to an almost total absence of drinkin' likker in these parts."

He hurried on from Gafsa to Tebessa and checked in at the nearby headquarters of General Lloyd R. Fredendall's II Corps, situated in a muddy, wooded ravine called "Speedy Valley." The press was lodged at Tebessa in a four-room mud house, heatless except for a smudgy blaze in a corner fireplace, which also feebly supplemented the candlelight illumination. These dubious comforts he quit for a pup tent at Corps, where the danger of bombing was so acute that it was forbidden to expose white laundry, and elaborate caves were being blasted into the side of the gully (to General Eisenhower's disdain when he saw them). It was wet and cold, but the mess tent was warmed by a stove, and Ernie often stayed on there after supper and chatted with Fredendall.

Transportation was scarce—everything was scarce—but Captain Ed Atkins, Corps headquarters commandant, wangled a jeep for him. Into it, each time Ernie made a trip, he loaded a heavy canvas bedroll stuffed with blankets and a pup tent, and tucked around it his musette bag, gas mask, helmet, canteen, shovel, and a dispatch case containing writing material. He wore coveralls, a long-billed cap, a soldier's mackinaw, and overshoes. He usually had a few cans of rations and plenty of Bull Durham. Ready-made cigarettes were uncommon at the front, except for obscure and unpopular brands, the better-known ones seldom getting farther forward than Algiers.

He got to be a familiar figure at command posts all along the front. Officers and men were glad to see him again; not just because he might be writing about their outfits, but because they liked him. And it worked both ways. Ernie's love affair with GI Joe was beginning. Here in Tunisia he got his first and indelible knowledge of the doughfoot's lot—the cold, the fear, the loneliness, the dreary sameness—and of the fortitude with which those burdens, unimaginable at home, were borne. He devoted himself wholeheartedly to an effort to convey to the people in America— many of whom persisted in picturing their sons as lolling in a lush tropic land—the truth of this ugly imitation of life. He confessed much later in a letter to General Eisenhower that this self-appointed task was impossible of real fulfillment, for nobody could visualize the soldier's life without experiencing it. But those who read the column got closer to the facts of war than they would have without him.

Soldiers who are a long time and distance from home get a feeling that they are forgotten and that the wretched life they lead is unappreciated. A visiting reporter is a token that they are still remembered. And in Ernie's very special case, when the clippings came back in the mail and the doughs read what he had written about themselves or men like them, they saw they had a champion. "My men always fought better when Ernie was around," General Omar N. Bradley was to tell Aunt Mary later on.

This was the sort of thing the soldiers liked to have their people read: "You can scarcely credit the fact that human beings—the same people you've known all your life—could adjust themselves so acceptingly to a type of living that is only slightly above the caveman stage. . . . They have not slept in a bed for months. They've lived through this vicious winter sleeping outdoors on the ground. They haven't been paid in three months. They have been on British rations most of the time, and British rations, though good, get mighty tiresome. They never take off their clothes at night, except their shoes. They don't get a bath oftener than once a month. . . . Very few of the front-line troops have ever had any leave. . . . I have just been with one artillery outfit in the mountains who were getting only one cold meal a day. Nurses tell me that when the more seriously wounded reach the hospital they are often so exhausted they fall asleep without drugs, despite their pain. . . .

"The discomfort is perpetual. You're always cold and almost always dirty. Outside of food and cigarettes you have absolutely none of the little things that made life normal back home. You don't have chairs, lights, floors, or tables. You don't have any place to set anything, or any store to buy things from. There are no newspapers, milk, beds, sheets, radiators, beer, ice cream, or hot water. You just sort of exist, either standing up working or lying down asleep. There is no pleasant in-between. The velvet is all gone from living. . . .

"Soldiers ask me for Heaven's sake to get over to the folks at home that Africa in winter is frigid. . . . The other day, along the road, I ran into a soldier in a half-track who had a kerosene stove—the old-fashioned kind they used to heat the school with, you know. I offered him fifty dollars for it—back home it would be worth about three. He didn't hesitate a second. He just said, 'No, sir,' and that was the end of that. It would have been just the same if I'd offered him five hundred. . . .

"You become eminently practical in wartime. A chaplain who recently went through the pockets of ten Americans killed in battle said the dominant thing he found was toilet paper. Careless soldiers who were caught without such preparedness have had to use twenty-franc notes. . . .

"Certainly there are great tragedies, unbelievable heroics, even a constant undertone of comedy. It is the job of us writers to transfer all that drama back to you folks at home. Most of the other correspondents have the ability to do it. But when I sit down to write, here is what I see instead: Men at the front suffering and wishing they were somewhere else, men in routine jobs just behind the lines bellyaching because they can't get to the front, all of them desperately hungry for somebody to talk to besides themselves, no women to be heroes in front of, damn little wine to drink, precious little song, cold and fairly dirty, just toiling from day to day in a world full of insecurity, discomfort, homesickness, and a dulled sense of danger. . . ."

His new way of life was described in a letter to Jerry: "Everything seems to get away from you when you're at the front. Time has no meaning; you never know what day it is, sometimes you can't even guess the date within a week. . . . You get so interested and become so much a part of the constantly changing war machine at the front, that you resent ever taking time off to be a newspaperman and do any writing. . . .

"My Army bedroll has three blankets under me and three over me. In addition I pile on my mackinaw and all the stuff I can find on top, and sleep with my clothes on. Everybody does. I shave and wash my feet about once a week in my steel helmet. Otherwise we never wash at all. I've slept in chicken houses, under wagons, in cactus patches, among fir trees on mountainsides, and in old vacant buildings on stone floors. Sometimes I'd put up my little tent if the wind was too bad; other times I'd just throw my bedroll on the ground and crawl in with no roof above but the stars. If anybody had ever told me I could stand to sleep right out on the ground and wake up with snow on my bedroll I'd have called him nuts; but I have, and you find you can stand almost anything. It snows some and rains some and blows a lot and gets down below freezing. It wouldn't be bad if you could ever get warm, but there's no heat anywhere so it's like living out in our backyard in Albuquerque all winter without any heat. . . .

"Being so constantly out in the cold and driving so much in an open jeep has given me a wind-burn like I've never had before in my life. My hair is completely white on the sides, and against my brown face it makes a funny sight. Once I worked back into an Army headquarters back of the lines where I know all the officers, and they set me up an 'igloo' tent to live in for a few days. I begged a couple of boxes from the supply sergeant, sat on one and put the typewriter on the other, and wrote for about three days. But it was bitter cold, my tent had no heat, I had to keep the flap open and sit in the tent door to get light, and my fingers would get so cold they were stiff, as was my mind also. . . .

"Army friends have given me various important little things such as this private jeep, extra cigarettes, stocks of canned rations, and one general gave me a brand-new combat suit, which is wonderfully warm and almost impossible to get. . . . We always wear tinted goggles when driving—the old-fashioned race-track kind—you have to wear them, for at the front we have to put the windshield down and cover it, so it won't glare in the sun, and hence driving is terribly cold and windy." That Armored Corps combat suit, which he wore throughout the campaign, was given him by General Fredendall.

Of the seventy-odd correspondents in North Africa, usually not more than half a dozen to two dozen were in Tunisia at one time. The majority were in Algiers. Most of them, for one thing, were obliged to write "the big picture," and accordingly had to be in touch with headquarters for the briefings and communiqués. But Ernie was footloose. And for years he had been used to working on his own rather than with others of the press. He broke himself of that to some extent, however, because of the danger of driving alone in a jeep with no passenger to watch for Stukas.

In those first few weeks he got to know every general in Tunisia, but spent most of his time with lesser officers and with enlisted men. An occasional letter or cable drifting down from Algiers made it plain that the column was going like a house afire. Malcolm W. Bingay wrote in the *Detroit Free Press* that Ernie was "doing the best job of war correspondence that has come out of this conflict." *Newsweek* led off a glowing article about him with: "Covering the war in North Africa are many score correspondents—and Ernie Pyle." New papers were subscribing to the column. Jerry was apparently doing well and preparing to go to work. Ernie's world, so dismal a few weeks before, was bursting out of the mists of confusion and indecision. (I refrained from telling him that the head of NEA Service had asked that Ernie be brought home so that NEA could send a sketch-artist to Africa in his stead, Eisenhower having barred new correspondents except as replacements. The proposal got short shrift.)

Ernie did have one grievous setback in this period. A letter from Sister Margaret Jane at Albuquerque told him that she had brought up with Jerry the question of a proxy remarriage and Jerry had declined, at least for the moment. "It was the first news I'd had from Albuquerque for so long," he wrote Jerry, "and I'd hoped all along that maybe the deed had been done. It was just dusk when I got the letter, and I sat on a stump all bundled up against the cold, and read it. I was so disappointed I almost felt like crying."

One cold night he drove across half of Tunisia in a great convoy of blacked-out vehicles—over switchback mountain roads, through silent Arab villages, and on by daylight across treeless plains where strafing Stukas occasionally sent everyone scrambling for the fields. "You learn to hate absolutely flat country where there are no ditches to jump into or humps to hide behind." He climbed to a little hillside command post within half a mile of the fighting for Ousseltia Pass, and recorded the grim flow of information about tactical movements and casualties: "One of the dead men apparently had been a special favorite. An officer who had been beside him when it happened came up with blood on his clothes. 'We hit the ground together,' he said. 'But when I got up, he couldn't. It took him right in the head. He felt no pain.' 'Raise up that tent and pack his stuff,' an officer told an enlisted man. Another one said, 'The hell of it is, his wife's due to have a baby any time now.'"

A bomber group he had known in England invited him to go along on a hazardous mission to Bizerte: "I knew the day of that invitation would come, and I dreaded it. Not to go brands you as a coward. To go might make you a slight hero, or a dead duck. Actually I never knew what I'd say until the moment came. When it did come, I said this: 'No, I don't see any sense in me going. Other correspondents have already gone, so I couldn't be the first anyhow. I'd be in the way, and if I got killed my death would have contributed nothing. I'm running chances just being here, without sticking my neck out and asking for it. No, I think I won't go. I'm too old to be a hero.' The reaction of the fliers astounded me. I expected them to be politely contemptuous . . . but their attitude was exactly the opposite. . . . 'Anybody who goes, when he doesn't have to, is a plain damn fool,' one of them said."

Ernie "never seemed to be trying 'to get a story,' " according to Lieutenant Colonel Horace Miner. "When you saw him, you chewed over old times, friends, and recent events. When this banter contained something Ernie could use, he would write it. He never tried to guide the conversation into channels which would be useful to him. I recall a night in Tebessa [in the house where the press was quartered]. It was cold as the devil. A lot of reporters were in other rooms writing stories. We were talking about some experiences around Gafsa. Ernie was just a little fellow who sat huddled at the side of the room and finally collapsed into his blankets and sleep. But it was a story for him."

CHAPTER 23

Retreat

ERNIE cabled that he was planning to go west for a breather in Morocco. But General Erwin Rommel, the Desert Fox, intervened.

It was on St. Valentine's Day of 1943 that German armor and infantry, secretly accumulated beyond Faïd Pass, came storming through the mountains and onto the plain with stunning surprise. American artillery positions near Sidi-bou-Zid were quickly overrun, two battalions of the 34th Division were cut off, and Sbeitla was in danger. The real objective appeared to be our supply base and corps headquarters at Tebessa, to the west beyond Sbeitla and Kasserine Pass.

Only a few days before this Ernie had left the command post of the 1st Armored Division, in a cactus patch outside Sbeitla, and had gone north to Maktar, above the Ousseltia Valley, where much of the division's strength was misguidedly concentrated. Now, in the teeth of the ominous news, he drove back to Sbeitla. "Without reporting in or anything, I just picked out a little open spot among the bushes, got out my shovel and started digging a hole to sink my pup tent into. I had the hole about four inches deep and only half long enough when I heard a shout, 'Here they come!' . . . Dive-bombers had come out of the sun and were on us almost before we knew it. My hole in the sand was still not large enough to harbor a man even as slight as myself. But, I assure you, its inadequacy did not deter me from diving into it."

An incident of that day was described by Noland Norgaard of

233

the Associated Press, who had driven up in a jeep with Graham Hovey, of International News Service: "Hovey had just come to Tunisia and had never seen or heard a shot fired in anger. We had left the command post and driven back onto the highway en route forward to get a look at the battle when some Stukas came over. We piled out of our jeep and got into some holes just before one of the planes dive-bombed the road. The bomb hit squarely on a jeep ahead of ours. The jeep and the three soldiers in it were blown to bits and our own jeep was riddled. After looking over the scene, trying to get our knees steadied, we ran onto Ernie. He walked back with us to the scene of the bombing, and it was then I began to get some idea of the strong personal feeling the 'little guy' had for the men and boys who did the fighting. We walked around picking up bits of paper in hopes of getting the identity of the three men, carefully trying to avoid the occasional fragments of flesh. There was nothing maudlin in Ernie's sympathy. He was rather silent and listened closely to Hovey's comments. That was the beginning of a close friendship between them. We walked to Ernie's pup tent in the cactus. He had already learned more about living in the field than many soldiers know yet. He was carefully and neatly dug in, so that his home was also his foxhole. I'm sure it was the neatest and cleanest nest in the camp. Then, with typical generosity, he lent us his jeep to get back to Tebessa. We got it back to him the next day, in time for him to participate in the retreat."

Next morning Ernie was up before dawn and caught a ride to a new forward command post of the 1st Armored, in another cactus patch on the way to Sidi-bou-Zid. Officers and enlisted men that he knew poured out to him the stories of their escape from the sudden onrush the day before. "The minute a man would start talking he'd begin drawing lines on the ground, with his shoe or a stick, to show the roads and how he came. I'll bet I had that battleground scratched in the sand for me fifty times." Then "one by one the men in the cactus patch stretched on the ground and fell wearily asleep at midday." He lay down and slept too.

Our armor was to counterattack that afternoon, and a general told Ernie with mistaken optimism that "we are going to kick hell out of them." A lieutenant took Ernie up to see the fight. They drove out among the waiting tanks and other vehicles, thousands of them spread over miles, awaiting the order to advance. Each tank's crew was "at its post inside—the driver at his controls, the commander standing with his head sticking out of the open turret door, standing there silent and motionless, just looking ahead like the Indian on the calendars. . . . Somehow it seemed like the cars lined up at Indianapolis just before the race starts—their weeks of training over, everything mechanically perfect, just a few minutes of immobility before the great struggle for which they had waited so long. Suddenly out of this siesta-like doze the order came. . . . They started off, kicking up dust and clanking in that peculiar 'tank sound' we have all come to know so well. They poured around us, charging forward. . . . The battle was on."

In a gully they found a colonel beside a radio vehicle. "We stood close enough to the radio to hear the voice of the battalion commander who was leading the tank attack. At the same time, through binoculars, we watched the fantastic surge of caterpillar metal move forward amidst its own dust. Far across the desert, in front of us, lay the town of Sidi-bou-Zid. . . . Over the radio came the voice of the battalion commander: 'We're in the edge of Sidi-bou-Zid and have struck no opposition yet.' . . . Suddenly brown geysers of earth and smoke began to spout. . . . Again the voice from the radio: 'We're getting shelled but can't make out where it's coming from.'" Then, through the glasses, Ernie could see the dust plumes of German tanks advancing to the attack, and he said to the lieutenant, "Let's get on up there."

They drove across sandy plains and fields of grain, past Arabs herding their camels and even plowing, past burned-out tanks from the battle that had covered this same area the day before until the enemy fell back to prepare a further thrust. They finally stopped about a mile behind the foremost tanks. Dive-bombers came over, and since there was no ditch anywhere "I psychopathically lay down behind an old dead bush about twelve inches high." Enemy shells dropped within two hundred yards. "German tanks had maneuvered in behind us, and were shooting up our half-tracks and jeeps. But, fortunately, we didn't know all this at the time." After watching for a while, unable to assess the fortunes of the sprawling melee, they drove back to the rear. Next evening Ernie returned to the main division command post outside Sbeitla, pitched his pup tent in the hole he had dug two nights before, and hit the sack.

At one a.m. a soldier awakened him and told him to pack his jeep. Ten minutes later the soldier returned and "said just five words: 'German tanks are in Sbeitla.' Brother, I had that tent down and my jeep packed in world-record time. . . . Suddenly a giant flame scorched up into the dark eastern sky. We had set off our gasoline dump." But the order to retreat had not yet been issued, and after two hours Ernie spread his bedroll on the ground; "I never slept sounder in my life than during the next three hours." When he awoke the retirement was under way, a rear guard holding the western part of Sbeitla to cover the retreat. He slipped his jeep into the stream of vehicles headed west for Kasserine Pass. It was dark and cold, and it began to hail.

The withdrawal was well managed and orderly, with American planes providing cover. "It was hard to realize, when you were part of it, that this was a retreat—that American forces in large numbers were retreating in foreign battle—one of the few times in our history." It was our worst defeat on land since Bataan. The important Thelepte airdrome was abandoned, as was Gafsa. And II Corps headquarters was quitting its gully near Tebessa without ever using the newly blasted caverns. Reinforcements were rushing from Oran, but the Germans got twenty-one miles beyond Kasserine Pass before being stopped, and we lost more than a hundred tanks, and some five thousand men, though fewer than two hundred killed—the rest were captured or wounded or both. General Fredendall was relieved of the command of II Corps, and a glittering personality was summoned to replace him—the swash-buckling tank expert, General George S. Patton, Jr. With him as second in command was General Omar N. Bradley.

Ernie drove nearly four hundred miles to Algiers and pulled up at the Aletti Hotel at three a.m. He found an extra bed in the room of Ed Beattie, of the United Press, and collapsed into it.

CHAPTER 24

A Message from Albuquerque
to Accra

O N AWAKENING, Ernie had his second bath in almost two months. "It took me two hours to bathe, shave, and wash my head," he wrote Jerry. "I'm going to try to get some laundry done. Did all my own washing up till about six weeks ago, and since then just simply haven't washed."

The amenities of the Aletti had a perverse reaction. "I've just come back to civilization after seven weeks at the front," the letter to Jerry said. "It seems odd to be living halfway normal again. It's mighty good in a way, and yet in another way you feel a strange sort of restlessness and keep halfway wishing you were back there shivering and sleeping on the ground and never taking your clothes off. Which must be proof that I have reached the final stages of insanity. . . .

"Darling, I've got one of your letters. It came to me in Tunisea[1] about a week ago. What has happened to all your others God only knows. It was so wonderful to see your writing again and to sense that you were all right. Do you realize that's the first letter I've had from you in three and a half months? The Postal Department is cruel when it keeps bringing completely misaddressed fan letters through in a couple of weeks, but yours correctly addressed just never get through. My little book says that I wrote you the

[1] He spelled Tunisia that way for months, until I chaffed him.

238

last time on January 25, nearly a month ago. I was shocked when I saw it, and thought the book must be wrong. And then I realized that I have been going so fast and so continuously that I hadn't written anybody during all that time, the folks or Lee either, and that I had actually written only seven columns when I should have written about twenty-five. I hope enough mail copy has arrived in Washington to carry over this period. . . .

"I really stayed out too long, a person should come back at least once a month to gather up his loose ends and sort of take inventory. I haven't written for so long now that everything is a jumble in my head, and I don't know whether I can untangle any decent columns out of the mental hodge-podge. . . .

"Lee has mentioned that he supposes I'll be coming home for a short rest after the Africa cleanup, so apparently the office would approve if I came home on a visit. If I should it will be later, in the summer. Whether I come at all depends on where you are and how you feel. I wish you'd sort of say what you'd like for me to do."

The bath was too much for him. He wrote me about a week later that he had a bad cold: "I got it the day after I came in from the front—as the result of taking a bath, I'm positive. . . . This place gets on my nerves, as it does everybody's. It's a minor Washington, only not so minor. It's overcrowded, the correspondents' corps is just as greedy and back-biting as in Washington, everything is devious. Thank goodness I don't have to play this game or even stay here."

Word had reached Algiers of the death of his friend Ben Robertson in a Clipper crash. "We feel plenty terrible about it," Ernie wrote. "This war has been tough on newspapermen. Bill Stoneman[2] has recovered from his wound and is here in the hotel with me. His piece the other day summing up the whole campaign so far—and which the UP cabled back to their men here as an example of good reporting—was gotten mostly from me (the last half of it rather) after I returned from the front. Also the New York UP cabled here that compared with 'Pyle, Stoneman, and Gallagher'

[2] Of the *Chicago Daily News*.

the UP reports looked poor. You see I go far out of my way to re-port a compliment to myself. There ain't very much pleasure of any other kind over here.

"I can't claim any 'narrow escapes.' But we're always close enough to get something if it happens to hit in the right place. . . . I try not to take any foolish chances, but there's just no way to play it completely safe and still do your job. The front does get into your blood, and you miss it and want to be back. Life up there is very simple, very uncomplicated, devoid of all the jealousy and meanness that floats around a headquarters city, very healthful despite the cold, and time passes so damned fast it's just unbelievable. . . . The field commanders are all grand, you can walk in and talk to anybody anytime you want, and they tell us everything with complete frankness. It's all such a contrast to the rigamarole and official red tape and high-and-mightiness of the Army in Washington that you feel you're in a different world.

"I've been in a better frame of mind the last couple of months, feeling that Jerry has been progressing, and being up where things were really vital. I hope the mental agony of the last two years never has to be repeated."

A letter from Cavanaugh told him America was "just getting around to being a fit country to live in. No cars, no gas, no gadgets, no salesmen, every other woman pregnant, no one can earn more than twenty-five thousand a year, and plenty of whisky to last the duration. Money ain't worth a damn and I'm glad I've lived to see the day. Everybody you talk to has a military secret. I have compiled my plans for the postwar world, and I find no place in it for you." Ernie replied: "I have been in the suburbs of one battle and four dive-bombings, but I know it will thrill you to hear that I've had no narrow escapes, haven't rescued any-body, haven't taken any prisoners, haven't rescued anybody, have-n't had my sleeve shot off, haven't carried any messages to Garcia, and haven't rescued anybody. . . . Whisky is as scarce as buried treasure. I've gone for weeks without a single drink, and actually

I feel a thousand times better too, though I hate to admit it. In town the other evening I had three drinks with a friend before dinner and was tighter than a coot. . . ."

A cable from Jerry announced that she was working. She had obtained a Civil Service appointment as a clerk in the Air Force supply office at Kirtland Field, Albuquerque. And she was moving back into the house.

In ten days Ernie wrote himself out—a great stack of copy about the breakthrough and retreat, as well as a lot of other stuff he had been carrying in his mind when that action started. His slate clean, he decided to hunt some warm weather. He wrote Jerry: "I figured that if I went back again [to the front] right now and stayed through to the end it would be too much of the same thing, and the columns would get repetitious. Also, this cold just hangs on. I really don't feel bad, but it sort of consumes me. . . . I'm terribly disappointed in the columns I've written since returning from Tunisia. I guess the subject was too big for me, and I waited too long to write it. But I'm not discouraged, for it isn't important—and anyway there's been enough good news from home lately to last me awhile." There was no reason for his disappointment—the columns were being read with enthusiasm in the States.

"I'm pleased that you're returning to the house," his letter continued, "for I like to think of you there; and yet somehow I feel sad and haunted to think of you being there alone. I do hope you'll try to make some arrangement to have somebody there with you. I really believe it's wrong for us to be alone so much, even though it is our wish and instinct. . . . Then, too, you can't have Cheetah with you unless there's somebody to stay with her during the day; and with you working it'll be too much for you to get your own meals—at least I know you well enough to know you won't eat properly if you're alone! I still think so damn much about Cheetah; it's ridiculous for a person to have such affection for a dog—especially a *bad* dog like her! It'll make me happy if you can have her with you again. . . . I'm so anxious to hear what your job is, and how you are standing it. I know the first few days were torture for you. But I know that after you've broken in and got into the swim and rediscovered you can do things the same as anybody else, only a lot better, your confidence in yourself will all come back. . . .

"If anything should ever happen to me, know that I am proud of you, and that you are the one thing in the world that means anything to me, and that I love you. I think of myself always as being there with you. And someday I will be. Be happy and cheerful and do lots of things, and don't ever worry about me, for I'm swell. . . ."

On March 3 he set out by air for Accra, on the far Gold Coast. The trip took four or five days. It was a case of up before daylight every morning, fly most of the day, stop at one or another airdrome, eat, go to bed, and repeat the process. First west to French Morocco, where he sent a rug and some leather hassock covers to Jerry. Then on south over the vast western bulge of Africa, skimming drearily across that same Sahara Desert he had once dreamed of crossing by automobile—drearily because the desert was so veiled in a haze of blowing sand that there was nothing at all to be seen except at fuel stops: "We landed at little pinpoints populated by a lonely dozen or two Americans in khaki shorts." Even the long-sought warmth was now too much of a good thing: "The desert was stifling when we came down upon it, and each time we pitied the fellows stationed there." He learned to nap in the plane, on sacks of mail. At an airdrome in Liberia "we stopped at a jungle field for lunch. It was hotter than hell. Most of the black natives were semi-naked. The whites were sitting around in a sort of boiling stupor." He still had on winter underwear and "felt as though somebody had poured hot gravy down my back." After carrying his luggage a quarter-mile through a blazing sun he took a shower: "I washed and washed until I was weak from overcleansing. And then I put on summer underwear and thin khaki. . . . For a couple of hours I felt the way one feels after fever—light and floating and strange."

At Accra, "the biggest American aerial operation anywhere outside the United States," he found real comfort—concrete and stucco quarters, bathrooms, one-day laundry, paved streets, refrigerators, movies every evening, a sun helmet by day but a blanket by night. An Albuquerque crony, Colonel C. R. Smith, was at Accra to make him welcome. "I was lucky enough to get here just the day before he left on a week's trip," Ernie wrote Jerry. "He insisted that I move into his room while he is gone, so here I am—it's as modern and comfortable and lovely as his own house in Albuquerque. And his black houseboy is lying on a mat outside the door, here to do anything for me that I command. It is my misfortune never to be able to think of anything I need or want. . . .

"It seems too cruel that so few of your letters have ever gotten to me—only two since I left London four months ago today. Two in four months isn't enough for a yearning fellow. . . . Oh I do hope that you are happy in being busy, and that you are still well and can sleep and wake up feeling enthusiasm instead of dread for the day. . . . Be good to yourself, darling, and don't be losing me out of your memory. Give my love to the Shaffers and Mounts and Livingstones and Hicks. And be sure and keep Cheetah in old shoes so she won't forget." [3] On March 11 he wrote me: "I do get depression periods at knowing I'll be away from Jerry so terribly long and that we will become strangers, and our hopes for the future seem to become dimmer and dimmer. But I guess it's best for me just to stay on until I can finally come home for good. I'm completely out of touch on this trip; it was useless to try to have mail or messages follow me; so I won't be able to hear from you or Jerry or anybody until I return to the north. . . ."

But a message did get through, late the next night, March 12. It was from the London office of the United Press. It said: "New

---

[3] Months after Ernie's death, when I was working on this book in Albuquerque, Cheetah was brought home from the kennels. She had never seen me. When she heard me typing at Ernie's desk, she ran into the room. There she stood for a minute or two, listening to this once familiar sound and eyeing me in perplexity, and then she settled down at my feet.

York reports you married former wife by proxy. How about giving us yarn. . . ."

Ernie cabled his thanks to the UP but said this was too personal a matter for him to write about. He cabled Jerry: "Just received word marriage from London. So happy could bust. Love you."

He had been a married man for two days before he learned of it. Jerry had asked me to relay the following message, but it was weeks in reaching him: "Have exercised proxy March ten. Soon settled in house with Cheetah. View still glorious. House dog and gal waiting for the master. All send love."

The ceremony took place during Jerry's lunch hour. Ed and Liz Shaffer picked her up at Kirtland Field and took her to the office of Judge Neil McNerney. Shafe, as "attorney in fact" for Ernie, made the responses in his stead. Liz Shaffer said later she suspected that there was a slight mixup in the way the judge put the questions and that actually he married Jerry to Shafe!

Ernie wrote his wife: "I can't tell you how relieved and glad and everything I am, for I know it means you are well and your old self again, and for me it fills up again the mere shell that living had become. . . . I think one of the reasons I wanted this is that if anything should happen to me before this war is over, I wanted to go out that way—as we were. Not that I'm counting on anything happening, but in a war as all-encompassing as this one, anything can happen, of course. At any rate, what I'm trying to say is that now I feel some peace with the world again; life was incomplete and purposeless before."

In a letter to me he said: "The tragedy of the whole thing came very near breaking me. But if Jerry is cured, all the suffering was worth while. No matter what happens, I'll never consider divorce again. Of course, this doesn't alter my plans to stay on over here; in fact I think it's best that I should stay." To Aunt Mary he wrote: "I do hope you'll write Jerry a little note telling her you're glad; I wish Papa would write a few words too. I feel so much better, now that things are back where they were."

CHAPTER 25

"We Want Ernie!"

ERNIE had written me that he planned to go on even farther south, "down to the place you used to mention
jokingly in your letters"—the Congo. From Accra he flew
some fifteen hundred miles to Léopoldville, capital of the Belgian
Congo. At a way station on the Slave Coast a lieutenant introduced himself. It was Walter Wichterman, of Indianapolis, who
had been a member of the college baseball team that Ernie accompanied to Japan twenty-one years earlier. "He asked me," Ernie
wrote, "if I remembered how we used to stand on the curb in
certain parts of Tokyo and, after the native custom, publicly
make our toilets. I did remember indeed. Well, Lieutenant Wichterman's ambition is to fight his way on around the world and
wind up the war by standing once again in Tokyo doing the same
thing."

He had a few days at Léopoldville and at Brazzaville, across the
Congo River, then returned through dirty weather to Accra.
Here he got fresh word of his pyramiding popularity at home. He
wrote Jerry: "Quentin Reynolds has just arrived from America,
on his way to Russia. He has always been one of my best promot-
ers, and he's practically running over this time. Says I'm the No. 1
correspondent now, and could double my salary by asking, and
make twenty thousand by writing a book. I told him I was indifferent to both ideas, and he says I'm crazy. I know we'll need all
the money we can get after the war, but I haven't the time or
material to write a book, and I couldn't ask the office for more

245

money after they've been so wonderful to me, and somehow it seems wrong anyhow to try to make more money when so many people have had to give up all their salaries. . . ." Some weeks before he had turned down a book proposition from the Crowell Publishing Company.

Ernie mentioned in the column an outdoor entertainment at Accra in which Quentin Reynolds and Martha Raye, the actress, participated: "The soldiers had apparently been affected by the heat that day, for they started yelling for me to get up on the stage too. . . . But that old phobia of mine—stage fright—took a firm grip and I couldn't have moved if you'd offered me a million dollars." Colonel Smith wrote to a friend in Albuquerque that when Reynolds on this occasion referred to Ernie as "unquestionably the greatest correspondent in Africa," the troops roared, "We want Ernie!" Ernie wouldn't talk, but the ovation was so big that "even the stars were jolted."

About this time William Sloane of Henry Holt & Company told me he was willing to pay Ernie an advance of twenty-five hundred dollars against royalties on a book that would simply be a collection of his African dispatches, plus a last chapter to be written specially. I cabled Ernie, but my messages were piling up in Algiers awaiting his return. Sloane came to Washington and said he could make it five thousand. Since few other books of reprint had been notably profitable, this sounded generous if not reckless. But within the next few weeks other publishers wrote, phoned, or came to see me. At least three of them, aside from Holt, were willing and eager to lay the same amount on the line.

Ernie's list of newspapers now numbered about eighty, and his revenue from United Feature had outstripped the hundred and seventy-five a week Scripps-Howard paid him. I assured him that "I haven't been laying it on too thick in the messages I've sent about how the column has been going. I'm telling you it's terrific —both the copy and the reaction." I quoted Louis Seltzer, editor of the *Cleveland Press*: "In all my newspaper experience I have not heard anyone so widely discussed and such extravagant praise heaped upon a man or woman for an outstanding journalistic job."

At Algiers, where Ernie arrived in early April after a circuitous flight via Khartoum and Cairo, a mass of mail and cables awaited him, including my messages about the book project. He replied: "Re Holt go ahead. Accept but with stipulation book always be advertised and presented as column reprints and not new book because fooling public would harm column."

He had intended to stay around Algiers a week or more, but after two days wrote me that he was leaving for the front at once. "I've certainly been flooded with praise," he added. "Harry Butcher[1] gave a little dinner for the correspondents in town, to tell them about his trip home. It was a pretty disheartening picture he gave, incidentally, of the people's mental attitude, their apparently distorted views of the European end of the war, their greed, and so on. But to get to the point, out of a clear sky he told the group that I was the most widely read and talked-about of any correspondent at home, and then he worked back to it and repeated it twice later. I was very flattered and pleased. . . . I wish there were some way I could send you back a representative batch of the fan letters that have come over. There were a hundred and twenty-seven here when I got back. I'm going to the front with seventy-five or a hundred of them unopened. I even get a lot of nice ones from soldiers over here. . . .

"I have a feeling I don't want to come home until I can come for good. I believe it would be better all around, for my own morale, and Jerry's, and for the column. . . . Somehow I feel rather good about Jerry. Nobody knows what a great thing she has done in pulling herself out of the abyss she was in."

Three letters from Jerry, plus her month-old wedding cable, had greeted him at Algiers, and he wrote her: "Your letters heartened me so, for you wrote how you really feel, and that's what I want to know. . . . I feel just as you do; you are with me all the time; I seldom write or do anything without subconsciously asking myself whether you would approve or think it wise. I've

[1] General Eisenhower's naval aide.

made some errors of judgment in my writing because you weren't here to guide me; but I haven't made any, I think, in behavior. I hope I'm not getting old-fashioned in my old age, but I'm getting so damn conservative, you might say, in conduct that when I take just two drinks before dinner I wake up next morning feeling that guilty sense of self-disgust. I guess all these months with very little to drink, and the two months in Tunisia with nothing at all, have made me soft, for I don't enjoy my few drinks any more. On this trip down south I ran onto a windfall of a case and a half of good whisky—twenty bottles, in fact. And do you know that I've wound up with exactly three bottles for myself? Gave all the others away. Never knew I was so damn generous before. How did I get off on a temperance lecture, anyway? Except it isn't a temperance lecture, for I still don't like people who don't drink.

. . . I love you very much and am happy for us. I have a feeling we're both better people for what we've been through, and that even this present long and tragic separation will be repaid by smoothness and beauty in our lives some day. . . ."

He wrote his "stand-in" at the remarriage: "My dear Mr. Shaffer: Oh, so you married my wife, did you? . . . The minute a fellow turns his back his best friend ups and runs off with his wife. And I suppose your own poor wife and ragged children sitting there at home crying their hearts out doesn't touch you at all?"

While in Algiers Ernie called on General Eisenhower, who suggested that he "go and discover Bradley," which he eventually did.

But now he went to Gafsa, a crippled, thoroughly vandalized city. This area, including El Guettar, had been cleared of the enemy in a hard battle, Patton throwing his 1st and 9th Infantry Divisions into the attack to relieve some of the pressure against the British Eighth Army on the south. Jack Thompson of the *Chicago Tribune* recalled that at Gafsa "our press camp was set up a couple of miles outside of town, on the edge of a beautiful swimming pool. We were using the little cubicles in the bathhouse as our 'offices.' We all were tired. It was a grind every day to leave our sanctuary and jeep to the front, out around El Guettar. At night we had trouble sleeping in our tents, around the swimming pool, because the Luftwaffe came over all the time and used the blazing white bathhouse and pool, by the light of their flares, as a pylon to turn on for the strafing and bombing runs over Gafsa and El Guettar. It was on a night like that when Ernie, all bundled up in his old GI mackinaw and his knit cap, came in from Algiers. And do you know what that little s.o.b. had done? All the way from Accra, through the fleshpots of Algiers and the thirsts of hundreds of men, he carried half a bottle of Johnny Walker that someone had given him; carried it so that his friends up here could have a drink."

The fight for Tunisia was approaching its crisis. General Montgomery had disposed of the Mareth Line, made contact with our own 9th Division advancing from Gafsa, and was charging northward along the coast. The bulk of Patton's II Corps was shifted from the Gafsa area for the climactic thrust against Mateur and Bizerte. Patton himself was withdrawn to prepare the Sicilian campaign, and Bradley took over the Corps.

Ernie and two other correspondents drove east, past burned-out tanks around El Guettar, up through ruined Sidi-bou-Zid and across the mine-fringed Faïd Pass, to the battered port of Sfax. Somewhere along the way he was told of a high British officer who visited a battlefield where General Terry Allen's 1st Division had just carved another notch in its gun: "American boys were still lying dead in their foxholes, their rifles still grasped in firing positions in their dead hands. And the veteran English soldier remarked time and again, in a sort of hushed eulogy spoken only to himself: 'Brave men. Brave men!' " It was this incident that would suggest the title for Ernie's third book.

For several days Ernie trailed the British Eighth Army up the coast and "came to look upon it almost with awe. . . . The spirit of our troops is good, but these boys from the burning sands are throbbing with the vitality of conquerors." He and his two fellow correspondents got to the sacred city of Kairouan shortly after the Germans had evacuated it in the face of Monty's men. To their astonishment they "found the streets lined with crowds waving and cheering and applauding each passing vehicle. Not knowing the difference, they gave us correspondents as big a hand as the rest. And we beamed and waved back just as though we'd run the Germans out ourselves. I might add on our behalf that we did feel like heels while doing it."

Then on north to a press-relations camp of the British First Army in a hillside apricot grove at Thibar, a few miles from General Bradley's new headquarters just being organized at Béja. That evening Ernie and several other correspondents, billeted in Thibar until Béja would be ready for them, were at a tavern when German bombers came over. The others stepped outside to watch, but Ernie was too tired to move. One five-hundred-pounder landed in a monastery garden near the press camp and holed a few tents, but nothing bigger than a frog was killed.

At Béja Ernie settled down in a tent with Chris Cunningham of the United Press. "Nothing happened that first night that was spectacular," he wrote, "yet somehow the whole night became obsessed with a spookiness that leaves it standing like a landmark in my memory. . . . The roll of artillery was constant. It never stopped once in twenty-four hours. Once in a while there were nearer shots which might have been German patrols or might not. We lay uneasily in our cots. Sleep wouldn't come. We turned and turned." Dogs howled, and guinea hens set up an outlandish cackling. "Concussion ghosts, traveling in waves, touched our tent walls and made them quiver. Ghosts were shaking the ground ever so lightly. Ghosts were stirring the dogs to hysteria. Ghosts were wandering in the sky peering for us in our cringing hideout. Ghosts were everywhere, and their hordes were multiplying as every hour added its production of new battlefield dead. . . . Next morning we spoke around among ourselves and found one by one that all of us had tossed away all night. It was an unexplainable thing. For all of us had been through dangers greater than this. On another night the roll of the guns would have lulled us to sleep. It's just that on some nights the air becomes sick and there is an unspoken contagion of spiritual dread, and you are little boys again, lost in the dark."

He wrote Jerry a day or two later: "Somebody says this is Easter Sunday, but some think it isn't, so I don't know. . . . I've spent the day 'carpentering.' Built a washstand onto a tree out of some old pieces of boards, made a washpan out of a gasoline can, wired up an old chair that was broken, and sort of made the place homelike. . . . This afternoon I was lying on my cot thinking about you and about seeing you, and of how far it is and how long it would take even if I started right now, and of how long it will have to be, and all of a sudden I almost felt like crying. And then it passed away. As long as I can keep real busy, which I am most of the time, my spirits are pretty good."

Life was not unpleasant at Béja. Arabs dug slit trenches in return for a few cigarettes. There were cots to sleep on. The countryside was a lush green, and marigolds blazoned a field nearby. Bathing facilities were limited, but Ernie was bothered neither by this—he swore that fleas boycotted the unwashed—nor by his scarcely glamorous appearance. He dressed "like a cross between Coxey's Army and the ski patrol. . . . The only way you can tell me from a private is that I'm too old." He was the oldest of the correspondents in Tunisia except for Gault MacGowan of the *New York Sun*.

My letter joshing him for his months-long misspelling, "Tunisea," finally reached him, and he replied: "We've all had a big laugh at my expense around camp. Just one of those blind spots that even a genius (ahem) hits now and then, I guess." He mentioned the book hopefully: "With good heavy pushing and concentration on the cities where the column runs, and pressing the idea of buying the book to have the columns in permanent form, don't you think they ought to sell fifty thousand?" He was far short of the mark on that one.

CHAPTER 26

The God-damned *Infantry*

"Now to the infantry," he wrote in the column, "the God-damned infantry as they like to call themselves." He had gone forward, to a battalion of the 1st Division in the rocky hills before Mateur, steppingstone to Bizerte itself. "I love the infantry because they are the underdogs. They are the mud-rain-frost-and-wind boys. They have no comforts, and they even learn to live without the necessities. And in the end they are the guys that wars can't be won without."

He was with the battalion a week, in a different spot almost every night. Half the time he slept on the ground with nothing over or under him except his clothes, but then he got a blanket and shared shelter halves with a British liaison captain until the latter was wounded. There was no hot food—only cold C rations, even cold coffee; the smoke of a fire could not be risked. Snakes, lizards, scorpions, and centipedes fretted him almost as much as the continuous artillery fire and the dawn dive-bombings. But he felt an "exaltation." It was an "unbelievable" week. "[I] was a part of about all the horror of war there is. . . . I don't see how any of the boys who live through it can ever be the same people again." For three days and nights he was under constant fire, "and it ain't play."

He was close to his deadline and had to turn out five columns in the field, with a pencil. He started writing in the shade of a big rock at the battalion command post. But the Germans had left

behind, on the very hill where he was working, a well dug-in and
camouflaged machine-gun sniper. "I would write for ten or fifteen
minutes, then suddenly machine-gun slugs would come singing
down from the hilltop and buzz past us overhead. Apparently my
paper made a target. . . . Four times in one day that fellow chased
me out of my shady place. The fourth time three bullets went
past so close they had fuzz on them, and the fourth went into the
ground with a squish just ten feet away." He abandoned the shady
spot and wrote in a foxhole, often with GIs reading over his
shoulder, until a particularly monstrous-looking reptile nudged
his leg—"A movie of me leaving that foxhole would look like a
shell leaving a rifle."

He wrote of a column of troops coming out of battle: "The
men are walking. They are fifty feet apart, for dispersal. Their
walk is slow, for they are dead weary, as you can tell even when
looking at them from behind. Every line and sag of their bodies
speaks their inhuman exhaustion. On their shoulders and backs
they carry heavy steel tripods, machine-gun barrels, leaden boxes
of ammunition. Their feet seem to sink into the ground from the
overload they are bearing. They don't slouch. It is the terrible
deliberation of each step that spells out their appalling tiredness.
Their faces are black and unshaven. They are young men, but the
grime and whiskers and exhaustion make them look middle-aged.
The line moves on, but it never ends. All afternoon men keep coming round the hill and vanishing eventually over the horizon. It is
one long, tired line of antlike men. There is an agony in your heart
and you almost feel ashamed to look at them. They are just guys
from Broadway and Main Street, but you wouldn't remember
them. They are too far away now. They are too tired. Their
world can never be known to you, but if you could see them just
once, just for an instant, you would know that no matter how
hard people work back home they are not keeping pace with these
infantrymen in Tunisia."

He went along with the battalion on some night marches.

Prolonged artillery fire, he found, was more oppressive than aerial bombings; it "comes very close to being unbearable, and we saw many pitiful cases of 'anxiety neurosis.' " On every march there was a constant fear of mines. The nights were chilly, and the ground damp with dew, and smoking was safe only in foxholes, under coats used as hoods. There were narrow escapes, like the time a shell—which turned out to be a dud—"hit the ground about thirty feet ahead of us, bounced past us so close we could almost have grabbed it, and finally wound up less than a hundred yards back of us." Nevertheless, "during all the time we were under fire I felt fine. The catch-as-catch-can sleep didn't seem to bother me. I never felt physically tired even after the marches. The days were so diverse and so unregimented that a week sped by before I knew it. I never felt that I was excited or tense except during certain fast-moving periods of shelling and bombing, and these were quickly over. When I finally left the line just after daylight one morning I never felt better in my life. And yet, once I was safely back in camp an intense weariness came over me. I slept almost every minute of two days and nights. I just didn't have the will to get up, except to eat. My mind was as blank as my body was lifeless. . . ."

The day after his return to Béja he found strength to get off a letter to Jerry: "By the time I get written up I expect the present phase of fighting will be over. The fighting has now moved forward far enough that we can just faintly hear the artillery at night. The other boys go to the front in daytime excursions, but I seem to be the only one who goes up and lives right with the troops. . . . I've had an Arab woman do some washing for me, but I'm gradually getting so dirty and disorganized I almost feel like throwing everything away when the African campaign ends and starting all over again. Our tent back here has a dirt floor and the wind blows dirt into everything and we haven't anyplace to set anything. . . . "

The British, French, and Americans, under overwhelming airpower, were closing in fast now on the trapped enemy, whose leader, Rommel, had cleared out. Early in May the pivotal Hill 609 fell to our 34th Division, and Mateur to the 1st Armored. The grand finale was on, and in a few days General Bradley would be able to report with economical eloquence: "Mission completed." Ernie got to Bizerte and Tunis—taken respectively by the Americans and the British—in time to goggle at the thousands of suddenly docile "supermen" for whom the war was over, and to see the carnivals of joy among the liberated. American troops were weighting themselves with souvenirs, and he got one himself. A *Volkswagen*, German counterpart of our jeep, was presented to him by somebody in the 1st Armored for "sweating it out with us at Faïd Pass." He was mighty proud of it, but a few days later a general order required all captured cars to be turned in. By that time, anyway, Ernie had found the *Volkswagen* far inferior to the jeep.

After surveying the scenes of victory he returned to the press camp at Béja. There was a message from me: "Recent copy has been absolutely terrific. Everybody proud of you." He replied: "I'm deeply appreciative of the morale-building wirelesses you've been thoughtful enough to keep coming to me all winter, and I hope I can continue to deserve them. Yesterday I had a grand two-and-a-half page letter from Roy [Howard], full of encomiums. . . . Christ, Miller, if something doesn't happen to stop all this nonsense, we're gonna get rich. Everything about the book deal sounds okay to me. I'm not nuts about the proposed title[1] but so far haven't been able to think of anything better. . . . Fred Painton of *Reader's Digest* has just spent a half day pumping me for a sort of profile. . . . He insisted on knowing how much money I made, so I told him thirteen thousand last year and maybe twenty-five thousand this year. I hate like hell for stuff like that to be in print but I suppose I've let myself into a position where nothing can be secret. . . . The UF [United Feature] take sounds

[1] Holt originally planned to call the book "With the Yanks in Africa."

magnifique, and I have no quarrels with anything. In fact the whole thing has got clear over my head and I don't even think about it. You just pile up the money for me, Doctor, and after awhile we'll go fishin'." He enclosed a power of attorney authorizing me to write checks against his bank account for paying his income tax and buying War Bonds.

He told Jerry of receiving a letter she had written on New Year's Eve—it was four and a half months on the way: "But I love even the old ones. I know I've read them each a dozen times. Your letters cheer me immensely, for they sound like you. . . . I am passively happy, knowing that some peacefulness and happiness have come to you. I don't seem to have any doubts about the future at all. My only concern is that after this is all over I, along with millions of others, will have such a terrible readjustment to make to normal life. The 'slowing down' period will be a dangerous one for all of us to go through. Even though my only goal and dream is to slow down to a complete stop, I know it will be difficult. I love you darling."

He and Will Lang set out from Béja to drive back to Algiers. During a stop at Constantine, the forward headquarters of the high command, "I ran onto scores of my old Air Corps friends I hadn't seen for months," he wrote Jerry. "I think within an hour I must have met a hundred of them, and it was one of those chaotic periods with too much talk and too many people that I never could stand, you know, even though enjoying it. At any rate about an hour later I began having a stomach pain like those I used to have after drinking egg-nog, and pretty soon was so sick I had to have a doctor. Damned if I didn't think I was going to die. I'm convinced it was purely from nervous tension and over-tautness. It was the beginning of our return to 'civilization', and I'm afraid I can't take crowds or commotion or the usual manifestations of social intercourse in bulk any more."

They followed the coastal road most of the way to Algiers and, he told Jerry, "I must admit that never anywhere have I seen more beautiful country or more thrilling sights. It is much like the Oregon coast, except inland there are scenes which are really lovelier than anything I ever remember seeing at home anywhere. Will and I drove in two-hour shifts; I enjoy traveling with him because we ride along and don't talk, just as you and I used to."

CHAPTER 27

A Pause at Zeralda

INVASION of Sicily had been decided on at Casablanca by Roosevelt and Churchill, but Ernie would not learn of this until three weeks after his return to Algiers, when General Eisenhower informed the correspondents.

The press camp was being moved from Béja to the shore at Zeralda, about twenty miles from Algiers, and Ernie decided to live at the camp while writing and resting. He wrote that his "antipathy to cities" had "doubled and tripled."

Messages from me had greeted him at Algiers: "If I could arrange quick air transport would you be interested in dashing home for few weeks." And: "Deacon [Parker] urges you take furlough home. Incidentally Walker [Stone] suggests your reactions to domestic scene on returning exbattle might make powerful and influential reading."

Our solicitude, it turned out, only intensified the jitteriness that bustling Algiers provoked in him. He wrote Jerry: "I guess my time at the front has completely spoiled me for 'civilization.' You know the tightness in the back of the head and the 'eyes out of focus' I used to have so much. Well, those completely disappeared; haven't had them for months. But back here with crowds and street noise and too many people you know, and correspondence and obligations, I have that old panicky swamped feeling again. . . . Much to my surprise and confusion, there were several cables here from Lee asking if I didn't want to dash home for a few weeks. I'd had no plans at all along that line, but now that they've

258

put it in my head of course it's something new to fret about. . . .
If I'm put to experting the home front I'm completely out of character; and as we know from our yearly returns to Washington even
in peacetime, a visit 'home' doesn't rest you but destroys you. I
really don't think I could stand crossing the ocean twice on a
hurry trip and the madness of two or three weeks in the States.
The one thing that makes my decision hard is the opportunity to
see you again. I can't know what would be best. Any visit would
be so brief it would be over before we could get our breaths back
from the original excitement. I know how hard it has been for you
to establish yourself in your new routine, and I think it might be
wrong to interrupt it. I somehow feel it would be better for us
both for me not to come until I could stay at home a month or
two entirely free of work. If I wait till next fall at the earliest or
next spring at the latest, you will have some leave coming and I
can take leave with a clear conscience. So I think in the end I will
probably wire them that I think it wiser to stay on over, although
I could almost cry at not seeing you when it might be possible.
My decision is all mixed up with a vague and probably false 'duty'
sense that I should stay on to face with the other thousands over
here what must be faced in this other-other world we're living in
now. I hope you won't feel I've done wrong if I don't come home
yet. . . . Underneath my consciousness all the time is the knowledge that what I'm really doing is just waiting out the intermin-
able months and years of distorted life until this is all over and we
can be ourselves together again. I know and appreciate that it is
far easier for me than it is for you, for there's always something
new and distracting here. . . ."

He wirelessed me: "Have definitely decided due tightness transportation and other things not come home now."

At Zeralda the press tents were pitched on low dunes within a
hundred yards of a sandy beach lapped by the Mediterranean, and
Ernie gradually made himself comfortable. He wrote Jerry that
he and Acme photographer Chuck Corte "have tents close
together and their ends form a sort of triangle, shadowed by

a scrub pine tree, which we call the patio. We have two straight-backed chairs and an easy deep wicker chair out there, and a grass mat on the sand. It's really a grand little nook. Also I have my tent fixed up nicely with a cot, two tables, grass mats all over the sandy floor, electric light over my cot, mosquito net, and everything. It's the homiest place I've had in seven months. . . . This morning I killed my first scorpion. He was sitting in the sand right in the door of my tent. Foot-long lizards crawl around the tent and once in a while onto the cot, but we don't pay any attention to them. I've seen only one snake here. . . . Our food is absolutely marvelous, and our site is isolated and as quiet as the middle of a desert."

In spite of the idyllic languor of Zeralda he worked energetically. Within a week he had turned out nine columns cleaning up the Tunisian campaign, a requested article for *Stars and Stripes*, and the five-thousand-word last chapter for his book, and was starting on a dozen columns of travelogue covering the latter part of his long swing around Africa in March and April.

Mail was pouring in, but none lately from Jerry. Shafe wrote that she was doing fine with her job. Sister Margaret Jane said she was working hard and enjoying it. Roz Goodman, who had stopped off at Albuquerque on a trip to the Coast, reported that she had "never seen Jerry looking so lovely." Walker Stone was there briefly too; he wrote that she looked better and seemed to feel better than in many years. "I'm jealous that everybody else is seeing you and I can't," Ernie wrote her. "Walker said you were proud of the job, that the house was more attractive than ever, and that a neighbor's dog called every morning for breakfast. I'm even jealous of the dog. . . ."

Some Red Cross people were giving a dinner party in Algiers and pressed him to come, so he left Zeralda for an evening which turned out to be a bibulous one, at least for Ernie. He wrote Jerry: "I got bit by the venomous worm—a stranger lo these many months—and having lost all immunity to its poison, I didn't last long. They said I insisted on maintaining my dignity while being carried upstairs, so they let me *think* I was walking up, and everything was all right. I stayed the night in Marty's[1] apartment. The last I remember he had been talking without interruption for two solid hours about raisin pie, of all things. The whole thing was such a novel experience I didn't even mind feeling bad next day. Marty thinks it's a great joke that, since I haven't slept in a bed for so long, they put me to bed but he found me next morning lying on the hard stone floor of his hallway, wrapped up in a rug like an Arab."

George Biddle, newly arrived as leader of a group of artists assigned by the War Department to make a graphic record of the war, visited Zeralda, and in his book *Artist at War* gave a size-up of Ernie: "This morning I did a drawing in red sanguine of Ernie Pyle. I only put into it, I am afraid, a small part of his rare personality. He seems Yankee to the core, though hailing from Indiana farm stock. Ascetic, gentle, whimsical, shy. Frugal in his habits. Like so many Americans, his expression is fundamentally sad, yet full of tenderness. Of course a stubborn, thin-lipped individualist, and probably hard as granite under his timid manner. I like to think of him as he sits on the beach toward sundown, a white and slender Gandhi, swathed in towels and wrappers, for he hates the cold as much as he fears the sun. He does not swim and dislikes bathing. So he spends his week's holiday as follows: he sleeps three hours each day; reads for three hours; and then, being at his wits' end what to do, he sits down and writes a column. He puts his whole life into his column: his shy love of human beings, his tenderness, and his hard, salty, Indiana-farmer humor."

The beach was less quiet now, as troops ticketed for Sicily were having maneuvers there, but by this time Ernie was taking it easy. "I've been working like a bastard trying to get all caught up," he wrote Cavanaugh, "and now I haven't got a thing left except to write a couple of dozen letters. You'd like it here. It's just damn near ideal, and I'll sure hate to go back to war. . . .

"I understand the secret is out at last. They tell me *Time* mag-

[1] Martin Codel of the Red Cross.

azine has arrived over here with a full-page piece about me, in which it estimates my annual income at twenty-five thousand. How much do you make incidentally? Think you ought to tell me now. Although of course I ain't coming right out and saying that *Time* is right. . . .

"The years are dealing heavily with me. No wine, no women, no song, no play—soon nothing will be left to me but my shovel and a slight case of athlete's foot. . . . I get mail from a lot of people, but am gradually sinking into my old-time funk (from which I've been free for several months) about Jerry. I've a premonition things have gone bad again. God, if they have I don't know what to do." He signed it "Mahomet."

He borrowed a copy of Sinclair Lewis's *Arrowsmith*. "I'm so glad I did," he wrote Jerry, "for I'm absorbed in it. When I read stories like Maugham's and Steinbeck's I think maybe I could really write someday, but when I read such broad, meticulous things as this I know I never could." When he had finished the story of Martin and Leora Arrowsmith he told her: "I'm very moved by it. In so many ways it is so much you and so much me that it sort of haunts me. In all his faults I can see so much of myself; his one-trackedness, his shallow wanderings from it, his self-centeredness, his neglects. And in her there is so much of you—the seeing beyond all sham, the patience with my childishness, that acute and automatic understanding of absolutely everything that of all the people I've ever known only you and Ruth Egan[2] possess. And maybe Cavanaugh. . . . Somehow I knew that Lewis would have her die in the book, and the book ended there for me. I finished it, but I wasn't interested after that. Possibly because I felt it might picture my own pathetic and wretched flounderings if you were ever gone. . . ." He asked Jerry to buy a few new books each month: "Maybe some day I'll have time to read them, and anyhow you know how I like to have more and more books around. . . ."

The column continued to evoke wide comment at home. *Time* called Ernie "America's most widely read war correspond-

[2] Wife of newspaperman Charles M. ("Chuck") Egan, of Washington.

ent." Mrs. Roosevelt said she "would not miss that column any day if I possibly could help it." Ben McKelway, assistant editor of the *Washington Star*—of which Ernie's own paper was a competitor—told him in a letter: "I wish to God I had you in the *Star*. . . . I envy you . . . because you are one of the newspaper people who are really making a contribution to winning this war." In New York the *World-Telegram* was spreading his stuff daily on page one in double-column ten-point. Walter Leckrone, editor of the *Indianapolis Times*, wrote that it was "the hottest feature we've got." Kermit McFarland of the *Pittsburgh Press* said it "has this town on fire." *Stars and Stripes* asked, and received, permission to print the column regularly. Ernie wrote to his father and aunt: "It looks from all the reports that I'm the No. 1 correspondent of the war. That's nice, but I'm glad I'm not at home and having to go through all the fuss that goes with it." Many letters from readers asked him to find out the details regarding the death of particular soldiers: "They're pathetic letters," he wrote to Dana, "but I can't do all that and keep the column going too. It would take a full-time staff." Occasionally there was a happier errand to perform, like fulfilling this request from a friend's wife, who had telegraphed it to me for forwarding: "Baby girl born June fourth Sandra. Tell Max thanks. Polla Kuehnert."

Fan letters were too numerous to answer, although he tried to reply to those from soldiers in Africa. Don Coe of the United Press, after a visit with a newly arrived division, said he could have made two hundred dollars selling Ernie's autographs if he'd had them. The first question every soldier asked, he reported, was whether he knew Ernie. Quentin Reynolds, after similar experiences, swore he was going to call his next book "Do You Know Ernie Pyle?"

On a trip to Algiers Ernie tried to collect five hundred dollars I had cabled him to replenish his expense kitty; because the cable spoke of "Ernie Pyle," while his credentials read "Ernest Taylor Pyle," it took half a day and an affidavit from the Army finance office "before these adamant asses would give me my money."

He was getting eager, and even a bit nervous, about the book. He estimated that he had written more than one hundred and fifty thousand words about Africa and was afraid Holt might have to cut this severely. In a message to me he said: "Assume you'll see they don't edit out the little asides and crackerbarrel stuff that make column." I was able to reply: "Holt volubly reassuring against bludgeoning of copy or undue shortening."

By this time he knew about the plans against Sicily and was prepared to go on the invasion. He had a booster shot of typhoid serum and had to take to his bed for a day. There was still no mail from Jerry, and he asked me by wireless to try to get a message from her. That same day Jerry was telegraphing me: "Cable Ernie heartsick letters don't reach him. Try to make him know how well things are with me for truly they are. Love work. Have had promotion. House would seem empty except always feel he is just around the corner. My existence centers on that. Saw Cheetah. She knew me and is beautiful. Inadequate but it is hard to span oceans and continents. Love."

He replied: "I'm sorry my spirits are so vulnerable to lack of mail from you, but I guess I'm so flexible that I come up as fast as I go down, and now I feel wonderful after hearing from you. . . . Your cable was lovely, and now I can finish my rest and start out again with a better heart. I'm so thrilled about your promotion; and so soon after you've started working too. I'm happy that Cheetah remembers you; I know she wouldn't me but I guess she could relearn. I relive in memory so many times her flattering hysterics that day I came back from Denver after being gone a week. . . . I don't believe you worry much about me, but in case you do I can assure you that I will be in very little danger. I can't of course tell you anything about the future, in fact know very little myself, but do know that whatever happens I will be only on the edges rather than in the thick of things. I'd still love a new picture of you."

Ernie was writing Jerry even oftener than usual. In one letter he said: "Lately I seem to be daydreaming so much about

what we can and will do after this is all over and we get back to
whatever we decide we want to have as normal. I suppose first of
all we will have to go through a period of great patience with each
other, for we will inevitably be a little changed after so long a
time. We will have forgotten how it is not to live alone, and I will
have to grow out of this world of living only with men, and with
all normal outlook on everything tensed and roughened, and you
will have had to create interests for and within yourself that I am
not acquainted with. That readjustment will have to come to
millions of people, and I'm glad we are us and know each other so
well, instead of the thousands who hardly knew each other before
they went away. And I hope you will help me have the courage to
give up this devastating job. Not that I want to sit, or even labor
under the illusion any more that I might like just to sit. If maturity—this maturity over here, I mean—has brought me anything, it is an awakening to the fact which you've probably long
known, that I've got to be hacking away at something. I don't
know why, but I've got to be trying all the time to accomplish
something. I'm sure it doesn't necessarily have to be writing; but
since I do like to write and do know my way around in that world,
perhaps it may as well be that as anything else. But not this all-
consuming every-day thing, which exalts a little and destroys
completely, unless I should find happiness in being devoured by it.
That can happen, I know, but it mustn't happen to me. It has too
nearly happened already, for us.

"If nothing happens to either of us, we should be able to pretty
well pick and choose when the war is over, as far as the economics
of life go. We could take time to rest and look around, and even
play at writing a book or something like that, knowing it wouldn't
kill us if it failed. It might be fun to build another house. There
are lots and lots of things we can do to keep occupied and be
happy, if we've the sense between us to do them. A little travel
still, and some sittin', and some dog-playing, and some daily
chores, and through it all something definite to tack to that has
some purpose in it. I'm so eager about the future that I'm grow-

ing as impatient as the soldiers are about the war getting over, and I think I'm getting homesick again. But I'll have to smother that, for even if I were back home none of this could happen until the war is over and everybody else is freed also to go his own damnfool way. . . ."

His backlog of copy in Washington was about to run out, but he picked up a series of five columns about the Wacs (or Waacs as they were then still known) in Algiers. The Wac officer who showed him through their downtown barracks, "after careful yoohooing and peeking ahead," pointed out clotheslines filled with stockings and underwear. "You're the first man who has ever seen this many pairs of Wac panties at one time," she told him. "Madam," Ernie said he retorted, "due to the rigors of old age and the encroachment of war work upon my spare time I have never seen even one pair of Wac panties before." The series sufficed to keep the column going, with only a one-day lapse, until he could start wirelessing about the Sicilian invasion.

On June 29 he wrote me that another letter had come from Jerry, the second within a week, and "hearing from home makes me kinda homesick and I might come home for a short spell this fall." A letter to his father and aunt, the same day, said: "I'm ready to start to work again. In fact am working now, and a jeep is waiting for me. . . . I'll be pretty busy for a while, so if you don't hear from me for a few weeks don't worry about it."

The jeep took him to Algiers, where he boarded a plane for Bizerte.

CHAPTER 28

Yesterday Is Tomorrow

AMONG the scores of ships in Bizerte harbor was the USS *Biscayne*, a converted seaplane tender that was serving as flagship for an admiral. Ernie was directed to board her at once, although she would not leave for a week. On the *Biscayne*, to his delight, he found ice-cream, Coca-cola, recent magazines, after-dinner movies, showers, beds with mattresses, meals at table with silverware. It was hot below, but the captain, Commander Rufus Young, had a cot and mattress put on the breeze-cooled deck for Ernie. Ernie, in turn, agreed to edit the ship's daily mimeographed newspaper, although this involved rising at three a.m. and spending two or three hours assembling and rewriting the news taken down by a radio operator.

It was the ship's first invasion, and her unblooded crew was a little apprehensive. But in the pre-dawn darkness one night, while Ernie was busy in the radio shack with his editing, German raiders came over Bizerte and she got her baptism of fire, an hour and a half of bedlam in which three men aboard were wounded and the ship's guns shot down one plane—or, as the gunnery officer exclaimed to the captain, "Sir, we got the son-of-a-bitch!" It did the crew a lot of good; their anxiety about how they might behave in action was gone in a wave of exultation.

Late one afternoon the *Biscayne* left her pier, took the solemn salute of a naval guard of honor on the Customs House roof, slipped past the breakwater, and joined one of the several fleets that made up the great invasion armada.

D-minus-one dawned ominously gray and misty, and the Mediterranean roughened; by afternoon it was breaking over the decks and seasickness was epidemic. Ernie, feeling queasy, turned in that night with his clothes on: "Never in my life had I been so depressed. I lay there and let the curse of a too vivid imagination picture a violent and complete catastrophe for America's war effort—before another dawn." The next thing he knew, the loudspeaker awoke him: "Stand by for gunfire. We may have to shoot out some searchlights." The ship had stopped a few miles off shore, and the silhouettes of Sicilian hills were visible. The storm had vanished. The matter of the lights was something else.

The *Biscayne* had been preparing to anchor, it developed, when searchlights on shore began sweeping the water. One of them picked out the flagship and four others quickly bunched on her. She was duck soup for the poorest gunner. One officer said later: "The fellow standing next to me was breathing so hard I couldn't hear the anchor go down. Then I realized there wasn't anybody standing next to me." After what seemed a very long time the five lights were unaccountably switched off, one by one. There had been no firing at all. A few minutes later, at approximately two forty-five a.m., July 10, the initial assault boats hit the beach.

The *Biscayne* was lying near the city of Licata, midway in the fourteen-mile expanse assigned to Major General Lucian K. Truscott's 3rd Infantry Division and an attached combat team of the 2nd Armored Division. Off to the right Terry Allen's veteran 1st Division was landing, in rough surf and against some gunfire, near Gela, and still farther east the 45th Division was having its troubles with rough water. But in Ernie's sector things were easy. Since the ship's paper was being omitted on D-day, after the searchlight incident he took a catnap until daylight, when enemy bombers precipitated a thunderous retort of ack-ack. Then Italian artillery opened up, from the hills, but with hospitable inaccuracy, although one shell finally dropped within fifty yards of the *Biscayne*: "Our ship wasn't supposed to do much firing, but that was too much for the admiral. He ordered our guns into action. And for the next ten minutes we sounded like Edgewood Arsenal blowing up." While transports circled defensively, the *Biscayne* raced along the shore, pouring shells into Licata and the gun positions. Then destroyers laid smoke, through which barges carried tanks ashore. After a few sample shots from the tanks, Licata surrendered.

About nine a.m. Ernie boarded an assault barge to take a look ashore. He waded in, east of Licata, found a ride into town, and spent the day watching the roundup of jittery Italian troops and suspect civilians, marveling at the sparseness of the anti-invasion defenses, and talking with soldiers who griped at the lack of action but found delight in the abundance of fresh tomatoes. Back on the ship, he wrote Jerry next day: " . . . counterattacks are developing and their air is getting heavier. It's noon now and we've had eleven raids since dawn. I am fine, except for the worst exhaustion I've yet experienced. Several days and nights with almost no sleep, and then the climax of the landings and all day barging around on the island and dodging raids, has left me worn out and dopey. . . ."

By nightfall on this second day the Americans and British had more than eighty thousand men ashore on a hundred-mile front. The 1st Division had weathered a crisis, beating off with the aid of naval gunfire a counterattack by a hundred tanks. That night occurred the ghastly incident in which twenty-odd transport planes, bringing in troops of the 82nd Airborne Division, were shot down by our own guns in the confusion of a coincidental German bombing.

After the third day few enemy planes were seen, and while Ernie busied himself at completing his account of the invasion from the naval viewpoint, life aboard ship settled back to normal. The *Biscayne* moved up and down the coast from time to time, and once Ernie went ashore briefly. "Luckily ran smack into the other correspondents," he wrote me, "and got my pitcher taken with the big general [Patton]." Some of the correspondents told him the 1st Division kept asking where he was; they wagged their heads and said he'd have a rough time explaining that he'd turned sailor. He wrote Jerry that his extra stint as editor of the ship's paper was wearing him out, "but everybody seems to appreciate it so much from the crew on up to the captain that I wouldn't think of stopping." And he added: "In two weeks I'll have a birthday. Good Lord, I was forty-one when I left America and now I'll be forty-three."

When it came time to quit the *Biscayne*, he left with regrets: "I hated to part from the friends I had made. Too, this taste of civilized living had been a strange delight, and yet for some perverse reason I seemed to look forward to going back to the old soldier's way of sleeping on the ground and not washing before breakfast and fighting off fleas." Patton meantime had swept across Sicily and taken Palermo, on the northern coast, so Ernie proceeded to that blitzed city. There he encountered Raymond Clapper, who was shocked by his gaunt appearance.

Ernie wanted to do some columns on the combat engineers. With Clapper he drove fifty miles east to 45th Division headquarters at Cefalù, where they parted. Clapper wrote: "It seemed sad to leave him there—a frail little fellow in Army fatigue coveralls, carrying a bedroll. It seemed as if he was being left all alone with the whole war."

Ernie joined up with the 120th Engineers Battalion, attached to the 45th Division. But before he could write anything he came down with a widespread malady which the doctors were calling battlefield fever, said to result from a combination of road dust, improper eating, inadequate sleep, high tension, and all-around exhaustion. "You ache all over and have a very high temperature. . . . You don't die of battlefield fever, but you think you're going to." They took him by ambulance to one of the 45th's clearing stations, a small tent hospital in an olive grove, where four or five days of rest and medication put him on his feet. During that time hundreds of wounded arrived at the station, and not all of them lived. "Dying men were brought into our tent, men whose death rattle silenced the conversation and made all the rest of us grave. When a man was almost gone the surgeons would put a piece of gauze over his face. He could breathe through it but we couldn't see his face well. Twice within five minutes chaplains came running. One of these occasions haunted me for hours. The man was still semiconscious. The chaplain knelt down beside him and two ward boys squatted alongside. The chaplain said, 'John, I'm going to say a prayer for you.' Somehow this stark announcement hit me like a hammer. He didn't say, 'I'm going to pray for you to get well,' he just said he was going to say a prayer, and it was obvious he meant the final prayer. It was as though he had said, 'Brother, you may not know it, but your goose is cooked.' He said a short prayer, and the weak, gasping man tried in vain to repeat the words after him. When he had finished the chaplain said, 'John, you're doing fine, you're doing fine.' Then he rose and dashed off on other business, and the ward boys went about their duties. The dying man was left utterly alone, just lying there on his litter on the ground, lying in an aisle, because the tent was full. Of course it couldn't be otherwise, but the awful aloneness of that man as he went through the last few minutes of his life was what tormented me. I felt like going over and at least holding his hand while he died, but it would have been out of order and I didn't do it. I wish now I had."

At the clearing station he got his first mail since leaving Algiers, and a wedding-anniversary wireless that Jerry had sent three weeks earlier: "House has been painted. Daisies in full bloom. And I am still as single-hearted as I was seventeen years ago today."

He replied: "Hope be in house before paint many months older."

Instead of rejoining the engineers he acted on General Eisenhower's suggestion at Algiers that he "discover" General Bradley. He went to II Corps headquarters, in the hills just west of Troina, a key village topping a dusty ridge where the Germans were making a desperate stand to cover the evacuation of scores of thousands of troops to the Italian mainland. Bradley, who had been made a lieutenant general after the Tunisian campaign, was scarcely more than a name in America, and not a particularly well-known name at that. Ernie spent three days with him and his staff. He took long rides with the General. From observation posts they watched the difficult struggle for Troina. At the end of the day there was usually a drop of Scotch, at the truck in which the General lived, to cut the dust.

Ernie and Bradley hit it off perfectly. Each respected and admired the other. The General said later on, "I have known no finer man, no better soldier"; he wrote Jerry that "the remembrance of his compassion for the lot of our soldiers will always fix him among the great and good men we have known." And Ernie declared: "If I could pick any two men in the world for my father except my own Dad, I would pick General Omar Bradley or General Ike Eisenhower. If I had a son, I would like him to go to Bradley or Ike for advice."

He sent in half a dozen pieces about the General, which quickly became the standard source for magazine writers doing pieces back home about Bradley. The other correspondents jollied him for deserting the GIs to hobnob with the high brass. Hal Boyle's daily greeting was: "There goes that social-climbing columnist!" Chris Cunningham predicted that soon Ernie would be making remarks like: "Well, I told Omar that his battle plan wouldn't work, but he insisted on trying it out anyhow." Jack Thompson accused him of being "seduced by the aristocracy." Actually the correspondents shared his regard for the General, whose plainness and modesty were in sharp contrast with the picturesque egoism of his then superior officer, Patton.

Bradley's G-2, Colonel B. A. ("Monk") Dickson, recalled that Ernie "roamed the Corps c.p. as quietly and unobtrusively as a leprechaun. He would come into the G-2 tent and perch on a map case amid the hullaballoo of duty officers howling over miles of field wire laid on the ground, pounded typewriters, Boche radio broadcast, etc. He'd ask a question or two. Then he would fade like a wraith. On several occasions he went up when I presented the G-2 situation to the General. He watched the Old Man work and his staff work and I don't think he missed a trick. . . . One day he asked me my estimate [of Bradley]. I replied, 'He has the greatness of simplicity and the simplicity of greatness.' Ernie quoted that. Mrs. Dickson spotted it and wrote me that she knew I had said it. It was Ernie's knack of reporting that when he selected a quotation it was so much on the beam that those who knew the quotee could spot it thirty-five hundred miles away."

In those days, according to Don Whitehead of the AP, "Ernie was always cautioning others against taking too many chances, but then he would go up himself with the doughboys and expose himself to all the dangers of the infantryman." Once he was caught in an air raid with no helmet and used his shovel to protect his head. During the battle for Troina the correspondents were sleeping in a peach orchard, loud with guinea hens, peacocks, ducks, turkeys, calves, and a donkey, beside the looted country home of an Italian baron, south of Cerami. The press room was in the dining room of the house. "Ernie had his typewriter," Whitehead recalled, "on a table just below a large and horrible painting of a string of glassy-eyed dead fish. Once he looked up at the painting and said, 'I wish those goddamned fish wouldn't keep staring like that. They make me nervous—and there's too much sympathy in their eyes.' "

It may have been under the sad-eyed fish that he wrote Jerry: "For some reason I've been awfully homesick in the last few weeks and I've definitely decided to come home for a while this fall. . . ."

That night German bombers kept him awake, and for a while "it looked as if I might never get to be forty-three." But he celebrated his birthday, next day, with an egg for breakfast—he traded cigarettes to a boy for it. He also managed to work in a toast or two, with Colonel Harry Goslee and Colonel Samuel L. Myers, and a bit of vermouth with Master Sergeant Don

Hutcheson and some other soldiers. The sergeant reported: "As he sat there talking to us, it was hard to believe that here was a man who had reached his goal. They don't say, 'There's Pyle, the writer.' Just 'Pyle' is enough. There is nothing conceited about him. He claims he weighs about a hundred and ten. Still, that hundred and ten pounds of man is more than any man I have ever met."

Two days later Ernie and Goslee and others watched through binoculars as Troina was given a tremendous final shellacking by air and artillery. That evening an officer broke out a bottle of champagne. "My palate has never been educated up to champagne," Ernie wrote, "and I'd just as soon have had a good swig of Bevo, but . . . you can't let your old friends down."

Troina fell next day. It took another ten days to wind up the Sicilian campaign—a tough ten days. Ernie wrote of a company runner in the 1st Division who was so exhausted that he "came slogging up to a certain commander and said excitedly, 'I've got to find Captain —— right away. Important message.' The Captain said, 'But I'm Captain ——. Don't you recognize me?' And the runner said 'I've got to find Captain —— right away.' And he went dashing off. They had to run to catch him." The fatigue of a hard campaign was described in this paragraph: "It's the perpetual dust choking you, the hard ground wracking your muscles, the snatched food sitting ill on your stomach, the heat and the flies and dirty feet and the constant roar of engines and the perpetual moving and the never sitting down, and the go, go, go, night and day, and on through the night again. Eventually it all works itself into an emotional tapestry of one dull, dead pattern—yesterday is tomorrow and Troina is Randazzo and when will we ever stop and, God, I'm so tired!" Back home the *Infantry Journal* was saying: "The war is not likely to see more accurate reporting" than Ernie's. During the closing days of the campaign he rejoined the 120th Engineers for a while, then moved over to the 10th Engineers, attached to Truscott's 3rd Division, which was racing along the north coast for Messina and the kill. At Point

Calava he saw this unit, in a single spectacular day and night, bridge an enormous hole blasted by the retreating enemy in the shelflike approach to a highway tunnel through which the 3rd must pass.

One night he sat with Don Whitehead in a lemon grove near Messina, looking at the stars and talking about death. "I'm afraid," he said. "War scares hell out of me. I guess it's because I don't want to die. But I know I'm not a coward, and that means a great deal. I know the longer we stay with this the smaller our chances are of getting out. But what the hell! We can't leave it and we know it."

Just before Messina fell he was ticketed by MPs three times in one day for not wearing his helmet and leggings, for which Patton was a celebrated stickler. Each ticket called for a forty-dollar fine. A few nights later a messenger handed him an envelope from his friend Major John Hurley, the provost marshal, containing the official conviction papers and this penalty: "You are hereby sentenced to recite ten times a night for the next thirty nights, as follows: 'I'm a good soldier and will try to conduct myself as such by wearing my helmet and leggins at all times.'"

He wrote Jerry: "I'm feeling very happy, for when I came back to camp last night after several days away there was considerable mail—no letters from you, but your pictures in a letter from Lee. It was so wonderful to see them. You look so fine, and so pretty. At first you looked strange and I couldn't figure it out, and then I realized it's that you look the way you used to look a long time ago. . . . And then this afternoon another batch of mail came in by courier, and in it was a V-letter from you, the second I've had since leaving Africa seven weeks ago. You said you had gone to bed that night with *Arrowsmith*. . . . Have you heard the German song called 'Lili Marlene,' which they say is so far the outstanding song of the war? I heard it just once over the German radio, and it is sad, lovely, repetitious, haunting sort of thing. . . . There were one hundred and fifty-three papers using the column on July 2. . . . People send me clippings of newspaper pieces written about me by people I've never heard of, most of which are ninety per cent misinformation, such as one which said that all my life I'd been plagued with people playing practical jokes on me! I hadn't been aware of that, but maybe I don't know a practical joke when I see one.

"The Sicilian campaign is just about over. The summer climate and its various foreign germs are beginning to catch up with us. A couple of days after getting back to normal from my spell of a couple of weeks ago, I contracted the famous military disease known as 'the GIs,' and have been considerably weakened by that, although didn't feel bad and kept on going. I guess I've suddenly passed the point in middle age where I can't take much any more. . . . This last trip I've been with the combat engineers, and the other day walked four miles with the infantry beyond where vehicles could go, and next day just had to lie down on the ground about half the time. And I feel sleepy all the time. It's disgusting because I know it's nothing but just the all-over cell collapse that comes with too many years—for I'm actually healthy and there's nothing wrong with me in the medical line. The other correspondents have been dropping off like flies with malaria. . . . The weather has been so grand that we don't bother with tents; just sleep on the ground in the open. I really like the outdoor life when the weather is good—it seems so much cleaner than being in a house. Of course I have no desire to make a permanent thing of it, however. I think I've looked at your pictures at least fifty times since they came last night. . . .

"I haven't been under fire very much during the Sicilian campaign. My time with the Navy and in hospital (guess I've picked that up from the British, saying 'in hospital' instead of 'in the hospital') used up about half the campaign, and then too as time goes on I find myself more and more reluctant to repeat and repeat the same old process of getting shot at. I don't know whether it's cowardice or experience or what, but the other correspondents who have been with it a long time say they are having the same reaction. When you get shells whining and falling around you, or on the infrequent occasions when bombers come over, you sort of cringe and say, 'Oh God, do I have to go through this all over again?'

"I'm so happy to hear you say that you feel your work is important, even though you can't place it in the 'big picture.' For it is important. The soldiers way down in the tropics so far away from the war are afflicted with a feeling that they're doing nothing, but I tried to tell them that it was something that had to be done, and in its way was just as important as the man who was getting shot at. I try to bulldoze myself and keep up my spirits by making believe that my work is important too in the war effort, but it's hard for me to convince myself when I see daily how easy my lot is compared to all the kids in there taking it constantly; and me making so much money out of it to boot. The only justification I can find for myself is that at least I'm making it the hard way, and not by sitting in New York or Washington pontificating over a typewriter. But the war gets so complicated and confused in my mind; on especially sad days it's almost impossible for me to believe that anything is worth such mass slaughter and misery; and the after-war outlook seems to me so gloomy and pathetic for everybody. . . ."

Ray Clapper returned to Washington, and told me how worn-out Ernie looked. I wirelessed at once: "Urge vacation homeward when feasible."

A few days after Messina fell to the 3rd Division—too late to prevent the escape to Italy of eighty-eight thousand enemy troops—Ernie went back to Palermo, and there made up his mind to go home. Before receiving my message he wirelessed me: "Returning headquarters city [Algiers] in few days and have pretty definitely decided start home in couple weeks. If any objections let me know. Have just sort bogged down and feel need mental refreshing."

As he put it later in the column: "I had come to despise and be revolted by war clear out of any logical proportion. I couldn't find the Four Freedoms among the dead men. Personal weariness became a forest that shut off my view of events about me. I was no longer seeing the little things that you at home want to know about the soldiers. . . . I just got too tired in the head."

At Palermo he was billeted "in a dungeonlike cell that overlooked an alley inhabited by a melee of Sicilians who screamed constantly and never cleaned up anything." Before going to bed the first night he inspected the sheets: "My haul was three bedbugs and a baby scorpion. Civilization, she is wonderful." He took a bath and was promptly assaulted by fleas.

When Bob Hope and his troupe came to Palermo Ernie spent most of a couple of days with them. On a Sunday he went out with them to the 45th Division and saw them do their stuff before nineteen thousand soldiers. Back in the city that night some of the press and public-relations men gave a party for Hope and singer Frances Langford, which ended in the small hours with a whopping German air raid.

Ernie flew to Algiers, and while awaiting transportation home dropped in to pay his respects to General Eisenhower, who congratulated him on some of the columns that had appeared in *Stars and Stripes*. John Steinbeck, whom Ernie had long admired but had never met, was at the Aletti, and Ernie decided to pay a call. As often happened with him, on the way to the hotel he began getting nervous. Perhaps Steinbeck would be busy. Probably he had never heard of Pyle. Maybe it would be better not to stick one's neck out. But he went on. Quentin Reynolds was there with Steinbeck, which made the introductions easy, and for Ernie and John it turned into a historic session of the mutual-admiration society. They dined at the country villa of an English official and, according to Reynolds, "acted like a couple of lovebirds courting each other. We sat there on the stone terrace of the villa, talking, almost until dawn. Then we decided to spend the night there. Our English pal put some blankets on the floor and we used them as beds. I dropped off to sleep about six a.m. and Ernie and John were still talking, exchanging ideas and finding that they agreed with each other on everything from bourbon to ranch life in the Southwest. It was the beginning of a beautiful friendship between two fine, humble men."

Steinbeck later wrote: "There are really two wars and they haven't much to do with each other. There is the war of maps and logistics, of campaigns, of ballistics, armies, divisions, and regiments—and that is General Marshall's war. Then there is the war of homesick, weary, funny, violent, common men, who wash their socks in their helmets, complain about the food, whistle at Arab girls, or any girls for that matter, and lug themselves through as dirty a business as the world has ever seen and do it with humor and dignity and courage—and that is Ernie Pyle's war. He knows it as well as anyone and writes about it better than anyone."

From Algiers Ernie flew west to Rabat, French Morocco, and caught a Clipper home.

CHAPTER 29

"It Came a Little Too Late"

I HAD been waiting for hours when the Clipper delivered Ernie at La Guardia Field. It was about four a.m. on September 7, 1943. We went to the Algonquin Hotel, where he tried to telephone Jerry in Albuquerque but could not get through. We sat and talked, while outside our window the Empire State Building materialized with the dawn. There was so much to say, on both sides, that a lot of the conversation was in unfinished sentences. Ernie was travel-tired as well as war-weary, but he was eager to hear about what was going on at home and he had a boyish curiosity about the new fame that awaited him. It was eight o'clock before we went to bed. And within ten minutes the ring of the phone shattered our dazed sleep. A few minutes later came another call, and another. The *World-Telegram* was sending a reporter. *Editor & Publisher* wanted an interview. An Army intelligence officer must question him—a wartime routine with returning correspondents. We had to give up the idea of sleep.

Radio people began telephoning. Ernie had written me that he might get up nerve to do a broadcast or two; perhaps he could do the GIs a service by telling, over the air, of the miseries they were undergoing so gallantly; and he might pick up a little money to compensate in a small way for magazine and other offers he had declined. A radio network had hopefully volunteered to "place some time at his disposal," but it had in mind getting his services free. Ray Clapper, who had done much radio work, told me Ernie shouldn't take less than fifteen hundred dollars for a broadcast. So, when a representative of one program now offered a few hundred dollars for an appearance by Ernie, I said fifteen hundred would be the minimum. The man sounded shocked. Within minutes there came another call: one of the chains would like to place him on a big-time program, and fifteen hundred was all right. But by this time our rooms were a three-ring circus, with interviewers and photographers and other visitors treading on one another's heels, and Ernie felt panicky and trapped. When I reported the fifteen-hundred offer he decided to turn it down.

Long-distance calls and telegrams were arriving, for the press associations had carried an item about his return. A lecture manager offered a twenty-five-thousand-dollar guarantee. Wives and friends of soldiers phoned to ask if he had any recent word of their men. And Ernie had errands to do—messages from soldiers to their folks, letters from John Steinbeck and Quentin Reynolds to their wives, courtesy calls on his New York bosses.

That night he reached Jerry by telephone and told her he would go to Washington and Dana first, so that on reaching Albuquerque he could forget everything else and relax. We got a few hours' sleep before the telephone started again. The Office of War Information wanted him to make some recordings. So did the Wac recruiting office. Indiana University asked him to address a convocation. "We, the People" wanted him on a War Bond program with Secretary Morgenthau and would pay five hundred dollars for three or four minutes; he decided to do this one, since it was a Bond show. The phone was never silent. A new call was waiting on the switchboard whenever we hung up. Finally we threw our gear together and raced for Penn Station, where a redcap of the wartime variety took one look at Ernie's heavy duffle bag and turned his back. Ernie shouldered it, and we ran. The train to Washington was moving as we stepped aboard. Ernie draped his trench coat over his head and slept.

Washington was more hectic than ever. The telephone became a plaguing hornet, even though all except long-distance calls were shut off. The merry-go-round was running full speed, and he couldn't get off. He was having fun in a way, but it was grinding him down. My efforts to protect him met with scant success. There were too many friends, too many duties, too much pleasure, too much drinking. There was the dentist to see; a lawyer friend, Glenn Simmon, came to straighten out his taxes; a Marine sergeant-correspondent, back from Guadalcanal, showed up to interview him for War Bond publicity; two girls from *Fortune* wanted material on anxiety neurosis among the troops; autograph hunters waited in the lobby. Pentagon asked him over for an interview with "five or six" officers; he went, with a hangover, and was confronted by fifty-odd officers, but he managed all right. Secretary of War Stimson asked him in for a private talk. On several occasions Ernie started to tell me a secret story about General Patton but was always interrupted, and it was weeks before he got a chance to relate, in confidence, the "slapping incident" at the 93rd Evacuation Hospital in Sicily.

Chesterfield offered five hundred dollars for the use of Ernie's picture in an advertisement. I suggested fifteen hundred, and Ernie settled for a thousand. Photographer Ruzzey Green came down from New York with a roomful of equipment and set up shop at Ernie's hotel, the Hay-Adams. I invited Deac Parker's secretary, Milton Pike, an amateur photographer, to drop in and try his hand too. Both produced fine pictures, Green a smiling color photo for the ad, Pike a grave one in black and white, eloquent of fatigue—it was used later on the jacket of *Brave Men*. The phone rang during the posing; it was Ray Clapper, who said that a Hollywood producer, Lester Cowan, had called from New York and wanted to talk to Ernie about a movie. Ernie agreed to meet Cowan next day in Washington. It developed that the War Department was urging a film about the infantry, and Cowan thought Ernie's copy would be ideal for it. After several sessions an agreement was reached to sell Cowan the film rights to the forthcoming book. Bigger producers had been making inquiries but were waiting to see whether the book sold well. Cowan was willing to take a chance.

The North American Newspaper Alliance sent an emissary to woo Ernie from Scripps-Howard with talk of a fifty-thousand-dollar-a-year guarantee. Ernie said no.

He forced himself to produce a few columns, after which we re-issued some forty favorites among the old ones, to keep the feature going. He had to write the copy for his "We, the People" interview with Morgenthau, which was to be broadcast from Jefferson's home outside Charlottesville, Virginia, but he was in such a funk he couldn't think. While he lay on a bed, gray as a ghost, I "interviewed" him and took down his answers on the typewriter. He was feeling stale and grim when he went to Charlottesville; somehow he got through the brief broadcast without too much stage fright.

He wanted to get out of uniform, but there were no clothes in storage except an old jacket. At a haberdashery he selected a pair of trousers and then asked for a lightweight hat. The salesman produced only heavyweight fedoras, and when Ernie said he'd look elsewhere the clerk demanded, "Don't you know there's a war on?" Ernie wrote a paragraph for the column about the smart aleck but killed it for fear it might cost the fellow his job.

He found time to dictate a lot of letters, most of them to the families of soldiers he had met. And he wrote Jerry: "The correspondents who had been home this summer and returned to Africa warned me that I would be smothered when I got home, but I never dreamed of it being this bad. . . . I hate every day that delays me from getting out there with you. I do hope you'll be really glad to see me." And to his father and aunt: "I'm just absolutely snowed under with hundreds of requests for everything under the sun. . . . Lee is acting as my 'manager' and 'secretary' and handling all the people who want things, but even so enough seeps through that it's about to drive me nuts.

. . . Three or four days will be the outside I can stay [in Dana], as I just must get on out to Albuquerque and begin my rest. That's all I came home for was to rest, and here in one week I'm more exhausted than I ever was at the front."

Scripps-Howard gave a big party for him at the Walker Stones' house, with a hundred or more guests, and it was a fine gay rally, but just about the last straw. He escaped to Dana, where he had a few fairly quiet days, then flew to Albuquerque.

Jerry's period of eager waiting while he was in the East had done her no good, easy prey as she was to tensions. The homecoming had its sorrowful aspects. Ernie unburdened himself in a letter to Roz: "I'd told Jerry not to meet me, but she and the two poor Sisters had been up since three a.m. meeting every plane that came in. I was shocked at how thin she was—she weighs only ninety-two pounds. Her job is so damned hard it's man-killing, but she likes it in a way and knows she must have it or she is lost. . . . The poor gal is fighting like hell, but she is an emotional wreck. . . . Occasionally misses a day's work, yet despite it is doing a superior job of her work and is constantly commended. . . . Sister [Margaret Jane] says that any unusual emotion upsets her. . . . She feels that another complete nervous collapse is inevitable. All that can be done is to help stall it off, and God knows Sister has done a magnificent job with her. It is saddening beyond words, but it has been my fear all the time. She does herself up so nicely that she looks pretty—yet even in repose there is a horrible anguish in her face. . . . I believe Sister when she says that her love for me is the dominant thing in her life, yet I believe it makes no difference eventually whether I should be here with her permanently or not. I mean, if I were to quit and stay here forever, it couldn't make any difference because her trouble is basic.

"Jerry has been a 'case' so long that my normal feeling of love for her has been sort of smothered in an academic viewpoint toward her, yet she is the only thing in the world that means anything to me, and she is so outstandingly wonderful that I can hardly look at her, or any of her things when she's away, without kind of crying inside at her awful tragedy—and mine. She has always been so alone inside. . . ."

In the column, later on, he wrote: "Our little house is still a gem. Now it has some Algerian rugs on the floor, Moroccan hassocks before the fireplace, Congo ivory on the mantle. We can still see eighty miles from our front window, and the sunsets are still spellbinding. Quail still peck in our front yard. Roaming neighborhood dogs come and visit us. So do children. The postman always has something pleasant to say. We have two cups of hot tea very early in the morning, and we are sitting here drinking it when the first dawn comes over the Sandias. The sun soon warms the desert, and the day grows lazy. . . ."

There were cozy evenings, sometimes alone with Jerry, sometimes with the Shaffers or the Mounts or other friends. The days were full of small missions. Ernie got his car out of storage, and a generous ration board gave him coupons for forty gallons of gasoline a week. Weeds had taken over his south lot, and he counterattacked. The shed was bulging with oddments that needed sorting and discarding. There was usually an errand or two downtown every day, which turned out agreeably. "People out here are swell," he wrote Roz. "Downtown they gather around everywhere I go and shake hands and say nice things, and then immediately go away as people should. As they overtake you in their cars they'll call, 'Welcome home, Ernie,' and then go right on, not hounding you with requests. I'm apparently the No. 1 citizen of the state, and they are glad I'm here, but they have a certain Western dignity which keeps them from badgering you."

There was much telephoning, telegraphing, and writing between Albuquerque and Washington. Cowan hadn't liked the original book title, and Ernie hit on "Here Is Your War," which Holt instantly accepted. (The film eventually was titled *The Story of GI Joe.*) Advance orders for the book were rolling in, and Holt had raised the print order to a hundred and fifty thousand copies. "What the hell we gonna do?" Ernie wrote me. "Let's retire. You've got to take a small portion of all this dough."

He insisted that Cavanaugh come from California for his vacation: "Just bring your overalls and some booze, that's all." Liquor was then hard to get in Albuquerque. Cavanaugh came, and Lester Cowan flew in too. Ernie, who had been skeptical of Hollywood in general, began to take to Lester. "He really had a wonderful time here," Ernie wrote me. "He fitted in well, and Jerry and Cavanaugh both liked him. . . . It wound up that we cooked ham and eggs here instead of going out to eat; he kept raving about how he liked the place, and he fell in love with Cheetah and wants to get a dog like her; and finally TWA called up and said there'd been a cancellation and he could fly to Los Angeles that night after all, and he told them on the phone to skip it, he was having too good a time to leave."

Cavanaugh was a tonic to Ernie: "He's so swell and old-shoe and has added a touch of lightness to Jerry's still-existing depression." He was also a fast man with a dishcloth or an ax. Ernie ordered a cord of firewood against the winter, and when it came in large blocks Cavanaugh split it all and stored it in the shed. Every morning he and Ernie would drive Jerry to work, have breakfast at the airport restaurant, then shop and plan dinner. In the late afternoon people would begin to drop in and dinner would be deferred, often until near midnight. "It wasn't easy for Jerry, it sure wasn't," Cavanaugh said later.

Strangers came past occasionally. The only one to whom Cavanaugh saw Ernie react uncivilly was a zealot campaigning for peace, who came up on a bicycle and started haranguing. Ernie said, "I'm sorry, Mr. ——, I've come eight thousand miles to get some rest, and I just can't talk to you. I'm sick of war." The man said, "Are you sick of peace too?" Ernie said, "Yes I am," and would have no more truck with his caller.

Ernie wrote Roz: "I give up. I started in this morning to answer absolutely personal and intimate letters, and had just one finished when the postman arrived with another wheelbarrow load. If I try to answer even just the personal mail, it'll take me eight hours a day for the next month, since I get started and write three or four pages to friends. So you're going to have to take onto your drooping shoulders the bulk of the personal mail too—for this emergency period."

Numerous requests for speeches and articles were turned down. "I'm getting depressed," he wrote me, "over what few obligations we have taken on, and we'll sink if we try to do anything more. I think you'll have to say no even to the semi-official and patriotic type of request. . . . Things aren't too bad here; but the time is almost up and I've been with Jerry so little and she is not in too good shape, confidentially, and I wake up and lie awhile before daylight every morning so blue about leaving that I can hardly bear it."

Finally Jerry went to pieces and he had to take her to the hospital. "She says, and I believe her," he wrote me, "that it *isn't* the result of too much chaos around here; actually it's emotional over our time being so short and my getting ready to go and her working all the time I was here and her job being so damned hard that just too much work piled up on her and she couldn't take it. . . . They're going to give her an assistant, so if the leaving isn't too big a crisis for her (Sister and I both have grave fears), maybe she can swing back into the routine shortly after I'm gone. She and we know that she *must* keep her job for her own survival."

She came home after a few days and arranged to stay off her job until Ernie's departure. "I believe she has herself in hand where she can get over the hump of my going," he wrote me. "This last week has been mad. Seems as though everything undone, and everybody who had held off, has been upon us. For the past several days I've had to make out a schedule to go by, in order to get everything done." He and Shafe had lunch with Governor Jack Dempsey, who appointed Ernie a New Mexico colonel, as Governors Tingley and Miles had done before. *Life* sent a photographer from Santa Fe to take pictures of the Pyles and their home. An Army hospital persuaded Ernie to make a two-hour visit by telling him that it was filled with wounded from Africa; when he got there he found there wasn't a soul from overseas, and never had been.

To resolve any doubts about the complete legality of their remarriage by proxy, he and Jerry had the ceremony repeated, at home, with Judge McNerney again officiating. It was, in a way, the third time they had married each other.

Jerry found a wool-lined sleeping bag as a going-away present. And on October 26 Ernie boarded the *Chief* for Chicago. Jerry managed the leave-taking without undue stress.

Ernie's first destination now was Clinton, Indiana, not far from Dana, where his father was in the hospital with an injured hip. "My dad is neither blind nor deaf," he wrote in the column, "but he is a little of each. . . . The night I arrived, several members of our family met the train and we drove right to the hospital. The folks hung back so I could go ahead into the room alone. So I went in and my father held out his hand, and we talked together for about a minute, and then the rest of them came in. He greeted them all, and then asked if they had been to the depot yet. They said yes, and then my dad said, 'Did Ernest come?' So they all howled and said, 'Who do you think you've been talking to the last few minutes?' 'Why,' he said, 'I thought it was Clyde Howard.' Clyde is the barber up at Dana. My dad was very chagrined."

Ernie was told about the time his father had a nightmare there at the hospital. He thought he was in a tent in the hospital grounds. And "while he was 'in the tent' he had to go to the toilet. He got out of bed and couldn't find the door to the bathroom. He got completely lost there in the dark. Then he felt the foot of the bed, and since he figured he was in a tent with no floor but the ground, what difference did it make? The nurses caught him at that and put him back to bed. I don't believe I've heard my father get as tickled in forty years as when he recounts the story." Ernie gave Mr. Pyle a little ivory kangaroo he had bought in Khartoum and a copy of *Here Is Your War*: "I notice he shows visitors the kangaroo first and says proudly, 'See what Ernest brought me from Egypt.' The book is dedicated to my father on the flyleaf, but he hasn't noticed it yet, and I haven't said anything to him about it."

Back in Washington he caught up with the reviewers' hearty reception of his book, including a handsome spread on page one of the *New York Times*' Sunday book section. After reading it, Ernie skimmed through the rest. "Why, the dirty so-and-so's," he complained, "they've also reviewed some other people's books in this issue!"

Mrs. Roosevelt praised *Here is Your War* in "My Day," and he sent her a thank-you note, which brought an invitation to tea. He explained to the First Lady's secretary, Miss Malvina Thompson, that the only coat he possessed was an old gray one with both elbows out, and she said to think nothing of it. Nevertheless he was nervous, and he paced Lafayette Park for twenty minutes before the appointed hour. Mrs. Roosevelt and Miss Thompson soon put him at his ease. Mrs. Roosevelt told him it took her about half an hour to write her column. "I told her it took me half a day, and she said, 'Yes, but you write a much better column than I do.' Since it is bad taste to dispute the opinion of the First Lady, I just spluttered into my tea." Presently he walked back across Lafayette Park to the Hay-Adams House, "feeling as light as a feather."

There were a number of conferences on the film with War Department officials and Cowan and Arthur Miller, the soon-to-be-famous playwright, who was on the Cowan payroll for a time. Lord Halifax, the British Ambassador, invited Ernie to the Embassy for a talk. There were scores of copies of the book to autograph for friends. There were inoculations to take and other nagging necessities. And when at last he was all clear it developed that somebody at the Pentagon had neglected to act on his application for air transportation, so there was a further delay. Meanwhile he resumed the column. "I've never hated to do anything as badly in my life as I hate to go back to the front," he wrote. "I dread it and I'm afraid of it. But what can a guy do? I know millions of others who are reluctant too, and they can't even get home. So here we go. The decision, it's true, is my own. Nobody is forcing me to go back. Probably that's the reason I feel so glum about it. Going back is all my own fault. I could kick myself." The *Boston Globe* spread that first piece under an eight-column headline on page one: "Ernie Pyle Writes Again."

In one column he had this to say about his new fame: "Once in a while you get resentful. Most of the time you just feel too rushed and a little bewildered, and kinda pleased. I suppose the main thing is that ninety-nine out of a hundred of us are born with a certain amount of vanity, or pride, or egotism, or whatever you want to call it. And when you hit a point where you're recognized every time you step out, you can't help but feel sort of sparkly inside. Furthermore, you get a lot of things by being 'known' that you'd never get otherwise. I mean stores will get 'shortage' articles from under the counter and sell them to you; railroad and airline men will give you a reservation after turning other people away; the plumber and the typewriter repairman, who aren't accepting calls before a week from Saturday, will come immediately. . . . But when the bolt of fame strikes, a guy better be mighty careful or he's going to wind up giving most of his time to his new career of being a celebrity, and practically no time at all to his family and real friends. And the job which gave him prominence in the first place will be done merely at odd moments, with his mind on something else. . . . I think that on the whole I'm fairly safe from the perils of celebrity. For one thing, it came a little too late. I'm forty-three, and it doesn't matter so much any more. My life has been pretty full and pretty pleasant; I've got most everything I ever wanted, but I've had some blows too; I've contributed a little and received a great deal. Through the years I did my job the best I could, and this is what happened. I didn't plan it, and I didn't ask for this. I could have done without it, but now that it's here, I'm pretty sure I can take it. . . . This is all kind of immodest. But it's all kind of true too."

As always, it was hard to resume production, and he felt uncertain about the propriety of those first pieces. But soon he was able to write Jerry: "People have been enthusiastic about the first two columns—such people as Deac and Lowell and the Mac-Kayes. I'm amazed; it gives me some encouragement to keep beating myself back to the typewriter."

Roy Howard was in town, and at lunch with Ernie expressed some disappointment that he was not going west, to the theater of Roy's friend MacArthur, but, as Ernie wrote Jerry, "I gave him my reasons for not wanting to go yet, and he was quite satisfied with it and perfectly nice." Glenn Simmon came around to go over his taxes again, and he wrote her: "Our income for this year figures around sixty-nine thousand dollars, and our income tax around twenty-nine thousand. Aren't those figures ridiculous? When we were compiling it, Simmie and I had to stop right in the middle of it and laugh. . . . I gave Lee a check for two thousand, because he's been so wonderful and has really done the work of a professional ten-per-cent agent. He didn't want to take it of course." Since I was Ernie's immediate boss, this transaction was rather unusual, but it was approved by my own bosses, Parker and Stone.

Ernie had been in Washington nearly three weeks before he could get away. At last, packed and ready to go, he wrote Jerry: "Darling, it's awful for us to face the start of another such long separation, but I want you to feel one thing—that you needn't worry about me. I'll be all right physically, for now that I've sort of been through the mill, I'm not going to take any unnecessary chances this time. . . . I'm glad you think I'm wonderful and great, but you know I think that about you too. Whatever this fame business is, you're as much responsible as I am; for you have given me more in character than anyone else in the world. If I could only have your depth of honesty and sincerity, I might think

I was really great. But great or not, we've both got so much to live for; we've got everything if we could just have ourselves, and I'm convinced that when I come back again we will have that. I love you, darling; I can't conceive of going on without you; so be there big and strong for me when I come back."

CHAPTER 30

The Beloved Captain

AN ARMY plane took Ernie to Miami, where he had to wait a few days. He was introduced to Al Jolson, who had been entertaining the troops in Africa and Sicily, and Jolson said to a reporter: "Everywhere I went the soldiers told me how wonderful Ernie Pyle was. Heck, he doesn't sing or dance, and I couldn't figure out what he did to entertain them, but they acted like he was Mr. God." Ernie wrote me: "I've had a good time here, but I'm tired of it now and hope to God we get out to-night. . . . Everything was swell in Washington, and I love everybody. But I'll be glad to get down to hard work again."

He did get out that night. The flight, via South America, took five days, and along the way he signed Short Snorter bills by the hundred. At one tropical stop a Major Bill Marsh asked him to mention in print that at last he had met somebody from Tekamah, Nebraska: "Major Marsh couldn't produce any proof there really is such a place, but he did have an honest face." Less than a year and a half later, a soldier from Tekamah was to help recover Ernie's body.

At the Aletti in Algiers it was old home week for sure. "Here I sit on the same balcony of the same room I was in a year ago," he wrote Jerry. "Everybody is nice, and officers I don't remember ever seeing before yell across the street and say 'Welcome back.'" Lots of friends were around—among them Dick Hollander, Hal Boyle, "Boots" Norgaard, Don Coe, Graham Hovey, George

293

Biddle, Ken Crawford, Fredric March, with a USO troupe, and Red Mueller of NBC, with whom Ernie shared a room.

He went on to Naples in a cargo plane but hadn't been there two hours "before I felt I couldn't stand it," so he got a ride up to the headquarters of General Mark Clark's Fifth Army at Caserta, north of Naples. There he was billeted with other correspondents in a mammoth royal palace—a drafty layout of many hundred rooms.

"The long winter misery has started," he wrote Jerry. "By this time tomorrow night I will be in the lines. Sometimes I've felt that I couldn't make myself go, but now that I'm here I want to take the plunge and get in and get the first return over with. . . . I feel very strange and lonely here, as I always do in new places. I wonder about you and think about you and hate myself for ever having left you, and yet I suppose I would have hated myself if I hadn't come back. . . ."

He went forward, to an artillery outfit he had known in England, and soon wrote her in a quite different mood: "I'm afraid my last letter was a little depressed, but this one isn't. I was feeling sort of pathetic about plunging back into the old fray again, but now that I've taken the plunge it's all right and I think I'm getting back into the old swing. It's hardly ever as bad once you're in it, as just thinking about it is. . . . You would glow if you could know what a joy my sleeping bag is. I slept in the open, on the ground, with it for the first time on this trip, and truly I kept as warm as a bug."

His next sortie was to the 36th Division, in the mountains, where the ridge-to-ridge fighting was being supplied by mule and by men on foot, laboring up trails with heavy packboards. A soldier of the 36th, writing to his father, said: "Ernie knows what the score is. He was sweating out the Jerry shells alongside of me for two nights, during which he had a suite of rooms in the only establishment open for business at that time—a remodeled pig shed. I say remodeled, because there was no pig in it. Old Ernie is a regular guy and all of us foot soldiers have a lot of respect for him." He climbed a rugged trail and visited a medical-aid station, situated in an old stone building which the Germans shelled occasionally. There, he reported to Jerry, a medical captain "broke out a bottle of Schenley bourbon. We sat in the attic or loft and nipped at this bottle for a couple of hours. Finally the Germans started shelling right close to it, and every one would shake the barn and the rubble would come tumbling down from the ceiling, but we felt so good by that time we didn't even pay any attention."

Back at Caserta, he wrote again: "I am in a room with Reynolds Packard of UP and Clark Lee of INS. At first it was a miserable place; big and bare and cold. Several of the windowpanes were blown out; the door was blown out; the place was cold and dirty. There were eight Italian cots in the room, but only three of us living in it. Well, one day an Italian showed up as our 'houseboy.' I haven't the remotest idea where he came from and neither does anybody else. He puttered around a couple of days and finally I gave him a small tip, and since then he practically drives us nuts with his attention. But he has really made the place livable. He scoured around and got workmen to come and put new windowpanes in, making it airtight. Then he dug up pieces of wood and started a fire in the funny Italian stove, and has kept it up daily since, so we are nice and warm all day long. Also he does our washing, in just a few hours; he cleans the place at least a dozen times a day; he brings flowers and lugs in tables and shelves for our stuff; we're so well organized it's going to be tough to leave. . . . The boy, whose name is Angelo, drives Packard crazy because he's the world's untidiest individual, and the boy keeps everything so neat and regimented he can't find a thing. But he's so nice we tolerate him. When I dry my razor after shaving, he runs and takes the other end of the towel and dries part of it. He looks over my shoulder when I'm writing and sits in the room all day trying to anticipate our wants. . . .

"Last night back here at base I got bit up pretty badly, and all I can figure is that I must have picked up some bedbugs in my sleeping bag somewhere at the front. If it happens again tonight I'll have to take steps. . . .

"Captain Hank Meyer, one of the censors who is an old friend of mine, came up and we played gin rummy and I won five straight games. You know how I love to win at anything, so it was a pleasant evening. . . . I get lonely on days like this, for although I like all the correspondents, most of them are new and there is no one I feel really close to. . . ."

Mail arrived, but "of course none from Geraldine," Ernie wrote Roz Goodman. "I am always a little bit startled . . . at Uncle Sam's great ability to sort one letter out of billions for constant losing, while delivering all the others so regularly. . . . Don't think I've met a soldier since returning that doesn't follow the column, and some of them are ecstatic. It's very gratifying to say the least. There is a rumor over here that I was wounded in Sicily, and all the soldiers ask me about it. I have to confess I merely had the GIs. . . . It's been pretty depressing where I've been the last week. I almost got my chin as low as I did in Sicily—too many dead men, and wounded and exhausted ones, for the good of the soul. . . . I'll write about five days and then go up again, which means I'll spend Christmas in the mud. . . . Am getting pretty good physically; beginning to get a little of the old ruggedness back. . . ." A letter to me said: "I've been to the front for my second stay; got considerable shelling and saw a spectacular battle; but back here to write up it sounds like the same old stuff and I'm having trouble getting going." A postscript, written next day, told how Sherman Montrose, the photographer, "produced a bottle of eau de vie, and yours truly got himself good and tight for the first time since arriving. Feel like death today but am sort of glad I did it, for I was really low and had the jerks yesterday, and something had to happen." It was on or about this day of hangover that he wrote one of his most famous columns, about a certain Captain Waskow.

Don Whitehead of the AP reminisced later on: "Ernie was all man, but there was something about him that made you want to

take care of him, to lend him a hand whenever possible. I suppose
we sensed that war was a heavier strain on him than on most of us
because he was more sensitive to cold and hunger and pain and the
shock of seeing men killed and wounded. Generally it was in
Ernie's room in the old Caserta palace where we gathered to drink
and talk. Usually he would be huddled in his bedding roll with
only his head sticking out, looking like a pixie in that knit cap. He
suffered some terrible fits of depression in Italy. The whole campaign was going badly, far more slowly than had been anticipated,
and the strain began to wear on everyone. One night I came in and
found Ernie at work. He had been up front to get a series of
stories on the mule-pack trains. 'I've lost the touch,' he said. 'This
stuff stinks. I just can't seem to get going again.' He tossed over
three columns and said, 'What do you think of 'em?' The first
one I picked up was the story of Captain Waskow. The simplicity
and beauty of that description brought tears to my eyes. This
was the kind of writing all of us were striving for, the picture we
were trying to paint in words for the people at home. 'If this is a
sample from a guy who has lost his touch,' I said, 'then the rest of
us had better go home.' "

Young Henry T. Waskow was commander of Company B,
143rd Infantry Regiment, 36th Division. He had graduated
in 1939 from Trinity University at Waxahachie, Texas, and the
next year, as a corporal in the Texas National Guard, he was called
to active service. Rapid promotions brought him to the command
of Company B in January of 1943. The devotion that he won
from his men was immortalized by Ernie. And the devotion was
mutual: in Waskow's will, written in Italy and addressed to his
parents, were these words: "When you read this I will have been
killed in action. . . . In your prayers, remember also my men."

He was killed on December 14, 1943, in the mountains near San
Pietro. Ernie's column was not published until January 10, 1944,
since Army regulations forbade the mention of casualties by name
in the press before next of kin had been notified. The dispatch,
as received by voice wireless from Algiers, had several garbled

phrases, but these were trivial. The column was given page-one display from coast to coast. The *Washington Daily News* devoted its entire first page to the column—not even a headline, just solid text. (The paper was completely sold out that day.) Radio commentators helped themselves to it. What follows is Ernie's original version, received later by mail:

Frontlines in Italy—In this war I have known a lot of officers who were loved and respected by the soldiers under them. But never have I crossed the trail of any man as beloved as Captain Henry T. Waskow, of Belton, Texas.

Captain Waskow was a company commander in the 36th Division. He had led his company since long before it left the States. He was very young, only in his middle twenties, but he carried in him a sincerity and a gentleness that made people want to be guided by him.

"After my own father, he came next," a sergeant told me.

"He always looked after us," a soldier said. "He'd go to bat for us every time."

"I've never knowed him to do anything unfair," another one said.

I was at the foot of the mule trail the night they brought Captain Waskow's body down. The moon was nearly full at the time, and you could see far up the trail, and even part way across the valley below. Soldiers made shadows in the moonlight as they walked.

Dead men had been coming down the mountain all evening, lashed onto the backs of mules. They came lying belly-down across the wooden pack-saddles, their heads hanging down on the left side of the mule, their stiffened legs sticking out awkwardly from the other side, bobbing up and down as the mule walked.

The Italian mule-skinners were afraid to walk beside dead men, so Americans had to lead the mules down that night. Even the Americans were reluctant to unlash and lift off the bodies at the bottom, so an officer had to do it himself, and ask others to help.

The first one came early in the evening. They slid him down

from the mule and stood him on his feet for a moment, while they got a new grip. In the half light he might have been merely a sick man standing there, leaning on the others. Then they laid him on the ground in the shadow of the low stone wall alongside the road.

I don't know who that first one was. You feel small in the presence of the dead men, and ashamed at being alive, and you don't ask silly questions.

We left him there beside the road, that first one, and we all went back into the cowshed and sat on water cans or lay on the straw, waiting for the next batch of mules.

Somebody said the dead soldier had been dead for four days, and then nobody said anything more about it. We talked soldier talk for an hour or more. The dead man lay all alone outside, in the shadow of the low stone wall.

Then a soldier came into the cowshed and said there were some more bodies outside. We went out into the road. Four mules stood there, in the moonlight, in the road where the trail came down off the mountain. The soldiers who led them stood there waiting. "This one is Captain Waskow," one of them said quietly.

Two men unlashed his body from the mule and lifted it off and laid it in the shadow beside the low stone wall. Other men took the other bodies off. Finally there were five, lying end to end in a long row, alongside the road. You don't cover up dead men in the combat zone. They just lie there in the shadows until somebody else comes after them.

The unburdened mules moved off to their olive orchard. The men in the road seemed reluctant to leave. They stood around, and gradually one by one I could sense them moving close to Captain Waskow's body. Not so much to look, I think, as to say something in finality to him, and to themselves. I stood close by and I could hear.

One soldier came and looked down, and he said out loud, "God damn it." That's all he said, and then he walked away. Another one came. He said, "God damn it to hell anyway." He looked down for a few last moments, and then he turned and left.

Another man came; I think he was an officer. It was hard to tell officers from men in the half light, for all were bearded and grimy dirty. The man looked down into the dead captain's face, and then he spoke directly to him, as though he were alive. He said: "I'm sorry, old man."

Then a soldier came and stood beside the officer, and bent over, and he too spoke to his dead captain, not in a whisper but awfully tenderly, and he said:

"I sure am sorry, sir."

Then the first man squatted down, and he reached down and took the dead hand, and he sat there for five full minutes, holding the dead hand in his own and looked intently into the dead face, and he never uttered a sound all the time he sat there.

And then finally he put the hand down, and then reached up and gently straightened the points of the captain's shirt collar, and then he sort of rearranged the tattered edges of his uniform around the wound. And then he got up and walked away down the road in the moonlight, all alone.

After that the rest of us went back into the cowshed, leaving the five dead men lying in line, end to end, in the shadow of the low stone wall. We lay down on the straw in the cowshed, and pretty soon we were all asleep.

Ernie had expected to go back to the 36th Division on Christmas Eve, but it didn't work out that way. There was a bar in the Caserta palace, stocked with that inferior stuff which Italians hopefully called cognac, and after writing the Waskow column he began catching up on his drinking. Others were doing the same. Particularly one of the photographers, who took too much and at dinner gave Colonel Kenneth Clark, chief public-relations officer of the Fifth Army, a tongue-lashing. When he refused to retract, Colonel Clark ordered him out of the theater. Ernie and several cameramen drank late with their banished colleague; next day Ernie did not feel up to the front lines, and by sundown—well, Clark Lee recalled it this way:

"It was in December that Ernie and I went on our notorious drunk in Caserta. It started Christmas Eve, when somebody issued some gin. For Ernie the relaxation was the result of a job well done. He had just written the Captain Waskow piece. For me it was a flight from a job to be done—a New Year's Day attack with the Special Service Force. Ernie was in one of his periods of being frightened. That's what I remember most about him—he would tell you, and convince you, that he was absolutely washed up—he simply couldn't stand the sound of another shell or bullet, or the sight of another bleeding guy—and the next thing he would turn up with some assault force, all the time protesting that he just couldn't take any more. Anyway, Ernie and I stayed there about a week, and the next thing we knew some guy was shoving needles in our arms, with B-1 vitamins in them, and we stopped it."

On one occasion during this holiday letdown Ernie mixed umbrage with his liquor at the officers' bar in the palace. "We had a couple of drinks," Don Whitehead said, "and Ernie made a casual remark to a colonel standing beside us. Ernie was dressed in his usual collapsible style, and the officer didn't recognize him. Instead, the colonel made some curt remark intended to show his rank. 'You know,' Ernie said to him, 'I was going to buy you a drink because I thought you were nice people. Come on, Don, let's find some nice people.' He went over to a table where two second lieutenants were sitting with two nurses. 'You look like nice people to me,' he said. 'Do you mind if we have our drinks with you?' So we sat with them for a couple of hours, talking about war, home, love, mud, the wounded, and how nice it would be sitting in the sun at Albuquerque."

There was a fair backlog of columns when the spree started, but after a few days it got dangerously low. According to Whitehead: "One evening in Ernie's room he announced, 'Tonight I'm through. I ain't goin' to touch another drop. I promise. I'll be out tomorrow.' Everyone agreed that was fine and started to break up the gathering. He asked me to stay behind for a few minutes. After they were gone he said, 'Close the door, Don.' I closed the door and came back to the bunk. 'If you'll just look under my cot you'll find a bottle,' he said. 'Now let's have just one more drink.' Next night Colonel Clark sent a young doctor around. The youth was awed by the little man lying in the cot with only his head sticking out from under the blanket and the knit cap on his gray head. Ernie looked at him owlishly. 'Here, Mr. Pyle,' the doc said. 'Take these pills and tomorrow you'll feel fine.' He was being very professional. 'What are they?' Ernie asked. 'They're sleeping pills. Take one and you'll get a good night's sleep.' 'Hell, Doc,' Ernie said, 'all I have to do is turn over and I sleep twelve hours straight. What I need is something to sober me up. Now you come back in the morning and give me something to get me out of this sack.' The young doctor pleaded, 'Please, Mr. Pyle, just take these pills and I'm sure you'll feel better.' Ernie swallowed them, just to make the doc feel better, more than anything else. But next morning he was out of bed and on the job again."

On New Year's Day he wrote Jerry about the holiday jag and added: "I'm not sorry, for I guess we had to relax somehow, and I was more than a week ahead with the columns, and also we stayed in our room most of the time and didn't bother anybody. When I finally got over the hangover I discovered I had some natural aches and pains unconnected with the debauchery that I didn't have before starting, but they're not serious. . . . I've been so homesick it's been hard to keep going. The dive back into this semibarbarian life is almost too much."

CHAPTER 31

Villa Vessels

ERNIE caught one of his celebrated colds at Caserta, and put off a return to the lines in favor of a comfortable billet at Naples, in an apartment maintained for the press by the Air Force. This establishment was famous among correspondents as "Villa Vessels," so called for Major Jay Vessels, the Minneapolis newspaperman who presided over it.

The "Villa," which was to be Ernie's home off and on for weeks, was an upper floor of a building overlooking the Bay of Naples. A system of smudge pots blotted out the view with an artificial fog when enemy bombers were around. The racket of the ack-ack was dominated, for Vessels' guests, by a Bofors gun a few steps from the apartment. Tracers from the Bofors seemed sometimes to be clipping the cornice of the building. The correspondents—there would be anywhere from one to ten living in the place and others dropping in—paid little attention to such routine manifestations of war.

Villa Vessels was a good place to relax and to work. Ernie was given a room to himself, so when he wanted to hole up and produce some columns he was well situated. The apartment had its own mess, with an Italian cook, and several soldiers to look after the correspondents' needs. Compared to the palace at Caserta, this was heaven. However, he wrote me, "I've got so serious and depressed about the war that I can't seem to write anything light any more. Even when I write a trivial piece it comes out heavy-handed. . . . Everybody is low, and the spirit is catching. Not about the outcome of the war or even the Italian campaign, but

303

because we're all bored and there's too much misery and things have been static for so long. I'm in an apartment looking down over what is certainly one of the most beautiful sights in the world, and I don't get even the tiniest thrill out of it. . . . I've deliberately chosen not to stick my neck out on something which you will understand by the time you get this letter.[1] If I'm going to get killed I'd rather wait and do it on a bigger show, such as France. . . ."

One of the Villa Vessels noncoms, Staff Sergeant Arthur W. Everett, Jr., of Bay City, Michigan, said later on: "Ernie was a lonely, unhappy man. Often in the dead of night he liked to talk —of his wife, her illness, their life together before the war, the friends they knew, and the little humorous incidents that brightened their nomadic path. His voice was tired and he never raised it. He was no saint; he liked to drink, and he liked the conviviality that went with it. He had definite opinions and was at home in a rousing argument, but he was by nature temperate. He was innately modest, but he knew he was famous and he was pleased. . . . Awakening one night from a sound sleep, he walked unthinkingly into the next room, clad only in a shirt and the bottom of his long underwear. There were several nurses in the room from the hospital across the street. Ernie walked gallantly over to the first girl, bowed low, and kissed the back of her hand. He gravely went from one girl to the next, repeating the performance, and then sat quietly and without embarrassment in a corner."

Villa Vessels had lots of callers. Lieutenant John Mason Brown, bookman turned naval officer, described one occasion for the *Saturday Review of Literature:* "No canteen was ever more crowded than these small rooms. There was a difference, however; a sense of veneration, a centering of interest, such as no canteen knows. Ernie was that center. These young people hovered around him like priests around an altar. He sat there like some benign god who refused to admit that he was being worshiped. More than

[1] The landing at Anzio.

hanging upon his words, these youngsters chinned themselves upon them. . . . He treated them with the solicitude most people reserve for brass hats. . . . He was more than a host. More than a wise uncle. More than an oracle too. He was their friend and confidant; a person who palpably shared their interests and seemed to share their age."

The news from home was both good and bad—good as to fame and fortune, which were skyrocketing; bad as to Jerry, since she was not writing him. He was not to learn until weeks later that she had suffered a nervous collapse, given up her job, and gone to the hospital.

The column was running in more than two hundred dailies and Ernie's checks from United Feature were larger each month— around eighteen hundred dollars now. *Here Is Your War* was high on the best-seller lists. Praise was pouring in. Quentin Reynolds was saying: "Three great discoveries of this war are the jeep, the Red Cross girl, and Ernie Pyle." Fred Painton reported to the *Saturday Evening Post* that Ernie "was probably the most prayed-for man with the American troops." *Life* said he "now occupied a place in American journalistic letters which no other correspondent in this war has achieved."

Karl Bickel, former president of the United Press, wrote concerning the Captain Waskow dispatch: "I'm going to hang it up and look at it every once in a while just to make me glad that I'm still hanging on to the 'game' by my fingernails but more because there are still men in it like Pyle who can write stuff like that." Grove Patterson, editor of the *Toledo Blade,* said: "When the war is over I predict it will be found that Ernie Pyle wrote the most beautiful lines that came out of the whole dark and bitter conflict. His story of the dead men coming down the hill is the most beautifully written newspaper story I have ever read."

Best of all, the column had come to be regarded as gospel by the soldiers themselves and by their leaders. The *Army and Navy Journal* referred to Ernie as "the seeing-eye reporter." *Stars and*

Stripes declared: "Whatever advantages Ernie Pyle finds in his new fame are more than deserved if the opinion of the soldiers in the ETO is any criterion." Jim Wright, a newsreel cameraman hospitalized in Italy, wrote Ernie: "When they wheeled me in here, I felt like a slow-motion tennis ball going over the net at Forest Hills. Everybody's head moved from left to right, and vice versa on the other side of the ward. You see, the grapevine had given out the news that a war correspondent was being wheeled in. I understand the tension was terrific until I came out of the morphia. The first question all and sundry asked me was not how I felt or what was wrong with me but—did I know Ernie Pyle. . . ."

Pfc. Robert O'Doherty, of the 88th Division, wrote: "I'll always remember the sight of that tiny, gray-haired man dressed in shabby ODs, surrounded by towering soldiers in ODs just as bedraggled. He never said much; just listened. All of us had the feeling, somehow, that when the chips were down he would do us more good than any high-powered senator in Washington." And Ernie was becoming a yardstick with which to measure other reporters. The *Des Moines Register* and *Tribune* advertised their writer in Italy, Gordon Gammack, as "Iowa's own 'Ernie Pyle.'" George Hicks, the radio correspondent, was billed as operating "à la Ernie Pyle, Scripps-Howard battlefront Boswell."

Word of these matters, however, had not penetrated *quite* universally. An American general with whom Ernie dined one night remarked that he had been reading the column in *Stars and Stripes* and volunteered his good offices in arranging for its syndication in the States.

Ernie had been driving out from Villa Vessels to visit Air Force units. Now he wrote me that he was going back with the foot soldiers: "Oddly enough, I find the Air Corps rather colorless and anticlimactic after so long with the infantry. They're doing a wonderful job, of course, and are grand people and wonderful to me, but I've grown to feel more at home with the doughfoots. . . . It's got to the point where it's a little hard to work—everywhere I go I'm treated like royalty or something, and people are always snapping pictures and getting out Short Snorters to sign. The other night I was with about fifty enlisted men in their mess hall and they wanted me to talk and I said I couldn't, but they started asking questions and it wound up that we talked sort of forum-like for two and a half hours. I sure don't want to get to the point where they're always asking me instead of me asking them. . . ."

He wrote Roz, on January 21: "Still feel lousy but am off for the front again tomorrow." It was on this "tomorrow" that the new Allied landing was made at Anzio-Nettuno, a hundred miles up the coast from Naples. Ernie explained in another letter to Roz why he did not go on this expedition—"partly because I was afraid to go with this cold, since I'd probably get wet and have to sleep on the ground for a week or so with no blankets or anything and I was scared of pneumonia; and partly because everybody [the correspondents] had to be pooled [2] and you can hardly pool a daily column. . . . So instead I went back to the infantry front before Cassino."

There he joined the 34th Division, veterans of Tunisia and Salerno, attaching himself to a company commanded by Lieutenant John J. Sheehy. He couldn't identify the company in his dispatches but later wrote in the margin of *Brave Men*: "It was Company E of the 168th Infantry of the 34th Division, God bless 'em." Sheehy told me he "felt like a million dollars because my company had been selected for him to visit."

As Ernie put it: "I've never seen a man prouder of his company than Lieutenant Sheehy, and the men in it were proud too. . . . A lot of people have morale confused with the desire to fight. I don't know of one soldier out of ten thousand who wants to fight. They certainly didn't in that company. The old-timers were sick to death of battle, and the new replacements were scared to

[2] The copy of all assault reporters was made available to the entire American press for the first day or so. Later, out of Normandy, Ernie's columns were distributed in this way to all the papers, including competitors of his clients.

death of it. And yet the company went on into battle and it was a proud company."

It was on that first afternoon, a thousand yards from the front line, that Sheehy introduced Ernie to Sergeant Frank ("Buck") Eversole, one of the few old-timers left in the company. Buck was of a breed revered by Ernie, who wrote about him: He "shook hands sort of timidly and said, 'Pleased to meet you,' and then didn't say any more. I could tell by his eyes and by his slow and courteous speech when he did talk, that he was a Westerner. Conversation with him was sort of hard, but I didn't mind his reticence, for I know how Westerners like to size people up first. . . . Later in the afternoon I came past his foxhole again, and we sat and talked a little while alone. We didn't talk about the war, but mainly about our West, and just sat and made figures on the ground with sticks as we talked. We got started that way, and in the days that followed I came to know him well. He is to me, and to all those with whom he serves, one of the great men of the war."

In peacetime, Buck had been a cowboy in Idaho and Nevada. Now he was a platoon sergeant. "He has been at the front for more than a year. War is old to him and he has become almost the master of it. He is a senior partner now in the institution of death. His platoon has turned over many times. . . . 'It gets so it kinda gets you, seein' these new kids come up,' Buck told me one night in his slow, barely audible Western voice, so full of honesty and sincerity. 'I know it ain't my fault that they get killed, and I do the best I can for them. But I've got so I feel like it's me killin' 'em instead of a German. I've got so I feel like a murderer. I hate to look at them when the new ones come in.' " Buck had a Purple Heart, and two Silver Stars for bravery. "He is cold and deliberate in battle. His commanders depend more on him than on any other man. He is the kind of man you instinctively feel safer with than with other people. He is not helpless like most of us. He is practical. He can improvise, patch and fix."

Buck had to leave the company on the day before a night march,

as he was due for five days at a rest camp. Ernie wrote that Buck
went to Sheehy "and said, 'Lieutenant, I don't think I better
go. I'll stay if you need me.' The Lieutenant said, 'Of course I
need you, Buck, I always need you. But it's your turn and I want
you to go. In fact you're ordered to go.' The truck taking the few
boys away to rest camp left just at dusk. It was drizzling and the
valleys were swathed in a dismal mist. Artillery of both sides
flashed and rumbled around the horizon. The encroaching darkness was heavy and foreboding. Buck came to the little group of
old-timers in the company with whom I was standing. You'd have
thought he was leaving forever. He shook hands all around. 'Well,
good luck to you all.' And then he said, 'I'll be back in just five
days.' He was a man stalling off his departure. He said good-by
all around and slowly started away. But he stopped and said
good-by all around again. And again he said, 'Well, good luck
to you all.' I walked with him toward the truck in the dusk. He
kept his eyes on the ground, and I think he would have cried if he
had known how, and he said to me very quietly, 'This is the first
battle I have ever missed that this battalion has been in. Even
when I was in the hospital with my arm, they were in bivouac.
This will be the first one I have ever missed. I sure do hope they
have good luck.' And then he said, 'I feel like a deserter.' "

Ernie went on the night march, then made his way to the rear
when the company moved into an attack soon after dawn. He
went past the rest center and asked its commanding officer if Buck
could go along with him for a few days, to give him "some information on the front lines."

Buck wrote to me after the war was over, from Green Forest,
Arkansas: "I am sending you a letter that Ernie wrote me, but I
please want it back. He was the best friend I ever had, and I am
very thankful for the reputation he gave me. I couldn't see why
he picked me to write about. I suppose when we met that we felt
pretty much the same towards each other. . . . He came to the
rest camp and got a pass for me to go to Naples. At that time GIs

were restricted from Naples. We stayed at the public-relations building, where I met Major Vessels and other nice people. Ernie and I and the gentlemen that roomed there had a few drinks that night, and talked. I also met Bill Mauldin there, the cartoonist for the *Stars and Stripes*. The next day Ernie had to catch up on some of his columns, so Major Vessels and two nurses and I went to Pompeii. I had a swell time. Ernie and I also visited the palace at Caserta." Buck was mustered out after developing arthritis from having his feet frozen, and at the time he wrote me was "living on a small farm that I rent for ten dollars a month. I am not able to buy any livestock so I just work at whatever I can get. . . . Give Captain Sheehy my regards when you write him. He was a gentleman."

Sergeant Bill Mauldin, mentioned in Buck's letter, was the subject of a column by Ernie, with the direct result of that magnificent ironist having his slender Army pay augmented by the income of a syndicate star. Mel Ryder, publisher of the unofficial soldier newspaper *Army Times* in Washington, read the piece and forthwith showed me a collection of Mauldin's cartoons, which he had been reprinting in his paper. I arranged for him to see George Carlin, and after some complicated negotiating, in which Ernie helped, an arrangement for syndication was concluded. The drawings were an overnight success. Incidentally, there was a smattering of unfavorable reaction from readers about the hobolike appearance of Mauldin's principal characters, Willie and Joe. One such complaint reached John H. Sorrells, executive editor of Scripps-Howard, who tended to agree until he got a letter from his paratrooper son overseas, who said: "I understand that a lot of people don't like Mauldin because they say our American youth doesn't look or act like that over here. Well, they do act and feel that way. He's the favorite here."

On Ernie's return from the 34th Division front he wrote Jerry about his night march with Sheehy's company: "They said it was the blackest night they'd ever seen in two years overseas. It was muddy and slippery, and every now and then somebody would go down and start cussing. We were all covered with mud by the time we finally got to the assembly area about four a.m. Shells were going over us constantly, and their echo against the low clouds made such a continuous crashing noise you could hardly hear anyone talk. It was so dark you just had to feel every step with your toes. . . . My typewriter is broken and I have to turn the cylinder by hand, but I can do that indefinitely. . . .''

Raymond Clapper was killed in a collision of carrier planes at Eniwetok in the Marshall Islands, and Ernie wrote Roz, "I'm so upset by it I can hardly think. It gives me the creeps, and makes more dominant that perpetual feeling we all have of 'When will my turn come?' The best we can do for Ray is to prattle about the best always getting it." He wrote me that he was "just floored" by Ray Clapper's death. "What a waste of intelligence and character—as the whole war is. The whole thing is getting pretty badly under my skin. I've got so I brood about it, about the whole thing, I mean, and I have a personal reluctance to die that is always in my mind, like a weight. Instead of growing stronger and hard as good veterans do, I've become weaker and more frightened. I'm all right when I'm actually at the front, but it's when I pull back and start thinking and visualizing that it almost overwhelms me. I've even got so I don't sleep well, and have half-awake hideous dreams about the war. . . ."

Another letter to me said: "I don't know what the hell has happened to all of us over here this winter. Everybody seems to have gone a little nuts. I've been drinking far more than I should; I think it was really that Christmas spree that weakened me so that I caught this damn cold. It was really much better last winter when there simply wasn't anything available. . . . We're all so damned homesick and weary of the war that it seems like a disease, and you take to the bottle now and then without planning on it."

One of the columns that followed his visit to the 34th Division was an appeal for extra "fight pay" for combat infantrymen: "Obviously no soldier would ever go into combat just to get extra 'fight pay.' That isn't the point. There is not enough money in the world to pay any single individual his due for battle suffering. But it would put a mark of distinction on him, a recognition that his miserable job was a royal one and that the rest of us were aware of it." Eventually extra pay of ten dollars a month was granted by law to combat infantrymen, for whom there was also designed a special badge.

Ernie had dinner with General Ira Eaker, and wrote Jerry: "He asked of you, of course. He is just like he always was, except looks tired and a little older. He sent me back in his own car, and when I got here I discovered he had sent a gift of a quart of rye and a carton of Camels. Sure was thoughtful of him. . . .

"Suppose you saw that General Bradley had been appointed to lead the American troops on the invasion. I am anxious to get to England and see him. Correspondents have been rolling out of here for England for the last month, but I am making my own deductions (without having any 'dope' at all) and I still think I'll be in plenty of time. Not that I even intend to go on the invasion, but I do want to be there when it happens. . . .

"Lee's cable just arrived, saying you had been sick since the first of the year. . . . I felt you must either be sick or had abandoned me altogether; I wasn't sure which. . . . I've been out of America almost three months and had only one letter from you. . . .

"I've been slightly acquainted with an Air Corps flight surgeon named Major Wendell Dove . . . and a few days ago he just happened to drop by to see me. He saw I wasn't feeling very chipper, so next day he showed up with a doctor from the Army hospital across the street, and a couple of attendants and all kinds of gadgets, and they bled and tested me all over the place. The result was that they have turned up with a verdict of secondary anemia, with a hemoglobin of only fifty. So now they've started on a big program of liver injections, poly-vitamin capsules, hydrochloric acid, and whatnot. I will continue working, although they said to take it rather easy and do no more drinking than one or two before supper. They said that within three to four weeks I'll feel better than I have in years, and I have a feeling I will too. . . .

Also, the soldiers who run our apartment and mess are grand and have gone scrounging and actually dug up some eggs (at twenty-five cents apiece) so that I now have the luxury of eggs and bacon for breakfast. Also an Army nurse at the hospital, who is the dietician and goes with one of the boys here, is sending me over some fresh meat, so I am really eating like a potentate. I'm glad Major Dove finally did something about me, for I never felt sick enough to go to a hospital myself but just kept dragging around. They said that in another month my condition would have been serious. . . ."

He wrote Roz that a number of readers had told him "they'd written Jerry for my overseas address and got prompt and charming answers. Wonder if I could get a letter out of her that way?"

I wrote that I was putting him up for the Pulitzer Prize and said, "Everybody here thinks it's in the bag." He replied that "I'll never get a Pulitzer Prize, because my stuff just doesn't fit their rules."

In another letter I said: "I suppose you will be in London when you get this. . . . Don't get too damned heroic. About the tenth echelon of the invasion will be soon enough."

But Ernie had not gone to London. He had gone, instead, to our hard-held beachhead at Anzio.

CHAPTER 32

Incident at Nettuno

ERNIE had intended remaining only a few days at Anzio, but his visit stretched out to nearly a month.

The Anzio-Nettuno beachhead had been confined by stout German resistance to such a limited area that every inch of it was vulnerable to the enemy artillery, to say nothing of bombers. As Ernie put it: "The beachhead is so small that you can stand on high ground in the middle of it and see clear around the thing. . . . You can drive from the rear to the front in less than half an hour, and often you find the front wider than the rear. . . . Never have I seen a war zone so crowded. . . . If a plane goes down in No-Man's Land, more than half the troops on the beachhead can see it fall."

The press was housed in a Nettuno waterfront building, and here Ernie had a close call. "Most of the correspondents lived in the part of the house down by the water," he reported, "it being considered safer because it was lower down. But I had been sleeping alone in a room in the top part because it was a lighter place to work in the daytime. We called it 'Shell Alley' up there because the Anzio-bound shells seemed to come in a groove right past our eaves day and night. On this certain morning I had awakened early and was just lying there for a few minutes before getting up. It was just seven and the sun was out bright. Suddenly the anti-aircraft guns let loose. Ordinarily I don't get out of bed during a raid, but I did get up this one morning. I was sleeping in long underwear and shirt, so I just put on

314

my steel helmet, slipped on some wool-lined slippers, and went
to the window for a look at the shooting. I had just reached the
window when a terrible blast swirled me around and threw me
into the middle of the room. I don't remember whether I heard
any noise or not. The half of the window that was shut was ripped
out and hurled across the room. The glass was blown into thousands of little pieces. Why the splinters or the window frame itself
didn't hit me I don't know. From the moment of the first blast
until it was over probably not more than fifteen seconds passed.
Those fifteen seconds were so fast and confusing that I truly can't
say what took place, and the other correspondents reported the
same. There was debris flying back and forth all over the room.
One gigantic explosion came after another. The concussion was
terrific. It was like a great blast of air in which your body felt as
light and as helpless as a leaf tossed in a whirlwind. I jumped
into one corner of the room and squatted down and just cow-
ered there. I definitely thought it was the end. Outside of that
I don't remember what my emotions were.

"Suddenly one whole wall of my room flew in, burying the
bed where I'd been a few seconds before under hundreds of
pounds of brick, stone, and mortar. . . . Then the wooden
doors were ripped off their hinges and crashed into the room.
Another wall started to tumble but caught only part way down.
The French doors leading to the balcony blew out. . . . As I
sat cowering in the corner, I remember fretting because my steel
hat had blown off with the first blast and I couldn't find it. Later
I found it right beside me. [Ernie had long since learned not to
buckle his helmet strap under his chin, lest a heavy concussion
knock off the helmet and break his neck.]

"I was astonished at feeling no pain, for debris went tearing
around every inch of the room and I couldn't believe I hadn't
been hit. But the only wound I got was a tiny cut on my right
cheek from flying glass. The first I knew of it was when blood
ran down my chin and dropped onto my hat. . . . My typewriter was full of mortar and broken glass but was not dam-

aged." He dug out his pants from under the debris and went below. "The boys couldn't believe it when they saw me coming in. Wick Fowler of the *Dallas News* . . . had just said to George Tucker of the Associated Press, 'Well, they got Ernie.' The German raiders had dropped a whole stick of bombs right across our area. They were apparently 500-pounders, and they hit within thirty feet of our house. Many odd things happened. . . . When I went to put on my boots there was broken glass clear up into the toes of them. When I went to get a cigarette after the bombing, I found they had all been blown out of the pack. . . . Sergeant Bob Geake had some iodine and was going around painting up those who had been scratched. Bob took out a dirty handkerchief, spit on it two or three times, then washed the blood off my face before putting on the iodine, which could hardly be called the last word in sterilization. . . .

"Since then little memories of the bombing have gradually come back into my consciousness. I recall now that I went to take my pocket comb out of my shirt pocket, to comb my hair, but instead actually took my handkerchief out of my hip pocket and started combing my hair with my handkerchief. Me nervous? Why, I should say not."

It is not true, although it has been printed, that Ernie was given a Purple Heart.

He stayed on at the beachhead and did a thorough job of covering both front and so-called rear. He wrote Jerry that he "went out for four days, took my sleeping bag, and slept in underground dugouts with the troops. . . . I'm so dirty I don't dare think about myself. Haven't any clean clothes with me here even if I did take a bath."

Back in Naples, finally, he wrote her again: "I do hope our little flurry of close squeaks on the beachhead didn't cause you to worry too much. I was tremendously lucky to come out alive. Twice 88s hit within twenty or thirty feet of me, and I didn't get hurt because the ground fortunately was muddy and absorbed the shell fragments. But the bombing of our

house was really a horrible thing to go through. . . . I had felt
that it just wasn't right for me to leave this theater without
going to the beachhead, and now I'm glad that I did, since
everything turned out all right. In a way I hate to leave this
theater—I've been with it so long and feel so much a part of it
that I almost feel like a deserter at leaving, and yet I'm sort of
glad in a way to be moving on, for this winter somehow has
been very depressing to me. . . .

"I am so distressed that you've suffered so, and wish until I
ache that there was something I could do. I've given up all
hope of ever hearing from you, but will keep on writing to you,
and hope you want me to. I have days when I feel so close to
you and long so to be with you that I can hardly keep from
crying to myself, and yet at other times when I try to write
to you like now, I feel that we've so lost contact that I hardly
know what to say to you. I can't and don't want to heckle
you about not writing, but how I do wish you could, just once
in a while.

"Lee reports that the book has dropped back to third place
[on the best-seller lists], but they've sold 225,000, so that's far
better than anyone could hope even if they don't sell any more.
Lee says the column is now in around 270 papers. . . . Of course
all that is nice to hear, and yet I'm more indifferent than I could
believe. . . .

"I continued to take my liver shots and other stuff on the
beachhead, and although my appetite never got ravenous as it
was supposed to do, I did respond, for the last blood count
showed my hemoglobin up to 90, and my red count at 4,810,000,
which was pretty good. And actually I feel much better. I guess
that's all now, darling. We're awfully far apart now in many
ways, but I do love you as I always have, your being well again
is the only thing that really means anything in my life, and if
my wanting you to means anything, you will keep on trying,
won't you? And if you feel that my being there would help,
let me know and I will come. Love again."

A letter to Roz said: "I've just finished devoting one full day and a half to answering letters, mostly from soldiers from over here. They are so fine they just have to be answered. I've been running about one hundred letters a week lately, from soldiers and the home folks put together." This was in addition to much mail being received in Washington, which Roz handled.

He went to see Noland Norgaard of the AP, who was in an Army hospital with pleurisy, and Norgaard has recalled: "When he left there was a silence, then from one of the ten other beds in the ward came the question, 'Say, who was that little guy?' I replied that it was Pyle, and back came the awed words, 'Gosh, I thought so.' For the next hour I was pumped about Ernie by those ten young officers, and thereafter I was quite a celebrity in the ward simply because I knew Ernie. When I was able to get out for afternoon strolls, they pressed upon me caps, scraps of paper, and even a handkerchief to be taken over to the press apartment for Ernie's autograph."

Passage to London was arranged, via the Air Transport Command, and Ernie took leave of Naples on April 5, 1944. He slept most of the way to Algiers and Casablanca. "The sun was just setting when I woke up. I've written many times that war isn't romantic to the people in it. . . . But here in that plane all of a sudden things did seem romantic. A heavy darkness had come inside the cabin. Passengers were indistinct shapes, kneeling at the windows to absorb the spell of the hour. The remnants of the sun streaked the cloud-banked horizon ahead, making it vividly red and savagely beautiful. We were high, and the motors throbbed in a timeless rhythm. Below us were the green peaks of the Atlas Mountains, lovely in the softening shroud of the dusk. Villages with red roofs nestled on the peak tops. Down there lived sheepmen—obscure mountain men who had never heard of a Nebelwerfer or a bazooka. Men at home at the end of the day in the poor, narrow, beautiful security of their own walls. And there high in the sky above and yet part of it all were plain Americans incongruously away from home. For a moment it seemed terribly dramatic that we should be there at all amid that darkening beauty so far away and so foreign and so old."

Ernie had a high priority, arranged by General Eaker, but bad weather held him at Casablanca for four or five days. Then he flew through the night to England, where there was bad news from Albuquerque. Ed Shaffer was dead.

CHAPTER 33

Prelude to the Big Show

ERNIE reached England in mid-April, nearly two months before Normandy D-day. "It's practically like old-home week every time I step out," he wrote Jerry, from whom he had at last received a letter in London. "All the old African gang and correspondents, and lots of soldiers and civilians from America that I know, and some British friends too. I just have to sort of hide in my room to get my work done. . . . I've never been stared at so much in my life. Everybody here dresses 'regulation,' in dress blouse and pinks. All city soldiers. But I arrived in British battle jacket, OD pants, and infantry boots, for it was all I had, and down there everybody wears anything he wants to. At least I was clean. Apparently they'd never seen anybody who looked like he might have come from the front, and I hate to go out on the street. Actually, I'll have to get regulation uniform or I'll be getting picked up by the MPs. . . .

"Another cable from Lee came, saying he was mailing me a letter from you, and that you were planning a series of special hospital treatments. I do hope you don't have to go through too much ordeal before you are better again. . . ."

He had also received from me a copy of the "presentation" I had prepared in submitting a selection of his columns to the Pulitzer Prize Committee. He wrote me: "If I should get the damn prize I think you ought to have it." I told him I was willing to bet he would win. "Sure I'll betcha I don't get it—want to make it a hundred dollars?" he wrote. I accepted. A week later Don Whitehead was at the Associated Press office in London when a bulletin came in announcing that Ernie had won a Pulitzer Prize for "distinguished correspondence." As Whitehead told it: "I telephoned Ernie the news. There was a silence and then he said, 'You wouldn't fool me, would you, Don?' No, I told him, it was true—and read him the dispatch. 'Well, I'll be goddamned!' he said. 'Now I lose a hundred dollars.'" (The prize was five hundred dollars, plus, of course, the prestige.) Ernie wrote me: "I truly didn't expect it. I've got fairly dulled to accolades, but when Don told me I damn near started to cry. I didn't realize it meant so much to me. I never enjoyed losing a bet more. . . ." He wirelessed me to deduct another hundred and buy everybody drinks. (I never found time.) The *London Express* reprinted his Captain Waskow column, under the impression that this was the prize-winner, whereas the award was for work published in 1943. The *St. Louis Star-Times*, piqued about some of the Pulitzer Prizes, polled Washington correspondents and found considerable disaffection regarding various of the awards—but unanimity in support of the one given Pyle. Ernie wrote to Dana: "The nicest thing is that all the other correspondents seem glad about it too, and I don't think anybody is jealous."

Another letter, written the day of the Pulitzer award but apparently before he got the word, was in a dark mood: "I worry about after the war. I want only to stop and let everything flow by; yet somehow I sense that nervousness and maladjustment and impatience with everything about me will be so great that no placidity will ever come. Being so close for so long to the high tension and fantastic massed suffering and tragedy of war seems to have robbed me of all ability to adjust myself to normal people. Being here in the big city again (and I do love London), with all these normal people leading pretty normal lives, is driving me crazy. I'm no longer content unless I am with soldiers in the field. I've learned to live on a wholly new basis, which is not a good basis nor a peacetime basis, and it frightens me. I find on returning here that I'm vastly impatient with gabby people, or 'smart' people, or people who know nothing about real war—and I hate myself for being that way. . . ."

A party given by Charles Collingwood and Ed Murrow, the broadcasters, brought Ernie together with Robert E. Sherwood and with Alfred Lunt and Lynn Fontanne, who were appearing in London in Sherwood's play, *There Shall Be No Night*. Lieutenant John Mason Brown was there too and has told how Ernie, receiving congratulations on the Pulitzer Prize, was "far prouder of having just been chosen the 'Year's Outstanding Hoosier.' " Ernie joined Sherwood in some strenuous singing, and, according to the playwright, "showed a great knowledge of various performances the Lunts had given and boundless curiosity about how they worked." [1]

There was a nice bit of news from Willys-Overland Motors. In a column written in Africa the year before, Ernie had given high praise to the jeep but had said the vehicle needed a better handbrake; the present one was "perfectly useless—won't hold at all. They should either design one that works or else save metal by not having one at all." The automobile company now wrote him that a new handbrake, developed as a result of his suggestion, would soon be installed in all new jeeps.

A devoted reader of the column, G. G. Blaisdell, president of the Zippo Lighter Company in Bradford, Pennsylvania, began sending him fifty Zippos a month to give soldiers and friends. Ernie was delighted, for, as he wrote me, "The Zippo lighter is honestly one of the most coveted things in the Army."

To keep the column running until D-day he wrote some pieces

---

[1] Sherwood has written: "In 1940 I used to read Ernie's pieces with great admiration but also with a kind of anger that anybody who was so obviously a fine observer and reporter could be so utterly indifferent to what was going on in the world. He seemed to mention everything that he saw and felt except the fact that there was a war on and it was daily getting closer to us. Then, suddenly, I experienced the great thrill of reading at the end of one of Ernie's pieces the statement that something inside him had told him he had to go to blitzed England and he was going. From then on, I never ceased to be deeply grateful for the existence and the enormous influence of Ernie Pyle."

about life among the invasion forces—for instance, about the vast officers' mess in Grosvenor House, so big it was called Willow Run and where it was forbidden to leave uneaten food on one's tray (a problem for the slight Pyle appetite). At a B-26 bomber base he encountered an officer from Houston, Clayton Smith, who was a friend of Deac Parker. Smith reported to Deac that Ernie "does the morale a lot of good. He turned down a nice room in a c.o. quarters to sleep with the enlisted gunners. He of course thinks Deac Parker hung the moon."

A letter to Jerry said: "The boys in the bomber squadron wanted me to go on a mission with them, but I told them I was allergic to missions. I did go on a sort of practice one with them, however, taking off in the dark just before dawn. We flew about two hours, and England in early dawn was so green and beautiful."

Ernie's room at the Dorchester Hotel was, according to Don Whitehead, "a gathering place for all sorts and kinds of people— you were as apt to find General Bradley there as a couple of GIs who just wanted to meet Ernie Pyle. I asked him for an autograph to send to my eleven-year-old daughter Ruth. He wrote her a note: 'Dear Ruth: I understand you are collecting autographs so I am sending you several of mine. Maybe you can trade them for fishworms.' He signed his name about a dozen times below the note.

"At dusk one day he telephoned me from the Dorchester. 'Come on over,' he said. 'I'm lonesome, and this waiting around for the invasion is getting on my nerves.' I found him finishing a column. There was a bottle of bourbon on the table, a rarity in those days. 'Some guy who said he was a friend of mine came in and left it,' Ernie said. We wound up having dinner with Gordon Gammack and Duke Shoop [correspondents] at a little restaurant in Soho. While Ernie was in the men's room, Duke explained to the waitress and to nearby tables that Ernie was our old professor, and that we were having a class reunion. He had taught us philosophy back in the States and now was over here on a mission for the gov-

ernment. He really shouldn't be in London, in view of his health
and years, but he felt it was his duty. 'The professor,' Duke said,
'doesn't look it, but he's almost seventy.' When Ernie returned to
the table you never have seen such deference from the waitress
and from those nearby. They all but lifted him back into his chair,
and the waitress hovered around as though he might drop a fork
and break a brittle leg. Gammack brought up the question of
ages, and Ernie asked the waitress, 'How old do you think I am?'
'Why, sir, you don't look a day over fifty-five,' she said. Ernie almost gagged on a bite of cabbage."

Back home, business was buzzing. I seldom got out of bed in the
morning before receiving two or three long-distance calls concerned with Ernie's affairs. Radio people in particular were bearing down. There were all kinds of offers, on a rising scale, which
culminated in a proposition by Westinghouse to pay him three
thousand dollars a week for simply reciting his newspaper columns into a wire recorder, the transcriptions to be broadcast
after publication. This caused considerable turmoil. Roy Howard, who had what seemed to me an almost unreasoning aversion to
radio (he once asked me who Bob Hope was), inquired rather
sharply, during a visit to the Washington office, whether I was
not spending too much time looking after Ernie's extracurricular
interests at the expense of energies I owed to Scripps-Howard. In
truth, my situation was an abnormal one. I was Ernie's boss and yet
at the same time I was representing him, although usually only to
the point of saying no, in conversations with numerous persons
and groups who wanted to make use of his popularity. In the normal course, an immensely sought-after writer might have retained
a professional agent. In Ernie's case, his fame had developed while
he was overseas, and I had simply acquired the role of agent by de-
fault. I tried to explain this to Roy, pointing out that Ernie was
the most important writing asset on the Scripps-Howard payroll, and mentioning that the half-share which Scripps-Howard's
United Feature Syndicate took out of the proceeds from selling
Ernie's column on the open market was far in excess of Ernie's

Scripps-Howard salary. I said that if even half of my time was being devoted to Ernie, I thought this was sound from a strictly business viewpoint. Roy was still huffy. I wrote a memorandum to Deac Parker suggesting that, if Roy's attitude was general among the managers of Scripps-Howard, it would be better for all involved if I were relieved of these special Pyle responsibilities, which could be turned over to an agent. Nothing came of it.

When the Westinghouse offer reached Ernie he decided against it. "I think I would have accepted," he wrote me, "if it hadn't been for Roy's and other brass-hat objections. I don't want to get crosswise with them, and yet I'm beginning to feel that Roy is a little free with his objections to my making some money. These offers will never come again, and I still don't have enough piled up to live on happily ever after. But, oh well—at least by bowing to his wishes I retain the freedom to quit writing the column any damn moment I want to, and one of these days I may up and do it, for I'm beginning to feel that I've run my race in this war and can't keep going much longer." This was written from Normandy a week or so after the invasion, when my letters and cables caught up with him. Not many days later he had a change of heart and cabled: "Have rethought Westinghouse offer. Feel perhaps made mistake downturning. Have downturned so much am beginning feel it hardly fair for office ask me forego something this size. So if not too late wish youd reopen talks."

It was too late. Someone else had been hired for the Westinghouse spot. Ernie wrote me that he was glad. And in a letter to Roz he said: "If nothing else ever happens to me, I can always think of myself as the man who turned down a hundred and fifty thousand dollars a year without batting an eye."

Plans were afoot for another book, again a compilation of the daily dispatches, to be called *Brave Men*. The movie was in the writing stage, and in a mess. A tentative script presented Ernie as a sort of yokel who had stumbled into the war, who stood in awe of other correspondents, and who got into his first battle by mistake while trying to get away from it. I told Cowan this approach would have to be discarded. Changes were made, but the Pyle role was never to jell satisfactorily—partly, I think, because Cowan had been oversold on the danger of putting words into Ernie's mouth that would strike the public as being out of character; the result was that the celluloid Pyle tended to posture wordlessly.

Jerry appeared to be improving. She had gone home from the hospital, with her two nurses, was not drinking, and was taking pleasure in gardening. In letters to her Ernie insisted that the invasion would not be very dangerous as far as his part in it was concerned. A letter to his father said: "It's hard for me to believe that I'll be forty-four this summer. Another couple of years and I'll be middle-aged."

He wrote Jerry: " . . . Among the big batch of letters was one from you, which made everything worth while. I was so pleased, and it lifted my spirits right up. It was such a nice letter, and sounded so like you. . . . I do hope the doctor can teach you to relax. I think you'll probably have to teach me when the war is over, for I seem to be so damn wound up most of the time. I'm afraid that I'm going to be so torn up inside and maladjusted by the time this is finished, that I'll take a lot of 'doin' with,' so I think your mission in life is to get well and ready to take care of me when I get back. . . . Darling I've just got to quit and get to bed. I've got to take a bath before going to bed too, which kills me. It's awful the way I don't take baths. Haven't had one now for about two weeks, although there's a big beautiful bathroom and constant hot water right here in my room. Now and then the maids give me the gentle hint by spreading out the bath mat and laying out the towels. They did it again tonight so I guess the time has come. . . . I know it's hard to be lighthearted in times like these, but try not to worry or be depressed by the state of the world. All my love. . . ."

Crowded London was beginning to thin out, almost imperceptibly at first, then more noticeably. Correspondents who frequented the Savoy bar would disappear, without good-bys. There was an eleventh-hour letter from Ernie to Cavanaugh, dated May 26: "I think I can spare a few moments this evening to give you the benefit of my studied opinion on various matters. In the first place I think the whole kaboodle of you better throw in the sponge and forget all about the movie and go back to the farm where you all belong.[2] . . . Burgess Meredith is a fine actor, but I don't think for me, do you? He's younger and handsomer and heavier than me. Everybody I mention it to, without one single exception, says Walter Brennan is just the guy. . . . I do hope the War Department will not get narrow about letting 'Lili Marlene' be used in the picture, provided Lester likes it. The way I visualized it being used was . . . as a soft background throughout the picture whenever you needed music, in a way that the audience would be almost unconscious of, until, through much repetition, it would come along toward the end to carry the spirit of sadness of the whole damn picture. . . . [3]

"This interlude of inability to plan and comparative nonproductiveness is very nerve-wracking on a guy trying to keep a daily column going. So after another day or two I'm going to give up the ghost for a few days, let the damn column drop, and just relax a little. I've been fighting the deadline so close, and holding tense against all the intrusions and petty details so much, that I am all tied up in knots in the back of my neck. . . . Sorry I can't write you another funny letter this time; I don't feel very funny right now. . . . (Signed) The Unhappy Warrior."

[2] Cavanaugh had been hired by Cowan as an authority on Ernie.
[3] Cowan eventually decided against "Lili Marlene." Instead, his wife, Ann Ronnell, composed a ballad much in the same vein, "Linda," which was used in the movie.

CHAPTER 34

A Beach Called Omaha

NEARLY five hundred American correspondents had gathered in England to cover the invasion. Twenty-eight of them were chosen to go along on the first phase of the assault, and Ernie, despite his avowed intention of waiting until a beachhead had been secured, was one of them. "During those last few weeks," he wrote, "we were called frequently for mass conferences and we were briefed by several commanding generals. We had completed all our field equipment, got our inoculations up to date, . . . and even sent off our bedrolls. . . . The old-timers sort of gravitated together, people such as Bill Stoneman, Don Whitehead, Jack Thompson, Clark Lee, Tex O'Reilly, and myself. . . . We felt our chances were not very good. And we were not happy about it. Men like Don Whitehead and Clark Lee, who had been through the mill so long and so boldly, began to get nerves. And frankly I was the worst of the lot, and continued to be. . . .

"The call came at nine o'clock one morning, and we were ordered to be at a certain place with full field kit at ten-thirty. We threw our stuff together. Some of us went away and left hotel rooms still running up bills. Many had dates that night but did not dare to phone and call them off. . . . The first night we spent together at an assembly area, an Army tent camp. . . . Next morning Jack Thompson said, 'That's the coldest night I have ever spent.' Don Whitehead said, 'It's just as miserable as it always was.' You see, we had all been living comfortably in hotels or apartments for the last few weeks. We had got a little soft. . . ."

Ernie was transferred to General Bradley's headquarters at Bristol. Colonel Samuel L. Myers of Bradley's staff subsequently recounted: "One of my clerks said, 'Colonel, there is a funny-looking guy outside with a stocking cap.' It was the first time I had seen Ernie since Sicily. Ernie said Chet Hansen [Bradley's aide] and General Bradley had invited him to cross the Channel on the *Augusta*,[1] but he felt there would be too much 'brass.' It was decided that he would ride along with me on board whatever LST fell to my lot.

"Long before daylight on May 31 we moved out, headed southwest for Cornwall. He elected to ride with Harry Goslee in a jeep, a decision which he much regretted before nightfall, because it was a very cold, dreary, rainy day. . . . The journey took about seven hours, and he was half frozen upon arrival. By nightfall we had boarded LST 353 in Falmouth harbor and anchored out in the stream."

Sergeant Arnold Diamondstein wrote his mother in Philadelphia: "We checked him on board as he walked up the gangplank. When he called out his name, as we checked on a roster of personnel, we could hardly believe it. He stopped a moment and said, 'Wish me luck, boys, I'll need it!' Well, we all did wish him luck. He was, so to speak, our spokesman. It was not that his column told us things we did not know or feel, but the fact that we knew you folks at home could read it, and get to know and understand. . . ."

Resuming Colonel Myers' narrative: "Late in the afternoon on June 3 we set sail, with the intention of making the coast of Normandy on the morning of the fifth, but a fierce storm was blowing in the Channel and we had no sooner crossed the breakwater than we were ordered back into Falmouth harbor.[2] Ernie went around making friends with all the crew, from the skipper to the last

[1] Flagship of Admiral Alan G. Kirk, the American naval commander for the invasion.
[2] The rough weather forced General Eisenhower to order a twenty-four-hour delay in the invasion.

grease monkey. He especially endeared himself to the crew of the three-inch gun aft by autographing their gun with a paint brush.

"Again we started out in the afternoon of June 4, towing a huge section of joined steel floats about twenty feet wide and sixty feet long.[3] The storm was still blowing rather strong, and before we reached the Isle of Wight, about three p.m. on June 5, we had lost our tow and one of the engines was acting up. Shortly before dark our convoy, which was so tremendous that the end of it could not be seen, turned south and headed straight for Omaha Beach. Ernie had taken his seasickness pills, so he was comfortably asleep most of the time. That night the port engine stopped completely, and the starboard engine was slowed down to less than one-third speed. Because of the strong southwest wind we were blown out of the convoy and, much to my trepidation, out of the swept channel. I went into the cabin about one a.m. on the sixth, told Ernie what had happened, and suggested that he come out on deck. He mumbled, 'Go on and leave me alone, I don't care what happens. I just want to sleep.' We finally got the motors going, caught up with the convoy, and arrived at the transport area about ten in the morning. General [William B.] Kean and General Bradley, aboard the *Augusta*, told me it was much too hot to make reconnaissance [for a First Army command-post site] that day. So I advised Ernie not to go ashore either."

Ernie wrote in his column: "Here we were in a front-row seat at a great military epic. Shells from battleships were whamming over our heads, and occasionally a dead man floated face downward past us. Hundreds and hundreds of ships laden with death milled around us. We could stand at the rail and see both our shells and German shells exploding on the beaches, where struggling men were leaping ashore, desperately hauling guns and equipment in through the water. We were in the very vortex of the war—and yet, as we sat there waiting, Lieutenant Chuck Conick[4] and I played gin rummy in the wardroom and Bing Crosby sang 'Sweet

[3] A "rhino," or landing ferry.
[4] The same Conick who had given Ernie a lift on his arrival in Africa in 1942.

Leilani' over the ship's phonograph. Angry shells hitting near us would make heavy thuds as the concussion carried through the water and struck the hull of our ship. But in our wardroom men in gas-impregnated uniforms and wearing lifebelts sat reading *Life* and listening to the BBC telling us how the war before our eyes was going. But it isn't like that ashore. No, it isn't like that ashore."

In Washington the switchboard girls at the *Daily News* were getting as many inquiries concerning Ernie's safety as about the progress of the invasion.

Returning to Colonel Myers' account: "Early on the morning of D plus 1, while the beach was still getting a liberal sprinkling of shell and mortar fire, Ernie went in aboard an LCVP and spent most of the day walking up and down. This was the day he wrote that very beautiful column about the beach."

What Ernie wrote was: "I took a walk along the historic coast of Normandy in the country of France. It was a lovely day for strolling along the seashore. Men were sleeping on the sand, some of them sleeping forever. Men were floating in the water, but they didn't know they were in the water, for they were dead. The water was full of squishy little jellyfish about the size of your hand. Millions of them. In the center each of them had a green design exactly like a four-leaf clover. The good-luck emblem. Sure. Hell, yes.

"I walked for a mile and a half along the water's edge of our many-miled invasion beach. You wanted to walk slowly, for the detail on that beach was infinite. The wreckage was vast and startling. The awful waste and destruction of war, even aside from the loss of human life, has always been one of its outstanding features to those who are in it. Anything and everything is expendable. And we did expend on our beachhead in Normandy during those first few hours. For a mile out from the beach there were scores of tanks and trucks and boats that you could no longer see, for they were at the bottom of the water—swamped by overloading, or hit by shells, or sunk by mines. Most of their crews were lost. You could see trucks tipped half over and swamped.

You could see partly sunken barges, and the angled-up corners of jeeps, and small landing craft half submerged. And at low tide you could still see those vicious six-pronged iron snares that helped snag and wreck them. On the beach itself, high and dry, were all kinds of wrecked vehicles. There were tanks that had only just made the beach before being knocked out. There were jeeps that had burned to a dull gray. There were big derricks on caterpillar treads that didn't quite make it. There were half-tracks carrying office equipment that had been made into a shambles by a single shell hit, their interiors still holding their useless equipage of smashed typewriters, telephones, office files. There were LCTs turned completely upside down, and lying on their backs, and how they got that way I don't know. There were boats stacked on top of each other, their sides caved in, their suspension doors knocked off.

"In this shoreline museum of carnage there were abandoned rolls of barbed wire and smashed bulldozers and big stacks of thrown-away lifebelts and piles of shells still waiting to be moved. In the water floated empty life rafts and soldiers' packs and ration boxes, and mysterious oranges. On the beach lay snarled rolls of telephone wire and big rolls of steel matting and stacks of broken, rusting rifles. On the beach lay, expended, sufficient men and mechanism for a small war. They were gone forever now. And yet we could afford it. We could afford it because we were on, we had our toehold, and behind us there were such enormous replacements for this wreckage on the beach that you could hardly conceive of their sum total. Men and equipment were flowing from England in such a gigantic stream that it made the waste on the beachhead seem like nothing at all, really nothing at all. . . .

"And standing out there on the water beyond all this wreckage was the greatest armada man has ever seen. You simply could not believe the gigantic collection of ships that lay out there waiting to unload. Looking from the bluff, it lay thick and clear to the far horizon of the sea and on beyond, and it spread out to the sides and was miles wide. Its utter enormity would move the hardest man. As I stood up there I noticed a group of freshly taken German prisoners standing nearby. They had not yet been put in the prison cage. They were just standing there, a couple of doughboys leisurely guarding them with tommy guns. The prisoners, too, were looking out to sea—the same bit of sea that for months and years had been so safely empty before their gaze. Now they stood staring almost as if in a trance. They didn't say a word to each other. They didn't need to."

His next column also concerned the beach: "Here in a jumbled row for mile on mile are soldiers' packs. Here are socks and shoe polish, sewing kits, diaries, Bibles, and hand grenades. Here are the latest letters from home, with the address on each one neatly razored out—one of the security precautions enforced before the boys embarked. Here are toothbrushes and razors, and snapshots of families back home staring up at you from the sand. Here are pocketbooks, metal mirrors, extra trousers, and bloody, abandoned shoes. Here are broken-handled shovels, and portable radios smashed almost beyond recognition, and mine detectors twisted and ruined. Here are torn pistol belts and canvas water buckets, first-aid kits and jumbled heaps of lifebelts. I picked up a pocket Bible with a soldier's name in it and put it in my jacket. I carried it half a mile or so and then put it back down on the beach. I don't know why I picked it up, or why I put it back down. . . .

"Always there are dogs in every invasion. There is a dog still on the beach today, still pitifully looking for his masters. He stays at the water's edge, near a boat that lies twisted and half sunk at the water line. He barks appealingly to every soldier who approaches, trots eagerly along with him for a few feet, and then, sensing himself unwanted in all this haste, runs back to wait in vain for his own people at his own empty boat. . . .

"The strong, swirling tides of the Normandy coastline shift the contours of the sandy beach as they move in and out. They carry soldiers' bodies out to sea, and later they return them. They cover the corpses of heroes with sand, and then in their whims they uncover them. As I plowed out over the wet sand of the beach on that first day ashore, I walked around what seemed to be a couple of pieces of driftwood sticking out of the sand. But they weren't driftwood. They were a soldier's two feet. He was completely covered by the shifting sands except for his feet. The toes of his GI shoes pointed toward the land he had come so far to see, and which he saw so briefly."

Ernie went back to the LST, wrote his copy, got a ride to the *Augusta* to file it, then went ashore again. John Mason Brown, who was on Admiral Kirk's staff, wrote: "We climbed down the *Augusta's* net into a small boat and headed for the beaches. With us was the Navy's Charles E. Thomas, photographer's mate first class. As is the way of photographers, Thomas was not traveling light. He was freighted down with a large movie camera, while I was carrying his no less sizable still camera. When we waded ashore Ernie was next to me. Halfway in he said, 'Come on, give it to me now. It's my turn.' I hesitated because he looked so frail. I soon realized, however, that Ernie meant what he said. His carrying it was a point of pride; a principle of behavior. His insistence made me understand all the more fully why, as we trudged down those improvised roads, dusty and traffic-jammed, one tired GI after another would smile upon seeing him, saying either, 'Jeez, there's Ernie Pyle,' or 'Hi-ya, Ernie. Glad to see ya.' "

He returned to the LST, tired and footsore. Next day he went ashore to stay, and made his way to General Bradley's First Army command post, in an orchard near Pointe de Hoe.

"Camp was being established," Colonel Myers related, "and a detail was hard at work removing bodies, mines, hand grenades, unexploded shells, and the million and one other items of debris common on the battlefield. Ernie pitched in to help the boys and picked up the yarn about the exhausted soldier[5] who lay down in a field and rolled up in his blanket, and in the morning discovered on his right side a dead Boche and on his left side an unexploded potato-masher grenade. Upon extricating himself the soldier

[5] Private Carl Vonhorn of Cooperstown, New York.

made that classic remark which became famous within the head-quarters: 'It was very distasteful.' Ernie, Colonel Sterling Wright,[6] Corporal William B. Wescott, and myself discovered that we had been so busy getting everyone else settled down that we didn't have a place to sleep ourselves. So we raided the medical dispensary and got a blanket apiece, found a couple or three K rations which we gobbled in short order, and lay down by the jeeps to sleep. About eleven o'clock a very heavy Boche raid came over. They laid a stick of bombs about one hundred and fifty or two hundred yards away, knocking the kitchen down and riddling a few tents, but causing no major casualties. Ernie and Sterling didn't wake up. But the flak was so bad, falling very much like hailstones, that I woke them up and told them to crawl under my jeep, where at least their heads would be protected. Ernie said, 'What good does it do to have your head protected when your belly sticks out? If you get a piece of shrapnel through the belly it will kill you.' I argued that the average piece of shrapnel[7] didn't have enough force to go through the clothing to injure the belly, but Ernie went to sleep still arguing that it would injure his belly just as much as his head. Sterling Wright squirmed all over the ground that night and finally found a nice soft piece of earth on which to place his head. He slept very comfortably, according to him, but in the morning discovered that his head had been pillowed all night on a rich pile of horse manure. Of course Colonel Wright, being a good cavalryman, had not noticed any unusual aroma."

Ernie busied himself visiting various units at the front, especially those of an old love from North Africa, the 1st Division, and of the 29th Division, these having been the two principal components of the bloody Omaha Beach victory. As soon as it was feasible he sent me a message: "How is Jerry? I am all right." She telegraphed me: "Cable Ernie that I am truly well.

---

[6] An aide to the Secretary of War and in France as an observer.
[7] Bomb and shell fragments were erroneously but almost universally called shrapnel.

Have been concerned about him but not upset by his going which he may feel. He must not worry about me."

On D plus 10 he wrote Roz: "I haven't had too bad a time, and yet the thing is about to get me down. Last night I was just abnormally terrified when the bombers were right over us all night, and if I had the courage I'd chuck the whole business. . . . I'm so sick of living in misery and fright."

The first mail reached the beachhead. "No letter from Jerry," he told Don Whitehead. "They'll be along later," Don said; "they've just been delayed." "No," Ernie replied. "Everybody else has got mail. There just wasn't any letter." And he went back to his tent alone.

CHAPTER 35

Hellfire at St. Lô

ENERAL J. Lawton Collins' VII Corps struck westward
across the base of the Cotentin Peninsula to Barneville
and the sea, then wheeled north to reduce Cherbourg.
Ernie joined one of Collins' divisions, the 9th, which he had known
in Tunisia and Sicily, and after some warming experiences among
the newly liberated and ecstatically hospitable Frenchmen, moved
north with the division for the Cherbourg assault. The 9th, under
Major General Manton S. Eddy, pressed the enemy so hard and
fast that its headquarters, where Ernie spent his nights, moved forward six times in seven days.

During the street fighting in Cherbourg, Ernie had a brisk esca-
pade, along with Charles Wertenbaker and photographer Robert
Capa, both of *Time* and *Life:* "It was about time for me to
go—out alone into that empty expanse of fifteen feet—as the infantry company I was with began its move into the street that
led to what we did not know. One of the soldiers asked if I didn't
have a rifle. Every time you're really in the battle lines they'll ask
you that. I said no, correspondents weren't allowed to; it was
against international law. The soldiers thought that didn't seem
right. Finally the sergeant motioned—it was my turn. I ran with
bent knees, shoulders hunched, out across the culvert and across
the open space. Lord, but you felt lonely out there. I had to stop
right in the middle of the open space, to keep my distance behind
the man ahead. I got down behind a little bush, as though that
would have stopped anything." There were snipers in some of the

buildings, and correspondents as well as soldiers were hugging the walls as they proceeded up the street. Wertenbaker watched Ernie's face and reported that "he was scared all right." They reached a military hospital, where, according to Capa in his book *Slightly Out of Focus:*

"About two hundred and fifty wounded prisoners from the 82nd Airborne Division were liberated—also a considerable supply of the very best French bottles in the basement. Ernie went to talk to the prisoners, Charlie interviewed the German doctor, and I made for the cellar. I was late. Every soldier of the 47th Infantry already had his arms, jacket, and pockets bulging with precious bottles. I begged one of them for just a single bottle, but he laughed and said, 'Only if you're Ernie Pyle.' With the next soldier my approach was different. I asked him for a bottle for Ernie Pyle, and he parted with it willingly. Soon I had collected my loot of Benedictine and brandy."

After that, as Ernie related it: "About a block beyond the hospital entrance two American tanks were sitting in the middle of the street. . . . I walked toward them. Our infantrymen were in doorways along the street. I got within about fifty feet of our front tank when it let go its 75-millimeter gun. The blast was terrific there in the narrow street. . . . As the tank continued to shoot I ducked into a doorway, because I figured the Germans would shoot back. . . . Suddenly a yellow flame pierced the bottom of the tank and there was a crash of such intensity that I automatically blinked my eyes. The tank, hardly fifty feet from where I was standing, had been hit by an enemy shell. . . . In a moment the crew came boiling out of the turret. Grim as it was, I almost had to laugh as they ran toward us. I have never seen men run so violently. They ran all over, with arms and heads going up and down and with marathon-race grimaces. They plunged into my doorway."

Wertenbaker had gone on ahead, and Ernie explained to him, upon catching up: "Some of those fellows that jumped out of that tank knew me from my picture so I had to stop and talk." They wanted his autograph, and he took down their names.[1] The tank had knocked out two German pillboxes before being hit. There was a third pillbox a little way forward, but the correspondents had had enough street fighting for their professional purposes, so they repaired to division headquarters and were luckily in time to get a look at the German commander of Cherbourg, General Carl Wilhelm von Schlieben, who had just surrendered. The German was furious when General Eddy sent for the photographers. He made some scathing remarks in German about the impertinence of the American press, to which Capa retorted, also in German, that he was bored with photographing defeated German generals.

After the fall of Cherbourg on June 27, Ernie went back to the area behind Omaha Beach, where a press camp had been established at Vouilly. There he wrote at length to Jerry: "Three days ago I came back to our base camp after the Cherbourg campaign was finished and had my first mail in well over a month. There was lots of it. . . . Since I hadn't written any letters for a month, I started writing, and wrote everybody else before you, hoping that before I finished one letter from you would arrive. And sure enough, late last night, two letters came—your June 14 and 16 letters. I am so happy about them. . . . I am as fully confident as you are that this time is it; that you've found a way to handle and control the inherent despair and nervousness within yourself. . . .

"Darling, I didn't lie to you about what I was to do on the invasion—at least I didn't at first and later there was no chance to tell you, although I probably wouldn't have anyway. I truly planned to go slow on this one—not to come over for two or three weeks, after things were well established. But what happened was this—a certain very important general let it be known informally that I and one other correspondent were very acceptable to go with him. That is something like an invitation from the White

---

[1] Two of them, Corporal Martin Kennelly of Chicago and Private Charles Rains of Kansas City, were killed a few weeks later, according to a marginal notation by Ernie in *Brave Men*.

House. Something you don't refuse. So there was really nothing else to do. . . .

"We are in six-man tents, on cots, in a grove. . . . They've cleared out a couple of rooms in a farmhouse for censors and a writing room for correspondents, but I've dug up a little folding table and sit on my cot and write. The only drawback is the mess, which is stinko. We correspondents are going to chip in a little extra so the mess officer can buy eggs and milk and stuff on the side. . . .

"In my tent are Don Whitehead of AP, Hank Gorrell of UP, Bert Brandt, photographer for Acme, Jack Lee (not Clark Lee) of INS, and Joe Liebling of *The New Yorker*. Don is about my best friend over here, as you know, and I like Hank too, and Bert and I tented together all through the Cherbourg campaign, so we've learned to fix up our corner a little together. I got him started on being neat in his tent and providing yourself with a few little common comforts, such as ash trays from ration cans, a box beside your cot to put things on, and such stuff. Bert fell in with the idea like a child, and since he's a natural-born scrounger, he comes back every evening with all the junk he can carry, mostly taken from captured German headquarters units. Yesterday he and Don went on a foraging trip and came back with a whole case of Ten-in-One rations, plus two dozen eggs and jam and a lot of other junk. Bert has a little Coleman stove, so every morning I get up and cook eggs and bacon for Bert and Don and me. But I'm afraid its popularity is going to devour it, for this morning we had six for breakfast instead of three, and I cook for about an hour before I get everybody fed and get to eat myself. . . .

"Perhaps you have heard me speak of Kay Garland, one of the British girls at the Ministry of Information, who was always so grand to us, clear back to the Blitz winter. Next to Gwyn [Barker] she was our best friend in England. Well, we've just heard that she was killed about ten days ago while attending church by one of the new flying bombs.[2] I suppose I've seen five hundred dead men just since landing in France, but when someone you know who isn't really connected with the war gets killed by war, you seem to feel it more. The correspondents were really very lucky on the invasion, especially the ones who landed at a certain beach on D-day. Don Whitehead and Jack Thompson have no right to be alive at all. Don always keeps saying he's going to slow up a bit, but he has such a sense of duty and loyalty to his office that he keeps on going. . . .

"My sleeping bag is still wonderful. . . . I had one of the little Coleman stoves in Italy, a brand-new one, but had to give it away because I didn't have weight allowance enough to carry it up to England. . . . I was just racking my brain thinking how I might lay hands on one, when yesterday came a letter from the Coleman people saying their employees were making me up a special one, with brass instead of steel fittings and all prettied up and everything, and had arranged with the Army to have it flown over. . . .

"The nights here are a little difficult for sleep, as the guns often go all night and a few German planes wander around and keep you apprehensive. . . . We have not been liquorless after the first few days of the campaign. The French had hid a little cognac from the Germans but not much. But after we began capturing various German headquarters we found German officers had stored up cognac by the hundreds of cases, so we had our share. For a while the only way we could get any sleep was to go to bed tight so you wouldn't hear the guns and planes, but it isn't so bad where we are now, so we don't have that pleasant excuse."

He wrote me: "The clippings were awfully nice and cheered me up. . . . Sometimes I get so obsessed with the tragedy and horror of seeing dead men that I can hardly stand it. But I guess there is nothing to do but keep going. . . . Charlie Wertenbaker showed me a cable from *Time* asking a lot of questions and saying they were planning a front cover. Jesus. The country surely must

[2] The first V-1 had fallen on London June 12.

have gone nuts. . . . A letter from George Carlin today. . . . George was full of fear and gravity and apparently has been praying constantly for my survival. There must be an awful lot of prayin' going on in America these days. I have seen one hell of a lot of guys that prayers didn't help any. . . .

"I had a letter today from Bill Mauldin. He's in hot water half the time for his cartoons lampooning the Base Sections and their strict discipline. He wants to come up here [from Italy] but says if he doesn't stop offending the local big-boys he won't be in any position to ask favors. . . . To my mind any attempt for Bill to change his mode in the slightest would be destructive of the fine thing he is doing. . . .

"I may not write again for a long time, for I'll probably be hitting the front pretty hard, and neither the circumstances nor the mood gets very good for writing often. But I hope you keep 'em rolling to me, for your letters and accolades and what not are about all I have to look forward to. . . ."

Ernie lived in the Vouilly press camp off and on for weeks. There was much drinking and much badinage. Ernie had an appreciative audience for racy bits from Cavanaugh's letters, and he would produce with mock pomposity various clippings and other testimonials to his popularity. Hal Boyle had for a long time been referring to himself facetiously as "the poor man's Pyle." There were various switches on this phrase. Ernest Hemingway, who was there as a correspondent, called himself "Ernest, the rich man's hemorrhoid." And eventually somebody, with that sacrilegiousness which chaplains in the field learned to close their ears to, accused Ernie of being "the poor man's God." In fact, according to Clark Lee: "One night, in the mail, a copy of the Indiana University alumni monthly came for Ernie. Somebody picked it up and read an article about him. It quoted some editorial saying that Ernie's writing was reminiscent of the Bible for its rugged simplicity and unadorned style and great strength. We looked at Ernie to see his reaction. He was pouting. Somebody asked if he didn't feel honored. 'Hell, no,' he said, with that chuckle of his. 'I never did think the Bible was very well written.' "

One of his tentmates, A. J. Liebling, conceded later on: "I thought then that he clung to his homespun manner the way a baseball player hangs on to a lucky bat, but that was probably unkind. I think now that he just didn't have any other manner— that if he hadn't been born into his honest Hoosier character (and for all I know he had), he had at least grown into it so solidly that he couldn't change. . . . Soldiers often came from outfits far up the line with gripes to lay before him, as if he could remedy abuses by speaking directly to General Bradley. I think that he actually did go to bat now and then. He was always on the soldiers' side, but he was a bit fine-grained, without physical health, and their coarseness sometimes revolted him. I remember him bawling out one drunken Army cook for obscenity and asking him how many times a week he wrote to his wife. The cook said his wife was an obscenity and he never wrote to her. Ernie bawled him out some more, and the cook cried. Sometimes he said things that surprised you. One day we were talking about a fellow none of us liked much who had just been killed, and I deferred to convention enough to say he had been a nice guy. 'Nonsense,' said Ernie, 'a sonofabitch is a sonofabitch even if he's dead.' "

There was a story about the cumulative effect that the obscenity of soldier language had on Ernie, who is supposed to have said of a certain short and vulgar verb: "I am sick and tired of that word ——. If I ever hear the ——ing word again I'm going to throw up!"

On the Fourth of July Ernie got a letter from Jerry, and replied: "You wrote it apparently on the evening of D-day, as it was mailed June 7—the one where you sat out in the patio till the moon came out and everything seemed so peaceful. It was such a beautiful note, darling—I lay down on the grass in an orchard and read it with nobody around, and I'm glad nobody was, for when I finished I was sort of choked up and couldn't have spoken to anybody. . . . In a way it seems incongruous that there should be such peacefulness and quiet as you felt there, and yet even here in the heart of war there are interludes of the same unbelievable peace. Long lulls when there is not a sound, and the apple trees and grass and hedgerows are so green and pretty, and cows will be mooing in the next field, and a bumblebee buzzing around and nothing else. These interludes are so false that they give you a spooky feeling. . . .

"I've only gradually learned, from little things dropped here and there, what a truly horrible time you had of it last winter and spring. . . . I'm still okay—get tired easily and really begin to feel old in numerous small ways—but actually my health is fine and I think my weariness is largely laziness and fed-upness with the war. I've even reached the advanced age where people call me 'Pappy,' but to hell with them. . . .

"I've been out for several days collecting a series on the Ordnance Department. . . . We did have one spooky night when I went up with them after midnight to pull out two German knocked-out tanks that they were afraid the Germans might try to recapture that night. But outside of that it was pretty prosaic. Which suits me, except it's hard to write about prosaic things and keep them interesting.

"Don Whitehead and I got so tickled at supper we got the giggles like children and could hardly eat. The AP had asked permission of UP to use the story I wrote about the other correspondents, in which I quoted Don. The story they put out was all right, but Don today had clippings back from his home paper in Kentucky, and the head on the piece said 'Harlan Man Talks in Foxhole.' Somehow that struck us so funny we almost got hysterical. . . . Do you remember reading in one column about my coming ashore with a Corporal Wescott, and I suggested that if anybody wanted to send his wife flowers that she worked for Southern Pacific Railway at Sixth & Main in Los Angeles? Today a long telegram came from the president of the SP himself, practically inarticulate with excitement, saying he had shared with Mrs. Wescott the thrill of it and the railroad had swamped her with flowers and what not. I suppose the outcome will be that she'll wind up marrying the president of the railroad and poor Wescott will be without a wife.

"Had a nice letter from Aunt Mary. Said they'd been flooded for two weeks with photographers and reporters—apparently in preparation for the *Time* piece. I do hope they did a nice job on it. Lee said they pumped him for five and a half hours; also their Los Angeles man worked on Cavanaugh and Chris Cunningham;[3] they sent men from Indianapolis to see the folks and talk to Iva Jordan and Mabel Campbell, who were my schoolteachers. And they had Wertenbaker send a long piece from here and Will Lang one from Italy.

"This morning while I was frying eggs a captain and a sergeant walked in wanting me to autograph a snapshot taken on the boat. Don, who was apparently asleep, was laughing about it later. He said before the eggs were half through I'd talked them out of three cans of tomato juice, two cans of bacon, two cans of grapefruit pieces, an empty can for boiling water, and three pounds of coffee. . . ."

From a letter to Roz: "I have a feeling I've used up all the chances a man is endowed with, and when I have to tempt Fate further I get the horrors inside. If I ever was brave, I ain't any more. Much of the time I'm quite depressed, and hang on only by the feeling that it can't be too long now. Writing is difficult these days—I seem bored with the war and impatient for the end. Wouldn't it be cute of me—now that I've got all the papers in the world and the prizes and the front cover of *Time*—just to quit and go into seclusion! . . ."

His avid anticipation of the article in *Time* turned to disap-

---

[3] Cunningham, of the United Press, had soldiered with Ernie in Africa and Sicily. Knowing from Ernie that Chris was overdue for home leave, I was cocked for action when the president of the UP telephoned me, plaintively, that only the rival AP and INS had "technical advisers" in Hollywood in connection with the Pyle film. Chris got his leave at once, after I telephoned producer Cowan and commandeered an invitation.

pointment when a copy of the magazine arrived. There on the cover was his portrait all right, and inside was a long article on which great pains had been expended, but while the piece was in large part excellent, it contained some fabulous inanities. The most glaring of these was an account of the alleged origin of Ernie's technique as a correspondent:

"Ernie himself was a little slow to recognize the nature of the new assignment. At first he tried to be a more or less conventional war correspondent, covering the news as others did. The change began one day in Africa when the press corps was invited to meet Admiral Darlan. Scripps-Howard cabled him to be sure to attend. He was hurrying across an airfield to the interview when a swarm of *Stukas* swooped down, began splattering bullets around him. He dived into a ditch just behind a GI. When the strafing was over he tapped his companion on the shoulder and said, 'Whew, that was close, eh?' There was no answer. The soldier was dead. Pyle sat through the interview in a daze, went back to his tent and brooded for hours. Finally he cabled his New York office that he could not write the Darlan story. Instead he wrote about the stranger who had died in the ditch beside him. For days he talked of giving up and going home. But when the shock wore off, he knew for sure that his job was not with the generals and their stratagems but with the little onetime drugstore cowboys, clerks and mechanics who had no one else to tell their stories. The GIs were slow to reciprocate the Pyle devotion. In the field Ernie, abnormally sensitive to cold, wraps his skinny frame in as many thicknesses of nondescript clothes as he can lay hands on, makes himself look like a ready-made butt for jokes. At first the GIs plagued the funny-looking little man unmercifully, 'scrounging' (*i.e.*, swiping) his blankets and water, knocking off his helmet to reveal the wad of toilet paper always kept there, ridiculing his passion for orderliness and his perpetual puttering, pouncing on him in howling droves when he modestly retired behind a bush to relieve himself. Then the letters from home began to arrive, mentioning the Pyle column or enclosing clippings of it. Slowly it dawned on the GIs that they had acquired a champion. . . ."

Ernie wrote to his wife: "The part about interviewing Darlan and getting strafed and jumping in a foxhole with a dead soldier is complete and utter fiction. I'd like to know where they got it. Nothing even remotely resembling that ever did happen. And then after that all the bunk about soldiers making fun of me is completely ridiculous. Nobody has ever played a practical joke on me. . . . My biggest disappointment was that they didn't use a picture of you and write something more about our place. I had asked Lee to ask them discreetly to soft-pedal the divorce if they would—for both our sakes—but they soft-pedaled so much that you seemed to be hardly a part of my life at all."

It appeared that the elaborate news-gathering machinery of *Time* had fallen on its face in Hollywood. A Cowan press agent had shown a *Time* correspondent an early draft of the Pyle movie script, prepared by writers who knew little about Ernie and who had constructed a Pyle career to suit their own ends. The *Time* man, unhappily, took these Hollywood imaginings as gospel. But it is remarkable that this magazine, with its vaunted army of researchers, did not spy out the obvious incongruities. For instance, Ernie did not reach Algiers until a week after Darlan's assassination.

Ernie's spleen about the piece did not moderate as the weeks passed; he wrote me: "I could slit Hollywood's throat for fouling up the latter part of that *Time* piece. Good God, all soldiers carry toilet paper in their helmets, and there's no joke about it. Actually I carry mine in my pocket, but so what? Through that *Time* piece they've created a legend that makes me a combination of half-wit and coward, and it'll grow and be perpetuated."

In the meantime more urgent matters engaged him. It was on July 25 that Eisenhower, delayed for weeks by ugly weather, launched the heavy attack with which Bradley's American First Army broke out of the beachhead area, through St. Lô, and opened a path for Patton's theretofore uncommitted Third Army. In preparation for the big thrust, Ernie had assigned himself to the 4th Infantry Division under Major General Raymond O. Barton. He spent one night "on the dirty floor of a rickety French farmhouse, far up in the lines, with the nauseating odor of dead cows keeping me awake," and next night "slept on the ground even farther up, snugly dug in behind a hedgerow so the 88s couldn't get at me so easily." On the following day the weather cleared and the attack was on: "If you don't have July 25 pasted in your hat I would advise you to do so immediately. At least paste it in your mind. For I have a hunch that July 25 of the year 1944 will be one of the great historic pinnacles of this war. . . .

"The various battalion staffs of our regiment[4] were called in from their command posts for a final review of the battle plan. Officers stood or squatted in a circle in a little apple orchard behind a ramshackle stone farmhouse. . . . Chickens and tame rabbits still scampered around the farmyard. Dead cows lay all around in the fields. The regimental colonel stood in the center of the officers and went over the orders in detail. Battalion commanders took down notes in little books. The colonel said, 'Ernie Pyle is with the regiment for this attack and will be with one of the battalions, so you'll be seeing him.' The officers looked at me and smiled and I felt embarrassed." General Barton made a little speech. Then everyone proceeded to his unit.

The infantry attack was to be prefaced with a tremendous aerial bombing by fifteen hundred "heavies" and a great many other aircraft, a highway a few hundred yards ahead of the waiting troops serving as deadline for the bombers. Ernie chose a farmyard half a mile away from which to watch the air barrage: "And before the next two hours had passed I would have given every penny, every desire, every hope I've ever had to be just another eight hundred yards farther back." For this was the occasion when a segment of the Air Force missed its mark, let its bombs fall far short, and killed hundreds of our own people, including Lieutenant General Lesley J. McNair. Ernie reported that the

[4] The 12th Infantry.

forward margin of the American forces had been marked with strips of colored cloth, as well as with colored smoke, to guide the airmen. The dive-bombers, leading the armada, hit their target zones perfectly. Then came the heavy bombers, in great successive masses. "From then on, and for an hour and a half that had in it the agonies of centuries, the bombs came down. . . . Individual noises did not exist. The thundering of the motors in the sky and the roar of bombs ahead filled all the space for noise on earth. Our own heavy artillery was crashing all around us, yet we could hardly hear it. The Germans began to shoot heavy, high ack-ack. Great black puffs of it by the score speckled the sky until it was hard to distinguish smoke puffs from planes. And then someone shouted that one of the planes was smoking. Yes, we could all see it. A long faint line of black smoke stretched straight for a mile behind one of them. And as we watched there was a gigantic sweep of flame over the plane. From nose to tail it disappeared in flame, and it slanted slowly down and banked around the sky in great wide circles, this way and that way, as rhythmically and gracefully as in a slow-motion waltz. Then suddenly it seemed to change its mind and it swept upward, steeper and steeper and ever slower, until finally it seemed poised motionless on its own black pillar of smoke. And then just as slowly it turned over and dived for the earth—a golden spearhead on the straight black shaft of its own creation—and it disappeared behind the treetops. But before it was done there were more cries of 'There's another one smoking,' and 'There's a third one now.' Chutes came out of some of the planes. Out of some came no chutes at all. One of white silk caught on the tail of a plane. Men with binoculars could see him fighting to get loose until flames swept over him, and then a tiny black dot fell through space, all alone. And all that time the great flat ceiling of the sky was roofed by all the others that didn't go down, plowing their way forward as if there were no turmoil in the world. Nothing deviated them by the slightest. They stalked on, slowly and with a dreadful pall of sound, as though they were seeing only something at a great distance and nothing existed in between. God, how you admired those men up there and sickened for the ones who fell. . . .

"As we watched, there crept into our consciousness a realization that windrows of exploding bombs were easing back toward us, flight by flight, instead of gradually forward, as the plan called for. Then we were horrified by the suspicion that those machines, high in the sky and completely detached from us, were aiming their bombs at the smokeline on the ground—and a gentle breeze was drifting the smokeline back over us!

"An indescribable kind of panic comes over you at such times. We stood tensed in muscle and frozen in intellect, watching each flight approach and pass over us, feeling trapped and completely helpless. And then all of an instant the universe became filled with a gigantic rattling as of huge, dry seeds in a mammoth dry gourd. I doubt that any of us had heard that sound before, but instinct told us what it was. It was bombs by the hundred, hurtling down through the air above us. Many times I've heard bombs whistle or swish or rustle, but never before had I heard bombs rattle. I still don't know the explanation of it. But it is an awful sound. We dived. Some got in a dugout. Others made foxholes and ditches and some got behind a garden wall—although which side would be 'behind' was anybody's guess. I was too late for the dugout. The nearest place was a wagon shed which formed one end of the stone house. The rattle was right down upon us. I remember hitting the ground flat, all spread out like the cartoons of people flattened by steamrollers, and then squirming like an eel to get under one of the heavy wagons in the shed. An officer whom I didn't know was wriggling beside me. We stopped at the same time, simultaneously feeling it was hopeless to move farther. The bombs were already crashing around us. We lay with our heads slightly up—like two snakes—staring at each other. I know it was in both our minds and in our eyes, asking each other what to do. Neither of us knew. We said nothing. We just lay sprawled, gaping at each other in a futile appeal, our faces about a foot apart, until it was over.

"There is no description of the sound and fury of those bombs except to say it was chaos, and a waiting for darkness. The feeling of the blast was sensational. The air struck you in hundreds of continuing flutters. Your ears drummed and rang. You could feel quick little waves of concussion on your chest and in your eyes. At last the sound died down and we looked at each other in disbelief. Gradually we left the foxholes and sprawling places and came out to see what the sky had in store for us. As far as we could see other waves were approaching from behind. When a wave would pass a little to the side of us we were garrulously grateful, for most of them flew directly overhead. Time and again the rattle came down over us. Bombs struck in the orchard to our left. They struck in orchards ahead of us. They struck as far as half a mile behind us. Everything about us was shaken, but our group came through unhurt. . . .

"An hour or so later I began to get sore all over, and by midafternoon my back and shoulders ached as though I'd been beaten with a club. It was simply the result of muscles tensing themselves too tight for too long against anticipated shock. And I remember worrying about war correspondent Ken Crawford, a friend from back in the old Washington days, who I knew was several hundred yards ahead of me." [5]

Later Ernie told me he could never go through another such experience and retain his sanity. Yet he wrote in the column: "I'm sure that back in England that night other men—bomber crews—almost wept, and maybe they did really, in the awful knowledge that they had killed our own American troops. But I want to say this to them. The chaos and the bitterness there in the orchards and between the hedgerows that afternoon have passed. After the bitterness came the sober remembrance that the Air Corps is the strong right arm in front of us. . . . Anybody makes mistakes. The enemy makes them just the same as we

[5] Crawford, encountering Ernest Hemingway just after the bombing, remarked in allusion to the sleeping-bag episode in *For Whom the Bell Tolls:* "It's true, Ernest, the earth *does* shake."

do. The smoke and confusion of battle bewilder us all on the ground as well as in the air. And in this case the percentage of error was really very small compared with the colossal storm of bombs that fell upon the enemy. The Air Corps has been wonderful throughout this invasion, and the men on the ground appreciate it."

The leading company of the battalion to which Ernie had attached himself had suffered severe casualties from the bombing, including many shock cases, and Ernie could not imagine the company being able to carry out its orders, which required it to spearhead the infantry attack forty minutes after the bombing had ceased. "And yet Company B attacked—and on time, to the minute! They attacked, and within an hour they sent word back that they had advanced eight hundred yards through German territory and were still going. Around our farmyard men with stars on their shoulders almost wept when the word came over the portable radio. The American soldier can be majestic when he needs to be."

He stayed with the 4th Division for a few days while the historic breakthrough was being accomplished, and then, near the end of his tether, returned to the press camp at Vouilly. He wrote Jerry: "I was up with the infantry for five days and nights, and although I felt fine when I came back to base camp, the second day here I came down with the aches all over and the famous Army diarrhea—just as I was starting to write up the stuff I'd gathered. . . . I'll have to keep my nose to the grindstone now for quite a while to keep even.

"I'm so glad you sent me the pictures. You look awfully thin in the black skirt. . . . And if you could possibly get some color pictures, how I'd love them. I believe the most appreciated gift over here is a color picture of family and gardens and dogs from home. . . . They are expensive, but hell, I guess we're getting pretty rich. . . .

"Lee is now in Hollywood trying to straighten out the movie. He cabled the other day that he had eliminated the worst asininities. . . . I'm trying to get them to play down my part in it. . . . Everybody still says Cowan's intentions are good, and I believe they are, but his Hollywood instinct to dramatize or make something better just gets the best of him. . . .

"Yes, Lee has written about the new book. . . . I think I will dedicate it to all the unnamed ones, as you suggest, or to all the ones who won't be reading books any more.[6]

"The office has lately been urging me to take a furlough, and even to come home right away if I wanted to; but I don't want to go to England, and it would be foolish to come home right now with the war in the status it is. . . ." (General Patton's Third Army had charged through the gap torn by the First and was brilliantly exploiting the Allied initiative.)

The Coleman stove arrived, "and it is a beauty—all chrome-plated and with my name engraved on it. It's so damn pretty I can hardly bear to use it and get it dirty. I'm not going to light it until Don Whitehead and Bert Brandt, who are furloughing in England, get back, for they were as anxious for it to come as I was. . . .

"I don't quite know how to explain to you the things I do that have worried you. The not-going on bombing missions has always been a kind of whim; I could justify myself in that, or rationalize or whatever you call it. But I haven't felt the same way about the ground. . . . I spend considerable time covering and trying to give credit to some of the rear echelon branches; but you can't just do that all the time; it wouldn't be fair to the troops who are doing the real fighting. This recent trip was a pretty tough one; almost as tough as anything I've been through; and yet it was one of the historic actions of the whole war, and we knew it ahead of time, and any correspondent who wasn't in it violated his right to be over here at all. . . .

"Day after tomorrow is my birthday. A couple of colonels

---

[6] *Brave Men* was dedicated: "In Solemn Salute To Those Thousands of Our Comrades—Great, Brave Men That They Were—For Whom There Will Be No Homecoming, Ever."

[Myers and Goslee] who helped me celebrate it in Sicily last year are still nearby, so I'm going over to their camp. . . ."

The circumstances of Ernie's forty-fourth birthday were set down by Colonel Myers: "General Hodges had taken over the First Army, and being as aggressive as General Bradley[7] liked to have his command post well up, so we moved to the vicinity of Canisy and set up in a very lovely 'parc' of the Comte de Corgolay, beside a charming little lake. Later we discovered that this château had been the headquarters of a German corps and was plotted on their maps. The first night a couple of JU 88s came across the c.p., each laying a stick of anti-personnel bombs right through the middle of the camp. Nobody was killed but it raised hell with the kitchen. The second night they came back again, and one of them laid a five-hundred-pounder right in the middle of the lake. So on the morning of August 3 there were quite a number of fish lying all over the place, and Ernie made one of his dry and apropos remarks: 'If those sons-of-bitches would just fry these damn fish too, I would have a real good birthday party.' That night we had his party—the second one that Harry Goslee and I had celebrated (the first being at Nicosia, Sicily, where, strange to say, our c.p. got bombed also). The celebration started early on a case of Hennessy which I had saved from Cherbourg, and by the time we sat down to eat I don't think any of us were quite sure who was there. Suffice it to say that we had a wonderful time."

The officers must have felt more festive than Ernie, for he wrote Roz that "my stomach was still too touchy to take more than about three drinks." He also told her: "I'm hearing from Jerry now quite regularly—a letter about every ten days. She is down to one nurse now. She is terribly proud of the lawn and the flowers, which they've spent a lot of time and work on. . . . During this recent spell of depression I've been terribly homesick. . . . Most of the correspondents have gone back [to London] for a 'rest' of a week or two, but I much prefer to stay right

[7] Now promoted to command of the Twelfth Army Group.

here. I believe I'm the only one of the original correspondents in France who hasn't yet taken a rest. . . .

"Ernest Hemingway is over here, and the funny part is that nine-tenths of the GIs think that he is me! I should think he would like to kick people in the face—spend twenty-five years at becoming one of America's two or three greatest writers, and then have everybody think he is Ernie Pyle! Three days ago he and Bob Capa got themselves caught in a townful of Germans and very nearly got killed. They had a corporal with them, and yesterday the corporal was telling one of our correspondents how he almost got killed with Ernie Pyle the day before! Hemingway seems like a hell of a nice fellow. . . ."

In a letter to Jerry, Ernie said: "I don't have much feeling one way or the other about our present fame. . . . It's nice in a way, but I'm afraid it's going to make life almost unlivable when I get home; at least we'll have to shut ourselves off in a shell to be able to endure. It's even starting to get bad over here; everywhere I go I have to autograph hundreds of franc notes for soldiers (although I always enjoy that); but now it's got so soldiers come to the camp just to see me, and they don't know when to leave and it slows me up. . . ."

His Albuquerque friend, Captain Arthur McCollum—one of the contractors who built his house—turned up, to spend a few days' leave, and Ernie took him on a tour. Not far west of the area where the Allied pincers were sealing the historic Falaise-Argentan gap, they ran into a story. Ernie wrote: "The ditches were full of dead men. . . . There was no live human, no sign of movement anywhere. Seeing no one, hearing nothing, I became fearful of going on into the unknown. So we stopped. . . . To our left lay two smashed airplanes in adjoining fields. The hedge was low and we could see over. They were both British fighter planes. One lay right side up, the other lay on its back. We were just ready to turn around and go back when I spied a lone soldier at the far end of the field. . . . I waved and he waved back. We walked toward each other. He turned out to be a second lieutenant—Ed Sasson, of Los Angeles. He is a graves registration officer for his armored division, and he was out scouring the fields, locating the bodies of dead Americans. He was glad to see somebody, for it is a lonely job catering to the dead.

"As we stood there talking in the lonely field a soldier in coveralls, with a rifle slung over his shoulder, ran up breathlessly and almost shouted, 'Hey, there's a man alive in one of those planes across the road! He's been trapped there for days!' We stopped right in the middle of a sentence and began to run. We hopped the hedgerow and ducked under the wing of the upside-down plane. . . . We dropped on our hands and knees and peeked through a tiny hole in the side. A man lay on his back in the small space of the upside-down cockpit. His feet disappeared somewhere in the jumble of dials and rubber pedals above him. His shirt was open and his chest was bare to the waist. He was smoking a cigarette [given him by the soldier who had found him]. He turned his eyes toward me when I peeked in, and he said in a typical British manner of offhand friendliness, 'Oh, hello.' 'Are you all right?' I asked stupidly. He answered, 'Yes, quite. Now that you chaps are here.' I asked him how long he had been trapped in the wrecked plane. He said he didn't know for sure as he had got mixed up about the passage of time. But he did know the date of the month he was shot down. He told me the date. And I said out loud, 'Good God!' For, wounded and trapped, he had been lying there for eight days!

"His left leg was broken. . . . His back was terribly burned by raw gasoline that had spilled. The foot of his injured leg was pinned rigidly under the rudder bar. His space was so small he couldn't squirm around to relieve his own weight from his paining back. He couldn't straighten out his legs, which were bent above him. He couldn't see out of his little prison. He had not had a bite to eat or a drop of water. All this for eight days and nights. Yet when we found him his physical condition was strong, and his mind was as calm and rational as though he were sitting in a London club. He was in agony, yet in his correct Oxford accent he even apologized for taking up our time to get him out."

Although other soldiers soon joined the little rescue party, it took almost an hour to get the pilot free, and during that time he told them what had happened. He was Flight Lieutenant Robert Gordon Fallis Lee. German fire had knocked out the motor of his night fighter, and he was too low to jump. He turned on his lights to attempt a crash landing, and then a machine-gun bullet got him in the right hand. The plane cut a fifty-yard groove before nosing over on its back in what turned out to be a very lively battlefield. "When I came to," he said, "they were shelling all around me." This his rescuers could well believe, for the field had erupted with hundreds of shell holes, some of them only a few yards from the plane; it was during this melee that a 20-millimeter shell struck his leg and exploded. Actually, according to later information, Flight Lieutenant Lee was trapped "only" five days.

Ernie and McCollum worked frantically with the others, ripping at the metal skin of the plane with pliers and whatever else could be found in vehicles nearby. Meantime a soldier was sent off to fetch a jeep-ambulance with a surgeon and corpsmen.

Ernie wrote: "The American boys worked faster than we believed possible. They tore their fingers on the jagged edges of the metal; they broke strong aluminum ribs with one small crowbar and a lot of human strength. Soon they had a hole big enough so that I could get my head and shoulders inside the cockpit. Somebody handed me a canteen of water and I shoved it through the hole to the pilot. He drank avidly. Somebody outside said not to let him drink any more right now. The pilot said, 'Would you pour some on my head?' I soaked my dirty handkerchief and rubbed his forehead. . . . Inside the plane the stench was shocking. My first thought was that there must be another man in the plane who had been dead for days. I said to the pilot, 'Is there someone else in the plane?' And he answered, 'No, this is a single seater, old boy.' "

Apparently the lieutenant's leg was gangrenous. When the surgeon arrived, his first step was to reach into the plane and inject morphine, but the airman was so strong in spite of his ordeal that the drug did not knock him out. Finally, with painful difficulty, and some help from a board that McCollum ripped off a fence to brace the pilot's back, they got him out and he said, "My God, that air! That fresh air!"

Ernie saw the lieutenant later, in a hospital, and was told that after some operations he would be all right.

CHAPTER 36

The City of Light—and Kisses

THE Americans closed in on Paris. Eisenhower would have preferred to surround the city and compel its surrender without risking an assault, but his hand was forced when the impatient Free French rose against the Nazi garrison. "It was necessary to move rapidly to their support," he wrote in *Crusade in Europe*. "Information indicated that no great battle would take place and it was believed that the entry of one or two Allied divisions would accomplish the liberation of the city. For the honor of first entry, General Bradley selected General LeClerc's French 2nd Armored Division."

The correspondents were champing at the bit. At First Army headquarters in a château, Maillebois, outside Alençon—about a hundred miles west of Paris—Colonel Myers was approached by Ernie, Jack Thompson, Clark Lee, Hank Gorrell, and others who wanted permission to go into Paris at once, now that the underground had showed its hand. "It was necessary to refuse," Myers told me. "We did arrange to have a Cub plane look over the situation to see if there was any possibility of getting a press camp into the Longchamps race track. The plane was fired at from various locations in Paris, and particularly at the race track, so we felt it was not advisable to move at that time. However, some of the correspondents did go in about the twenty-third or twenty-fourth and got there as soon as or perhaps ahead of some of the combat troops, so that when Paris actually capitulated they had liberated the Hotel Scribe and were well entrenched."

Ernie moved on to General LeClerc's headquarters at Rambouillet, about thirty miles from Paris, and wrote Jerry on August 24:

"If you could see where I am writing you'd either laugh or cry. I'm in a shed about ankle-deep in straw. This morning we are sort of stymied as far as moving is concerned, so in order not to waste a day I dug up a white metal table out of a nearby garden, brought it in the shed, and am sitting here in the straw writing. It is raining cats and dogs and is so dark in mid-forenoon that I can hardly see; but at least it's dry in here. I've just been neck and neck with the columns every day for two or three weeks. Too, I have had one of my low spells—you know, homesick and fed up with the war and feeling like you couldn't take it any longer. . . . We are all so wet and thoroughly crummy, I'll be glad when at last we get to a big city and move into a hotel. The last few days we've been going rough again. Sleeping on the ground and eating hit and miss, and I've got so it kind of gets me. . . ."

A correspondent of the *Omaha World-Herald*, Lawrence Youngman, recalled: "After finishing his letter he lay down on the straw, pulled a funny little black beret down over his eyes, and went through the motions of napping. As he lay there he looked so feeble and emaciated that I couldn't escape the feeling that I should try to help him. But when time came to shove off it was Mr. Pyle who came lugging my typewriter and bedroll out to the jeep."

On August 25 LeClerc's division entered the City of Light. It was a day to remember. "I had thought that for me there could never again be any elation in war," Ernie wrote. "But I had reckoned without the liberation of Paris—I had reckoned without remembering that I might be a part of this richly historic day. We are in Paris—on the first day—one of the great days of all time. . . . We drove through a flat, garden-like country under a magnificent bright sun and amidst greenery, with distant banks of smoke pillaring the horizon ahead and to our left.

And then we came gradually into the suburbs, and soon into Paris itself. . . . The streets were lined as by Fourth of July parade crowds at home, only this crowd was almost hysterical. The streets of Paris are very wide, and they were packed on each side. The women were all brightly dressed in white or red blouses and colorful peasant skirts, with flowers in their hair and big, flashy earrings. Everybody was throwing flowers, and even serpentine.

"As our jeep eased through the crowds, thousands of people crowded up, leaving only a narrow corridor, and frantic men, women, and children grabbed us and kissed us and shook our hands and beat on our shoulders and slapped our backs and shouted their joy as we passed. . . . We all got kissed until we were literally red in the face, and I must say we enjoyed it. . . . Everybody, even beautiful girls, insisted on kissing you on both cheeks. Somehow I got started kissing babies that were held up by their parents, and for a while I looked like a baby-kissing politician going down the street. The fact that I hadn't shaved for days, and was gray-bearded as well as bald-headed, made no difference. Once when we came to a stop some Frenchman told us there were still snipers shooting, so we put our steel helmets back on. . . . Above the din we heard some not-too-distant explosions— the Germans trying to destroy bridges across the Seine. And then the rattling of machine guns up the street, and that old battlefield whine of high-velocity shells just overhead. Some of us veterans ducked, but the Parisians just laughed and continued to carry on. . . ."

The street in front of the Hotel Scribe, where the correspondents took up headquarters, was jammed with women. According to Clark Lee: "Several guys kept going back and forth through the mass of feminine worshipers just to get kissed and hugged and embraced on the way in and out of the hotel. Ernie made it once and then stood up on a balcony to watch the mad scene in the street below. Finally, after about an hour, he delivered his considered opinion, with that well-known chuckle,. 'Anybody who doesn't sleep with a woman tonight is just an exhibitionist.' "

Two days later I got a wireless: "Eyem about done up and would like start homeward negotiations in a few days. Now that Paris is over feel it all right to leave. Eyem all right physically but bogged clear down inside and can barely keep columns going. Have you any objections?"

I replied: "All hands say come arunnin. Copy been finest but you cant go on forever without letup."

During a night raid on Paris Ernie lay alone in bed and was so frightened he was physically sick. "I would have given anything in the world just to go down the hall and be with someone," he said, "but I guess I was too proud." He wrote Roz: "For six weeks I've been dragging lower and lower, from mental exhaustion and just a sort of unendurable blur of too much war. As I dragged lower I kept setting up my date for coming home. A week ago I decided to be there by mid-October. But today I decided it had to be very soon, so I've cabled Lee. . . . 'I've had it,' as the saying goes. I can't take any more war—at least not now. . . . I'd give a fortune right now never to have to write another column. . . . Your news of Jerry [which was unfavorable] only confirmed what I had begun to suspicion. I would rather know than not know; that's what made my homecoming to Albuquerque the last time so horrible, because everybody had been so kind and lied to me. Her letters do continue fine. . . . I haven't been around Paris much yet. I'm so indifferent to everything I don't even give a damn that I'm in Paris."

Sergeant Mack Morriss wrote in *Yank* of a conversation with Ernie in a hotel bar. A Medical Corps captain came over and asked, "Aren't you Ernie Pyle?" Ernie said he was. "I just want to thank you," said the captain. "You've done some great things for us in your column." Ernie grinned. "You won't be reading it much longer. I'm going back to the States in a couple of days." Morriss said that something like relief passed over the medic's face. "Are you?" he said. "By God, I'm glad. You've seen enough of it. I'm glad you're going."

Sergeant Morriss commented: "War-weary or khaki-happy or whatever he is, Ernie is leaving a hemisphere in which he has produced some real contributions to the American doughfoot. . . . 'So you're a war correspondent?' an infantryman will say. 'Know Ernie Pyle? There's a guy who knows how it is.' "

A message came to me: "Am back with Army in field out of Paris madhouse and regaining little sanity."

And two days later: "Am back in Paris after two days fruitless traveling. Plan stay here now until departure."

Before leaving for London Ernie wrote a valediction: "This is the last of these columns from Europe. By the time you read this, the old man will be on his way back to America. After that will come a long, long rest. And after the rest—well, you never can tell. Undoubtedly this seems to you to be a funny time for a fellow to be quitting the war. It is a funny time. But I'm not leaving because of a whim, or even especially because I'm homesick. . . . I have had all I can take for a while. I've been twenty-nine months overseas since this war started; have written around seven hundred thousand words about it; have totaled nearly a year in the front lines. I do hate terribly to leave right now, but I have given out. . . . The hurt has finally become too great. All of a sudden it seemed to me that if I heard one more shot or saw one more dead man, I would go off my nut. And if I had to write one more column I'd collapse. So I'm on my way. . . . I cannot help but feel bad about leaving. Even hating the whole business as much as I do, you come to be a part of it. And you leave some of yourself here when you depart. Being with the American soldier has been a rich experience. To the thousands of them that I know personally and the other hundreds of thousands for whom I have had the humble privilege of being a sort of mouthpiece, this then is to say good-by—and good luck."

He drove to the headquarters of General Bradley at Chartres, to say good-by. Bradley told him that when he got home he ought to stay there. Keenly as the General appreciated Ernie's friendship, as well as his value to morale, he thought the correspondent had done his share and warned him that he couldn't keep on at this trade indefinitely without getting hurt.

In London a correspondent of the *Chicago Sun*, W. A. S. Douglas, noticed an unusual crowd of soldiers in the mail room at Army press headquarters. Ernie had arrived that morning, and they were waiting to see him. "Pretty soon 'the little fella' came in, and I was surprised over how frail and worn he looked. . . . It seemed as though he had put on ten years in ninety days. . . . The GIs crowded around Ernie, slapping his shoulders, shaking both his hands. It was an ovation such as I have never seen any other newspaperman receive from either soldiers or civilians. The packages were brought out, broken open, the contents distributed, and about an hour later Ernie and I walked out into the sunlit square; he had kept only two bundles out of twenty-odd—presents from his own relatives. The alert had been on all morning. Two robot bombs had fallen on London inside the last hour while Ernie had been passing out his cigars, cigarettes, and candy. And as we leaned on the railing of Grosvenor Square Garden a third V-1 putt-putted to a roar, passed directly over our heads, came down about half a mile away. We felt the impact. The ambulances and fire engines came roaring by. . . . 'I feel like I'm running out,' said Ernie."

CHAPTER 37

Respite

H E CAME home on the *Queen Elizabeth*, which should have
been more restful than an airplane. But he had a cold.
And since the ship was bringing back many of the soldiers
wounded in France, he devoted much of his time to them. One
boy, with a leg off, confided that he had not written to his family about the amputation; they thought he was only slightly
wounded and he didn't know how to tell them. Ernie wrote the
letter for him: "Your son is healthy and happy. . . . Don't feel
too badly about it. . . ." (The soldier's parents, Mr. and Mrs.
Joseph Murawski of Pittsburgh, replied that "although the news
was bad, the letter made it easier for us.") Most of the
men had been reading the columns and had seen the one in which
Ernie told of his decision to go home. He said to a reporter in
New York: "They wanted to tell me they understood. There I
was, unhurt physically, standing over those kids with arms and
legs and eyes gone, all battered to hell, and they told me they
understood." A sergeant aboard the ship, Byron Deerr of Belle
Plaine, Iowa, told the *Indianapolis Times*: "He seemed worn
out. None of us blamed him for coming home, for he sure did his
job—more than his job. All he could think of on the ship was how
we GIs were getting along."

I met him in New York, with a letter from Jerry: "My dear
dear Ernie—You are back—I am humbly—and numbly, thankful
—Had I any feeling beyond that, I believe I would be ashamed
to admit it—but I have not—You will know I am waiting, eagerly

—I shall try not to be impatient—but I can't guarantee that! For if you linger in the East until frost takes the flowers—and nips the lawn—well! Love, darling."

New York was feverish and wearing. Ernie telephoned Jerry that he would be delayed—he had agreed to stay on four or five days to let Jo Davidson do a sculpture of his head. The sittings at Jo's studio on Fortieth Street were in the afternoons. The mornings and evenings were as crowded as they had been a year earlier, with a multiplicity of guests and telephone calls and errands. Roz Goodman came up from Washington to help out. The John Steinbecks came to visit. Fredric March looked in one night and found Ernie already bedded down, exhausted. There was an interview with Dwight Bentel, of *Editor & Publisher*, who wrote: "He's just himself—just like his column. . . . There he sprawls across one end of a settee with his paratrooper's boots thrust out into the middle of the room, GI shirt unbuttoned at the throat, relaxed as a fresh-boiled noodle and the strain of months of tense living on the European battlefronts rolling off the ends of his toes and tips of his fingers by the yard. You can just feel the pain and heartache draining out of him. . . . Across the room from Ernie sits his boss and best friend of twenty years, Lee Miller, managing editor of the Scripps-Howard newspapers, his bare feet stuck into moccasin slippers and pulled up under him. Rosamond Goodman, Ernie's attractive and gracious white-haired secretary, swings one leg from the edge of a table between jumping after the doorbell and the two telephones. Happy? They're happy as June bugs—Mrs. Goodman and Miller because Ernie's back, and Ernie because he's so glad to be back, and they're carrying on like zanies. 'You'll just have to excuse us,' says Ernie, 'we're all a little mad.' And they are. But it's a happy, infectious kind of madness that you're glad to be a part of for a few minutes. You can practically see Ernie's nerves untangling themselves right there before your eyes. This madness is good medicine—nature's medicine—for a guy who has been wound up like a steel spring through months, and months of close squeaks and near misses. . . ."

Ernie telephoned messages to the wives of colleagues and other friends, sent off to Tom Treanor's widow in California the personal papers of that gallant correspondent, killed in an accident in France, and wrapped up little gifts of perfume and other things bought in Paris. Dozens of radio and magazine and lecture offers were declined. When a heartsick soldier who had served in Sicily telephoned from Chicago, he promised to write the boy's estranged wife and explain that patience was needed when a fighting man was readjusting to home.

Jo Davidson's studio was usually crowded. There Helen Keller ran her fingers over Ernie's face. Charles Ervin, a grand old man of labor and liberalism, came past, and Ernie said, "My God, Charlie, I thought you were dead!" Roy Howard and practically the whole of the Scripps-Howard high command looked in. A newspaper vendor at a nearby corner said, "Jeest, it's Oinie!" and refused payment for a paper.

Roy invited Ernie and me to dinner at his home one night. That afternoon, after returning from the studio to the hotel, we had quite an influx of guests. As we left, I made a mental note from a scribbled memorandum of the Howards' address—20 East Sixty-fourth Street—and, giving the address to the taxi driver, proceeded to forget it. So did the driver. We had the right street but couldn't remember the number. I telephoned the *World-Telegram* from a drugstore, but was told it was forbidden to give out Howard's address. The man did consent to telephone Roy and call me back. We arrived at the house in less than good humor. A maid admitted us and was taking us up by elevator when Ernie, thinking it must be an apartment house and not realizing the maid was one of the Howards' staff, nudged me and said, "Let's go in with chips on our shoulders." When dinner was over we all had to listen to a Dewey campaign speech, during which Ernie slept in a chair. So did a Scripps-Howard executive who was among the guests.

Finally Ernie got off to Dana. He had asked me to request a priority for airplane passage from Indianapolis to Albuquerque, and I applied to the Pentagon, since the Army controlled passenger priorities on the commercial airlines. I was turned down. A society editor, no less, said she could easily arrange it, but I thought of Commander Max Miller, of the Navy, which was eager to have Ernie see some naval warfare in the Pacific. Max picked up a telephone and arranged the booking in a minute's time. Next day four Army officers had occasion to telephone me, requesting various services by our Mr. Pyle. I explained that Ernie was dreadfully in need of a rest but that I would forward their inquiries. Each time I found a way to mention that the Army had denied Ernie a priority. They all expressed dismay, and each time I assuaged the gentleman's sorrow by explaining, "Oh, it's all right, the Navy has taken care of it." It sort of took the wind out of their sails.

When Ernie arrived at the Albuquerque airport his impedimenta included a dressed chicken from Aunt Mary, in a shoebox. He was met not only by Jerry and her nurse, Mrs. Ella Streger, but by Paige Cavanaugh, just in from Hollywood.

Ernie wrote to his father and aunt: "Jerry is much better than I had expected. . . . The house and the yard are so beautiful I can hardly stand to look at them. The lawn is the nicest in Albuquerque, and Jerry and the nurse have flowers growing everywhere. Jerry has to keep to her routine of resting at periods during the day and going to bed early. And not having much excitement."

Lester Cowan arrived, and his director, "Wild Bill" Wellman, came for a day. The mirage of an unbroken siesta in the sun was once again short-lived. There were always people—with problems. Of course Cavanaugh wasn't "people"—he was one of those rare phenomena, an old friend so completely attuned to Ernie by background and temperament and by mutual nostalgias that he was as relaxing as Ernie's treasured vista of mountain and mesa. And Cowan, belying the standard concept of Hollywood's producers, fitted himself into the little household quite comfortably. But he did have problems with the movie, which had to be thrashed out. "Jerry has stood up well under these three days' chaos," Ernie wrote me. "She is very far from a well woman, but she has improved tremendously, especially in control of herself. . . . I don't think she can ever recover, but she has tried terrifically and she has made great progress." In a week or so he was writing Roz: "Jerry had a relapse and has been very sick for almost a week now. What happened was apparently a delayed reaction to the excitement of my coming home, and the interruption to her rigid routine of 'relaxing' and taking her B-1 shots. The effect is a terrible muscle ache all over which just has her in agony. For days she lay and cried with pain, and it damn near broke my heart and Mrs. Streger's. . . . Her illness of last winter was much graver than I had known, in fact she was close to death for a month, and the long illnesses have wracked her terribly. She has aged fifteen years since I saw her last. . . . Please don't mention around about Jerry's showing the effects of her physical illness so much; for I know she knows it and is sensitive about it. . . .

"We've not been bothered very much locally by callers or phone calls, as Dan Burrows[1] has been good enough to keep it out of the papers that I am here. We do get a lot of long-distance calls though, both from friends and people wanting me to speak everywhere, from Seattle to Minneapolis. In one day I turned down long-distance requests from Bob Hope, Eddie Cantor, and the Treasury Department. . . . No, I can't give Fame much myself. I certainly have ceased to have any life or time of my own. In my peculiar circumstances there's so much that you simply can't hide or run away from. Such as all this correspondence with soldiers I've known, and letters to families of friends, and being polite to requests from people I know and who are good intentioned. Even though I say no to damn near everything, even that is a burden. I wish to God the war was over so I could drop the column and let my name die out."

The University of New Mexico asked him to accept an honor-

---

[1] Burrows succeeded Shaffer as editor of the *Albuquerque Tribune*.

ary degree, Doctor of Letters. He said yes. Dean Edmondson of Indiana University, now retired and living in Pasadena, came to Albuquerque with the word that I.U. also desired to honor him, and Ernie agreed to this too. He heard from me that Roy Howard had telephoned about a wishful rumor that Ernie was about to endorse Dewey for President, which gave him a laugh—that is, at the idea of his endorsing *anybody* for political office. (Once he wrote me: "Suppose you're head over heels in the election right now. Who's running?") An American Legion press agent telephoned from Indianapolis wanting him to say something handsome about the Legion's new commander, whom Ernie had never even heard of.

He wrote me: "I'm tentatively figuring on being on the way to the Pacific early in December—but I don't know. I hate and dread to go so terribly that when I let myself think about it I get clear down in the dumps."

Cavanaugh persuaded him to go to Hollywood, where the scriptwriters were still having troubles. Ernie didn't want to go to the studio, so the movie people were brought out singly and in small groups to talk with him in the Cavanaugh backyard. He showed some asperity at their unfamiliarity with his writings, on which the film was supposed to be based: "Well, why in hell don't you read my goddamn books?" Director Wellman clattered out on his motorcycle and spent a day. "I don't think the picture ever would have been made," Ernie wrote me later, "if they hadn't got Wellman on the scene. He's an enthusiastic guy and put life into everybody. I must say that Lester has some pretty able-looking key men around. I was very pleased with Meredith, and he's keen to play the part. He's a little guy, even shorter than I am. And he's got some brains. I was very pleased when he and I saw some point different from Wellman, and he stood up alongside of me and screamed for two hours to win his point." Wellman told Cavanaugh, "I see the thing now. It's a love story. Ernie falls in love with the lousy infantry, and leaves it, and finds he has to go back to it." Cowan wired me: "Ernie's visit here of inestimable value. He took time to infuse every technician with understanding of soldier and his point of view. It will be source of inspiration to all during making of picture."

Lincoln Barnett arrived to do a full-dress article on Ernie for *Life*. He was enchanted with the sometimes slapstick camaraderie of Pyle and Cavanaugh and quoted the latter as saying: "I got awful sick of Pyle this last year. The whole country is so intent on making him a god-darned little elf." One night, according to Barnett, Cavanaugh heard Ernie sighing and tossing in his bed. "What's the matter?" Cavanaugh called. "I can't sleep," Ernie replied. "That's because you're so damn rich," said Cavanaugh. A little later Pyle heard Cavanaugh tossing around. "Now what's the matter with *you?*" he asked. "I can't sleep either," Cavanaugh said. "That," said Ernie, "is because you're so damn poor." Cavanaugh laughed, then remarked thoughtfully, "I got an idea. You give me half of your dough and then we can both get to sleep."

Ernie told Barnett he dreaded going back to war but said there was one bright spot about the Pacific: "I'll be damned good and stinking hot. Oh boy!" Barnett's article concluded: "However long the war may last, Pyle is determined to cover it to the last shot. This resolution disturbs many of his admirers who regard Ernie Pyle as a nonexpendable national asset. . . . He is not afraid to die, but he looks forward very much to a day when he can jump into a car with unlimited gasoline and drive once again with Jerry by his side down the long white roads of the Southwest. 'I can't bear to think of not being here,' he says. 'I like to be alive. I have a hell of a good time most of the time.' "

Ernie was due in Albuquerque for the academic ceremonies at the University of New Mexico, so he caught the Santa Fe's overnight *El Capitan,* and sat up in a coach. He got into a bibulous conversation with two Marine veterans of Saipan and had only a few hours' sleep before reaching Albuquerque in the morning. He had little more than time to shave before an escort of faculty dignitaries arrived. It had been agreed that no speech by Ernie was required, which was as well. He went through the formalities, before a considerable crowd, in a sleepy haze. Judge Sam Bratton of the United States Circuit Court of Appeals, chairman of the University Board of Regents, bestowed the degree: "Ernest Taylor Pyle, writer, journalist, war correspondent, world traveler, and interpreter of the American way of life, sympathetic and understanding friend of our soldiers on the fields of battle, friend and comforter of thousands of relatives whose loved ones have fallen in the service of their country."

After writing autographs for an hour, a haggard "Doctor" Pyle returned in cap and gown to his home, a few blocks from the campus, and sought some sleep. He didn't get much. Helen Richey, by now with the Wasps, happened to be ferrying an A-20 across the country. She put down at Albuquerque and telephoned Ernie, who demanded that she come right over. She wangled an Army car and driver, and the latter was big-eyed on being asked to drive to Ernie Pyle's house. He may have been somewhat differently impressed upon arrival, for Ernie emerged from the front door in rumpled pajamas and greeted the good-looking Helen with, "What's been holding you up, you old bag!"

He wrote Roz: "When I got back from California there was the goddamnedest mountain of mail, packages, telegrams, requests, demands, and pleas stacked up that you ever saw in your life. I spent one whole day merely sorting the stuff. A Mrs. Collis comes early every morning and takes dictation for a couple of hours, and now Shirley Mount, between semesters, has been helping me daily. The days are full of interruptions, people coming and phoning. . . . Jerry has relapsed again. We finally had to put her back in the hospital. She'll be in for a long time, and even I can't see her. . . ."

CHAPTER 38

"Everything Was Blood"

"**R**ELAPSE" was an understatement. Ernie wrote me: "This is a hard letter to write. Poor Jerry finally did it. She didn't succeed, but she sure butchered herself up. She will be in the hospital for a month, and even I am not allowed to see her.

"I might as well begin at the beginning and tell the whole thing. This of course is for you only; only a few people here will know it, and outside of here, only you, Po, and Cavanaugh will know it. As I told the doctor, I don't give a damn, but he wants it kept secret for Jerry's sake and the effect on any possible future recovery.

"When I came home, she was mentally herself for the first time in many years; at least she was herself in that she was unlikkered and undoped. She had aged about fifteen years and obviously was far from recovered either physically or mentally, but she had made wonderful progress and God how she had tried this time.

"She was fine the first week, then had that bad relapse, which was really physical and not mental. Then she was good again for about a week. And then the day before I got back from California, she started into one of those things that psychologists call manic depressions. The doctor says it was probably caused by nothing specific at all, that it was just the swing of the cycle.

"Well, she concealed it from me until last Thursday, acting perfectly normal and fine. But Mrs. Streger told me later that it started the Tuesday before, and the doctor has now revealed some telephone conversations from her which show it started even before that. But beginning on last Thursday evening, she became so low she took part in nothing. She just sat and stared. She wouldn't answer when you talked to her. She almost stopped eating. She would get up early each morning and bathe and dress, and then sit bolt upright on the edge of her bed all day long, just staring. It was pretty horrible. The doctor came daily and sometimes oftener. On Sunday he said, 'I might as well tell you, we're in for a rough time ahead.' He predicted that it would get worse for about five days, finally reaching a crisis by her becoming rigid and lying and screaming. At that point he planned to begin electrical shock treatments, similar to the insulin shock treatments you've read about. We made preparations for it as though you were preparing for a storm. Lined up extra nurses, called off the visit this week-end of the Hollywood people, got stocked up with drugs, etc.

"That was Sunday noon. He said there was a very slight chance that she would pull out of it herself. Shortly after Mrs. Streger (her wonderful nurse) went home around five o'clock Sunday evening, she *did* begin pulling out of it. She asked if she could cook my dinner and I said certainly, so she did, and we ate together and talked and, although she wasn't wholly normal, she seemed practically so compared to the previous several days. She went to bed seemingly happy, and a couple of times during the night (she sleeps, even with hypos, only three and four hours a night) she came into the room and we talked a little, and I became convinced she was pulling out of it.

"Yesterday morning she had slipped back into the silences some, but still was better than she had been. Mrs. Streger came at eight-thirty, so I could have the car to go downtown to a dentist's appointment at nine. (I've been having a long daily siege with the dentist.) Mrs. Streger and I both were very encouraged by her appearance yesterday morning. I was downtown two hours. When I drove into the driveway at eleven o'clock

Mrs. Streger was out in the yard, crying and wringing her hands and calling, 'Oh, Ernie, she's stabbed herself all over and now has locked herself in the bathroom.' I'd broken that bathroom door open once before about three years ago. So I took two lunges at it, and on the second one down it went. Jerry was standing at the washbowl, looking into the mirror. She turned and looked at me with that awful stare and never said a word or changed expression. She was blood from head to foot. She had dressed all up that morning in a linen suit. Everything was blood.

"Mrs. Streger had already got the doctors on the way. There was nothing we could do but sit her on the bed and hold her. At first glance you would have thought she would be dead in a few minutes. But after a minute or so I realized her face wasn't getting the death pallor, and that the blood was clotting and not flowing very fast. She had around twenty wounds in her. Most of them were superficial. But three were bad. There was a ghastly hole in the right side of her neck, an inch and a half long, an inch wide and an inch and a half deep. A smaller one, but still big, was in the same spot on the left side of her neck, just below the jaw and ahead of the ear. And the third one was right in the middle of her neck, below the Adam's apple, where she had jammed scissors into her neck and then pounded on them with her other hand. It went into the windpipe. She also hacked her left wrist, and cut her breast about fifteen times with a razor blade. But they were small cuts.

"To go back—Mrs. Streger, after I left, had asked her to go out in the yard as usual, but Jerry told her to leave her alone. She was sitting on the bed in her room. Mrs. Streger went into my room (adjoining, you know) to make my bed. When she finished she sat down on the hassock in my room to sew on a button or something. The doors to both rooms were open, and she heard no sound from Jerry's room except a slight clicking, which she thought was Jerry snapping her fingernails, which she does when she's nervous. It was Cheetah with a dog's instinct that probably saved her life. Cheetah came dashing into my room and, although not greatly affectionate usually nor demonstrative, jumped up twice on Mrs. Streger's lap, ran around in circles and kept dashing back into Jerry's room. Finally Mrs. Streger followed her. And there was Jerry, standing before her little writing desk, absolutely covered with blood, and pounding the scissors into her neck. They were those long narrow scissors, incidentally, that the Barnum & Bailey man (what was that famous press agent's name?[1]) gave us years ago on his annual spring trip. You may have a pair. They're about a foot long and very narrow, and have Barnum & Bailey and Ringling Brothers Circus engraved on them.

"Well, Jerry stared at her hatefully as though daring her to interfere, continuing all the time to pound the scissors into her neck. Mrs. Streger dashed toward her and Jerry ran behind the big chair, still pounding. When Mrs. Streger got too close she pulled the scissors out and started at Mrs. Streger with them. Finally Mrs. Streger did get them away from her but in her excitement laid them on the book shelf, and in a moment Jerry had them back again and started jabbing her wrists. Once more Mrs. Streger got them away from her and ran out of the room with them, then ran to the phone. Fortunately she got right through and got the doctor on the way. But while she was telephoning Jerry got in the bathroom and locked herself in. Mrs. Streger couldn't break the door. Then she ran out into the yard looking for help, and just then I drove up.

"The doctor got there in about ten minutes, took a quick look, and said she had missed every vital point. In a few minutes the surgeon arrived with all his gear and began sewing her up. She never uttered a sound all the time, but just stared at us. He used no anesthetic at all while he worked on her, yet she never flinched a muscle as he sewed her up. They washed and powdered the wounds with sulfa and gave her hypos and tetanus and gas gangrene shots.

"Mrs. Streger by now had got almost hysterical, sitting in my

[1] Dexter Fellows.

room crying her heart out, and blaming herself for it. So we had to work on her awhile. We got another nurse up in about half an hour. But there was actually nothing to do, except keep constant watch on her, and clean up the bloody house. The doctor said for me to take Mrs. Streger home, but she said she couldn't bear to be in her house alone and would rather stay here and work, and I thought that wiser too. For the thing certainly was a horror to her. So we worked around the house till about four o'clock, when the Nazareth San[itarium] out north of town finally made room for her, then called an ambulance and took her out. The only words Jerry had said all afternoon were to ask me once for a cigarette. When the ambulance came they brought the stretcher in the front room, and I went into Jerry's room and said, 'Darling, we're going to the hospital now.' She got out of bed instantly and walked right out to the front room and lay down on the stretcher.

"Mrs. Streger and I followed out in the car. She got off the stretcher in the hall [at the sanitarium] and walked into her room. But at the bed she turned and said, 'You can't do this to me. I don't deserve this.' So I said 'But, Jerry, this is where you asked to come.' Which was true—previously. She's had one of those psychological breaks with Sister Margaret Jane, you know, and had often said that if she ever had to go to the hospital again she didn't want to go to St. Joseph's. So when I told her she had asked to come to Nazareth she didn't remember it, of course, but it stopped her and she lay down. I sat down beside her and she said, 'May I ask you something?' So I leaned over and she whispered in my ear, 'Are you Ernie Pyle?' I told her I certainly was, and she said, 'I don't believe it,' and then she began staring and said no more until I left the hospital.

"The doctor went back about seven last night and said he talked with her for about an hour, and that she was rational and talked to him willingly and seemed quite a bit out of her depression. He queried her indirectly about what had happened and is convinced that she remembers nothing about it. She told him the first thing she remembered of yesterday was when the surgeon was sewing up her neck, and she wondered how it happened. Both the doctor and I are inclined to believe it. He thinks it was not premeditated at all, but a sudden blinding whim of the moment. She has not been drinking or doping up at all. But she had become intoxicated almost to the point of mental blankness by this desperate depression.

"None of us had sensed any suicidal instincts. Of course I lived for ten years in a horror that she would commit suicide, but in recent years Po and I and the various doctors had decided she never would—that her indirect threats were all part of her act. She had tried it a couple of times in the past but botched them up so badly they were almost laughable and convinced us she was acting. In the last couple of years I had ceased to worry that she would ever do it. There has been nothing at all lately to indicate she was thinking along that line, even as an act. But brother this one was no act.

"What to do now? I've long ago given up hope for Jerry, yet there's nothing to do but hope. The doctor is still confident. He is starting the electrical shock treatments just as soon as he's sure her windpipe is healing and that all danger of infection from her wounds is passed. These treatments are drastic. It's the same as electrocution, only they stop in time. It induces a convulsion, and unconsciousness for about two hours. The doctor says it is the same as dying each time. She will have one a day for thirty days. No one can see her. I saw her for the last time yesterday when we took her to the hospital. After the thirty days they will take her to some different place for convalescence. The theory of this thing, the best I can make of it, is that it breaks up all the maze of 'thought patterns' that are attached to each other. As the doctor says, Jerry is in a condition similar to ringing a doorbell, but instead of a bell ringing at the other end of the wire, twenty sticks of dynamite go off. These treatments are to disconnect the wire from the dynamite, as he puts it, although the dynamite will still be there. . . . It's too goddamned deep for me and I have little faith in it, but there's no harm in trying. He says that out of two thousand cases on which records have been kept, not all were successful, but that there isn't a single case made worse by them. . . .

"The doctor who has had her since last spring is a very smart guy and does some pretty good thinking about her. He says that I've been going away for years and she is the one to stay behind; this time if she recovers fast enough he wants her to be the one to go away on a trip and me stay behind—even though I'd leave the very next day for the Pacific. For that and other reasons— helping in the 'reassembling' and month of convalescence after the shock treatments—he hopes I can stay in America through December. And I may decide to do that. In fact I've been toying with it even before this happened. I'd originally figured to be on the way to the Pacific early in December, but goddamn it I'm not ready to go yet—I still have a dread of it, I still have a dread of starting to write again, I haven't had any real rest or peace yet. In other words, I just don't feel ready to go yet, and if I go feeling like that I'm afraid I can't last long without cracking up. . . . Since the first three days I don't think I've sat on our little sunny terrace a total of two hours. When I came back from California and faced this mountain of stuff piled up here, and when I tried for two days to get it worked out and in those two days hit an all-time peak wave of callers, calls, and unfair interruptions, for the first time I began to get bitter and resentful at the whole thing and to feeling I couldn't take it. . . ."

CHAPTER 39

Crowded Hours

J ERRY'S wounds mended, and the shock treatments were begun. Ernie wrote me: "She has been somewhat cheerful they
say, and rational too. For about a week she went in cycles of
depression and normalcy and was batty as hell. Some of it
was funny. Once she thought the doctor was Tom Dewey with
his mustache shaved off and conjured up all kinds of evil plots the
Democrats or Republicans, I forget which, were waging against
her. . . ."

Copies of *Brave Men* arrived, and Ernie went through one of
them making marginal notes: "Three weeks after Tommy
Clayton returned to the lines he was killed. It saddened me terribly, for I felt very close to him." "A few weeks later Major Lee
was dreadfully wounded by a mine." "Captain Perrin was killed
two months later at Cassino." "Lieutenant Robert Drew, Sr.,
was killed in a bomber crash in Labrador on his way overseas,
ironically meeting the fate his son had cheated."

He had to go to Indiana now to accept his second doctorate.
A special convocation had been arranged at the University. The
Bloomington city schools as well as University classes were dismissed for the day. Stores were closed during the ceremony. The
degree was that of Doctor of Humane Letters, the first ever
presented by I. U.

Ernie arrived from Dana, with his father and Aunt Mary, and
at the University auditorium was helped into cap and gown by
friends of his college days. Four thousand persons had crowded

380

into the auditorium, although it was well understood that Ernie was to make no speech. A bit of banter was provided on the rostrum by his classmate James S. Adams, a New York business executive. Adams produced a round white hat with a narrow black band, which he said was Ernie's old Sphinx Club hat and was nowadays to be found under the pillows of freshmen with literary ambitions. Adams also displayed five SAE pins, which, he said, Ernie had "hung" on five coeds in his day. There was some whispering between Ernie and President Herman Wells, and the audience thought that perhaps Mr. Pyle was going to change his mind and say a few words, but he was only asking, "Hermie, do I take my cap off or keep it on when I get the degree?" And Wells proceeded: "Ernest Taylor Pyle, homespun Hoosier, world traveler, discerning reporter, unexcelled interpreter of the minds and hearts of men in peace and in war, advocate for the rights of the soldiers in the ranks, in recognition of your achievements, your University gladly confers upon you the degree Doctor of Humane Letters. . . ."

The program over, Ernie spied a red-haired matron whom he had not seen in twenty-one years and walked over to kiss her. It was his college sweetheart, Harriett, who had turned him down those many years ago.

He went on to Washington for various errands in preparation for going to the Pacific. People made a procession in and out of his room at the Hay-Adams House. General Bradley's wife brought a carton of then scarce cigarettes. Sculptor Max Kalish, who had been commissioned by Willard Kiplinger, the Washington news-letter man, to execute bronze statuettes of the leading figures of the day in Washington, seized this chance for a sitting. (The collection is in the Smithsonian Institution.) *Brave Men* went on sale while Ernie was in Washington, and the critics were enthusiastic. A *Chicago Sun* executive sought me out to report a rumor that Ernie was unhappy in his present affiliation and to suggest that the *Sun* would be glad to take him away from all that. I disenchanted him. Olive Clapper, widow of Ray, was making a lecture tour. The story went that at her first engagement, in Toledo, after delivering a prepared address she braced herself for the scheduled question period, wondering what complex phase of international or domestic politics might be thrust at her from the audience. The first question was, "Can you tell us how Ernie Pyle's health really is?"

Back again in Albuquerque, he wrote Roz: "I was allowed to see Jerry for the first time last night. Her improvement in just the last few days has been remarkable. . . . It has really been grand here alone these four days. . . . I got Cheetah out of the kennel, and she was almost hysterical at the reunion. . . ."

Jerry was insisting on leaving the hospital, and in spite of many objections was coming home next day, with nurses around the clock. She had been told he was going to the Pacific, "and accepts it as inevitable, but for the first time in her life is trying to influence me not to go, which makes it harder—since I dread to go anyway." And, about Washington, he told Roz wistfully: "Our 'little family' is such a grand bunch, and you are all so kind and good to me." In the same vein he wrote Eleanor Shamel, my secretary, "I wish I weren't so damn sentimental. I can hardly think of not seeing you all for another year (if I'm lucky) without an overwhelming sadness. I don't know what I would do without my little Washington gang—without your sweetness and your devotion."

Jerry was brought home but, Ernie wrote Roz, ". . . immediately went to pieces. Within five hours she was back in the hospital. Yet she pulled out of that and is home again, and is happy and fairly normal. . . . Her memory is at least fifty per cent gone. She asks about people who have been dead for years. She asked me yesterday if we had been divorced once. It is pathetic, and yet there are still signs of the possibility of recovery, and when she is halfway normal she is so damn sweet. . . ."

He wrote "Dear Papa & Auntie": "I'm trying to get everything straightened up before I leave, for Jerry can't handle the financial things. I know you don't need any money right now, but I'm sending you each a little, just for emergencies. I am making an awful lot of money right now, but of course most of it goes back to the government. My federal income taxes this year are the fantastic figure of $105,000. We are not really rich as rich people go, but do have enough built up to take care of Jerry the rest of her life if anything should happen to me. . . . Please don't mention to friends about my taxes . . . for it is misleading. . . ."

Jerry had begun to show substantial progress. When somebody recommended to Ernie a private hospital in Pasadena, California, much to his surprise she readily agreed to spend the winter there. Mrs. Streger was to stay at the hospital with her. On December 20 Ernie and Jerry came to the Albuquerque airport to say hello to me when my plane stopped briefly on its way west; I was going to the Southwest Pacific for a few months as a correspondent—with a stopover in Hollywood. That night, with Mrs. Streger, they took a train to Pasadena. Ernie thought that he had made a firm arrangement by telephone with the hospital, but now he wrote Roz: "Well, everything is changed. Christ, what a rat race my life is. Jerry and Mrs. Streger went out to the hospital this morning to look it over themselves and talk to the doctors. They came back very discouraged. Those doctors expect us to sit in a hotel and wait till they make room, and they won't say whether it might be two days or two months. So Jerry and Mrs. Streger are going back to Albuquerque; Jerry volunteers to go into the hospital there and stay till Dr. Lovelace feels she's capable of staying at home again."

They quit their Pasadena hotel and moved in with the Cavanaughs. Before going home, Jerry consented, in spite of her nervousness, to take a look at Hollywood's famous night life, at Cowan's invitation. He arranged a ringside table at Ciro's, and Ernie and Jerry danced together for the first time in years.

Finally, at the railroad station, there was a tremulous parting. And there was a longhand note: "My darling: I love you terribly, and always have and always will. Leaving is brutal for us both, but there'll be a better day, and just keep on keeping yourself for us when I come back. You're wonderful, and doing wonderfully. I'm so proud of you. Your Ernie."

He stayed on for a few more days. The making of the movie was well under way, and we spent a good deal of time watching both the shooting and the rushes. Ernie was upset by two or three of the scenes. He couldn't understand, for instance, how the various battle-experienced technical advisers lent by the Army could have overlooked such a blunder as having only a single blackout curtain over the entrance to a front-line command post. (There should be two, so that a soldier can pass through without exposing light.) And there was a melodramatic scene, based on the German breakthrough in Tunisia, in which an officer gasped out an order to "Burn the papers!" Ernie thought this was ludicrous.

One night in Dave Chasen's restaurant, Joe E. Brown, the actor, who had spent much time entertaining troops overseas, asked Cowan to introduce him to Pyle. They had a long conversation, of which I overheard one fragment:

Brown: "Ernie, those GIs are wonderful—every single last one of them."

Ernie: "Oh, Joe, that's a lot of bull——, and you know it."

Brown was taken aback, but he knew as well as anybody that in an army of millions of men the concept of universal wonderfulness was less than exact.

Cowan had wanted Ernie to meet W. C. Fields, and Ernie was eager to do so, but Fields could not be found. He got the message after Ernie had departed, and called Cowan to express his disappointment. "I love that little fella," he drawled, and Cowan replied, "Ernie loves you too, Bill." The comedian had the last word: "Is that so, Lester! Do you suppose he'd marry me?"

Ernie accepted an invitation to call on Hedda Hopper, the Hollywood columnist. Cavanaugh and a press agent and I went along. Miss Hopper led us to a large drawing room in which were stacked hundreds of Christmas presents. "Ernie," she said, "this is what *fear* does to Hollywood."

On New Year's Day he called on Burgess Meredith and Paulette Goddard. Olivia De Havilland and Jinx Falkenberg dropped in, but Ernie, tuckered out, had crept upstairs for a nap. He revived in time to kiss the girls good-by. The Cowans took him to dinner and then, as he wrote Roz, "they poured me and all my Pacific gear on the nine o'clock train." He greeted a porter with, "Pardon me, sir, but what is your position with this company?"

He had been persuaded to break the trip to San Francisco with a stop at Camp Roberts, and he wrote Jerry: "I had to get up at two a.m.—with a smashing hangover. The General commanding Camp Roberts was there in person to meet me, with his aide and driver, and then we had to drive two hours to camp, and then I started right in with the soldiers, long before daylight. Boy, it was a hell of a day. I couldn't see half the time, and almost got sick at my stomach a couple of times. Went all day long till after five-thirty, when I went back to the General's house to have dinner with him. Fortunately he gave me a couple of drinks before dinner. Actually he was awfully nice and completely honored my request to be with the men and not have a 'tour' made of it. Then the sergeants picked me up again, and we went down to the Noncommissioned Officers Club, where the overseas veterans gather of an evening to drink beer. But the manager of the club winked and called us back to his office, and we sat there drinking his whisky for a couple of hours."

"I was at the tag end of nothing when we arrived here [San Francisco]," he wrote Roz. "I decided not to call a soul for a couple of days, for I must get cleared up on my neglected work. I stopped all calls, even though I thought nobody knew I was in town. How it gets around I don't know, for telegrams started coming in, and one call got through by mistake. It was a Red Cross girl I'd known in Italy whose husband was killed over there." She came to the hotel, and they talked for five hours.

He telephoned Jerry almost daily, and he wrote her: "Don't be too discouraged and disheartened if you do break down again, darling, for I think it's possible and normal that you may once or twice before you become completely well. You've got one thing on your side lately that you didn't use to have—and that is that you're trying so earnestly and sincerely, and that you *want* to get well."

She wrote to him: " . . . Ernie I am all right—or I'm going to be soon—so don't worry about me—at all—I'm a long way from reaching the honest humility I should have—but I see it clearly enough in moments to long for it—I am sorry fear and apprehension and dread and shame figure so strongly in the desire— but it couldn't be otherwise—I want one day for pride in me to be a real factor in your love for me—I don't know the way—but hope and believe I may find it, dear—I do care about what you have come to mean to people in this country—but in my heart I care only because they love you—and feel close to you, for what you are—and in my own true heart, I think you know that is how I love and have loved you—and shall go on loving you all my life."

I arrived from Hollywood, and Max Miller from Washington. The Navy had assigned Max to show Ernie the ropes. A note to Jerry: "Your letters keep coming in, and I'm glad you are so good to write me often just before I leave, and I'm ashamed I have not been equally good about writing you. After the first couple of days of being here 'secretly,' it has been the usual rat race, with me feeling pressured and kind of frantic. The loss of time is largely due to my inability to say 'No' to anybody, and thus isn't anyone's fault except my own. However, I am about all cleaned up except the batch of columns I wanted to write before going. I've only got one and a half done. . . . To write columns like these out of your head, I need not a half day here and a half day there, but a whole week absolutely uninterrupted so I can finally get in the mood of it and stuff will automatically come rolling out. . . .

"At eight-thirty Monday morning the Army picked us up for a tour of Port of Embarkation—at their request. First we went to see the general [C. H. Kells] in command, who was very nice, and went on his private yacht over to Angel Island, where all the troops either headed for or returning from the Pacific come through." A young steward on the boat, fetching coffee, noticed Ernie's war-correspondent patch and said to him, "Gee, a war correspondent, eh? You mean just like Ernie Pyle?" I said, "Just who do you think this is?" He looked again and almost dropped his tray.

"When the yacht docked," Ernie continued, "here was a fifty-piece Army band on the pier to serenade us! The colonel commanding [J. T. Hogan] asked if I would mind saying a few words to some of the boys he'd had assemble in the drill hall. I said, 'Oh my God, no, I can't speak. Never do.' But it was too late. They had me trapped. We all walked into the drill hall, where a thousand soldiers were sitting waiting. The band was there again, playing. Lee and I and these three colonels had to get up on the stage, and the colonel made a little flattering speech about me, and then I had to step up and face it. I said about half a dozen sentences, something to this effect: 'I can't make you a speech, because I was born tongue-tied. This is the first one I've ever made, and I hope the last one. I've been two and a half years on the other side of the war, and now I'm headed for your side. A lot of you are too. So wish me luck and I'll wish you luck and thanks a lot.' My voice cracked toward the end, and I shook like a leaf for an hour afterward, but Lee said I did all right and I sure got a big hand! . . .

"I went shopping yesterday afternoon and got your ring and had it mailed from the store. Unaccustomed as I am to buying wedding rings, I don't know whether it was a good selection or not. Most of them had diamonds, and I thought you wouldn't want diamonds.[1]

"I'm sorry, darling, but it's too late now to back out on this

[1] Jerry, who had never had a wedding ring, had written him asking for one.

trip. You know that I don't want to go any more than you want me to go, but the way I look at it it's something almost beyond my control. I hate it, but there's just nothing else I can do. . . . You ask me to tell you what I would most wish you to do. Darling, it's almost impossible to answer that specifically. I just want above all, of course, for you to be your old self. I want your mind to be calm and clear and for you to enjoy being alive, and to be interested in things. . . .

"You say you want to learn to pray. That has to be up to you, of course, but it is so different from anything you or I have ever felt. I want you to get well but I wouldn't want you to become pious—for then you wouldn't be *you*. I don't think you can get well by any mystic device or even willing it so; but you can by devoting yourself to calmness and a routine that is full, and in trying to accept things that make you unhappy. You are good inside and always have been; you are big inside; it seems unfair that you have been so cursed with inner turmoil. But I feel you are going to come out of this whole again. . . . And one other thing I would like you to do—is not to hate yourself, not blame yourself, not be so contrite. I've noticed both before and after your last relapse that you were damning yourself unmercifully for the things you had done and hadn't done, and looking upon yourself as bad, which you are not. . . . Your last letter touched me deeply; I know how you love me, and I am grateful for that. . . ."

A letter, which he would not receive for some weeks, was being written him by President James B. Conant of Harvard: "It is a pleasure to inform you that the Governing Boards of Harvard University have voted to confer upon you the honorary degree of Master of Arts on Commencement Day, Thursday, June 28, 1945, if you can be present at that time to receive it. . . ." And General Bradley would be writing him in a few days, during a breather after the Battle of the Bulge: "Dear Doctor: May I extend my belated congratulations on the honor recently bestowed on you by two universities. The honor was well deserved and we here were all very pleased to learn of the awards. All of us over here miss you very much. . . ."

There was a letter to Jerry: "I'm grateful for these few days of unexpected delay in taking off, for with luck I'm going to get clear after all. For a few days it looked hopeless. . . . Thursday at breakfast John Steinbeck called up. He and Gwyn came and stayed till about seven. They asked Max and me to go to dinner with them, but I was too washed up, and just went downstairs and ate alone and then went to bed. . . . I've got another big envelope of clippings, pictures, and what not which I'll mail to you. Some of the pieces sort of embarrass me. You say a word or two about hating to go back to war and not getting much rest at home, and they seize on it and dramatize it out of all proportion. . . .

"Is your memory still improving? I don't know whether this might help you or not, but when Dr. McLin was trying to put into layman's language for me what the shock treatments were for, he illustrated it like this: He said supposing a person's mind was like a pile of blocks, each block being a 'thought pattern,' some good and some bad. He said the shock treatment just knocks this pile of blocks down and scatters them. He said it couldn't segregate the good from the bad and destroy the bad. They were all still there but scattered. And then after the treatments were over, the blocks or 'thought patterns' were to be rebuilt. It seems to make sense to me, and I believe you are now starting the rebuilding and that's the reason your mind sort of fluctuates and you can't see any clear path, because the blocks are still scattered and the rebuilding isn't finished yet. . . .

"Two letters came this afternoon—your last two. When I come back we'll do something about the money, but let's not now. I've never aspired for all this money as you know. I do like the security it gives us, but not the obligations and sidelines that go with it. We'll live simply when I get back—and we'll have time for ourselves, or else. I couldn't go on forever leading this frenzied goldfish life of the past few months. We'll just have to drift out of the limelight and let it die its natural death, that's all. . . . I certainly have no objection to your donating to the Tingley hospital fund or anything else. But I do know how generous you are, and I know that you might give every cent you have to some charity, and then have nothing to pay your bills. That's the reason I limited what is to be in the bank. So you can give a hundred dollars or two hundred to any charities or individuals you want to, but please don't go all out, for if you do Fred[2] will simply have to pay your bills. When I get back we can talk things over and then give lots more if we decide to.

"Well, the word has come. We are leaving tomorrow afternoon. I'll send you a telegram tomorrow, but I've decided not to call you. It's too hard on us both to actually say good-by. We've said it in our hearts and our minds and in our love for each other. . . . There's nothing we need to say—for we *know*. There should never have been any doubt in your mind, and there surely isn't now, that I love you above everything, always have and always will. . . ."

A telegram to Jerry: "This is it. Can't phone you. My great love darling."

---

[2] Fred White, an Albuquerque banker with whom Ernie had left money for emergencies.

CHAPTER 40

The War
of Magnificent Distances

RNIE slept much of the way to Pearl Harbor, on blankets spread on the "deck" of the Navy plane, and was reasonably refreshed upon setting foot on warm Oahu soon after daybreak on January 15, 1945. He telephoned me—I had preceded him by a few days—and I found him comfortably situated with Captain H. B. ("Min") Miller, the Navy's new public-relations chief in the Pacific, in a house near Admiral Nimitz' headquarters. The Navy was almost overdoing a promise it had made to protect him from intrusion while he wrote some preliminary columns. In fact, it looked for a time as if there was going to be a little Army-Navy spat. When word was passed to Pearl Harbor that Lieutenant General Robert C. Richardson, Jr., Commanding General, U. S. Army Forces, Pacific Ocean Areas, wanted to see Mr. Pyle, the Navy answered that Ernie was cloistered for a day or two, and this did not go down too well at Fort Shafter. After Ernie got his work done he made his call on the General.

"Anybody who has been in war and wants to go back is a plain damn fool in my book," he wrote in the column. "I'm going simply because there's a war on and I'm part of it and I've known all the time I was going back. I'm going simply because I've got to, and I hate it. . . . One man said to me one day in complete good faith, 'Tell me, now, just exactly what is it you don't like

391

about war?' I think I must have turned a little white, and all I could do was look at him in shock and say, 'Good God, if you don't know, then I could never tell you.' It's little things like that which make returning soldiers feel their misery has all been in vain."

Most of his four nights on Oahu were claimed by the admirals. There was dinner one night with Vice Admiral Marc A. Mitscher, commanding the great Task Force 58, and the correspondent and the Admiral pitched horseshoes.

Ernie was already suffering a dual nostalgia—for Albuquerque and for the European Theater of Operations. He wrote about being "far, far away from everything that was home or seemed like home . . . from Sidi-bou-Zid and Venafro and Troina and Ste.-Mère-Eglise—names as unheard of on this side of the world as are Kwajalein and Chichi Jima and Ulithi on the other side. The Pacific names are all new to me too, all except the outstanding ones. For those fighting one war do not pay much attention to the other war. Each one thinks his war is the worst and the most important war. And unquestionably it is."

This observation caused some eyebrows to rise in the Pacific. So did a remark he made in an interview with Corporal Charles Avedon of the *Midpacifican*, a service newspaper published in Honolulu: "I understand there's an island complex in the Pacific. A claustrophobia. But even though I appreciate the monotony your GIs face, I can't go overboard on sympathy. Not after I've seen the misery and cold and mud and death in Europe. Of course, boys are dying on Luzon and other spots in the Pacific, but I haven't been there yet."

He spoke from his heart, but he should not have said it. Even troops stationed cozily in the Hawaiian Islands had come to feel sorry for themselves, as soldiers on garrison duty far from home probably always will. As for the men to the west who had sweated and stunk and suffered the fevers and funguses of New Guinea and Guadalcanal and the terrors of Tarawa and Peleliu and Leyte, they deserved better.

Ernie made a sentimental pilgrimage to the cottage at Waikiki that he and Jerry had occupied during their visit in 1937. Earl Thacker, a Honolulu businessman he had met on that earlier trip, and Mrs. Thacker gave a dinner party for him complete with native women singers. Ernie was so bewitched by the soft island melodies, with possibly some assistance from the refreshments, that soon after dinner began he left his seat beside the hostess and joined the singers in the next room, where he remained as one course after another was removed untouched from his vacant place at table.

Ernie and Max Miller got their orders for Guam, and Captain Min Miller and I rode with them to the naval airfield. At the entrance a tall Marine flagged us down. Captain Miller identified himself and said the rest of us were all right. The Marine, however, gave each of us a searching look and then, directing a smart salute at the four-striper, said, "I don't know you, Captain, but I recognize Mr. Pyle. Go right ahead."

At Pearl Harbor Ernie had switched from the khaki necktie of the Army to the black tie of the Navy, and now as they set out by way of Johnston and Kwajalein Islands for Guam he adopted the no-tie-at-all etiquette that prevailed in all services west of Oahu.

On Guam the Navy continued to treat him as a personage rather than a reporter. Instead of being housed with other correspondents he was put up in the senior officers' quarters, with Max Miller virtually standing guard to prevent even old cronies from intruding. The constant shepherding and very-important-person treatment were alien and confusing. Ernie was glad to get away to nearby Saipan. This island, seized in sanguinary fighting the previous summer, had become a base for the bombing of Japan by B-29 Superfortresses. Ernie was already acquainted with Brigadier General Emmett ("Rosie") O'Donnell, Jr., commanding the 73rd Bombardment Wing on Saipan. He also encountered there a shipmate of his voyage to Africa on the *Rangitiki* in 1942—Lieutenant Colonel John H. Griffith (later lost in an incendiary attack on Japan). Here also was his "nephew," Lieutenant Jack Bales, who greeted him as "Uncle Shag." Jack was a step-grandson of Ernie's Aunt Mary.

At last there was some surcease from social pressures, and Ernie was able to work in a normal way. Saipan had a grim story to report on, for many B-29s were being lost on the long haul to Japan and back. The fourteen-hour missions were so wearing that, as Ernie wrote in the column, most of the time between flights was spent by the crews lying on their cots doing nothing. In fact, he emphasized this predilection for "sack time" so strongly that an officious brigadier in Washington dispatched some sharp questions implying that these gallant men were leading too languorous a life.

Returning to Guam, Ernie wrote Jerry: "I certainly hit the jackpot on mail yesterday and today. I had five letters from you. . . . I'm so pleased to hear just now for it's the last mail I will be able to get for quite a while. . . . I've been on Jack's island for almost a week and really did enjoy it. And feel good because I accomplished a lot in addition. Jack lives in a hut with nine chief pilots, all grand guys, and they set up a cot for me and I lived with them. . . . Jack's squadron commander turned out to be a man I'd known in Africa [Colonel Griffith]. They've built him a cute little house right down on the beach, so the last three days I was there I went down to his house and wrote on his porch. I was all alone and there were no interruptions and it was about the best place I've ever had to write. With the three days there, and two hard days since I've been back here, working like mad— I've turned in a batch of seventeen columns today! That equals my all-time world record for one sitting. You remember I once wrote seventeen columns in one batch when we were in Helena, Montana. Too bad I couldn't have got one more and broken the record. But there just wasn't time. There is no quality in the columns but quantity is what I am after now. . . . I'm beginning to get back a little into the swing of working. The first couple of weeks almost killed me; I felt I just never could force myself to write again. And also I seem to have thrown off that awful inner horror of coming back that had obsessed me. I guess it was partly being up with the B-29 boys, where I was left alone and really loafed a while and felt relaxed and wasn't constantly pestered. And partly because of realizing that their outlook is so much gloomier than mine. At any rate, I don't feel any fear at all now. . . .

"The Navy has been wonderful to me. Lots of people I know are here—Fred Painton and John Lardner among the correspondents, and many service people. . . . Ed Waltz, who used to be Bob Scripps' secretary, is a yeoman in the Navy out here, and works in the public-relations office. I've talked with him, and he will be delighted to take on the job of answering the fan letters and handling my mail. Ed is a nice guy, sensitive, and widely experienced as a secretary.

"Things over here are so different—the distances, and the climate, and the whole psychological approach—that I still haven't got the feel of it. Also censorship is much different, due to a different type of security necessity, and I'm afraid I may be frustrated quite a bit in trying to give the average guy's picture of the war. . . . If I do get going all right, I'll hang on this time just as long as I can, even if it's a year or more, bolstered by the one vow that when I come home next time, it's for good. I'd rather stay out a year and a half if necessary than ever to go through the ordeal of returning to war again. . . . They've introduced a bill in the New Mexico legislature to make my birthday 'Ernie Pyle Day' in New Mexico. For Christ's sake! [The bill was subsequently enacted.]

"*An hour later*—Darling. This is wonderful. Two more letters just came in. I'm so pleased with them. Your letters have come in so fast that although I've read them all twice, I haven't really got them digested yet, so I am taking them with me to reread and tide me over the time I won't be getting any. . . ."

He had not been able to tell Jerry about his next mission—a voyage aboard a carrier that was to participate in the first great naval air strikes on Japan proper, including Tokyo, as well as in the direct tactical support of the Marines' invasion of Iwo Jima. He and Max Miller flew several hundred miles to Ulithi, an atoll occupied a few months earlier for use as a fleet anchorage and base. Here the carriers were "making up." And not alone the carriers. "Out there on that dark blue water lay the United States fleet," Ernie wrote. "Hundreds and hundreds of ships. The Navy says officially that it was the greatest concentration of fighting ships ever assembled in the history of the world. . . . Battleships and cruisers and carriers and uncountable destroyers. And all the swarm of escorts and tugs and oilers and repair ships that go with them. And this wasn't the only fleet. Others started from other anchorages scattered out over the Pacific, hundreds and thousands of miles from us. They started on a timetable schedule, so that they would all converge in the upper Pacific at the same time. . . . Whatever happened to you, you would sure have a hell of a lot of company."

Commodore O. O. ("Scrappy") Kessing, island commandant at Ulithi, was a good host. There is a photograph of the commodore and the correspondent, inscribed by the former: "To Ernie Pyle—the only guy in the world who can call me what he did and get away with it." According to Robert E. Sherwood, who was among those waiting at Ulithi to go on the strike, "Life for us on that remote atoll was one long series of parties and hangovers."

Ernie had requested assignment to one of the smaller carriers, and was given orders for the veteran *Cabot.* "Her battle record," he wrote later, "sounds like a train-caller. Listen—Kwajalein, Eniwetok, Truk, Palau, Hollandia, Saipan, Chichi Jima, Mindanao, Luzon, Formosa, Nansei Shoto, Hong Kong, Iwo Jima, Tokyo— and many others." There was a notation by Commander D. J. Welsh, executive officer of the *Cabot*, in the ship's mimeographed "Plan of the Day": "We are fortunate in having aboard the famous press correspondent Ernie Pyle. All hands will cooperate with him in every way and make available any information of interest to him. Welcome to the *Cabot!*"

From the *Cabot* Ernie sent off a note to Jerry: "This letter is velvet, as I hadn't thought I would get to write again. . . . You are trying wonderfully for yourself, but I feel you need someone to guide you, someone who is professional about it. . . . The only person that I know of really is Dr. McLin.[1] This isn't a definite expression that I want you to go back with him, for that wish would have to come from you. . . . I know you must feel unsure of yourself, but if there's one thing I can implant in your mind from this distance, I'd like it to be this—don't self-accuse yourself, darling. You have never done anything bad; your wants are modest and you're not doing wrong in having our house and car. It would be wrong for you not to have them. . . . I want you to get well as I've never wanted it before, and I know you do too and that helps me. . . ."

It was on February 19 that the V Marine Corps, supported by the Fifth Fleet of which Ernie's ship was a part, landed on Iwo Jima. He did not see that furiously defended island, nor did he see bombs rain on Tokyo, except through the eyes of returning fliers. But he was crammed with mental notes; and since he was unable to get off any dispatches while at sea, he arranged to transfer to a destroyer escort which was returning to Guam. He wrote a message to the men of the *Cabot*: "Many of you have expressed a disappointment that you didn't have more excitement to show me on this trip. Don't worry about that. I've had two and a half years of 'excitement' on the other side of the world, and I can do with a little monotony now. Monotony suits me fine. . . ." The skipper of the *Cabot*, Captain Walter W. Smith, noted that the morale of his crew had never been higher, and that one of the reasons was the presence aboard of "a famous war correspondent."

From Guam Ernie wrote Jerry: "I've been at sea for three weeks, and much to my amazement and delight I didn't get sea-sick. . . . I went with the carriers to the Japan area and then

---

[1] Jerry had dismissed Dr. McLin, as she had done before with other doctors and would do again.

back to Iwo Jima. . . . I later transferred to a destroyer escort, which is a tiny little ship, and came clear back to base on it. They sure do bob around in the ocean. You should have seen me being transferred from one ship to another, in rough weather, in a bos'n's chair pulled across a line attached to the two ships in mid-ocean. I made three such transfers in one day.[2]

"Everybody was grand, I had good quarters and fine food. It was such a contrast to what I'd known for so long in Europe that I felt almost ashamed. It's hard for me to keep my mouth shut when some of the boys squawk about their conditions, when they're actually safe and living like kings and don't know it. But it was cold up there. They broke out long underwear for the whole crew, and we put on everything else we could find, and were still cold. . . . I'm beginning to get a little interested in telling the whole Navy story, although I do have to readjust myself completely in order to keep a perspective on it, for it is so devoid of the mass misery of the infantry. I had the most wonderful letter from General Eisenhower. . . .

"Whatever you decide to do about painting the house is all right, darling. . . . I know you fret about these decisions, and others that are less important, and are worried whether you've made the right decisions or not. But the way I look at it, the fact that you do make the decisions is the important thing. Even if you make a decision which later you might think was unwise, still there is no great harm done. . . .

"The Navy has taken pictures of me about every two minutes ever since I've been out here, so another batch will be along. It seems to me I'm getting to look awfully old and ugly. But I'm well and healthy; everybody here remarks about how much better I look than when I left. I did get a lot of air and ate like a horse. . . .

"Aunt Mary said they had such a nice letter from you. They've

---

[2] From the *Cabot* to the escort carrier *Windham Bay*, thence to the destroyer *Moale*, thence to the destroyer escort.

been going to 'revival meetings' every night and having a hell of a time! . . ."

He wrote to Eleanor Shamel at Scripps-Howard: "You are a great woman, Mrs. Shamel. Will you marry me? If you did that you could do all these wonderful things for me and the office wouldn't even have to pay you. You really are sweet to send me all the clippings and quotes and 'little things' that make life bearable. Between you and Roz, I don't know what I would do without you, and isn't that a hell of a back-end sentence? . . . The stack of mail awaiting me looked like the Empire State building, thank God. . . . Many thanks for your kind words about the column. But I think you're practicing morale-building on me. I like it though."

The letter from General Eisenhower which Ernie mentioned to Jerry:

15 December, 1944

Dear Ernie:

A few days ago I wrote you a note acknowledging receipt of your latest book [*Brave Men*]. Now I have read it.

I enjoyed it all. The last chapter strikes me—although I am a bit hesitant to admit it because of a most flattering personal reference—as a remarkably fine piece of writing. I think it well expresses the reactions of decent people to this bloody business.

But the one thing in your book that hits me most forcibly is a short sentence at the top of the fifth page where you announce yourself as a rabid, one-man army, going full out to tell the truth about the infantry combat soldier. This sentence gives me an idea for a useful postwar job. I should like you to authorize a hundred per cent increase in your army, (I mean in size, not in quality) and let me join. I will furnish the " brass" and you, as in all other armies, would do the work. In addition, I will promise a lot of enthusiasm because I get so eternally tired of the general lack of understanding of what the infantry soldier endures that I have come to the conclusion that education along this one simple line might do a lot toward promoting future reluctance to engage in war. The difference between you and me in regard to this infantry problem is that you can express yourself eloquently upon it; I get so fighting mad because of the general lack of appreciation of real heroism—which is the uncomplaining acceptance of unendurable conditions—that I become completely inarticulate. Anyway I volunteer. If you want me you don't have to resort to the draft.

Thanks again for your book.

With best wishes,

Sincerely,
Dwight D. Eisenhower

Ernie's reply:

Feb. 27, 1945

Dear General Ike—

Your grand letter of Dec. 15 has just now showed up. It was a long time reaching me. It doesn't require an answer, but I wanted to tell you how much I appreciate it anyway.

Yes, I think I'll allow you to join my army. But I think we're both fighting a losing cause—for I've found that no matter how much we talk, or write, or show pictures, people who have not actually been in war are incapable of having any real conception of it. I don't really blame the people. Some of them try hard to understand. But the world of the infantryman is a world so far removed from anything normal that it can be no more than academic to the average person.

As you know, I've spent two and a half years carrying the torch for the foot-soldier, and I think I have helped make America conscious of and sympathetic toward him, but I haven't made them *feel* what he goes through. I believe it's impossible. But I'll keep on trying.

I'm out in the Pacific now. Came about six weeks ago. It's very hard for me to get adjusted to the tempo of things out here. Distances are so vast; the time lag between planning and execution is so great; living conditions are so much better; most of the time you're just preparing for or traveling to a war. Now and then I have to pinch myself to realize this is war.

As much as I grew to hate the war, I miss my friends and the camaraderie of misery of the Western Front. But lots of the boys both in the Mediterranean and on the German front continue to write me and give me all the little front-line gossip, so I don't feel entirely lost. I suppose I shall be out here in the Pacific for a year or more. Are you all coming over to join us when you get your business finished?

I had to chuckle when I read your letter, and others you've written me. For some evil soul started a rumor in Washington, shortly after I came home from France last fall, that you had kicked me out of the European Theater for something I wrote that displeased you. The rumormonger would have enjoyed reading over my shoulder. I wonder why there have to be people in the world like that?

Please give my best to Butch and Tex and General "Beetle." And to General Bradley again when you see him. I had the pleasure of squiring his wife and daughter around Washington some last November. And good wishes to you. I don't know how you have stood up under the burdens you've had to bear these past three years. I fervently hope the bloody mess is soon finished.

Most sincerely,
Ernie Pyle

In the Philippines I had a letter from him: "I don't figure I'll get on over there for three months or more yet. There's so much to do in this part of the Pacific, and I work so slowly. And I guess there's still plenty of time yet anyhow. Wonder if you're coming on back here? This is an amazing place. If you do come the Navy would put you up well. I have a private room, all alone, in a BOQ, with fine bed and running water in the room and nice view and all the privacy I want. Couldn't have a better place to work. . . . Max and I stayed together until we went on separate ships about three weeks ago, and I haven't heard from him since. He is a wonderful guy—I grew to like him more than ever and we did have a lot of fun—but I'm much better off alone. . . . Had a number of letters from Jerry. Mrs. Streger's letters reporting on her are still worried, but Jerry's own letters seem marvelous. . . . Her memory is still bad, and she is very confused and unsure of herself, yet she seems better to me than in a long while. She writes regularly twice a week. . . ."

Turning in the first handful of his carrier series, he ran into trouble. Censors scissored out all the names of *Cabot* personnel. This was a difficulty that other correspondents had repeatedly protested to no avail. Ernie made an issue of it. He wrote Walker

Stone: ". . . The biggest thing I'm writing about is censorship. It finally came to a head today, and I've lost almost the whole day dealing with it. It is momentarily settled in our favor, but the settlement is not official, and I'm not too trustful of it. It's a fundamental policy which forbids the mention (in most cases) of names. There was a good reason for it in the beginning when we were weak, because it would identify ships. But it is now long antedated. Everybody agrees; from admirals on down through censors to the sixty or so correspondents who have been trying to outlaw it for months. Yet it still exists, and nobody can get it off the books. Apparently it stems clear back to Washington, and the final answer will be there.

"At any rate, if applied, it means that half the columns I write will be thrown out, because they are based on people. This present dull carrier series which I am trying to write will be half thrown away if the rule holds. And in the future I would have to become either a commentator or a writer of nothing but logistics, for I could not name names as I've always done. The PRO and the censors are turning heaven and earth to try to get the rule modified (not just for me but for everybody), and they now tell us to go ahead and put in names. I was told that two days ago, yet when my carbons came back from the censors all the names were gone. We're told afresh this evening to put them back in. Yet it is an informal decision, and no official, signed black-and-white Navy directive has been put out on it. . . . Under present regulations I can't even write about a Seabee who mixes concrete on this remote island, absolutely out of reach of the Japs, and name him.

"I told them this afternoon that unless the thing were definitely settled I would simply have to cable you that because of Navy censorship I was forced to leave the theater and either go on to the Philippines or come home. It is no personal quarrel whatever; everybody is grand and we're all on the same side. But it is a fundamental policy which has been a thorn out here for months and which hamstrings everybody trying to tell the honest story of the Navy. I don't know what the outcome will be, but if I suddenly pull stakes and go to the Philippines one of these days, you will know why. The head PRO [Min Miller] out here is a wonderful guy, probably the finest I've ever dealt with, and he is sensitive to all these things and tries to liberalize everything, and although he does have tremendous influence still he doesn't have the final authority. . . .

"I'm quite ashamed of this carrier series, and I've struggled like hell with it, but damned if I know how to make it any livelier. I'm trying hard not to get myself worked up into a complex about things out here, but I really don't see any way to keep my copy from being uninspired and dull . . . for the next several months. One way to solve it is to go in with the Marines on some theoretical future Iwo Jima landing, and although I have sworn I would never make another one, I may have to. . . ."

The restriction on names was subsequently removed for keeps.

Ernie found time, between columns, to answer a few letters from Army friends in Europe. Pfc Bob Ball wrote from the ETO that "I know there isn't a guy in the line who isn't glad that you are going to be warm this winter," and Ernie replied, "I suppose one of these days when I get a ship shot out from under me I will wake up and realize that this also is the real thing." There was also a letter to a former Dana neighbor, Joseph Staats, who was now ninety-eight years old and living in Florida: "Methuselah is going to get jealous after a while. . . . I admire your spirit a lot, and am proud to have been born and raised down the road from you. . . . People tell me that you still read my columns through one eye. From the quality of them at present I think that is a lot better than reading them with two eyes. . . ."

Guam had outdoor movies every night, which Ernie occasionally attended. He made some little tours of the island, sometimes with the photographer Edward J. Steichen, a captain in the Naval Reserve. Steichen told later how pleased Ernie was on a visit to an outfit of Negro stevedores. Within half an hour they issued a mimeographed extra of their camp newspaper, the main story and picture devoted to him.

Max Miller took Ernie to call on Admiral Raymond A. Spruance, commander of the Fifth Fleet, and later reported: "Ernie had always been afraid of Spruance, just as Spruance was afraid of reporters. But I had some other admiral friends there, to whom I said, 'Make Spruance talk.' And I went up to Spruance myself, with the help of a couple of bourbons, and said, 'Admiral, I wish you would talk to that little boy sitting over there on the davenport. He's afraid of you because he has heard you are hard.' The great fighting admiral replied, 'But Mr. Pyle really wouldn't want *me* to talk with him, would he?' I said, 'Admiral, you really ought to, and you would like it.' So they sat on the davenport and talked and talked and fell in love with each other."

Ernie wrote Cavanaugh: "Dear Mr. DeMille: Your epistles, montages, dirty digs, commentaries, and essays on the art of the silver screen keep rolling in, and largely I have no idea what you are talking about. Now that you're using the word 'great' so often I figure you've lost your head and can't be depended upon. . . . Will you do something for me? Call up Hedda Hopper (or have Lester call her if you're afraid) and tell her that I got pally the other night with a couple of rough guys (rough I mean in that they do work that makes the Rangers look tame) and that one of them, Lieutenant Arthur Choate, said Hedda's son is under him, and that he is a wonderful guy, and will come back a better man for what he's doing (not that he wasn't a fine man to begin with). And tell her not to wangle this around into something for the column, because this ain't publicity, this is genuine. . . .

"Why don't you and Mrs. Cavanaugh just quit and go to the poorhouse? You're both over forty and don't have any fun anyway. Neither do I. (Signed) The Sad One."

He wrote Roz that some of the papers had been cutting his column in an "embarrassing" way: "For instance, I wrote about the fine beds and how comfortably you live; and then went on in the next paragraph to explain that everybody didn't live that way. That it was just the staff. . . . Some papers cut out that explanatory paragraph, making the piece infer that everybody out here lived in private rooms and on Simmons beds. Things like that harm me terribly and begin to destroy the men's faith in me."

He never saw an open letter addressed to him by the editors of an Air Force magazine called *brief*, published in Honolulu: "So now it's happened to you, Ernie. We were all glad when we heard that you had decided to come west. We all liked the idea; we thought here, at last, is a guy who is going to give us a break, here is somebody who is going to tell the folks at home that there is a war out here, too. . . . Then you made a remark in one of your first columns from the Pacific. You said that you had never heard of Kwajalein. That stopped everybody cold, Ernie. . . . Not to have heard of Kwajalein, and from a journalist, a guy who claims to represent the little guy in this war! Out here, Ernie, you speak of Kwajalein the same way you speak of Gettysburg. After that crack, we began to worry. There was no way to pass it off—it was worse than civilian talk.

"Then you came to Saipan. You didn't say you hadn't heard of that battle or that island. But you came to Saipan, looked around for six days and wrote another column. Saipan, you said, was a great place to soldier, it was a paradise, or words to that effect. That was after six days. . . . If you had asked around a little, Ernie, any Pfc could have told you that six or sixteen or twenty-six months on an island like Saipan or smaller than Saipan does something funny to you. You begin to think that just one more day of sun and wind and coral and water and 'paradise' and something inside you is going to snap. A lot of guys kid about it. They call it going 'rock happy' and a lot of other names. But it isn't funny. And it isn't something you can find out about in six days. . . .

"Then you got on an aircraft carrier—a ship with the best possible living conditions in the Navy. And in another column you wrote about some enlisted sailors who complained to you about the time they spent away from home—sometimes a whole year. And you explained to them about soldiers in Europe who often had to spend two years away from home. That made the sailors shut up. It should. But why didn't you do the job right and tell the folks at home and those soldiers in Europe about this theater you are supposed to be covering? Why didn't you tell them about the men in the Army here, the men on any of these damned islands? . . . You would have to tell that for every guy spending two years in Europe there are guys spending three years here. . . .

"None of us can question your courage. You proved that enough times in Europe to satisfy everybody. And you proved that you could, for the sake of honest reporting, live the tough life of the GI under the worst circumstances. But if you were finally fed up with that life (and who could blame you if you were?), why didn't you just call it quits after you came home? Why come out here and live like no GI ever lived and tell the folks back home that this is 'paradise'?

"You're making liars out of a lot of soldiers here, Ernie. Or is it the other way around?"

Now came word that Operation Iceberg—the seizure of Okinawa—was imminent. Ernie was extremely hesitant about making the landing. According to Max Miller: "Before he finally settled the question in his own mind, he spent three sleepless days and nights. Repeatedly he said he knew he would be killed if he hit another beachhead. Then on the fourth morning his mind was made up. 'Now I feel all right again,' he explained. 'I think I'll come through it after all.' "

He wrote Jerry bleakly: "In one letter darling, you asked me not just what I was doing, but what I was thinking and feeling these days. Well most of the time I feel perfectly all right— easy and unconcerned in spirit, that is. But once in a while I'll get a low spell when the war and its details of death and misery get too real in my mind, and then I get kind of down in the mouth. It's just that I'd like so much to be home, and not personally ever see any more war ever. I don't expect to see as much out here as I did in Europe, but I'll have to see a little eventually, and I dread that. When I lie and think about it too clearly I feel afraid that if I am ever in combat again, I'll crack wide open and become a real case of war neurosis. . . .

"I am less worried about home than in a long time. I feel good about you, and that often makes me doubly homesick, for I feel that if I could be there maybe I could help you more than I'd ever been able to do before. I want that for you and for me both, and for me alone I want almost desperately just to sit down for a period with no predetermined end to it, have no responsibilities and no nothing, and just sit there quietly until I got good and sick of it. But I don't suppose that could ever happen now, unless we built a wall around ourselves. . . .

"You know darling that a separate life, as you term it, is something that I have never wanted and couldn't tolerate. I feel just the same as you do, and always have. All I want you to do is keep on trying just the very best you can until I get home again for keeps, and then we can at last have time to try together. . . . If I should ever feel that I am getting to the breaking point, I'll quit and come on home. . . .

"Did I write you that I'd had a list of the client papers from George Carlin, and he says the column is in almost four hundred dailies and nearly three hundred weeklies—almost seven hundred papers altogether? He says it has passed what Pearson or Winchell had. . . ."

Ernie wrote Cavanaugh: ". . . I wouldn't give you two cents for the likelihood of me being alive a year from now. And I'm not joking. I sure as hell wish I was sitting in your backyard drinking your booze. . . ."

There was a cable from Walker Stone: "Censors scissoring you considerably but your copy still by far best coming out of any ocean."

One of Jerry's letters said: ". . . Walker sent you the cable I should have sent—and had the impulse to send—about your col-

umns—They are marvelous columns—I'm sorry they came so hard
and that you feel the way you do about them—I'm reading more
clearly than I did—and so I can judge better—I guess—These columns are the first things I've been able to feel really certain
about—

"That you could ever become a victim of war neurosis is one of
the things I have believed—and still believe—couldn't happen—I
believe it without knowing why—Just as I believe that in spite
of everything you will come through—You say when you lie and
think about it you feel afraid—It's a different kind of fear—and has
an all too real basis—but in a way—it's rather like mine—and I'm
sorry now when I waken too early—(Did Mrs. Streger tell you
I'm sleeping naturally now? I'm almost afraid to mention it, for
fear I'll break the spell, the way I'd be afraid to mention that I'll
never take another of what is no temptation to me now at all—
even when I am pretty down.)

"That you do feel not worried about me, Ernie, makes *me* feel
maybe I'm helping you a little—Please keep on feeling that way
even though my letters may sometimes sound a little off key—
It's very hard for me to write—

"I hope you can 'just sit quietly' for a long while after you get
back, Ernie—and I think maybe you can—and maybe I can, too—
and when I think like that, everything seems all right—

"Yesterday Liz, Mrs. Streger and I went out with Mrs. Long
to look at shrubs and trees—Where I had been clear in the morning about what I thought I wanted—I got blank—plain blank—
and after it was all over, I suddenly felt I was going way beyond
what I could afford to do—and then I felt sunk—There are things
I don't know how to say to you—Do you remember how we used
to scoff at Pulitzer Prizes—and things like that? Your column on
what adulation, publicity and fame bring with them first made
me think, I guess—and to know how faulty my own consideration has been—Now you have been honored by a State—I have
lived in Our home—Your home in that State for four years—I've
neglected that home—and because I have, do you see how I feel—

I can't make up anything by suddenly getting the house and grounds in order—and between us, it makes no real difference so far as the factual aspect goes—but Ernie, do you understand— I want the home to fit in with the honor—well, not that—but to better justify being yours—the way I feel about myself—The outward appearance, which I used to argue with Roz—and about which I thought I cared nothing—does mean something—when it's properly backed up—It means a great deal—My old attitude now seems false to me—and it was, to the best in me—

"Ernie, promise me that you will not stay away until you get to the breaking point—and not because of any fear of coming home—There is enough straight in my mind now to make me see that I can keep it that way by trying—and to try for you, with you here—darling—In a strange, unclear way, I have always known how greatly I love you—Now it is clear—and deep and wanting—Ernie, sometimes when I feel you *must* be here, I have come into the house and opened your door, almost but not quite believing that I'd find you—but so much, that I wouldn't have been startled to find you—Someday you will be there—Darling how long is a long time—There is work for you here, Ernie—To be able to really help you—I *will* be able to—I will, Ernie. . . .

"A bright morning, darling. My love reaches out to you—so strongly—and wants so much for you—Bless you my Ernie."

CHAPTER 41

Operation Iceberg

I N EUROPE the war was approaching a denouement. The Pacific was another story. The Philippines were ours, except for the ugly work of "mopping up" (a phrase bandied blithely in communiqués but anathema to tired soldiers rooting out a desperate enemy). Our submarines and our airpower, both carrier and land-based, had constricted Japan's oceanic lifelines to the starvation point. The Jap Navy was finished. Yet it was agreed that the subjugation of Japan itself, where two million troops were ready to defend the beaches and the Mikado, would cost us enormous casualties. Okinawa—Operation Iceberg—was to be a sort of semi-final before the bloody assault on the homeland. Okinawa, in the Ryukyus, lies less than four hundred miles from the Japanese mainland, and the enemy's strong garrison could be expected to resist desperately. Ernie's forebodings, as Iceberg drew near, were entirely realistic.

"Sometimes I get so mad and despairing I can hardly keep from crying," he wrote Roz. "I've got so I worry so much about what might happen to me, I've even gotten to brooding about it and sometimes can't sleep. I'm feeling pretty low tonight." He gave Ed Waltz a memorandum: "If anything fairly fatal should happen to me, please send Jerry's letters back to her. . . ."

There were some grim attempts at merriment on Guam as the days of waiting diminished. Sherwood remembered a party in Max Miller's room: "We sang a lot, and Ernie told a number of Cockney and GI stories. He typed out a lyric of a song for me, one I had not known before, and one of the funniest and dirtiest of them all." Sherwood was in the Pacific as a sort of unofficial reporter for President Roosevelt. "I do not think I ever successfully persuaded Ernie," he said, "how much the President depended on him for information about the realities of the war that he could not get from any other source, certainly not through the regular 'channels.' But that night, when I had to leave, Ernie came out into the corridor with me and spoke very emotionally. He said, and I could not forget these words, 'Tell him I love him.' I promised to do so and told Ernie we would be getting together again soon. He shook his head and said, 'I am not coming back from this one.' I laughed and said, 'You said that about Sicily, Normandy, and every other operation—and you are still here.' He said, 'I always believed it when I said it, and I believe it now, and sometime I have got to be right.' We were both somewhat tight and tears were shed when we parted. I cried a lot more when I heard the news that this time Ernie *was* right."

Max Miller and Captain Steichen saw Ernie off for Ulithi, which was again his staging point, and at the airstrip he asked Max to "tell Jerry this will be my last landing."

At Ulithi Ernie cleared his decks. In two days he sent off ten columns. "This island," he wrote his father and Aunt Mary, "is a tiny little thing, about as long as from our house to Will Bales', and just a couple of hundred yards wide.[1] But it is very pretty and tropical looking, with white sand and lots of coconut trees. It isn't too hot; it's just right. I sleep on a cot with only a sheet over me." He told Aunt Mary he hoped his readers wouldn't pester her too much with requests for recipes—he had mentioned in print her special method of canning fried chicken for mailing abroad—but "I guess a lot of boys overseas will be surprised and pleased, though, to be getting some fried chicken from home."

[1] The island of Asor, which is the principal component of Ulithi atoll.

Perhaps it was visions of fried chicken that made him say: "I think I'm as homesick as I ever have been while overseas. . . . I may not stay out a year as I had planned."

Ulithi bustled as the day of departure neared. Scores of correspondents had gathered, many of them strangers to Ernie. Harold Smith of the *Chicago Tribune* recalled that most of his colleagues bashfully ignored Ernie "out of the corners of their eyes." Jack Dempsey, the former heavyweight champ and now a Coast Guard commander, was there too, and Ernie saw quite a lot of him.

The last day ashore, according to Robert Sherrod of *Time*, "we went out to Rear Admiral Lawrence Reifsnider's flagship, the *Panamint*, for the final briefing. The landing was going to be something horrendous—worse than Iwo. As we filed out Ernie turned to me and said, 'What I need now is a great big drink.' We did have a drink. Many of them. That night at the Black Widow, the officers' club, Scrappy Kessing threw a big party for the correspondents. High-ranking officers from the Navy ships in the harbor and from the 1st and 6th Marine Divisions were there. And so were, miraculously, about seventy women—nurses off the hospital ships in the anchorage, plus two Norwegian women, radio operators off a freighter. Everybody got drunk, including Ernie, as people always do the last night ashore. Jay Eyerman made some pictures, but *Life* never used them because people didn't look their best. Ernie was the lion of the party. He must have signed a Short-Snorter bill for everyone present."

In the morning he was hung over and gloomily preoccupied, though not too much so to hear out a plaintive seaman who told about his wife and eight destitute children and wondered if Mr. Pyle knew a way to get him home. Ernie promised to speak to Kessing—who knew the case well, and explained that the eight benighted children had been sired by a homesick imagination. Ernie went to the dock to see off a number of correspondents who were embarking earlier than he. Somebody shouted, "Keep your head down, Ernie," and he replied, "Listen, you bastards, I'll take a drink over every one of your graves," and then put up his fists at Dempsey and said, "Want to fight?" That afternoon he was sent out to his ship, an APA (assault transport) carrying units of Major General Pedro A. del Valle's 1st Marine Division. He was scarcely aboard before a signal came inviting him to go ashore for some drinks and then to dinner on an admiral's flagship. He arranged to take a Marine colonel along. After two hours of drinking, on top of his hangover, a blackout descended on him, at least so far as any recollection of subsequent events was concerned. "The colonel said we stayed over there till ten o'clock," Ernie wrote to Max Miller. "Everybody got tighter than ticks, the admiral and I sang a song on the dock for the delectation of all, and the admiral's aide fell in the ocean trying to get into the boat and we had to fish him out. We delivered the admiral and his aide at their ship, we all agreed on to hell with dinner, and then the night was so black and rough that we had to stop past three different ships to get our directions, and finally found our own ship in the darkness only by compass. I came aboard under my own power, thank goodness, but don't remember it. . . . The next thing I knew I was in my own bunk on my own ship, and the room was full of Marines having a party, in which I proceeded to join without ever getting out of bed. . . . We sailed next day. You can imagine how we felt." But he had managed a hurried postscript on a letter to Jerry: "Because of censorship I can't tell you where I am, or why, or what happens. They are waiting for me so I must go now. I hate it that this letter is so short, so inadequate. I love you and you are the only thing I live for."

Ernie shared a cabin with a Marine veteran of Guadalcanal, Major Reed Taylor, of Kensington, Maryland, and they hit it off fine. The sea was smooth, and the air soporific, and Ernie napped often. With the Marines he swapped reminiscences and rumors, worries about Okinawa, and drinks. "The more we heard about it the worse it became," his letter to Max Miller said, "and I'm willing to admit that I had the woolies pretty bad. But the

Marine officers I was with had them just as bad, so I didn't have to feel ashamed. Every day that passed and we'd be further briefed, things looked darker. And every day that passed I found myself being edged closer and closer to H-hour, when I had actually hoped not to go in till D plus one or two." Scrappy Kessing had given him three bottles of whisky. "On the way up we were all so gloomy that we drank two of my bottles and all the Marines' 'beachhead' liquor. I poured the last bottle in my canteen, so did have that for shoreside."

All too soon it was the day before L-day, or Love Day, as the invasion date was designated. Such gaiety as had been mustered on the transport was gone. Two days' K rations and some invasion yen—occupation money—were issued. Ernie was asked to write something to the men aboard ship, and what he wrote was: "In a message like this, it is the usual thing for a person to say that he's happy to be aboard. If I said that, I would be a liar for sure. Tomorrow, as you know, is our day. For some of you, this business tomorrow is new, and you are curious. For some of us, it is old stuff. None of us likes it. But we have to do it, and wishing doesn't change it. In writing about tomorrow and the days that will follow, I'll try to give the folks at home an honest picture of what happens—so that they can understand enough to give you the credit you deserve. I'll do the best I can. And so to you on the ship, and you in the boats, and you on the beaches—good luck. And I hope you wish me the same. I'll need it too!"

He wrote Jerry: "I'm on another invasion. I never intended to. But I feel that I must cover the Marines, and the only way to do it honestly is to go with them. So here I am. But I promised Max Miller, and I've promised myself, and I promise you, that if I come through this one I will never go on another one."

There was turkey for dinner. Ernie packed the few things he could carry ashore, took a bath, and hit the sack. He felt nervous and weak. His sleep was troubled.

At four o'clock on Easter morning they turned him out. He

put on green herringbone-twill fatigues, breakfasted on ham and eggs, and went onto the still darkish deck with his gear. The galley made him up a bag of turkey wings, bread, oranges, and apples.

The ship was well out from shore. LCVPs, carried on deck, were swung out by derrick to the level of the rail, Marines clambered aboard, and the boats were lowered onto the East China Sea. Ernie's, the first boat off, chugged through the dawn to its control ship, one of dozens that formed a picket line two miles off the beach. From the control ship Ernie watched as ten battleships and scores of lesser units pounded Okinawa with tens of thousands of shells and rockets, and planes from the carriers dropped napalm (a viciously incendiary petroleum compound) on the beaches. "The ghostly concussion set up vibrations in the air—a sort of flutter—which pained your ears and pounded upon you as though some almighty were beating you with invisible drumsticks." He was getting jittery. Some officers he knew came aboard and wanted to talk, but "I simply couldn't carry on a conversation." He got a drink of water, "though I wasn't thirsty." He felt miserable. "There's nothing romantic whatever in knowing that an hour from now you may be dead."

The task force shifted its shelling inland, and after a strafing sweep by one hundred and twenty-eight carrier planes the first wave of the invasion—amphibious tanks—hit the beach. "We looked at the shore through binoculars. We could see tanks moving across the fields and the men of the second wave walking inland, standing upright. . . . We couldn't make out any real fire coming from the shore. . . . The weight began to lift. . . . I found myself talking more easily with the sailors, and somehow the feeling gradually took hold of me that we were to be spared. The seventh wave was to pick us up as it came by. I didn't even see it approaching. Suddenly they called my name and said the boats were alongside."

Sailors shouted, "Good luck!" He boarded another LCVP, jammed with Marines shivering from the spray. But this was still not the final conveyance. Because of the underwater reef that flanged the beach, three or four hundred yards out, the LCVPs had to transfer their passengers to amphibious tractors. Then the last lap began. Ernie peered from the amtrac at the beach and still could see no hostile fire. A canteen was passed, and he took a swig that unexpectedly jolted him. It was brandy. The amtrac lumbered over the reef. And about ten o'clock, an hour and a half after H-hour, Ernie set foot on Beach Yellow at Okinawa. There wasn't a Jap within sight or earshot, nor an American casualty, nor a wrecked boat or burning tank. "You wouldn't believe it," he wrote. "And we don't either. It just can't be true. And yet it is true." Everybody had expected a shambles. "There was some opposition to the right and to the left of us, but on our beach nothing, absolutely nothing." The 5th Marine Regiment got ashore with only two cases for the medics—one Marine hurt his foot, and another was prostrated by the heat. Ernie recorded for history the first words he heard spoken on Okinawa—by a Marine: "Hell, this is just like one of MacArthur's landings!" One exultant sergeant wanted to "wear Ernie Pyle around his neck as a good-luck charm."

The regimental staff and headquarters company settled down for a while at the foot of a chalky bluff, near a cave full of dead Japs, and Ernie's eye for the incongruous began to record little paragraphs—a Marine with a vase crying, "Here's the first souvenir of Okinawa!"; a signalman leading a white nanny goat; another Marine with a commandeered horse; another with a bicycle. Ernie opened his bag of grub. Captain John N. Popham, a Marine, said: "He laughed a lot and repeated how he had enjoyed a picnic lunch three hundred and fifty miles from the Japanese homeland."

During the afternoon the outfit moved a mile and a half inland, on foot, and the old campaigner found that six months in the States and with the Navy had taken the temper out of his legs. It was unexpectedly hot, and he was wearing two pairs of pants and carrying a blanket rolled in a poncho, a musette bag, two canteens, three rubber life preservers (for sleeping on), a shovel, a typewriter, and two jackets, plus assorted knives, kits, etc. He couldn't keep up. He had to sit down awhile. After reaching the bivouac he dug a foxhole and presently was making coffee to wash down the K rations.

The heavy load of gear that made Ernie's legs sag came in handy now as night fell. He seemed to be the only man who had brought a blanket. And when he inflated those life jackets and laid them side by side to form an air mattress, a trick he had discovered in Normandy, Marines gaped and wondered audibly why they hadn't thought of it.

Three Jap planes came over and were shot down in a hurricane of ack-ack from the fleet. At dusk the mosquitoes came in clouds, warships began shooting parachute flares over Okinawa to expose any attempts at counterattack, and two or three naval shells a minute passed overhead with that "window-shade rustle" Ernie remembered so well. Field telephones and radios of the regimental c.p. were only a few yards from Ernie's foxhole, and officers sat at them taking and giving orders. Occasionally there was a rifle shot, or a flurry of them, and now and then a machine gun spoke. "All night it went like that. Flares in the sky ahead, the crack of big guns behind us, then of passing shells, a few dark figures coming and going in the night, muted voices at the telephones, the rifle shots, the mosquitoes, the stars, the feel of the damp night air under the wide sky—back again at the kind of life I had known so long. The old familiar pattern, unchanged by distance or time from war on the other side of the world. A pattern so imbedded in my soul that, coming back into it again, it seemed to me as I lay there that I'd never known anything else in my life. And there are millions of us."

Ernie stayed with the regiment for two days before moving back to the APA for a day's writing. At the town of Sobe, he ran into a Marine public-relations man, Tech/Sergeant Frank Acosta, Jr., who had been a reporter on the *Washington Daily News*. Acosta wrote me not long afterwards: "Ernie was as grateful as any of us that the landing here was so unbelievably easy. He swore he wasn't going in to the beach another time. Of course I didn't know him very well, but he remembered me, and we had a hell of a good talk. We talked about the office, and he said several times that you were the best friend he had."

Ernie went up to join a company of the 5th Regiment commanded by Captain Julian Dusenbury, from Claussen, S. C. Ernie was wearing a Navy jacket, with "U. S. Navy" stenciled on the back, when Dusenbury took him on a tour of the company area. A Marine spotted the "U. S. Navy" and Ernie's gray hair and remarked to his buddies, "That guy's an admiral. Look at the old gray-haired bastard. He's been in the Navy all his life. He'll get a medal out of this, sure as hell." Another Marine greeted him gravely with, "Good evening, Colonel."

Next morning the company marched to a new bivouac at the edge of a blasted village where a few dead Okinawans lay in the street. The temperature was fine, and during the march they all "felt that sense of ease when you know nothing very bad is ahead of you." As they were settling down, a couple of terrified Jap soldiers were rooted out from some bushes. They had rifles and grenades but made no move to use them. Ernie's "contribution to the capture consisted of standing to one side looking as mean as I could." To Jerry he wrote: "Fortunately they happened to be the surrendering kind, rather than the fight-to-death kind, or they could have killed several of us. They were the first Jap prisoners I'd ever seen in the raw before capture." That was the only ground "action" Ernie saw on Okinawa; the Marines, for a change, had lucked into a soft sector, while the Army's XXIV Corps, to the south, was running into resistance.

CHAPTER 42

The End of the Story

ERNIE left his muddy clothing-roll with the Marines and went out on the night of April 7 to the command ship *Panamint*, to scrape off the dirt and whiskers, do some writing, and get some rest. He was "too tired to wash . . . before supper," but after a long sleep wrote Jerry: "Everything is fine with me now. You can't know the relief I felt, for I had dreaded this one terribly. Now it is behind me, and I will never make another landing. . . . I do hope things have gone well with you since I heard from you last. In another couple of weeks your wonderful spring weather should start. I can visualize you planting your flowers and vines and wish I could be there to putter around and help. . . ." And to the folks at Dana he wrote that "outside of an accident of some kind, I feel now that at last I have a pretty good chance of coming through the war alive."

A cold sent him to the sick bay, where he wrote Max Miller: "I've got almost a spooky feeling that I've been spared once more and that it would be asking for it to tempt Fate again. So I'm going to keep my promise to you and to myself that that was the last one. I'll be on operations in the future, of course, but not on any more landings. . . . I'm in a spic and span little four-bed ward, and I'm the only patient here, so it's like a private room. Have a bath and everything. They bring my meals to me, the two doctors are solicitous, and I'm ruining all the corpsmen's lives because I don't want anything. . . . I've had no mail at all since I left you in Guam."

There was on the way to him a letter he never received, from Jerry. She wrote that Max, home from the Pacific, had telephoned "the message that you had made your last landing—There won't be any such thing as that for me until you are really home— but if it means no more such landings as you have described in your columns, I am thankful for that, Ernie—I am thankful for whatever it is that has made me feel through the years that as long as you were somewhere, nothing could be completely wrong—or hopeless—Is that something the way you have felt about me Ernie—in spite of everything? It transcends all other human things. . . ."

Major General A. D. Bruce, commanding the 77th Infantry Division, came aboard the *Panamint* with his staff. He had just received orders to seize an outlying islet, Ie Shima, and the assault was scheduled for April 16. Told of the impending action against Ie, Ernie said he would go ashore, though not on the first day. He did not seem to feel that a visit to the island after D-day would violate his pledge against any more invasion landings.

The ship's wireless received the stunning news of President Roosevelt's death. Ernie wrote to Dana that it was "such a shock to us. The war will go on just the same, but I don't know of anybody with the knowledge and strength to help arrange the peace. I don't know the slightest thing about Truman."

By April 15, the day before the Ie Shima assault, he was out of bed and back at work. Word had come that Fred Painton had dropped dead on Guam, and Ernie wrote: "The wear and the weariness of war is cumulative. To many a man in the line today fear is not so much of death itself, but fear of the terror and anguish and utter horror that precede death itself. I have no idea how Fred Painton would have liked to die. But somehow I'm glad he didn't have to go through the unnatural terror of dying on the battlefield. For he was one of my dear friends and I know that he, like myself, had come to feel that terror."

To "Papa and Aunt Mary" he sent a letter dated April 16: ". . . The war in Europe looks as though it couldn't last much longer.

In a way I wish I could be there at the finish, having been with it for so long. When I finally return from the Pacific, and have rested a while, I think maybe I'll go back to Europe and go over the devastated countries that I haven't seen, and write about them. . . ."

He wrote a tentative draft of a column he had thought of sending back for use whenever the Germans surrendered, which they did in about a month. The article was found in his pocket: "My heart is still in Europe, and that's why I'm writing this column. It is to the boys who were my friends for so long. My one great regret of the war is that I am not with them when it has ended. For the companionship of two and a half years of death and misery is a spouse that tolerates no divorce. . . ."

Ie Shima is a mere ten square miles—though at that it is bigger than Iwo Jima—and is dominated by a six-hundred-foot-high peak called Iegusugu and known more familiarly to the 77th Division as "the Pinnacle." It is, or was, an island of fishermen and hog-raisers, of windowless one-story farmhouses, and of men hardy enough to drink a sweet-potato liquor which, according to a soldier newspaper, assayed at 190 proof in Army medics' tests. It was also an island where the Japs had installed three airstrips. The strips were the prime reason we wanted Ie; secondarily, it would be a useful radar outpost.

The 77th assaulted Ie after a blasting by two battleships and sundry lesser craft, airplanes, and artillery emplaced a few miles away on tiny Minna Shima. Surprise was achieved, in spite of the preliminary blasting, because General Bruce chose to put his men ashore not at the obvious point, but over a treacherous coral reef on a poor beach. As a result the initial advance was rapid, and the airstrips and the western two-thirds of the island were taken with slight casualties.

The other correspondents went ashore on D-day. Ernie did his observing from the ship. That night he attended a briefing of the correspondents by General Bruce, who warned them not to be misled by the ease of the surprise landing and predicted bitter fighting. Events justified the warning. The division, which had fought on Guam and Leyte, "was to meet the stiffest opposition in its experience," according to the official history of Okinawa operations.

"We have never had a tougher fight," an officer of the 77th wrote, "for the Japs defended the ground from caves, some as deep as three stories, and absolutely impossible to reach with artillery, naval gunfire, or aerial bombardment. The infantry had to dig them out." Corporal Alexander Roberts wrote: "Not one Jap soldier surrendered. He killed until he was killed. He remained hidden until our troops passed him, and then he fired at their backs. He came out of hiding at night, every night, to kill as many Americans as he could before he was cut down; he made a living bomb of himself and threw himself under tanks and into foxholes and against groups of GIs. He planted five-hundred-pound aerial bombs, converted them into antipersonnel or antivehicle mines by attaching a detonating fuse requiring not more than the pressure of a little finger for activation, so that when a GI stepped on the mine he just disintegrated." In the six-day fight the 77th lost 172 killed in action, 902 wounded, and 46 missing. Attached units suffered additional casualties. Nearly five thousand Japanese were killed, including some civilians.

On April 17 Ernie and other correspondents stepped into a Higgins boat. On the way to shore he put on a jacket, as the sea breeze was chilly and he didn't want to renew that cold. "I'm like the one-hoss shay," he said to Bill McGaffin of the *Chicago Daily News*. "I'll probably go to pieces all at once."

They landed on Red Beach No. 2 and waited for a guide to lead them to the command post of the 305th Regiment (a component of the 77th Division), since without guidance they might get into a mined area. None showed up, so they followed an ammunition train, watching warily for snipers. They passed several vehicles that had hit mines, including a heavy amtrac and its still unburied crew; also the bodies of Japs killed during the landing. At the command post they were briefed on the tactical situation, and then scattered in search of copy. Lieutenant Charles Kane, a public-relations officer, escorted Ernie and Milton Chase, correspondent of station WLW, Cincinnati, to an observation post a thousand yards forward. "There was much evidence along that road of what would happen to the man who stepped on a land mine," Kane wrote. One soldier stepped on a mine before their eyes, according to Chase, and Ernie said, "I wish I was in Albuquerque!"

From the observation post Ernie watched as the 307th Regiment, which had been in reserve, came charging up the beach, heading toward the Pinnacle. A battalion commander, Lieutenant Colonel Ed Chalgren, Jr., of Minneapolis, was hit in the arm. He refused to be evacuated until the medics took him to meet Ernie. "Mr. Pyle," he said, "I'd just like to shake your hand and take a good look at you." Ernie and Chase and the Lieutenant returned through the mines to the command post. Kane and Chase were going back to the ship, but Ernie had decided, before coming ashore, to spend the night on Ie. He told Kane, "I'll meet you at 1400 [2 p.m.] tomorrow and go back to the ship."

During the afternoon he talked to many people, doughs and officers. He was in his element—the infantry. His cold was gone; his fears had abated; things looked good—except for the day's evidence that the taking of Ie was no mere formality. He spent the evening in a former Jap dugout, swapping talk with Brigadier General Edwin H. Randle, Assistant Division Commander, and others who drifted in and out. The conversation was punctuated with reports of Japs trying to infiltrate, but finally he slept, there in the dugout.

Next morning, Wednesday, April 18, Ernie had an early chat with General Bruce. "I gave him all the latest dope and our future plans," the General said. "I was surprised and pleased that he came to the same conclusions as I did as to how long the battle would last. He also felt the same as I did about the importance of this objective and why we were pushing the battle so hard in order to get it over quickly and take advantage of Ie's fine airfields. I can remember vividly now his smile of approbation and his slight nod of concurrence. Again his mind was on the individual doughboy. As soon as I left him to issue some orders he was surrounded by soldiers. I did not know that he was going forward."

One of the soldiers Ernie talked to was Sergeant Thomas Kirby, of Baltimore, a medical corpsman, who said later: "We told him the news about the new combat medic's badge being approved in Washington. He told us he had worked a long while to get approval for the medics to wear a special insigne, but that this was the first time he had heard it had been approved. He grinned and looked happy as hell when we told him. Then he got into a jeep and drove off."

The jeep was that of Lieutenant Colonel Joseph B. Coolidge, of Helena, Arkansas, commanding officer of the 305th, who wanted to look for a new site for his regimental c.p. Three other men were in it—Major George H. Pratt, of Eugene, Oregon; T/4 Dale W. Bassett, a radio operator, of Baush, Colorado, and the driver, T/5 John L. Barnes, of Petersburg, Virginia.

They set out about ten o'clock through rolling green country, up the same narrow, one-way road Ernie had traversed the day before, a road that paralleled the beach, two or three hundred yards inland. An occasional red cloth indicated a mine. In front of them towered the Pinnacle. The road itself had been cleared of mines, and hundreds of vehicles had passed over it. "Except for artillery and mortar fire it seemed perfectly safe," General Bruce said later, but he pointed out that the rapidity of our advance had not allowed time to seek out and mop up all the caves and other hideouts. "Many Japs lay doggo from twenty-four to seventy-two hours in camouflaged caves or pillboxes and would come out at night to raid behind the lines or would snipe whenever the opportunity presented itself. One of our severest raids came on our artillery well behind the lines."

It was no lonely road. Another jeep preceded Coolidge's. And just ahead of that were some two-and-a-half-ton trucks. "Every indication pointed to a fairly calm trip," the Colonel said later, "except for occasional mortars dropping into the open fields on either hand, where two infantry battalions had dug in for the night. These men were finishing breakfast and preparing to move forward to new positions."

As the jeep reached a road junction, some hundreds of yards short of the village of Ie, the high-voiced chatter of a .31-caliber Nambu machine gun was heard on the left and somewhat ahead of the party. Apparently it was firing from a shell-battered coral ridge about a third of a mile away. Dust danced in the field on their left. Barnes braked the jeep in a hurry and the five men bolted for shallow roadside ditches—Barnes to the left, the others to the right.

Why the Jap gunner let the other vehicles pass and opened fire on this one can never be known positively. It is possible that he caught a glint from the antenna of Colonel Coolidge's radio and reasoned that this meant a commanding officer.

Ernie and Coolidge and Bassett were fairly safe in their ditch only as long as they hugged the ground, for the Jap had a clear field of fire from his elevated nest. Major Pratt was a little ahead of them, beyond a small intersecting road that dammed the ditch at this point. Ernie and Coolidge raised their heads to look around for the others. When they located Major Pratt, Ernie smiled and asked, "Are you all right?" Those were his last words. "The Jap let go again," Colonel Coolidge wrote later. "He had had time to adjust his sights on us. Some shots chewed up the road in front of me and ricocheted over my head. After ducking I turned around to ask Ernie how he was. He was lying face up, and at that time no blood showed, so for a second I could not tell what was wrong." Ernie had been struck in the left temple.

The Colonel called across the fields to some soldiers and asked if a medic was available. None was, but it did not matter.

Ernie was buried a hundred yards or so from where the East

China Sea washes the shore of Ie. He was buried with his helmet on—"the way we thought he would have wanted it," the chaplain said. "A lot of the men thought he looked more natural that way." Soldiers fashioned a coffin from flimsy boards, and they put him in a long row of graves, among other soldiers, an infantry private on one side of him, an engineer on the other. At the services the Navy and the Marine Corps as well as the Army were represented, and a correspondent or two were there. All wore helmets, by order of General Bruce, as there was danger of Jap shellfire. The ceremony took about ten minutes. Then the soil of Ie Shima was returned to its place.

Epilogue

WORD of Ernie's death was communicated to Albuquerque before its release to the press. Jerry received it bravely. At Dana, a neighbor heard the news by radio before an official call could get through, and brought it to Mr. Pyle and Aunt Mary Bales.

President Roosevelt had been dead only six days. At Lingayen, on Luzon, I was shaving out of my helmet when I heard a radio in a nearby hut quoting President Truman: "The nation is quickly saddened again by the death of Ernie Pyle. No man in this war has so well told the story of the American fighting man as American fighting men wanted it told. He deserves the gratitude of all his countrymen."

In Europe General Bradley had just sat down to dinner when the news was brought in; he put his head in his hands and could say nothing. In Leipzig Hal Boyle woke up other correspondents with, "Ernie got it!" As Bob Capa wrote: "We all got up and drank ourselves stupid in silence." General Eisenhower said, "The GIs in Europe—and that means all of us here—have lost one of our best and most understanding friends." Bill Mauldin put it this way: "The only difference between Ernie's death and the death of any other good guy is that the other guy is mourned by his company. Ernie is mourned by the Army."

There were many posthumous honors. A Medal of Merit, bestowed jointly by the War, Navy, and State Departments, was accepted by Jerry at a ceremony in Washington. Her broken health soon went into a final decline, and she died in Albuquer-

427

que on November 23, 1945. The little house was given to the city, for use as a branch library.

At the site of Ernie's death a crude marker was put up, bearing the words:

<blockquote>
At This Spot
The 77th Infantry Division
Lost a Buddy
ERNIE PYLE
18 April 1945
</blockquote>

This was succeeded by a monument, similarly inscribed.

After the war the body was moved, first to an Army cemetery on Okinawa, then to the new National Memorial Cemetery of the Pacific in Punchbowl Crater, near Honolulu.

Index